Soft Computing

This book explores soft computing techniques in a systematic manner starting from their initial stage to recent developments in this area. The book presents a survey of the existing knowledge and the current state-of-the-art development through cutting-edge original new contributions from the researchers. Soft Computing: Recent Advances and Applications in Engineering and Mathematical Sciences presents a survey of the existing knowledge and the current state-of-the-art development through cutting-edge original new contributions from the researchers.

As suggested by the title, this book particularly focuses on the recent advances and applications of soft computing techniques in engineering and mathematical sciences. Chapter 1 describes the contribution of soft computing techniques towards a new paradigm shift. The subsequent chapters present a systematic application of fuzzy logic in mathematical sciences and decision-making. New research directions are also provided at the end of each chapter. The application of soft computing in health sciences and in the modeling of epidemics including the effects of vaccination are also examined. Sustainability of green product development, optimum design of 3D steel frame, digitalization investment analysis in the maritime industry, forecasting return rates of individual pension funds are among some of the topics where engineering and industrial applications of soft computing have been studied in the book. The readers of this book will require minimum prerequisites of undergraduate studies in computation and mathematics.

This book is meant for graduate students, faculty, and researchers who are applying soft computing in engineering and mathematics. New research directions are also provided at the end of each chapter.

Edge AI in Future Computing

Series Editors:
Arun Kumar Sangaiah
SCOPE, VIT University, Tamil Nadu
Mamta Mittal
G. B. Pant Government Engineering College, Okhla, New Delhi

Soft Computing Techniques in Engineering, Health, Mathematical and Social Sciences
Pradip Debnath and S. A. Mohiuddine

Machine Learning for Edge Computing: Frameworks, Patterns and Best Practices
Amitoj Singh, Vinay Kukreja, and Taghi Javdani Gandomani

Internet of Things: Frameworks for Enabling and Emerging Technologies
Bharat Bhushan, Sudhir Kumar Sharma, Bhuvan Unhelkar, Muhammad Fazal Ijaz, and Lamia Karim

Soft Computing: Recent Advances and Applications in Engineering and Mathematical Sciences
Pradip Debnath, Oscar Castillo, and Poom Kumam

For more information about this series, please visit:
https://www.routledge.com/Edge-AI-in-Future-Computing/book-series/EAIFC

Soft Computing

Recent Advances and Applications in Engineering and Mathematical Sciences

Edited by

Pradip Debnath
Department of Applied Science and Humanities,
Assam University Silchar, India

Oscar Castillo
Tijuana Institute of Technology, Mexico

Poom Kumam
Department of Mathematics, King Mongkut's University of
Technology Thonburi, Thailand

CRC Press
Taylor & Francis Group
Boca Raton London New York

CRC Press is an imprint of the
Taylor & Francis Group, an **informa** business

First edition published 2023
by CRC Press
6000 Broken Sound Parkway NW, Suite 300, Boca Raton, FL 33487-2742

and by CRC Press
4 Park Square, Milton Park, Abingdon, Oxon, OX14 4RN

CRC Press is an imprint of Taylor & Francis Group, LLC

ISBN: 978-1-032-31831-8 (hbk)
ISBN: 978-1-032-31917-9 (pbk)
ISBN: 978-1-003-31201-7 (ebk)

DOI: 10.1201/9781003312017

Typeset in Times
by codeMantra

Contents

Preface.....vii
Editors.....ix
Contributor.....xi

Chapter 1 A Study on Approximate Fixed Point Property in Intuitionistic Fuzzy n-Normed Linear Spaces.....1

Pradip Debnath

Chapter 2 Sequential Extended Parametric and Sequential Extended Fuzzy b-Metrics with an Application in Integral Equations.....15

Marija V. Paunović, Samira Hadi Bonab, Vahid Parvaneh, and Farhan Golkarmanesh

Chapter 3 Analytical Sequel of Rational-Type Fuzzy Contraction in Fuzzy b-Metric Spaces.....29

Nabanita Konwar

Chapter 4 Weak-Wardowski Contractions in Generalized Triple-Controlled Modular Metric Spaces and Generalized Triple-Controlled Fuzzy Metric Spaces.....45

Marija V. Paunović, Samira Hadi Bonab, and Vahid Parvaneh

Chapter 5 Some First-Order-Like Methods for Solving Systems of Nonlinear Equations.....67

Sani Aji, Poom Kumam, and Wiyada Kumam

Chapter 6 Cubic Inverse Soft Set.....87

Srinivasan Vijayabalaji and Kaliyaperumal Punniyamoorthy

Chapter 7 Inverse Soft-Rough Matrices 97

Srinivasan Vijayabalaji

Chapter 8 New Observations on Lacunary $\mathcal{I}$-Invariant Convergence for Sequences in Fuzzy Cone Normed Spaces 107

Ömer Kisi, Mehmet Gürdal, and Erhan Güler

Chapter 9 Some Convergent Sequence Spaces of Fuzzy Star-Shaped Numbers 125

Erhan Güler and Ömer Kisi

Chapter 10 Digitalization Investment Analysis in Maritime Industry with Interval–Valued Pythagorean Fuzzy Present Worth Analysis 141

Eda Boltürk

Chapter 11 Composite Mapping on Hesitant Fuzzy Soft Classes 153

Manash Jyoti Borah and Bipan Hazarika

Chapter 12 Ulam Stability of Mixed Type Functional Equation in Non-Archimedean IFN-Space 167

K. Tamilvanan, S. A. Mohiuddine, and N. Revathi

Chapter 13 Optimum Design of 3D Steel Frames with Composite Slabs Using Adaptive Harmony Search Method 179

Mehmet Polat Saka, Ibrahim Aydogdu, Refik Burak Taymus, and Zong Woo Geem

Chapter 14 Fostering Sustainability in Open Innovation, to Select the Right Partner on Green Product Development 211

Ricardo Santos, Polinho Katina, José Soares, Anouar Hallioui, Joao Matias, and Fernanda Mendes

Index 233

Preface

This book collects chapters from eminent contemporary researchers across the countries working on the theory and applications of soft computing techniques. The book presents a survey of the existing knowledge and also current state of the art development through cutting-edge original new contributions from the researchers. As suggested by the title, this book particularly focuses on the recent advances and applications of soft computing techniques in engineering and mathematical sciences. The first Chapter presents a study on approximate fixed point property in a generalized fuzzy normed space. Chapters 2–4 consist of new fixed point results and thier applications in different types of metric spaces such as fuzzy b-metric spaces and controlled fuzzy metric spaces. Chapter 5 describes new first order-like methods for solving nonlinear equations. Cubic inverse soft sets have been studied in Chapter 6, whereas inverse soft-rough matrices are introduced in Chapter 7. Some new convergence results concerning fuzzy normed spaces and fuzzy numbers have been described in Chapters 8 and 9, respectively. Digitalization investment analysis in maritime industry with picture fuzzy sets are studied in Chapter 10. Chapter 11 contains a study on composite mapping on hesitant fuzzy soft classes. In Chapter 12 we have Ulam stability of mixed type functional equation in fuzzy normed space. An interesting investigation on optimum design of 3D steel frames with composite slabs has been presented in Chapter 13. Finally, in Chapter 14, we discuss fostering sustainability in open innovation to select the right partner on green product development.

This book is meant for graduate students, faculties and researchers willing to learn and apply fuzziness and soft computing in engineering and mathematics. New research directions have been presented within the chapters to enable the researchers to further advance their research. The readers of this book will require minimum pre-requisites of undergraduate studies in computation and mathematics.

Editors

Pradip Debnath is an Assistant Professor (in Mathematics) at the Department of Applied Science and Humanities, Assam University, Silchar (a central university), India. He received his Ph.D. in Mathematics from the National Institute of Technology Silchar, India. His research interests include fixed point theory, nonlinear functional analysis, soft computing and mathematical statistics. He has published more than 60 papers in various journals of international repute and is reviewer for more than 40 international journals. Dr. Debnath is also a reviewer for "Mathematical Reviews" published by the American Mathematical Society. He is the Lead Editor of the books "Metric Fixed Point Theory - Applications in Science, Engineering and Behavioural Sciences" (2021, Springer Nature), "Soft Computing Techniques in Engineering, Health, Mathematical and Social Sciences" (2021, CRC Press) and "Fixed Point Theory and Fractional Calculus: Recent Advances and Applications" (2022, Springer Nature). He has successfully guided Ph.D. students in the areas of fuzzy logic, soft computing and fixed point theory. He has recently completed a Basic Science Research Project on fixed point theory funded by the UGC, the Government of India. Having been an academic gold medalist during his post-graduation studies from Assam University, Silchar, Dr. Debnath has qualified several national-level examinations in mathematics in India.

Oscar Castillo holds the Doctor in Science degree (Doctor Habilitatus) in Computer Science from the Polish Academy of Sciences (with the Dissertation "Soft Computing and Fractal Theory for Intelligent Manufacturing"). He is a Professor of Computer Science in the Graduate Division, Tijuana Institute of Technology, Tijuana, Mexico. In addition, he is serving as Research Director of Computer Science and head of the research group on Hybrid Fuzzy Intelligent Systems. Currently, he is President of HAFSA (Hispanic American Fuzzy Systems Association) and Past President of IFSA (International Fuzzy Systems Association). Prof. Castillo is also Chair of the Mexican Chapter of the Computational Intelligence Society (IEEE). He also belongs to the Technical Committee on Fuzzy Systems of IEEE and to the Task Force on "Extensions to Type-1 Fuzzy Systems". He is also a member of NAFIPS, IFSA and IEEE. He belongs to the Mexican Research System (SNI Level 3). His research interests are in Type-2 Fuzzy Logic, Fuzzy Control, Neuro-Fuzzy and Genetic-Fuzzy hybrid approaches. He has published over 300 journal papers, 10 authored books, 40 edited books, 200 papers in conference proceedings, and more than 300 chapters in edited books, in total 910 publications according to Scopus (H index=63, and more than 1050 publications according to Research Gate (H index=74 in Google Scholar). He has been Guest Editor of several successful Special Issues in the past, like in the following journals: Applied Soft Computing, Intelligent Systems, Information Sciences, Non-Linear Studies, Fuzzy Sets and Systems, JAMRIS and Engineering Letters. He is currently Associate Editor of the Information Sciences Journal, Applied Soft Computing Journal, Engineering Applications of Artificial Intelligence,

Granular Computing Journal and the International Journal on Fuzzy Systems. Finally, he has been elected IFSA Fellow in 2015 and MICAI Fellow member in 2017. He has been recognized as Highly Cited Researcher in 2017 and 2018 by Clarivate Analytics because of having multiple highly cited papers in Web of Science.

Poom Kumam received the B.S., M.Sc., and Ph.D. degrees in mathematics from Burapha University (BUU), Chiang Mai University (CMU), and Naresuan University (NU), respectively. In 2008, he received a grant from Franco-Thai Cooperation for short-term visited at the Laboratoire de Mathematiques, Universite de Bretagne Occidentale, France. He was also a Visiting Professor for a short-term research with Professor Anthony To-Ming Lau at the University of Alberta, AB, Canada. He is currently a Full Professor with the Department of Mathematics, King Mongkut's University of Technology Thonburi (KMUTT), where he is also the Head of the KMUTT Fixed Point Theory and Applications Research Group since 2007 and also leading of the Theoretical and Computational Science Center (TaCS-Center) in 2014 (now, became to TaCS-Center of Excellence in 2021). He has successfully advised 5 master's, and 44 Ph.D. graduates. He had won of the most important awards for mathematicians. The first one is the TRF-CHE-Scopus Young Researcher Award in 2010 that is the award given by the corporation from three organizations: Thailand Research Fund (TRF), the Commission of Higher Education (CHE), and Elsevier Publisher (Scopus). The second award was in 2012 when he received the TWAS Prize for Young Scientist in Thailand, which is given by the Academy of Sciences for the Developing World TWAS (UNESCO) together with the National Research Council of Thailand. In 2014, the third award is the Fellowship Award for Outstanding Contribution to Mathematics from International Academy of Physical Science, Allahabad, India. In 2015 Dr. Poom Kumam has been awarded Thailand Frontier Author Award 2015, Award for outstanding researcher who has published works and has often been used as a reference or evaluation criteria of the database Web of Science. Moreover, In 2016 Dr. Poom Kumam has been awarded 2016 Thailand Frontier Researcher Awards on Innovation Forum: Discovery, Protection, Commercialization By Intellectual Property & Science, and Thomson Reuters. Dr. Poom Kumam has been Highly Cited Researcher (HCR 2015, 2016, 2017). Moreover, he has been received KMUTT-HALL OF FAME 2017, In Honour of the Recipients of Academic Awards, KMUTT Young Researcher Awards, Excellence in Teaching Awards for 2016. In 2019 he received 2019 CMMSE Prize Winner: The CMMSE prize is given to computational researchers for important contributions in the developments of Numerical Methods for Physics, Chemistry, Engineering and Economics, from CMMSE Conference June 30 to July 6, 2019, Rota, Cadiz - Spain. He has also been listed and ranked in the 197th Place in General Mathematics among the Top 2% Scientists in the World 2021 (Published by Stanford University in USA).

He served on the editorial boards of various international journals and has also published more than 800 papers in Scopus and Web of Science (WoS) database and also delivers many invited talks on different international conferences every year all around the world. Furthermore, his research interest focuses on Fixed Point Theory, fractional differential equations and Optimization with related with optimization problems in both pure science and applied science.

Contributors

Sani Aji
Department of Mathematics
Faculty of Science
King Mongkut's University of Technology Thonburi (KMUTT)
Bangkok, Thailand
and
Department of Mathematics
Faculty of Science
Gombe State University
Gombe, Nigeria

Ibrahim Aydogdu
Department of Civil Engineering
Akdeniz University
Antalya, Turkey

Eda Boltürk
Istanbul Settlement and Custody Bank Inc.
Istanbul, Turkiye

Samira Hadi Bonab
Department of Mathematics, Ardabil Branch
Islamic Azad University
Ardabil, Iran

Manash Jyoti Borah
Department of Mathematics
Bahona College
Jorhat, India

Zong Woo Geem
College of IT Convergence
Gachon University
Seongnam, Korea

Farhan Golkarmanesh
Department of Mathematics, Sanandaj Branch
Islamic Azad University
Sanandaj, Iran

Erhan Güler
Department of Mathematics
Faculty of Science
Bartin University Bartin, Turkey

Mehmet Gürdal
Department of Mathematics
Faculty of Arts and Sciences
Suleyman Demirel University
Isparta, Turkey

Bipan Hazarika
Department of Mathematics
Gauhati University
Guwahati, India

Polinho Katina
Department of Informatics
University of South Carolina Upstate
Spartanburg, South Carolina

Ömer Kisi
Department of Mathematics
Faculty of Science
Bartin University

Nabanita Konwar
Department of Mathematics
Birjhora Mahavidyalaya
Bongaigaon, Assam

Wiyada Kumam
Applied Mathematics for Science and Engineering Research Unit (AMSERU)
Department of Mathematics and Computer Science
Faculty of Science and Technology
Rajamangala University of Technology Thanyaburi (RMUTT) Pathum Thani, Thailand

Joao Matias
Department of Economics, Industrial Engineering and Tourism – GOVCOPP
University of Aveiro
Aveiro, Portugal

Fernanda Mendes
ESAI
Lisbon, Portugal

S. A. Mohiuddine
Department of General Required Courses, Mathematics
The Applied College
King Abdulaziz University
Jeddah, Saudi Arabia
and
Operator Theory and Applications Research Group
Department of Mathematics, Faculty of Science
King Abdulaziz University
Jeddah, Saudi Arabia

Vahid Parvaneh
Department of Mathematics, Gilan-E-Gharb Branch
Islamic Azad University
Gilan-E-Gharb, Iran

Marija V. Paunović
Faculty of Hotel Management and Tourism
University of Kragujevac
Kragujevac, Serbia

Kaliyaperumal Punniyamoorthy
Department of Mathematics
Rajalakshmi Engineering College (Autonomous)
Chennai, India

N. Revathi
Department of Computer Science
Periyar University PG Extension Centre
Dharmapuri, India

Mehmet Polat Saka
Department of Engineering Sciences
Middle East Technical University
Ankara, Turkey

Ricardo Santos
GOVCOPP
University of Aveiro
Aveiro, Portugal

José Soares
Department of Management – ADVANCE
University of Lisbon
Lisbon, Portugal

Anouar Hallioui
Department of Industrial Engineering
Sidi Mohamed Ben Abdellah University
Fez, Morocco

K. Tamilvanan
Department of Mathematics, Faculty of Science & Humanities
R.M.K. Engineering College
Tamil Nadu, India

Refik Burak Taymus
Department of Civil Engineering
Yuzuncu yil University
Van, Turkey

Srinivasan Vijayabalaji
Department of Mathematics (S&H)
University College of Engineering Panruti (A Constituent College of Anna University)
Panruti, India

1 A Study on Approximate Fixed Point Property in Intuitionistic Fuzzy n-Normed Linear Spaces

Pradip Debnath
Assam University

CONTENTS

1.1 Introduction 1
1.2 Preliminaries 2
1.3 Approximate Fixed Points in IFnNLS 3
1.4 Intuitionistic n-Fuzzy Contraction and Nonexpansive Mappings 5
Bibliography 12

1.1 INTRODUCTION

Fuzzy set theory [31] has widespread applications in different branches of mathematical science such as theory of functions [18,28], topological and metric spaces [10,14, 19], and approximation theory [1]. It has also been applied in control of chaos [13], quantum physics [22], computer programming [16], population dynamics [3], and nonlinear dynamical systems [17].

The initial notion of fuzzy norm was put forward by Katsaras [20]. It was further improved and re-defined by various mathematicians considering particular areas of application [2,12,19,22,29]. The notion of an intuitionistic fuzzy n-normed linear space (IFnNLS) [23] generalizes an intuitionistic fuzzy normed space which was introduced by Saadati and Park [24].

The concept of fixed point property of mappings plays a significant role in the investigation of analytic properties of a normed linear space. In this chapter, we introduce the concept of approximate fixed point property in an IFnNLS. We also establish the relation between asymptotic regularity and fixed point property. Further, we introduce and investigate the properties of various types of intuitionistic n-fuzzy contraction mappings and their connection with fixed point property.

DOI: 10.1201/9781003312017-1

The definition of convergence of a sequence in an IFnNLS is crucial for the investigation of its analytic properties. A new and modified definition of convergence was introduced in [25,26]. The results of this chapter are established on the basis of this definition. For more relevant work, we refer to [4–7,11,15].

1.2 PRELIMINARIES

The same topology is induced by an intuitionistic fuzzy metric and a fuzzy metric [15]. Hence, to generate original and new results in intuitionistic fuzzy setting, it was necessary to re-define the notion of intuitionistic fuzzy norm [21,30]. To serve this purpose, an improved definition of an IFnNLS was put forward by Debnath and Sen [8,9] as given next.

Definition 1.1 *The five-tuple $(V,\eta,\gamma,*,\circ)$ is called an IFnNLS, where V is a vector space of dimension $d \geq n$ over a field F, $*$ is a continuous t-norm, $\circ$ is a continuous t-conorm, η,γ are fuzzy sets on $V^n \times (0,\infty)$, η signifies the degree of membership, and γ signifies the degree of non-membership of $(u_1,u_2,\ldots,u_n,t) \in V^n \times (0,1)$. The following conditions are satisfied for every $(u_1,u_2,\ldots,u_n) \in V^n$ and $s,t > 0$:*

(i) $\eta(u_1,u_2,\ldots,u_n,r) = 0$ *and* $\gamma(u_1,u_2,\ldots,u_n,r) = 1$ *for all non-positive real number* t,

(ii) $\eta(u_1,u_2,\ldots,u_n,r) = 1$ *and* $\gamma(u_1,u_2,\ldots,u_n,r) = 0$ *for all positive* r *if and only if* $u_1,u_2,\ldots,u_n$ *are linearly dependent,*

(iii) $\eta(u_1,u_2,\ldots,u_n,r)$ *and* $\gamma(u_1,u_2,\ldots,u_n,r)$ *are invariant under any permutation of* $u_1,u_2,\ldots,u_n$,

(iv) $\eta(u_1,u_2,\ldots,cu_n,r) = \eta(u_1,u_2,\ldots,u_n,\frac{t}{|c|})$ *and* $\gamma(u_1,u_2,\ldots,cu_n,r) = \gamma(u_1,u_2,\ldots,u_n,\frac{r}{|c|})$ *if* $c \neq 0, c \in F$,

(v) $\eta(u_1,u_2,\ldots,u_n,s) * \eta(u_1,u_2,\ldots,u_n',r) \leq \eta(u_1,u_2,\ldots,u_n+u_n',s+r)$,

(vi) $\eta(u_1,u_2,\ldots,u_n,s) \circ \gamma(u_1,u_2,\ldots,u_n',r) \geq \gamma(u_1,u_2,\ldots,u_n+u_n',s+r)$,

(vii) $\eta(u_1,u_2,\ldots,u_n,r) : (0,\infty) \to [0,1]$ *and* $\gamma(u_1,u_2,\ldots,u_n,r) : (0,\infty) \to [0,1]$ *are continuous in* r,

(viii) $\lim_{r\to\infty} \eta(u_1,u_2,\ldots,u_n,r) = 1$ *and* $\lim_{r\to 0} \eta(u_1,u_2,\ldots,u_n,r) = 0$,

(ix) $\lim_{r\to\infty} \gamma(u_1,u_2,\ldots,u_n,r) = 0$ *and* $\lim_{r\to 0} \gamma(u_1,u_2,\ldots,u_n,r) = 1$.

Definition 1.2 *[25,26] Let $(V,\eta,\gamma,*,\circ)$ be an IFnNLS. A sequence $v = \{v_k\}$ in V is called convergent to $\varsigma \in V$ with respect to the intuitionistic fuzzy n-norm (IFnN) $(\eta,\gamma)^n$ if, for every $\varepsilon \in (0,1)$, $r > 0$ and $u_1,u_2,\ldots,u_{n-1} \in V$, there exists $k_0 \in \mathbb{N}$ such that $\eta(u_1,u_2,\ldots,u_{n-1},v_k-\varsigma,r) > 1-\varepsilon$ and $\gamma(u_1,u_2,\ldots,u_{n-1},v_k-\varsigma,r) < \varepsilon$ for all $k \geq k_0$. We denote it by $(\eta,\gamma)^n - \lim v = \varsigma$ or $v_k \overset{(\eta,\gamma)^n}{\to} \varsigma$ as $k \to \infty$.*

proposition 1.1 *[27] In an IFnNLS V, $(\eta,\gamma)^n - \lim v = \varsigma$ if and only if for every $r > 0$ and $u_1,u_2,\ldots,u_{n-1} \in V$, $\eta(u_1,\ldots,u_{n-1},v_k-\varsigma,r) \to 1$ and $\gamma(u_1,\ldots,u_{n-1},v_k-\varsigma,r) \to 0$ as $k \to \infty$.*

Definition 1.3 *[25,26] Let $(V,\eta,\gamma,*,\circ)$ be an IFnNLS. A sequence $v = \{v_k\}$ in V is said to be Cauchy with respect to the IFnN $(\eta,\gamma)^n$ if, for every $\varepsilon \in (0,1)$, $r > 0$*

and $u_1, u_2, \ldots, u_{n-1} \in V$, *there exists* $k_0 \in \mathbb{N}$ *such that* $\eta(u_1, u_2, \ldots, u_{n-1}, v_k - v_m, r) > 1 - \varepsilon$ *and* $\gamma(u_1, u_2, \ldots, u_{n-1}, v_k - v_m, r) < \varepsilon$ *for all* $k, m \geq k_0$.

Definition 1.4 *An IFnNLS V is complete with respect to the IFnN* $(\eta, \gamma)^n$ *if every Cauchy sequence in it is convergent.*

proposition 1.2 *[27] If every Cauchy sequence in an IFnNLS V has a convergent subsequence, then V is complete.*

1.3 APPROXIMATE FIXED POINTS IN IFNNLS

Now we are ready to present our main results. First we define the concept of an intuitionistic n-fuzzy approximate fixed point (InFAFP) in an IFnNLS as given below.

Definition 1.5 *Let* $(V, \eta, \gamma, *, \circ)$ *be an IFnNLS and* $\Gamma : V \to V$ *be a mapping.* $\varpi_0 \in V$ *is said to be an intuitionistic n-fuzzy approximate fixed point (InFAFP) of* Γ *if for every* $\varepsilon > 0$ *and* $\omega_1, \omega_2, \ldots, \omega_{n-1} \in V$ *we have*

$$\mu(\omega_1, \omega_2, \ldots, \omega_{n-1}, \Gamma(\varpi_0) - \varpi_0, s) > 1 - \varepsilon$$
$$\text{and } \nu(\omega_1, \omega_2, \ldots, \omega_{n-1}, \Gamma(\varpi_0) - \varpi_0, s) < \varepsilon$$

for all $s > 0$. *We denote the set of all InFAFP of* Γ *by* $AFP_\varepsilon(\Gamma)$.

Further, we say that the mapping Γ *has the InFAFP property if the set* $AFP_\varepsilon(\Gamma)$ *is nonempty for every* $\varepsilon > 0$ *and* $\omega_1, \omega_2, \ldots, \omega_{n-1} \in V$.

The example below illustrates Definition 1.5.

Example 1.1 *Let* $V = (0,1)^n$, $\omega_i = (\omega_{i1}, \omega_{i2}, \ldots, \omega_{in}) \in (0,1)^n$ *for each* $i = 1, 2, \ldots, n$ *with*

$$\|\omega_1, \omega_2, \ldots, \omega_n\| = abs\left(\begin{vmatrix} \omega_{11} & \cdots & \omega_{1n} \\ \vdots & \ddots & \vdots \\ \omega_{n1} & \cdots & \omega_{nn} \end{vmatrix} \right),$$

and let $a * b = ab$, $a \circ b = \min\{a + b, 1\}$ *for all* $a, b \in [0,1]$. *Now for all* $w_1, w_2, \ldots, w_n \in (0,1)^n$ *and* $r > 0$, *let us define* $\eta(w_1, w_2, \ldots, w_n, r) = \frac{r}{r + \|w_1, w_2, \ldots, w_n\|}$ *and* $\gamma(w_1, w_2, \ldots, w_n, r) = \frac{\|w_1, w_2, \ldots, w_n\|}{r + \|w_1, w_2, \ldots, w_n\|}$. *Then* $((0,1)^n, \eta, \gamma, *, \circ)$ *is an IFnNLS.*

Consider the mapping $\Gamma : V \to V$ *defined by*

$$\Gamma(\theta_1, \theta_2, \ldots, \theta_n) = (\theta_1^1, \theta_2^2, \ldots, \theta_n^2)$$

for all $(\theta_1, \theta_2, \ldots, \theta_n) \in V$. *Clearly,* Γ *has no fixed point in* V. *Hence, we try to investigate its InFAFP.*

We observe that for every $\varepsilon > 0$, $w_1, w_2, \ldots, w_{n-1} \in (0,1)^n$ *and* $r > 0$, *there exists* $\mathrm{u} \in (0,1)^n$ *such that*

$$\eta(w_1, w_2, \ldots, w_{n-1}, \Gamma(\mathrm{u}) - \mathrm{u}, r) = \frac{r}{r + \|w_1, w_2, \ldots, w_{n-1}, \Gamma(\mathrm{u}) - \mathrm{u}\|} > 1 - \varepsilon$$

and

$$\gamma(w_1,w_2,\dots,w_{n-1},\Gamma(u)-u,r)=\frac{\|w_1,w_2,\dots,w_{n-1},\Gamma(u)-u\|}{r+\|w_1,w_2,\dots,w_{n-1},\Gamma(u)-u\|}<\varepsilon.$$

Hence, we conclude that Γ has InFAFP property.

Definition 1.6 *Let $(V,\eta,\gamma,*,\circ)$ be an IFnNLS and $\Gamma : V \to V$ be a mapping. Γ is said to be intuitionistic n-fuzzy asymptotic regular (InFAR) of Γ if for every $\varpi \in V$, $s>0$ and $\omega_1,\omega_2,\dots,\omega_{n-1}\in V$ we have*

$$\lim_{k\to\infty}\mu(\omega_1,\omega_2,\dots,\omega_{n-1},\Gamma^{k+1}(\varpi)-\Gamma^k(\varpi),s)=1$$
$$\text{and } \lim_{k\to\infty}\nu(\omega_1,\omega_2,\dots,\omega_{n-1},\Gamma^{k+1}(\varpi)-\Gamma^k(\varpi),s)=0.$$

Theorem 1.1 *Let $(V,\eta,\gamma,*,\circ)$ be an IFnNLS and $\Gamma : V \to V$ be a mapping. If Γ is InFAR, then it has InFAFP property.*

Proof. Let $\varpi_0 \in V$. Since Γ is InFAR, we have for every $s>0$ and $\omega_1,\omega_2,\dots,\omega_{n-1}\in V$ that

$$\lim_{k\to\infty}\mu(\omega_1,\omega_2,\dots,\omega_{n-1},\Gamma^{k+1}(\varpi)-\Gamma^k(\varpi),s)=1$$
$$\text{and } \lim_{k\to\infty}\nu(\omega_1,\omega_2,\dots,\omega_{n-1},\Gamma^{k+1}(\varpi_0)-\Gamma^k(\varpi_0),s)=0.$$

In this case, for every $\varepsilon>0$, there exists $k_0\in\mathbb{N}$ such that

$$\mu(\omega_1,\omega_2,\dots,\omega_{n-1},\Gamma^{k+1}(\varpi_0)-\Gamma^k(\varpi_0),s)>1-\varepsilon$$
$$\text{and } \nu(\omega_1,\omega_2,\dots,\omega_{n-1},\Gamma^{k+1}(\varpi_0)-\Gamma^k(\varpi_0),s)<\varepsilon$$

for every $k\ge k_0$. If we denote $\Gamma^k(\varpi_0)$ by ϑ_0, we have

$$\begin{aligned}&\mu(\omega_1,\omega_2,\dots,\omega_{n-1},\Gamma^{k+1}(\varpi_0)-\Gamma^k(\varpi_0),s)\\&=\mu(\omega_1,\omega_2,\dots,\omega_{n-1},\Gamma(\Gamma^k(\varpi_0))-\Gamma^k(\varpi_0),s)\\&=\mu(\omega_1,\omega_2,\dots,\omega_{n-1},\Gamma(\vartheta_0)-\vartheta_0,s)>1-\varepsilon\\&\text{and}\\&\nu(\omega_1,\omega_2,\dots,\omega_{n-1},\Gamma^{k+1}(\varpi_0)-\Gamma^k(\varpi_0),s)\\&=\nu(\omega_1,\omega_2,\dots,\omega_{n-1},\Gamma(\Gamma^k(\varpi_0))-\Gamma^k(\varpi_0),s)\\&=\nu(\omega_1,\omega_2,\dots,\omega_{n-1},\Gamma(\vartheta_0)-\vartheta_0,s)<\varepsilon.\end{aligned}$$

This proves that ϑ_0 is an InFAFP of Γ. □

1.4 INTUITIONISTIC N-FUZZY CONTRACTION AND NONEXPANSIVE MAPPINGS

In this section, we introduce the concepts of intuitionistic n-fuzzy contraction and nonexpansive mappings in an IFnNLS and investigate their properties.

Definition 1.7 *Let $(V,\eta,\gamma,*,\circ)$ be an IFnNLS and $\Gamma : V \to V$ be a mapping. Γ is said to be intuitionistic n-fuzzy contraction (InFC) if there exists $p \in (0,1)$ such that for any $s > 0$ and $\omega_1,\omega_2,\ldots,\omega_{n-1} \in V$ we have*

$$\mu(\omega_1,\omega_2,\ldots,\omega_{n-1},\Gamma(\theta)-\Gamma(\phi),ps) \geq \mu(\omega_1,\omega_2,\ldots,\omega_{n-1},\theta-\phi,s)$$
$$\text{and } \nu(\omega_1,\omega_2,\ldots,\omega_{n-1},\Gamma(\theta)-\Gamma(\phi),ps) \leq \nu(\omega_1,\omega_2,\ldots,\omega_{n-1},\theta-\phi,s).$$

for all $\theta,\phi \in V$.

Theorem 1.2 *Let $(V,\eta,\gamma,*,\circ)$ be an IFnNLS and $\Gamma : V \to V$ be an InFC. Then $AFP_\varepsilon(\Gamma)$ is nonempty for every $\varepsilon \in (0,1)$.*

Proof. Fix $\omega_1,\omega_2,\ldots,\omega_{n-1} \in V$ and $s > 0$. Also let $\varpi \in V$. Then

$$\begin{aligned}
&\mu(\omega_1,\omega_2,\ldots,\omega_{n-1},\Gamma^k(\varpi)-\Gamma^{k+1}(\varpi),s)\\
&\quad= \mu(\omega_1,\omega_2,\ldots,\omega_{n-1},\Gamma(\Gamma^{k-1}(\varpi))-\Gamma(\Gamma^k(\varpi)),s)\\
&\quad\geq \mu(\omega_1,\omega_2,\ldots,\omega_{n-1},\Gamma^{k-1}(\varpi)-\Gamma^k(\varpi),\frac{s}{p})\\
&\quad\geq \mu(\omega_1,\omega_2,\ldots,\omega_{n-1},\Gamma^{k-2}(\varpi)-\Gamma^{k-1}(\varpi),\frac{s}{p^2})\\
&\quad\geq \ldots\\
&\quad\geq \mu(\omega_1,\omega_2,\ldots,\omega_{n-1},\varpi-\Gamma(\varpi),\frac{s}{p^k})
\end{aligned}$$

and

$$\begin{aligned}
&\nu(\omega_1,\omega_2,\ldots,\omega_{n-1},\Gamma^k(\varpi)-\Gamma^{k+1}(\varpi),s)\\
&\quad= \nu(\omega_1,\omega_2,\ldots,\omega_{n-1},\Gamma(\Gamma^{k-1}(\varpi))-\Gamma(\Gamma^k(\varpi)),s)\\
&\quad\leq \nu(\omega_1,\omega_2,\ldots,\omega_{n-1},\Gamma^{k-1}(\varpi)-\Gamma^k(\varpi),\frac{s}{p})\\
&\quad\leq \nu(\omega_1,\omega_2,\ldots,\omega_{n-1},\Gamma^{k-2}(\varpi)-\Gamma^{k-1}(\varpi),\frac{s}{p^2})\\
&\quad\leq \ldots\\
&\quad\leq \nu(\omega_1,\omega_2,\ldots,\omega_{n-1},\varpi-\Gamma(\varpi),\frac{s}{p^k}).
\end{aligned}$$

For $p \in (0,1)$, as $k \to \infty$, we have $\frac{t}{p^k} \to \infty$. Thus, using the properties of the intuitionistic fuzzy norm, we have that

$$\mu(\omega_1,\omega_2,\ldots,\omega_{n-1},\Gamma^k(\varpi)-\Gamma^{k+1}(\varpi),s) \to 1$$

and

$$\nu(\omega_1, \omega_2, \ldots, \omega_{n-1}, \Gamma^k(\varpi) - \Gamma^{k+1}(\varpi), s) \to 0$$

as $k \to \infty$. Therefore, we conclude that $AFP_\varepsilon(\Gamma)$ is nonempty for every $\varepsilon \in (0,1)$. □

Example 1.2 *Consider the IFnNLS $(V = (0,1)^n, \eta, \gamma, *, \circ)$ as in Example 1.1. Also, consider the mapping $\Gamma : V \to V$ defined by*

$$\Gamma(\theta_1, \theta_2, \ldots, \theta_n) = (\frac{\theta_1}{2}, \frac{\theta_2}{2}, \ldots, \frac{\theta_n}{2})$$

for all $(\theta_1, \theta_2, \ldots, \theta_n) \in V$. Clearly, Γ has no fixed point in V.

We prove that Γ is an InFC mapping.

For every $w_1, w_2, \ldots, w_{n-1} \in (0,1)^n$ and $s > 0$, and for all $\mathfrak{u}, \mathfrak{v} \in (0,1)^n$ we have that

$$\begin{aligned}\eta(w_1, w_2, \ldots, w_{n-1}, \Gamma(\mathfrak{u}) - \mathfrak{v}, \frac{s}{2}) &= \frac{\frac{s}{2}}{\frac{s}{2} + \|w_1, w_2, \ldots, w_{n-1}, \Gamma(\mathfrak{u}) - \mathfrak{v}\|} \\ &= \eta(w_1, w_2, \ldots, w_{n-1}, \mathfrak{u} - \mathfrak{v}, s)\end{aligned}$$

and

$$\begin{aligned}\gamma(w_1, w_2, \ldots, w_{n-1}, \Gamma(\mathfrak{u}) - \mathfrak{v}, \frac{s}{2}) &= \frac{\|w_1, w_2, \ldots, w_{n-1}, \Gamma(\mathfrak{u}) - \mathfrak{v}\|}{\frac{s}{2} + \|w_1, w_2, \ldots, w_{n-1}, \Gamma(\mathfrak{u}) - \mathfrak{v}\|} \\ &= \gamma(w_1, w_2, \ldots, w_{n-1}, \mathfrak{u} - \mathfrak{v}, s).\end{aligned}$$

Now, for any $\varepsilon \in (0,1)$, we have

$$\begin{aligned}\eta(w_1, w_2, \ldots, w_{n-1}, \mathfrak{u} - \Gamma(\mathfrak{u}), s) &= \eta(w_1, w_2, \ldots, w_{n-1}, \mathfrak{u} - \frac{\mathfrak{u}}{2}, s) \\ &= \eta(w_1, w_2, \ldots, w_{n-1}, \frac{\mathfrak{u}}{2}, s) \\ &= \frac{s}{s + \|w_1, w_2, \ldots, w_{n-1}, \frac{\mathfrak{u}}{2}\|} \\ &> 1 - \varepsilon.\end{aligned}$$

Similarly, we can prove that

$$\gamma(w_1, w_2, \ldots, w_{n-1}, \mathfrak{u} - \Gamma(\mathfrak{u}), s) < \varepsilon.$$

Hence, Γ has InFAFP property.

Definition 1.8 *Let $(V, \eta, \gamma, *, \circ)$ be an IFnNLS and $\Gamma : V \to V$ be a mapping. If there exists $\kappa \in (0,1)$ and $\mathfrak{L} > 0$ such that for any fixed $\omega_1, \omega_2, \ldots, \omega_{n-1} \in V$, we have*

$$\begin{aligned}\eta(\omega_1, \omega_2, \ldots, \omega_{n-1}, \Gamma(\theta) - \Gamma(\phi), s) \geq\ & \eta(\omega_1, \omega_2, \ldots, \omega_{n-1}, \theta - \phi, \frac{s}{\kappa}) \\ & * \eta(\omega_1, \omega_2, \ldots, \omega_{n-1}, \phi - \Gamma(\theta), \frac{s}{\mathfrak{L}})\end{aligned}$$

and

$$\gamma(\omega_1,\omega_2,\ldots,\omega_{n-1},\Gamma(\theta)-\Gamma(\phi),s) \leq \gamma(\omega_1,\omega_2,\ldots,\omega_{n-1},\theta-\phi,\frac{s}{\kappa})$$
$$\circ\,\gamma(\omega_1,\omega_2,\ldots,\omega_{n-1},\phi-\Gamma(\theta),\frac{s}{\mathfrak{L}})$$

for all $s>0$ and $\theta,\phi\in V$, then Γ is called an intuitionistic n-fuzzy weak contraction operator (InFWCO).

Theorem 1.3 *Let $(V,\eta,\gamma,*,\circ)$ be an IFnNLS and $\Gamma : V\to V$ be an InFWCO. Then $AFP_\varepsilon(\Gamma)$ is nonempty for every $\varepsilon\in(0,1)$.*

Proof. Fix $\omega_1,\omega_2,\ldots,\omega_{n-1}\in V$. Also let $\varpi\in V$, $\varepsilon\in(0,1)$ and $s>0$. Then

$$\begin{aligned}
&\mu(\omega_1,\omega_2,\ldots,\omega_{n-1},\Gamma^k(\varpi)-\Gamma^{k+1}(\varpi),s)\\
&=\mu(\omega_1,\omega_2,\ldots,\omega_{n-1},\Gamma(\Gamma^{k-1}(\varpi))-\Gamma(\Gamma^k(\varpi)),s)\\
&\geq\mu(\omega_1,\omega_2,\ldots,\omega_{n-1},\Gamma^{k-1}(\varpi)-\Gamma^k(\varpi),\frac{s}{\kappa})\\
&*\,\mu(\omega_1,\omega_2,\ldots,\omega_{n-1},\Gamma^k(\varpi)-\Gamma^k(\varpi),\frac{s}{\mathfrak{L}})\\
&=\mu(\omega_1,\omega_2,\ldots,\omega_{n-1},\Gamma^{k-1}(\varpi)-\Gamma^k(\varpi),\frac{s}{\kappa})*1\\
&=\mu(\omega_1,\omega_2,\ldots,\omega_{n-1},\Gamma^{k-1}(\varpi)-\Gamma^k(\varpi),\frac{s}{\kappa})\\
&\geq\mu(\omega_1,\omega_2,\ldots,\omega_{n-1},\Gamma^{k-2}(\varpi)-\Gamma^{k-1}(\varpi),\frac{s}{\kappa^2})\\
&*\,\mu(\omega_1,\omega_2,\ldots,\omega_{n-1},\Gamma^{k-1}(\varpi)-\Gamma^{k-1}(\varpi),\frac{s}{\mathfrak{L}})\\
&=\mu(\omega_1,\omega_2,\ldots,\omega_{n-1},\Gamma^{k-2}(\varpi)-\Gamma^{k-1}(\varpi),\frac{s}{\kappa^2})*1\\
&=\mu(\omega_1,\omega_2,\ldots,\omega_{n-1},\Gamma^{k-2}(\varpi)-\Gamma^{k-1}(\varpi),\frac{s}{\kappa^2})\\
&\geq\ldots\\
&=\mu(\omega_1,\omega_2,\ldots,\omega_{n-1},\Gamma^{k-(k-1)}(\varpi)-\Gamma^{k-(k-2)}(\varpi),\frac{s}{\kappa^{(k-1)}})\\
&=\mu(\omega_1,\omega_2,\ldots,\omega_{n-1},\Gamma(\varpi)-\Gamma^2(\varpi),\frac{s}{\kappa^{(k-1)}})\\
&\geq\mu(\omega_1,\omega_2,\ldots,\omega_{n-1},\varpi-\Gamma(\varpi),\frac{s}{\kappa^k})\\
&*\,\mu(\omega_1,\omega_2,\ldots,\omega_{n-1},\Gamma(\varpi)-\Gamma(\varpi),\frac{s}{\mathfrak{L}})\\
&\geq\mu(\omega_1,\omega_2,\ldots,\omega_{n-1},\varpi-\Gamma(\varpi),\frac{s}{\kappa^k})*1\\
&=\mu(\omega_1,\omega_2,\ldots,\omega_{n-1},\varpi-\Gamma(\varpi),\frac{s}{\kappa^k}).
\end{aligned}$$

Similarly, for the non-membership function γ, we have

$$\begin{aligned}
&\gamma(\omega_1,\omega_2,\ldots,\omega_{n-1},\Gamma^k(\varpi)-\Gamma^{k+1}(\varpi),s)\\
&=\gamma(\omega_1,\omega_2,\ldots,\omega_{n-1},\Gamma(\Gamma^{k-1}(\varpi))-\Gamma(\Gamma^k(\varpi)),s)\\
&\leq\gamma(\omega_1,\omega_2,\ldots,\omega_{n-1},\Gamma^{k-1}(\varpi)-\Gamma^k(\varpi),\frac{s}{\kappa})\\
&\circ\gamma(\omega_1,\omega_2,\ldots,\omega_{n-1},\Gamma^k(\varpi)-\Gamma^k(\varpi),\frac{s}{\mathfrak{L}})\\
&=\gamma(\omega_1,\omega_2,\ldots,\omega_{n-1},\Gamma^{k-1}(\varpi)-\Gamma^k(\varpi),\frac{s}{\kappa})\circ 0\\
&=\gamma(\omega_1,\omega_2,\ldots,\omega_{n-1},\Gamma^{k-1}(\varpi)-\Gamma^k(\varpi),\frac{s}{\kappa})\\
&\leq\gamma(\omega_1,\omega_2,\ldots,\omega_{n-1},\Gamma^{k-2}(\varpi)-\Gamma^{k-1}(\varpi),\frac{s}{\kappa^2})\\
&\circ\gamma(\omega_1,\omega_2,\ldots,\omega_{n-1},\Gamma^{k-1}(\varpi)-\Gamma^{k-1}(\varpi),\frac{s}{\mathfrak{L}})\\
&=\gamma(\omega_1,\omega_2,\ldots,\omega_{n-1},\Gamma^{k-2}(\varpi)-\Gamma^{k-1}(\varpi),\frac{s}{\kappa^2})\circ 0\\
&=\gamma(\omega_1,\omega_2,\ldots,\omega_{n-1},\Gamma^{k-2}(\varpi)-\Gamma^{k-1}(\varpi),\frac{s}{\kappa^2})\\
&\leq\ldots\\
&=\gamma(\omega_1,\omega_2,\ldots,\omega_{n-1},\Gamma^{k-(k-1)}(\varpi)-\Gamma^{k-(k-2)}(\varpi),\frac{s}{\kappa^{(k-1)}})\\
&=\gamma(\omega_1,\omega_2,\ldots,\omega_{n-1},\Gamma(\varpi)-\Gamma^2(\varpi),\frac{s}{\kappa^{(k-1)}})\\
&\leq\gamma(\omega_1,\omega_2,\ldots,\omega_{n-1},\varpi-\Gamma(\varpi),\frac{s}{\kappa^k})\\
&\circ\gamma(\omega_1,\omega_2,\ldots,\omega_{n-1},\Gamma(\varpi)-\Gamma(\varpi),\frac{s}{\mathfrak{L}})\\
&\leq\gamma(\omega_1,\omega_2,\ldots,\omega_{n-1},\varpi-\Gamma(\varpi),\frac{s}{\kappa^k})\circ 0\\
&=\gamma(\omega_1,\omega_2,\ldots,\omega_{n-1},\varpi-\Gamma(\varpi),\frac{s}{\kappa^k}).
\end{aligned}$$

Since $\frac{s}{\kappa^k}\to\infty$, as $k\to\infty$, using the properties of the intuitionistic fuzzy n-norm, we conclude that an InFWCO has approximate fixed point property. □

Finally, we introduce and study the properties of an intuitionistic n-fuzzy nonexpansive mapping and establish its connection with approximate fixed point property.

Definition 1.9 *Let $(V,\eta,\gamma,*,\circ)$ be an IFnNLS. The mapping $\Gamma:V\to V$ is said to be intuitionistic n-fuzzy nonexpansive if for every $\omega_1,\omega_2,\ldots,\omega_{n-1}\in V$ and $s>0$, we have*

$$\eta(\omega_1,\omega_2,\ldots,\omega_{n-1},\Gamma(\varpi)-\Gamma(\theta),s)\geq\eta(\omega_1,\omega_2,\ldots,\omega_{n-1},\varpi-\theta,s)$$

and

$$\gamma(\omega_1,\omega_2,\ldots,\omega_{n-1},\Gamma(\varpi)-\Gamma(\theta),s)\leq\gamma(\omega_1,\omega_2,\ldots,\omega_{n-1},\varpi-\theta,s)$$

for all $\varpi,\theta\in V$.

Definition 1.10 *Let $(V,\eta,\gamma,*,\circ)$ be an IFnNLS and $\mathcal{J} \subset V$. Then $\mathcal{J}$ is said to have intuitionistic n-fuzzy approximate fixed point (InFAFP) property if every intuitionistic n-fuzzy nonexpansive mapping $\Gamma : V \to V$ satisfies the property that for fixed $\omega_1,\omega_2,\ldots,\omega_{n-1} \in V$ and $s > 0$, we have*

$$\sup\{\eta(\omega_1,\omega_2,\ldots,\omega_{n-1},\varpi - \Gamma(\varpi),s) : \varpi \in V\} = 1$$

and

$$\inf\{\gamma(\omega_1,\omega_2,\ldots,\omega_{n-1},\varpi - \Gamma(\varpi),s) : \varpi \in V\} = 0.$$

Theorem 1.4 *Let $(V,\eta,\gamma,*,\circ)$ be an IFnNLS having InFAFP property and $\mathfrak{J}$ be a dense subset of V. Then $\mathfrak{J}$ has InFAFP property.*

Proof. Let $\Gamma : V \to V$ be an intuitionistic n-fuzzy nonexpansive mapping. First we prove that for fixed $\omega_1,\omega_2,\ldots,\omega_{n-1} \in V$, $t > 0$ and $s > 0$,

$$\sup\{\eta(\omega_1,\omega_2,\ldots,\omega_{n-1},\varpi - \Gamma(\varpi),t) : \varpi \in \mathfrak{J}\}$$
$$= \sup\{\eta(\omega_1,\omega_2,\ldots,\omega_{n-1},\theta - \Gamma(\theta),s) : \theta \in \mathfrak{J}\}$$

and

$$\inf\{\gamma(\omega_1,\omega_2,\ldots,\omega_{n-1},\varpi - \Gamma(\varpi),t) : \varpi \in \mathfrak{J}\}$$
$$= \inf\{\gamma(\omega_1,\omega_2,\ldots,\omega_{n-1},\theta - \Gamma(\theta),s) : \theta \in \mathfrak{J}\}.$$

Since $\mathfrak{J} \subset V$, we have that

$$\sup\{\eta(\omega_1,\omega_2,\ldots,\omega_{n-1},\theta - \Gamma(\theta),s) : \theta \in \mathfrak{J}\}$$
$$\geq \sup\{\eta(\omega_1,\omega_2,\ldots,\omega_{n-1},\varpi - \Gamma(\varpi),t) : \varpi \in \mathfrak{J}\}$$

and

$$\inf\{\gamma(\omega_1,\omega_2,\ldots,\omega_{n-1},\theta - \Gamma(\theta),s) : \theta \in \mathfrak{J}\}$$
$$\leq \inf\{\gamma(\omega_1,\omega_2,\ldots,\omega_{n-1},\varpi - \Gamma(\varpi),t) : \varpi \in \mathfrak{J}\}.$$

Let $\theta \in V$. For $\mathfrak{J}$ is dense, there exists a sequence $\{\theta_k\}$ in $\mathfrak{J}$ such that $\theta_k \overset{(\eta,\gamma)^n}{\to} \theta$. We know that for each $k \in \mathbb{N}$ and $t,s > 0$,

$$\begin{aligned}
&\sup\{\eta(\omega_1,\omega_2,\ldots,\omega_{n-1},\varpi - \Gamma(\varpi),t) : \varpi \in \mathfrak{J}\}\\
&\quad \geq \eta(\omega_1,\omega_2,\ldots,\omega_{n-1},\theta_k - \Gamma(\theta_k),t)\\
&\quad \geq \eta(\omega_1,\omega_2,\ldots,\omega_{n-1},\theta_k - \theta + \theta - \Gamma(\theta) + \Gamma(\theta) - \Gamma(\theta_k),t)\\
&\quad \geq \eta(\omega_1,\omega_2,\ldots,\omega_{n-1},\theta_k - \theta,\frac{t}{3}) * \eta(\omega_1,\omega_2,\ldots,\omega_{n-1},\theta - \Gamma(\theta),\frac{t}{3})\\
&\quad * \eta(\omega_1,\omega_2,\ldots,\omega_{n-1},\theta_k - \Gamma(\theta_k),\frac{t}{3})
\end{aligned}$$

and

$$
\begin{aligned}
&\inf\{\gamma(\omega_1,\omega_2,\ldots,\omega_{n-1},\varpi-\Gamma(\varpi),t):\varpi\in\mathfrak{J}\}\\
&\quad\le\gamma(\omega_1,\omega_2,\ldots,\omega_{n-1},\theta_k-\Gamma(\theta_k),t)\\
&\quad\le\gamma(\omega_1,\omega_2,\ldots,\omega_{n-1},\theta_k-\theta+\theta-\Gamma(\theta)+\Gamma(\theta)-\Gamma(\theta_k),t)\\
&\quad\le\gamma(\omega_1,\omega_2,\ldots,\omega_{n-1},\theta_k-\theta,\frac{t}{3})*\gamma(\omega_1,\omega_2,\ldots,\omega_{n-1},\theta-\Gamma(\theta),\frac{t}{3})\\
&*\gamma(\omega_1,\omega_2,\ldots,\omega_{n-1},\theta_k-\Gamma(\theta_k),\frac{t}{3}).
\end{aligned}
$$

Since Γ is intuitionistic n-fuzzy nonexpansive, it is clearly intuitionistic n-fuzzy continuous.

If $\theta_k \overset{(\eta,\gamma)^n}{\rightarrow} \theta$, we have

$$\eta(\omega_1,\omega_2,\ldots,\omega_{n-1},\Gamma(\theta_k)-\Gamma(\theta),t)\ge\eta(\omega_1,\omega_2,\ldots,\omega_{n-1},\theta_k-\theta,t)\to 1$$

and

$$\gamma(\omega_1,\omega_2,\ldots,\omega_{n-1},\Gamma(\theta_k)-\Gamma(\theta),t)\le\gamma(\omega_1,\omega_2,\ldots,\omega_{n-1},\theta_k-\theta,t)\to 0$$

as $k\to\infty$.

Thus, we have $\Gamma(\theta_k) \overset{(\eta,\gamma)^n}{\rightarrow} \Gamma(\theta)$ when $\theta_k \overset{(\eta,\gamma)^n}{\rightarrow} \theta$. Hence, from the last inequality, we have

$$
\begin{aligned}
&\sup\{\eta(\omega_1,\omega_2,\ldots,\omega_{n-1},\theta-\Gamma(\theta),t):\theta\in\mathfrak{J}\}\\
&\qquad\qquad\ge\eta(\omega_1,\omega_2,\ldots,\omega_{n-1},\varpi-\Gamma(\varpi),\frac{t}{3})
\end{aligned}
$$

and

$$
\begin{aligned}
&\inf\{\gamma(\omega_1,\omega_2,\ldots,\omega_{n-1},\theta-\Gamma(\theta),t):\theta\in\mathfrak{J}\}\\
&\qquad\qquad\le\gamma(\omega_1,\omega_2,\ldots,\omega_{n-1},\varpi-\Gamma(\varpi),\frac{t}{3})
\end{aligned}
$$

for all $\varpi\in V$ and $t>0$ with fixed $\omega_1,\omega_2,\ldots,\omega_{n-1}\in V$.

Thus if we assume $\frac{t}{3}=t'$, then

$$
\begin{aligned}
&\sup\{\eta(\omega_1,\omega_2,\ldots,\omega_{n-1},\theta-\Gamma(\theta),t):\theta\in\mathfrak{J}\}\\
&\qquad\qquad\ge\sup\{\eta(\omega_1,\omega_2,\ldots,\omega_{n-1},\varpi-\Gamma(\varpi),t'):\varpi\in\mathfrak{J}\}
\end{aligned}
$$

and

$$
\begin{aligned}
&\inf\{\gamma(\omega_1,\omega_2,\ldots,\omega_{n-1},\theta-\Gamma(\theta),t):\theta\in\mathfrak{J}\}\\
&\qquad\qquad\le\inf\{\gamma(\omega_1,\omega_2,\ldots,\omega_{n-1},\varpi-\Gamma(\varpi),t'):\varpi\in\mathfrak{J}\}.
\end{aligned}
$$

Thus, our first claim is proved.

Now consider any intuitionistic n-fuzzy nonexpansive mapping $\Gamma_{\mathfrak{J}} : \mathfrak{J} \to \mathfrak{J}$. Since $\mathfrak{J}$ is dense, there exists a sequence $\{\theta_k\}$ in $\mathfrak{J}$ such that $\theta_k \overset{(\eta,\gamma)^n}{\to} \theta$ for any $\theta \in \mathfrak{J}$.

Since an intuitionistic n-fuzzy nonexpansive mapping is continuous, $\Gamma_{\mathfrak{J}}$ is intuitionistic n-fuzzy continuous and it can be extended on V by defining

$$\Gamma(\theta) = (\eta,\gamma)^n - \lim_{k\to\infty} \Gamma_{\mathfrak{J}}(\theta_k).$$

Hence, Γ may be considered as an intuitionistic n-fuzzy nonexpansive mapping on V.

Thus, we have

$$\begin{aligned}
&\eta(\omega_1,\omega_2,\ldots,\omega_{n-1},\Gamma(\theta)-\Gamma(\varpi),t)\\
&\quad= \limsup_{k\to\infty} \eta(\omega_1,\omega_2,\ldots,\omega_{n-1},\Gamma(\theta_k)-\Gamma(\varpi_k),t)\\
&\quad\geq \limsup_{k\to\infty} \eta(\omega_1,\omega_2,\ldots,\omega_{n-1},\theta_k-\varpi_k,t)
\end{aligned}$$

and

$$\begin{aligned}
&\gamma(\omega_1,\omega_2,\ldots,\omega_{n-1},\Gamma(\theta)-\Gamma(\varpi),t)\\
&\quad= \limsup_{k\to\infty} \gamma(\omega_1,\omega_2,\ldots,\omega_{n-1},\Gamma(\theta_k)-\Gamma(\varpi_k),t)\\
&\quad\leq \limsup_{k\to\infty} \gamma(\omega_1,\omega_2,\ldots,\omega_{n-1},\theta_k-\varpi_k,t)
\end{aligned}$$

for all $\theta,\varpi \in V$ and $t > 0$ with fixed $\omega_1,\omega_2,\ldots,\omega_{n-1} \in V$.

Since V has InFAFP property, we have

$$\begin{aligned}
&\sup\{\eta(\omega_1,\omega_2,\ldots,\omega_{n-1},\varpi-\Gamma(\varpi),t) : \varpi \in \mathfrak{J}\}\\
&\qquad= \sup\{\eta(\omega_1,\omega_2,\ldots,\omega_{n-1},\theta-\Gamma(\theta),s) : \theta \in \mathfrak{J}\} = 1
\end{aligned}$$

and

$$\begin{aligned}
&\inf\{\gamma(\omega_1,\omega_2,\ldots,\omega_{n-1},\varpi-\Gamma(\varpi),t) : \varpi \in \mathfrak{J}\}\\
&\qquad= \inf\{\gamma(\omega_1,\omega_2,\ldots,\omega_{n-1},\theta-\Gamma(\theta),s) : \theta \in \mathfrak{J}\} = 0.
\end{aligned}$$

Thus, given any intuitionistic n-fuzzy nonexpansive mapping Γ on $\mathfrak{J}$, we have

$$\sup\{\eta(\omega_1,\omega_2,\ldots,\omega_{n-1},\varpi-\Gamma(\varpi),t) : \varpi \in \mathfrak{J}\} = 1$$

and

$$\inf\{\gamma(\omega_1,\omega_2,\ldots,\omega_{n-1},\varpi-\Gamma(\varpi),t) : \varpi \in \mathfrak{J}\} = 0$$

and $\mathfrak{J}$ has InFAFP property. This completes the proof. □

Bibliography

1. G. A. Anastassiou, Fuzzy approximation by fuzzy convolution type operators, *Comput. Math. Appl.* **48** (2004), 1369–1386.
2. T. Bag and S. K. Samanta, A comparative study of fuzzy norms on a linear space, *Fuzzy Sets Syst.* **159** (2008), 670–684.
3. L. C. Barros, R. C. Bassanezi, and P. A. Tonelli, Fuzzy modelling in population dynamics, *Ecol. Model.* **128** (2000), 27–33.
4. P. Debnath, Lacunary ideal convergence in intuitionistic fuzzy normed linear spaces, *Comput. Math. Appl.* **63**, no. 3 (2012), 708–715.
5. P. Debnath, Results on lacunary difference ideal convergence in intuitionistic fuzzy normed linear spaces, *J. Intell. Fuzzy Syst.* **28**, no. 3 (2015), 1299–1306.
6. P. Debnath, Some Results on Cesaro summability in Intuitionistic Fuzzy n-normed linear Spaces, *Sahand Commun. Math. Anal.* **19**, no. 1 (2022), 77–87.
7. P. Debnath and S. A. Mohiuddine, *Soft Computing Techniques in Engineering, Health, Mathematical and Social Sciences*. CRC Press: Boca Raton, FL (2021).
8. P. Debnath and M. Sen, Some completeness results in terms of infinite series and quotient spaces in intuinionistic fuzzy *n*-normed linear spaces, *J. Intell. Fuzzy Syst.* **26**, no. 2 (2014), 975–982.
9. P. Debnath and M. Sen, Some results of calculus for functions having values in an intuinionistic fuzzy *n*-normed linear space, *J. Intell. Fuzzy Syst.* **26**, no. 6 (2014), 2983–2991.
10. M. A. Erceg, Metric spaces in fuzzy set theory, *J. Math. Anal. Appl.* **69** (1979), 205–230.
11. M. Erturk, V. Karakaya and M. Mursaleen, Approximate fixed points property in IFNS, *TWMS J. App. and Eng. Math.* **12**, no. 1 (2022), 329–346.
12. C. Felbin, Finite dimensional fuzzy normed linear spaces, *Fuzzy Sets Syst.* **48** (1992), 239–248.
13. A. L. Fradkov and R. J. Evans, Control of chaos: Methods and applications in engineering, *Chaos Solitons Fractals* **29** (2005), 33–56.
14. A. George and P. Veeramani, On some result in fuzzy metric space, *Fuzzy Sets Syst.* **64** (1994), 395–399.
15. V. George, S. Romaguera, and P. Veeramani, A note on intuitionistic fuzzy metric space, *Chaos Solitons Fractals* **28** (2006), 902–905.
16. R. Giles, A computer program for fuzzy reasoning, *Fuzzy Sets Syst.* **4** (1980), 221–234.
17. L. Hong and J. Q. Sun, Bifurcations of fuzzy nonlinear dynamical systems, *Commun. Nonlinear Sci. Numer. Simul.* **1** (2006), 1–12.
18. G. Jäger, Fuzzy uniform convergence and equicontinuity, *Fuzzy Sets Syst.* **109** (2000), 187–198.
19. O. Kaleva and S. Seikkala, On fuzzy metric spaces, *Fuzzy Sets Syst.* **12** (1984), 215–229.
20. A. K. Katsaras, Fuzzy topological vector spaces, *Fuzzy Sets Syst.* **12** (1984), 143–154.
21. F. Lael and K. Nourouzi, Some results on the IF-normed spaces, *Chaos Solitons Fractals* **37(3)** (2008), 931–939.
22. J. Madore, Fuzzy physics, *Ann. Phys.* **219** (1992), 187–198.
23. A. Narayanan, S. Vijayabalaji, and N. Thillaigovindan, Intuitionistic fuzzy bounded linear operators, *Iran J. Fuzzy Syst.* **4** (2007), 89–101.
24. R. Saadati and J. H. Park, On the intuitionistic fuzzy topological spaces, *Chaos Solitons Fractals* **27** (2006), 331–344.
25. M. Sen and P. Debnath, Lacunary statistical convergence in intuitionistic fuzzy *n*-normed linear spaces, *Math. Comput. Modell.* **54** (2011), 2978–2985.

26. M. Sen and P. Debnath, Statistical convergence in intuinionistic fuzzy n-normed linear spaces, *Fuzzy Inf. Eng.* **3** (2011), 259–273.
27. S. Vijayabalaji, N. Thillaigovindan, and Y. B. Jun, Intuitionistic fuzzy n-normed linear space, *Bull. Korean. Math. Soc.* **44** (2007), 291–308.
28. K. Wu, Convergences of fuzzy sets based on decomposition theory and fuzzy polynomial function, *Fuzzy Sets Syst.* **109** (2000), 173–185.
29. J. Z. Xiao and X. H. Zhu, Fuzzy normed spaces of operators and its completeness, *Fuzzy Sets Syst.* **133** (2003), 389–399.
30. Y. Yilmaz, On some basic properites of differentiation in intuitionistic fuzzy normed spaces, *Math. Comput. Modell.* **52** (2010), 448–458.
31. L. A. Zadeh, Fuzzy sets, *Inform. Cont.* **8** (1965), 338–353.

2 Sequential Extended Parametric and Sequential Extended Fuzzy *b*-Metrics with an Application in Integral Equations

Marija V. Paunović
University of Kragujevac

Samira Hadi Bonab, Vahid Parvaneh, and Farhan Golkarmanesh
Islamic Azad University

CONTENTS

2.1 Introduction 15
2.2 Main Results 17
2.3 Some Fixed Point Theorems 19
2.4 Sequential Extended Fuzzy *b*-Metric Spaces 23
2.5 Application 25
Bibliography 27

2.1 INTRODUCTION

In recent years, metric spaces have been generalized by many authors, which are expressed in different approaches. Many interesting spaces of the two-variable metric type are: $b-$metric space [2,5], rectangular metric space [4], parametric metric space [1,16,26], extended parametric *b*-metric space [29], sequential extended *S*-metric space [20], *JS*-metric space [17], extended *b*-metric space [19,30], modular metric space [25], multiplicative metric space [3], cone *b*- metric space [12], C^*-algebra valued metric space [27,28], vector-valued metric space [13,14], etc.

The purpose of this chapter is to introduce a new type of generalized metric spaces, called the sequential extended parametric *b*-metric space (SEPbMS), as a

DOI: 10.1201/9781003312017-2

generalization of extended parametric b-metric space [29], using JS-contractive type mappings. Also, we prove some fixed point theorems for JS-contractive type mappings in SEPbMSs, and we obtain some new fixed point results in triangular sequential extended fuzzy b-metric spaces (SEFbMSs) induced by this new structure. An example and an application are given to confirm the results.

For further details, the readers are referred to the book [6] and the references therein.

Definition 2.1 *[29] In a nonempty set $\mathcal{V}$, the mapping $\rho : \mathcal{V}^2 \times (0,+\infty) \to [0,+\infty)$ is said to be a parametric metric on $\mathcal{V}$ provided that,*

1. $\rho(\hbar,\hbar',\varsigma) = 0$ if and only if $\hbar = \hbar'$;

2. $\rho(\hbar,\hbar',\varsigma) = \rho(\hbar',\hbar,\varsigma)$ for all $\varsigma > 0$;

3. $\rho(\hbar,\hbar',\varsigma) \leq \rho(\hbar,\upsilon,\varsigma) + \rho'_{\hbar}(\upsilon,\hbar',\varsigma)$ for all $\hbar,\hbar',\upsilon \in \mathcal{V}$ and for all $\varsigma > 0$.

Then $(\mathcal{V},\rho)$ is called a parametric metric space.

Definition 2.2 *[32] In a non-empty set $\mathcal{V}$ a mapping $\rho : \mathcal{V}^2 \times (0,+\infty) \to [0,+\infty)$ is said to be an extended parametric b-metric (EPbM) if for all $\hbar,\hbar',\upsilon \in \mathcal{V}$ and $\varsigma > 0$:*

(a) $\rho(\hbar,\hbar',\varsigma) = 0$ implies $\hbar = \hbar'$ for all $\varsigma > 0$;

(b) $\rho(\hbar,\hbar',\varsigma) = \rho(\hbar',\hbar,\varsigma)$ for all $\varsigma > 0$;

(c) $\rho(\hbar,\hbar',\varsigma) \leq \Omega(\rho(\hbar,\upsilon,\varsigma) + \rho(\upsilon,\hbar',\varsigma))$,

where $\Omega : [0,\infty) \to [0,\infty)$ is an unto strictly increasing continuous function with $\Omega^{-1}(\varsigma) \leq \varsigma \leq \Omega(\varsigma)$.

Then $(\mathcal{V},\rho)$ is called an EPbMS with control function Ω.

Obviously, for $\Omega(\varsigma) = s\varsigma$, the EPbM reduces to parametric b-metric.

Let $\mathcal{V}$ be a non-empty set and $\vartheta_g : \mathcal{V}^2 \to [0,\infty]$ be a mapping. For any $\hbar \in \mathcal{V}$, let us define the set

$$C(\vartheta_g,\mathcal{V},\hbar) = \{\{\hbar_n\} \subset \mathcal{V} : \lim_{n\to\infty} \vartheta_g(\hbar_n,\hbar) = 0\}. \tag{2.1}$$

Definition 2.3 *[17] Let $\vartheta_g : \mathcal{V}^2 \to [0,\infty]$ be a mapping which satisfies:*

1. $\vartheta_g(\hbar,\hbar') = 0$ implies $\hbar = \hbar'$;

2. for every $\hbar,\hbar' \in \mathcal{V}$, we have $\vartheta_g(\hbar,\hbar') = \vartheta_g(\hbar',\hbar)$;

3. if $(\hbar,\hbar') \in \mathcal{V}^2$ and $\{\hbar_n\} \in C(\vartheta_g,\mathcal{V},\hbar)$, then $\vartheta_g(\hbar,\hbar') \leq p \limsup_{n\to\infty} \vartheta_g(\hbar_n,\hbar')$, for some $p > 0$.

The pair $(\mathcal{V},\vartheta_g)$ is called a JS-metric space.

Since the Banach fixed point theorem is very attractive and practical, many researchers have tried to generalize it in recent years. These generalizations have either been done in generalized metric spaces or constructing the new contractions in which the Banach contraction being obtained as a special case of these new contractions. Of course, the generalization of Banach's fixed point theorem is not limited to metric spaces. Rather, the Cartesian product of metric spaces and the Darbo's theorem in terms of measure of noncompactness are also generalizations of Banach's fixed point theorem. Each of these theorems, in turn, has been studied in various ways by many authors.

It should be noted that by obtaining these beautiful results, the existence and uniqueness of the solution for the functional integral equations, fractional integral equations, differential equations, differential fractional equations, and matrix equations have been proved.

Unswerving with Ref. [18], consider the family of all functions $\theta:(0,\infty)\to(1,\infty)$ so that:
(θ_1) θ is increasing;
(θ_2) $\lim_{n\to\infty}\theta(\rho_n)=1$ iff $\lim_{n\to\infty}\rho_n=0$ for each sequence $\{\rho_n\}\subseteq(0,\infty)$;
(θ_3) $\lim_{\rho\to 0^+}\frac{\theta(\rho)-1}{\rho^\kappa}=\lambda$ for some $\kappa\in(0,1)$ and for some $\lambda\in(0,\infty]$ is signified by $\mathcal{J}_0$.

Theorem 2.1 *[17,18] A self-mapping Υ on a complete metric space $(\mathcal{V},d)$ so that*

$$\hbar,\hbar'\in\mathcal{V},\quad d(\Upsilon\hbar,\Upsilon\hbar')\neq 0\Rightarrow\theta(d(\Upsilon\hbar,\Upsilon\hbar'))\leq\theta(d(\hbar,\hbar'))^\alpha$$

where $\theta\in\mathcal{J}_0$ and $\alpha\in(0,1)$ possesses a unique fixed point.

Reminder that the Banach contraction principle is a specific instance of Theorem 2.1.

We denote by $\mathcal{J}$ the family of functions $\theta:(0,\infty)\to(1,\infty)$ so that:
(θ_1) θ is continues and increasing;
(θ_2) $\lim_{n\to\infty}\theta(\rho_n)=\theta(\rho)$ iff $\lim_{n\to\infty}\rho_n=\rho$ for each sequence $\{\rho_n\}\subseteq(0,\infty)$;

In this chapter, via combination of Kannan contractions, Chatterjea contractions, and JS-contractions, we state and prove some fixed point results in two classes of generalized metric spaces.

2.2 MAIN RESULTS

In this section, first we introduce a new type of EPbMSs. To expand such a concept, we first define,

$$\eth(\rho,\mathcal{V},\hbar):=\left\{\{\hbar_n\}\subset\mathcal{V}:\lim_{n\to\infty}\rho(\hbar_n,\hbar,\varsigma)=0\text{ for all }\varsigma>0\right\},$$

where $\rho:\mathcal{V}^2\times(0,+\infty)\to[0,+\infty)$ is a given mapping.

Definition 2.4 *In a non-empty set $\mathcal{V}$, a mapping $\rho:\mathcal{V}^2\times(0,+\infty)\to[0,+\infty)$ is said to be a SEPbM if for all $\hbar,\hbar'\in\mathcal{V}$ and for all $\varsigma>0$:*

(a) $\rho(\hbar,\hbar',\varsigma)=0$ for all $\varsigma>0$ implies $\hbar=\hbar'$;

(b) $\rho(\hbar,\hbar',\varsigma)=\rho(\hbar',\hbar,\varsigma)$ for all $\varsigma>0$;

(c) $\rho(\hbar,\hbar',\varsigma)\leq\Omega\left(\limsup_{n\to\infty}\rho(\hbar_n,\hbar',\varsigma)\right)$, where $\{\hbar_n\}\in\eth(\rho,\mathcal{V},\hbar)$ and $\Omega:[0,\infty]\to[0,\infty]$ is an unto strictly increasing continuous function with $\Omega^{-1}(\varsigma)\leq\varsigma\leq\Omega(\varsigma)$ for all $0\leq\varsigma<\infty$.

The triplet $(\mathcal{V},\rho,\Omega)$ is called a SEPbMS. For simplicity, we denote it by $(\mathcal{V},\rho)$.

Definition 2.5 *Let $(\mathcal{V},\rho)$ be a SEPbMS, $\{\hbar_n\} \subseteq \mathcal{V}$ and $\hbar \in \mathcal{V}$.*

(i) $\{\hbar_n\}$ is said to be convergent and converges to $\hbar$, if $\{\hbar_n\} \in \eth(\rho,\mathcal{V},\hbar)$.

(ii) $\{\hbar_n\}$ is said to be Cauchy, if $\lim\limits_{n,m\to\infty} \rho(\hbar_n,\hbar_m,\varsigma) = 0$ for all $\varsigma > 0$.

(iii) $(\mathcal{V},\rho)$ is said to be complete, if every Cauchy sequence is a convergent sequence.

Example 2.1 *Let the triplet $(\mathcal{V},\rho,\Omega)$ be an EPbMS. If we define $\rho(\hbar,\hbar',\varsigma) = e^{\varsigma(\hbar-\hbar')^p}$ $(p \geq 1)$, then the pair $(\mathcal{V},\rho)$ will be a SEPbMS on $\mathcal{V}$ for $\Omega(\varsigma) = e^{2^p\varsigma}$ for all $\varsigma \geq 0$.*

proposition 2.1 *If $(\mathcal{V},\rho)$ be a parametric b-metric space with parameter s, then ρ is also a SEPbM on $\mathcal{V}$.*

Proof. If $(\mathcal{V},\rho)$ be a parametric b-metric space, then ρ undoubtedly fulfills the first two circumstances of Definition 2.4. We just indicate that ρ also gratifies the third condition of Definition 2.4.

Since ρ is a parametric b-metric, then for all $\hbar,\hbar' \in \mathcal{V}$ and for any sequence $\{\hbar_n\} \in \eth(\rho,\mathcal{V},\hbar)$, according to triangle inequality we have, $\rho(\hbar,\hbar',\varsigma) \leq s\limsup\limits_{n\to\infty} \rho(\hbar_n,\hbar',\varsigma)$ for all $\varsigma > 0$.

Then if we choose $\Omega(\varsigma) = s\varsigma$ for all $\varsigma \in [0,\infty]$, then we have $\rho(\hbar,\hbar',\varsigma) \leq \Omega\left(\limsup\limits_{n\to\infty} \rho(\hbar_n,\hbar',\varsigma)\right)$ for all $\hbar,\hbar' \in \mathcal{V}$, for all $\varsigma > 0$ and for all $\{\hbar_n\} \in \eth(\rho,\mathcal{V},\hbar)$. Therefore, $(\mathcal{V},\rho)$ is also a SEPbMS. □

Definition 2.6 *Let $(\mathcal{V},\rho)$ and (Y,ρ^*) be two SEPbMSs. A mapping $\Upsilon : \mathcal{V} \to Y$ is called continuous at a point $\hbar \in \mathcal{V}$ if for any $\varepsilon > 0$ there is $\delta_\varepsilon > 0$ such that for any $\upsilon \in \mathcal{V}$, $\rho^*(\Upsilon\upsilon,\Upsilon\hbar,\varsigma) < \varepsilon$ whenever $\rho(\upsilon,\hbar,\varsigma) < \delta_\varepsilon$, for all $\varsigma > 0$. Υ is said to be continuous on $\mathcal{V}$ if Υ is continuous at each point of $\mathcal{V}$.*

proposition 2.2 *In a SEPbMS $(\mathcal{V},\rho)$, if a sequence $\{\hbar_n\}$ is convergent, then it converges to a unique element in $\mathcal{V}$.*

Proof. Suppose $\hbar,\hbar' \in \mathcal{V}$ and $\varsigma > 0$ be arbitrary such that $\hbar_n \to \hbar$ and $\hbar_n \to \hbar'$ as $n \to \infty$. Then we have, $\rho(\hbar,\hbar',\varsigma) \leq \Omega\left(\limsup\limits_{n\to\infty} \rho(\hbar_n,\hbar',\varsigma)\right)$ which implies that $\rho(\hbar,\hbar',\varsigma) \leq \Omega(0) = 0$, *i.e.*, $\hbar = \hbar'$. □

proposition 2.3 *Let $(\mathcal{V},\rho)$ be a SEPbMS and $\{\hbar_n\} \subset \mathcal{V}$ converges to some $\hbar \in \mathcal{V}$. Then $\rho(\hbar,\hbar,\varsigma) = 0$.*

Proof. Since $\{\hbar_n\}$ converges to $\hbar \in \mathcal{V}$, so $\lim\limits_{n\to\infty} \rho(\hbar_n,\hbar,\varsigma) = 0$. Therefore, we have

$$\rho(\hbar,\hbar,\varsigma) \leq \Omega\left(\limsup_{n\to\infty} \rho(\hbar_n\hbar,\varsigma)\right) = \Omega(0) = 0,$$

which implies $\rho(\hbar,\hbar,\varsigma) = 0$. □

proposition 2.4 *For a Cauchy sequence $\{\hbar_n\}$ in a SEPbMS $(\mathcal{V},\rho,\Omega)$ such that Ω^{-1} is continuous, if $\{\hbar_n\}$ has a convergent sub-sequence $\{\hbar_{n_k}\}$ which converges to $\hbar \in \mathcal{V}$, then $\{\hbar_n\}$ also converges to $\hbar \in \mathcal{V}$.*

Proof. From condition (c) of Definition 2.4 we have, $\rho(\hbar_n,\hbar,\varsigma) \leq \Omega\left(\limsup_{k\to\infty}\rho(\hbar_n,\hbar_{n_k},\varsigma)\right)$ which implies that $\Omega^{-1}(\rho(\hbar_n,\hbar,\varsigma)) \leq \limsup_{k\to\infty}\rho(\hbar_n,\hbar_{n_k},\varsigma)$ for all $n \in \mathbb{N}$ and $\varsigma > 0$.

Because of the Cauchyness of the sequence $\{\hbar_n\}$, it follows that $\lim_{n,k\to\infty}\rho(\hbar_n,\hbar_{n_k},\varsigma) = 0$ and thus, $\Omega^{-1}(\rho(\hbar_n,\hbar,\varsigma)) \to 0$ as $n \to \infty$ which implies that $\rho(\hbar_n,\hbar,\varsigma) \to 0$ as $n \to \infty$, since Ω^{-1} is continuous. Hence, $\{\hbar_n\}$ converges to $\hbar \in \mathcal{V}$. □

proposition 2.5 *In a SEPbMS $(\mathcal{V},\rho)$, if a self-mapping Υ is continuous at $\hbar \in \mathcal{V}$, then $\{\Upsilon\hbar_n\} \in \eth(\rho,\mathcal{V},\Upsilon\hbar)$ for any sequence $\{\hbar_n\} \in \eth(\rho,\mathcal{V},\hbar)$.*

Proof. Let $\varepsilon > 0$ be given. Since Υ is continuous at $\hbar$, then there exists $\delta_\varepsilon > 0$ such that $\rho(\upsilon,\hbar,\varsigma) < \delta_\varepsilon$ implies $\rho(\Upsilon\upsilon,\Upsilon\hbar,\varsigma) < \varepsilon$.

As $\{\hbar_n\}$ converges to $\hbar$, so for $\delta_\varepsilon > 0$, there exists $N \in \mathbb{N}$ such that $\rho(\hbar_n,\hbar,\varsigma) < \delta_\varepsilon$ for all $n \geq N$. Therefore, for any $n \geq N$, $\rho(\Upsilon\hbar_n,\Upsilon\hbar,\varsigma) < \varepsilon$ and thus $\Upsilon\hbar_n \to \Upsilon\hbar$ as $n \to \infty$, that is, $\{\Upsilon\hbar_n\} \in \eth(\rho,\mathcal{V},\Upsilon\hbar)$. □

Let $(\mathcal{V},\rho)$ be a SEPbMS with associate function Ω. Define,

$$\mathcal{B}(\hbar,\eta) := \{\hbar' \in \mathcal{V} : \rho(\hbar,\hbar',\varsigma) < \rho(\hbar,\hbar,\varsigma) + \eta \text{ for all } \varsigma > 0\}$$

and

$$\mathcal{B}[\hbar,\eta] := \{\hbar' \in \mathcal{V} : \rho(\hbar,\hbar',\varsigma) \leq \rho(\hbar,\hbar,\varsigma) + \eta \text{ for all } \varsigma > 0\}$$

for all $\hbar \in \mathcal{V}$ and for all $\eta > 0$.

Remark 2.1 *Evidently,*

$$\tau_\rho := \{\emptyset\} \cup \{\mathcal{V}(\neq \emptyset) \subset \mathcal{V} : \textit{for any } \hbar \in \mathcal{V}, \textit{ there is } \eta > 0 \textit{ so that } \mathcal{B}(\hbar,\eta) \subset \mathcal{V}\}$$

forms a topology on $\mathcal{V}$.

2.3 SOME FIXED POINT THEOREMS

In this section, we suppose that $\theta \in \mathcal{J}$.

Theorem 2.2 *Let $(\mathcal{V},\rho)$ be a complete SEPbMS and $\Upsilon : \mathcal{V} \to \mathcal{V}$ be a mapping such that:*

(i) $\theta(\rho(\Upsilon\hbar,\Upsilon\hbar',\varsigma)) \leq \theta(\rho(\hbar,\hbar',\varsigma))^\alpha$ for all $\hbar,\hbar' \in \mathcal{V}$ and for some $\alpha \in (0,1)$,

(ii) there is $\hbar_0 \in \mathcal{V}$ so that

$$\delta(\rho,\Upsilon,\hbar_0) := \sup\{\rho(\Upsilon^i\hbar_0,\Upsilon^j\hbar_0,\varsigma) : i,j = 1,2,\ldots,\ \varsigma > 0\} < \infty.$$

Then Υ has at least one fixed point in $\mathcal{V}$. Moreover if $\hbar$ and $\hbar'$ are two fixed points of Υ in $\mathcal{V}$ with $\rho(\hbar,\hbar',\varsigma) < \infty$ then $\hbar = \hbar'$.

Proof. We define,
$\Delta(\rho,\Upsilon^{p+1},\hbar_0) := \sup\{\rho(\Upsilon^{p+i}\hbar_0,\Upsilon^{p+j}\hbar_0,\varsigma) : i,j = 1,2,\ldots,\ \varsigma > 0\}$, for all $p \geq 1$.
Clearly,
$\Delta(\rho,\Upsilon^{p+1},\hbar_0) \leq \Delta(\rho,\Upsilon,\hbar_0) < \infty$ for all $p \geq 1$.
Then for all $p \geq 1$ and for all $i,j = 1,2,\ldots,$

$$\begin{aligned}\theta\left(\rho(\Upsilon^{p+i}\hbar_0,\Upsilon^{p+j}\hbar_0,\varsigma)\right) &\leq \theta\left(\rho(\Upsilon^{p-1+i}\hbar_0,\Upsilon^{p-1+j}\hbar_0,\varsigma)\right)^{\alpha}\\ &\leq \theta(\Delta(\rho,\Upsilon^{p},\hbar_0))^{\alpha},\end{aligned}$$

which implies, for all $p \geq 1$,

$$\begin{aligned}\theta\left(\Delta(\rho,\Upsilon^{p+1},\hbar_0)\right) &= \theta\left(\sup_{i,j\geq 1}\rho(\Upsilon^{p+i}\hbar_0,\Upsilon^{p+j}\hbar_0,\varsigma)\right)\\ &\leq \theta\left(\Delta(\rho,\Upsilon^{p},\hbar_0)\right)^{\alpha}\\ &\leq \theta\left(\Delta(\rho,\Upsilon^{p-1},\hbar_0)\right)^{\alpha^2}\\ &\ \ \vdots\\ &\leq \theta\left(\Delta(\rho,\Upsilon,\hbar_0)\right)^{\alpha^{p}}.\end{aligned}$$

Let $\hbar_i = \Upsilon\hbar_{i-1} = \Upsilon^i\hbar_0$ for all $i \in \mathbb{N}$. For all $m > n \geq 1$ we have,

$$\begin{aligned}\theta\left(\rho(\hbar_n,\hbar_m,\varsigma)\right) &= \theta\left(\rho(\Upsilon^{n}\hbar_0,\Upsilon^{m}\hbar_0,\varsigma)\right)\\ &= \theta\left(\rho(\Upsilon^{n-1+1}\hbar_0,\Upsilon^{n-1+(m-n+1)}\hbar_0,\varsigma)\right)\\ &\leq \theta\left(\Delta(\rho,\Upsilon^{n},\hbar_0)\right)\\ &\leq \theta\left(\Delta(\rho,\Upsilon,\hbar_0)\right)^{\alpha^{n-1}} \longrightarrow 1 \text{ as } n\to\infty.\end{aligned}$$

Therefore, $\{\hbar_n\}$ is a Cauchy sequence in $\mathcal{V}$. From the completeness of $\mathcal{V}$, $\{\hbar_n\}$ is convergent. Let $\lim_n \hbar_n = \hbar \in \mathcal{V}$. Now, $\theta(\rho(\Upsilon\hbar,\Upsilon\hbar_n,\varsigma)) \leq \theta(\rho(\hbar,\hbar_n,\varsigma))^{\alpha} \to 1$ as $n\to\infty$. Therefore, $\hbar_{n+1} \to \Upsilon\hbar$ as $n\to\infty$. Hence, by Proposition 2.2, we have $\Upsilon\hbar = \hbar$, *i.e.*, $\hbar \in \mathcal{V}$ is a fixed point of Υ.

Now, if $\hbar$ and $\hbar'$ be two fixed points of Υ in $\mathcal{V}$ with $\rho(\hbar,\hbar',\varsigma) < \infty$, then

$$\theta(\rho(\hbar,\hbar',\varsigma)) = \theta(\rho(\Upsilon\hbar,\Upsilon\hbar',\varsigma)) \leq \theta(\rho(\hbar,\hbar',\varsigma))^{\alpha},$$

which gives $\rho(\hbar,\hbar',\varsigma) = 0$, hence $\hbar = \hbar'$. □

Theorem 2.3 *Let $(\mathcal{V},\rho)$ be a complete SEPbMS and $\Upsilon : \mathcal{V} \to \mathcal{V}$ so that:*
(i)

$$\theta\left(\rho(\Upsilon\hbar,\Upsilon\hbar',\varsigma)\right) \leq \theta\left(\Omega^{-1}\left[\frac{\rho(\hbar,\Upsilon\hbar,\varsigma)+\rho(\hbar',\Upsilon\hbar',\varsigma)}{2}\right]\right)^{\gamma},$$

for all $\hbar,\hbar' \in \mathcal{V}$ and for some $\gamma \in (0,1)$,

(ii) there is $\hbar_0 \in \mathcal{V}$ so that

$$\Delta(\rho, \Upsilon, \hbar_0) := \sup\left\{\rho\left(\Upsilon^i \hbar_0, \Upsilon^j \hbar_0, \varsigma\right) : i, j = 1, 2, \ldots,\ \varsigma > 0\right\} < \infty.$$

Then the Picard iterating sequence $\{\hbar_n\}$, $\hbar_n = \Upsilon^n \hbar_0$ for all $n \in \mathbb{N}$, converges to some $\hbar \in \mathcal{V}$. If $\rho(\hbar, \Upsilon\hbar, \varsigma) < \infty$, then $\hbar \in \mathcal{V}$ is a fixed point of Υ. Furthermore, if $\hbar'$ is a fixed point of Υ in $\mathcal{V}$ such that $\rho(\hbar, \hbar', \varsigma) < \infty$ and $\rho(\hbar', \hbar', \varsigma) < \infty$, then $\hbar = \hbar'$.

Proof. For all $p \geq 1$ and for all $i, j = 1, 2, \ldots$, $\theta\left(\rho(\Upsilon^{p+i}\hbar_0, \Upsilon^{p+j}\hbar_0, \varsigma)\right)$
$\leq \theta\left(\Omega^{-1}\left[\frac{\rho(\Upsilon^{p-1+i}\hbar_0, \Upsilon^{p+i}\hbar_0, \varsigma) + \rho(\Upsilon^{p-1+j}\hbar_0, \Upsilon^{p+j}\hbar_0, \varsigma)}{2}\right]\right)^{\gamma} \leq \theta(\Delta(\rho, \Upsilon^p, \hbar_0))^{\gamma}.$

This implies that

$$\theta\left(\Delta(\rho, \Upsilon^{p+1}, \hbar_0)\right) = \theta\left(\sup_{i,j\geq 1} \rho(\Upsilon^{p+i}\hbar_0, \Upsilon^{p+j}\hbar_0, \varsigma)\right) \leq \theta\left(\Delta(\rho, \Upsilon^p, \hbar_0)\right)^{\gamma}$$

for all $p \geq 1$.

Then continuing in an analogous technique as in Theorem 2.2, it can be effortlessly exposed that $\{\hbar_n\}$ is a Cauchy sequence in $\mathcal{V}$ and by the completeness of $\mathcal{V}$ there is some $\hbar \in \mathcal{V}$ such that $\lim_n \hbar_n = \hbar$.

Now,

$$\begin{aligned}
\theta(\rho(\hbar_{n+1}, \Upsilon\hbar, \varsigma)) &= \theta(\rho(\Upsilon\hbar_n, \Upsilon\hbar, \varsigma)) \\
&\leq \theta(\Omega^{-1}[\rho(\hbar_n, \Upsilon\hbar_n, \varsigma) + \rho(\hbar, \Upsilon\hbar, \varsigma)])^{\gamma} \\
&\leq \theta(\Omega^{-1}[\rho(\hbar_n, \hbar_{n+1}, \varsigma) + \rho(\hbar, \Upsilon\hbar, \varsigma)])^{\gamma},
\end{aligned}$$

for all $n \geq 0$, which implies that

$$\limsup_{n\to\infty} \theta(\rho(\hbar_{n+1}, \Upsilon\hbar, \varsigma)) \leq \theta(\Omega^{-1}[\rho(\hbar, \Upsilon\hbar, \varsigma)])^{\gamma} < \infty.$$

On the other hand,

$$\begin{aligned}
\rho(\hbar, \Upsilon\hbar, \varsigma) &\leq \Omega\left(\limsup_{n\to\infty} \rho(\hbar_{n+1}, \Upsilon\hbar, \varsigma)\right) \\
&\leq \Omega\left(\theta^{-1}(\theta(\Omega^{-1}[\rho(\hbar, \Upsilon\hbar, \varsigma)])^{\gamma})\right).
\end{aligned}$$

If $\rho(\hbar, \Upsilon\hbar, \varsigma) > 0$ then,

$$\Omega^{-1}(\rho(\hbar, \Upsilon\hbar, \varsigma)) \leq \theta^{-1}\left(\theta(\Omega^{-1}[\rho(\hbar, \Upsilon\hbar, \varsigma)])^{\gamma}\right) < \Omega^{-1}\left(\rho(\hbar, \Upsilon\hbar, \varsigma)\right),$$

a contradiction. Hence, $\Upsilon\hbar = \hbar$, i.e., $\hbar \in \mathcal{V}$ is a fixed point of Υ.

Now, if $\hbar'$ is a fixed point of Υ in $\mathcal{V}$ with $\rho(\hbar, \hbar', \varsigma) < \infty$ and $\rho(\hbar', \hbar', \varsigma) < \infty$, then we have

$$\theta(\rho(\hbar, \hbar', \varsigma)) = \theta(\rho(\Upsilon\hbar, \Upsilon\hbar', \varsigma)) \leq \theta\left[\rho(\hbar, \Upsilon\hbar, \varsigma) + \rho(\hbar', \Upsilon\hbar', \varsigma)\right]^{\gamma} = 0,$$

as $\rho(\hbar', \hbar', \varsigma) = 0$, therefore $\hbar = \hbar'$. □

Theorem 2.4 *In a complete SEPbMS $(\mathcal{V},\rho)$, if $\Upsilon:\mathcal{V}\to\mathcal{V}$ be a mapping so that:*

(i) $\theta(\rho(\Upsilon\hbar,\Upsilon\hbar',\varsigma))\leq\theta\left(\frac{[\rho(\hbar,\Upsilon\hbar',\varsigma)+\rho(\hbar',\Upsilon\hbar,\varsigma)]}{2}\right)^{\beta}$ *for all $\hbar,\hbar'\in\mathcal{V}$, for all $\varsigma>0$ and for some $\beta\in(0,1)$,*

(ii) there is $\hbar_0\in\mathcal{V}$ so that
$\Delta(\rho,\Upsilon,\hbar_0):=\sup\{\rho(\Upsilon^i\hbar_0,\Upsilon^j\hbar_0,\varsigma):i,j=1,2,\ldots,\ \varsigma>0\}<\infty$,
then, the Picard iterating sequence $\{\hbar_n\}$, $\hbar_n=\Upsilon^n\hbar_0$ for all $n\geq 1$, converges to some $\hbar\in\mathcal{V}$. If $\limsup_{n\to\infty}\rho(\hbar_n,\Upsilon\hbar,\varsigma)<\infty$, then $\hbar\in\mathcal{V}$ is a fixed point of Υ, and if $\hbar'$ is a fixed point of Υ in $\mathcal{V}$ such that $\rho(\hbar,\hbar',\varsigma)<\infty$, then $\hbar=\hbar'$.

Proof. By parallel argument as in Theorem 2.2, $\{\hbar_n\}$ is a Cauchy sequence in $\mathcal{V}$, and by completeness of $\mathcal{V}$ it converges to an element $\hbar\in\mathcal{V}$.

Now, for all $n\in\mathbb{N}\cup\{0\}$, we have

$$\begin{aligned}\theta(\rho(\hbar_{n+1},\Upsilon\hbar,\varsigma))&=\theta(\rho(\Upsilon\hbar_n,\Upsilon\hbar,\varsigma))\\&\leq\theta\left([\rho(\hbar_n,\Upsilon\hbar,\varsigma)+\rho(\hbar,\Upsilon\hbar_n,\varsigma)]\right)^{\beta}\\&\leq\theta\left([\rho(\hbar_n,\Upsilon\hbar,\varsigma)+\rho(\hbar_{n+1},\hbar,\varsigma)]\right)^{\beta},\end{aligned}$$

which implies that

$$\theta(\limsup_{n\to\infty}\rho(\hbar_{n+1},\Upsilon\hbar,\varsigma))\leq\theta(\limsup_{n\to\infty}\rho(\hbar_n,\Upsilon\hbar,\varsigma))^{\beta}$$

and hence $\limsup_{n\to\infty}\rho(\hbar_n,\Upsilon\hbar,\varsigma)=0$. Therefore,

$$\rho(\hbar,\Upsilon\hbar,\varsigma)\leq\Omega\left(\limsup_{n\to\infty}\rho(\hbar_n,\Upsilon\hbar,\varsigma)\right)=\Omega(0)=0$$

and as a result, $\Upsilon\hbar=\hbar$.

If $\hbar'$ be a fixed point of Υ in $\mathcal{V}$ with $\rho(\hbar,\hbar',\varsigma)<\infty$, then we have

$$\begin{aligned}\theta(\rho(\hbar,\hbar',\varsigma))=\theta(\rho(\Upsilon\hbar,\Upsilon\hbar',\varsigma))&\leq\theta\left(\frac{[\rho(\hbar,\Upsilon\hbar',\varsigma)+\rho(\hbar',\Upsilon\hbar,\varsigma)]}{2}\right)^{\beta}\\&=\theta(\rho(\hbar,\hbar',\varsigma))^{\beta},\end{aligned}$$

which implies $\rho(\hbar,\hbar',\varsigma)=0$, therefore, $\hbar=\hbar'$. □

Example 2.2 *Consider $\mathcal{V}=[0,1]$ and $\rho(\hbar,\hbar',\varsigma)=(\varsigma|\hbar-\hbar'|)+\ln(1+\varsigma|\hbar-\hbar'|)$ for all $\hbar,\hbar'\in\mathcal{V}$ and for all $\varsigma>0$. Then ρ forms a SEPbM on $\mathcal{V}$ with the function $\Omega(s)=s+\ln(1+s)$ for all $s\geq 0$.*
Define $\Upsilon:\mathcal{V}\to\mathcal{V}$ by $\Upsilon\hbar=\frac{\hbar}{4}$ for all $\hbar\in\mathcal{V}$. Then Υ gratifies all the circumstances of Theorem 2.2 for $\alpha=\frac{1}{2}$, $\theta(\varsigma)=e^{\varsigma}$ and evidently, Υ has a unique fixed point $0\in\mathcal{V}$, because

$$\begin{aligned}\theta(\rho(\Upsilon\hbar,\Upsilon\hbar',\varsigma))&=e^{(\varsigma|\hbar/4-\hbar'/4|+\ln(1+\varsigma|\hbar/4-\hbar'/4|))}\\&\leq[e^{(\varsigma|\hbar-\hbar'|+\ln(1+\varsigma|\hbar-\hbar'|))}]^{1/2}\\&\leq\theta(\rho(\hbar,\hbar',\varsigma))^{1/2}.\end{aligned}$$

For more details, the readers are referred to the book [11].

2.4 SEQUENTIAL EXTENDED FUZZY *B*-METRIC SPACES

In this section, stimulated by the work existing in Ref. [16], we present the perception of a SEFbMS. We generate an association between SEPbM and SEFbM and present some new fixed point results in SEFbMS. For more details on fuzzy metric and its generalization, the readers are referred to [7]– [10], [21–24] and the references therein.

Definition 2.7 *(Schweizer and Sklar [31]) A binary operation* $\star : [0,1]^2 \to [0,1]$ *is called a continuous t-norm if:*

(T1) $\star$ *is commutative and associative;*
(T2) $\star$ *is continuous;*
(T3) $\hbar \star 1 = \hbar$ *for all* $\hbar \in [0,1]$;
(T4) $\hbar \star \hbar' \leq \Re \star \Re'$ *when* $\hbar \leq \Re$ *and* $\hbar' \leq \Re'$, *with* $\hbar, \hbar', \Re, \Re' \in [0,1]$.

Definition 2.8 *[29] A triplet* $(\mathcal{V}, M, *)$ *is supposed to be a fuzzy metric space if* $\mathcal{V}$ *is an unselective set,* $*$ *is a continuous t-norm (CTN) and* M *is a fuzzy set on* $\mathcal{V}^2 \times (0,\infty)$ *so that, for all* $\hbar, \hbar', \upsilon \in \mathcal{V}$ *and* $\varsigma, s > 0$,

(i) $M(\hbar, \hbar', \varsigma) > 0$;
(ii) $M(\hbar, \hbar', \varsigma) = 1$ *for all* $\varsigma > 0$ *if and only if* $\hbar = \hbar'$;
(iii) $M(\hbar, \hbar', \varsigma) = M(\hbar', \hbar, \varsigma)$;
(iv) $M(\hbar, \hbar', \varsigma) * M(\hbar', \upsilon, s) \leq M(\hbar, \upsilon, \varsigma + s)$;
(v) $M(\hbar, \hbar', \cdot) : (0,\infty) \to [0,1]$ *is continuous;*

The function $M(\hbar, \hbar', \varsigma)$ *means the degree of closeness among* $\hbar$ *and* $\hbar'$ *regarding t.*

Definition 2.9 *[16] A fuzzy b-metric space is an ordered triplet* $(\mathcal{V}, B, \star)$ *such that* $\mathcal{V}$ *is a nonempty set,* $\star$ *is a continuous* ς*-norm and* B *is a fuzzy set on* $\mathcal{V}^2 \times (0,\infty)$ *so that for all* $\hbar, \hbar', \upsilon \in \mathcal{V}$ *and* $\varsigma, s > 0$,

(F1) $B(\hbar, \hbar', \varsigma) > 0$;
(F2) $B(\hbar, \hbar', \varsigma) = 1$ *if and only if* $\hbar = \hbar'$;
(F3) $B(\hbar, \hbar', \varsigma) = B(\hbar', \hbar, \varsigma)$;
(F4) $B(\hbar, \hbar', \varsigma) \star B(\hbar', \upsilon, s) \leq B(\hbar, \upsilon, b(\varsigma + s))$ *where* $b \geq 1$;
(F5) $B(\hbar, \hbar', \cdot) : (0,+\infty) \to (0,1]$ *is continuous from the left.*

Definition 2.10 *[29] An ordered quadruple* $(\mathcal{V}, B, \star, \Omega)$ *in which* $\mathcal{V}$ *is a nonempty set,* $\star$ *is a CTN and* B *is a fuzzy set on* $\mathcal{V}^2 \times (0,\infty)$ *so that for all* $\hbar, \hbar', \upsilon \in \mathcal{V}$ *and* $\varsigma, s > 0$,

(F1) $B(\hbar, \hbar', \varsigma) > 0$;
(F2) $B(\hbar, \hbar', \varsigma) = 1$ *if and only if* $\hbar = \hbar'$;
(F3) $B(\hbar, \hbar', \varsigma) = B(\hbar', \hbar, \varsigma)$;
(F4) $B(\hbar, \hbar', \varsigma) \star B(\hbar', \upsilon, s) \leq B(\hbar, \upsilon, \Omega(\varsigma + s))$;
(F5) $B(\hbar, \hbar', \cdot) : (0,+\infty) \to (0,1]$ *is continuous from the left,*
is an extended fuzzy b-metric space.

Now, let $\mathcal{V}$ be a non-empty set and B be a fuzzy set on $\mathcal{V}^2 \times (0,\infty)$. For any $\hbar \in \mathcal{V}$, let

$$\eth(B,\mathcal{V},\hbar) = \{\{\hbar_n\} \subset \mathcal{V} : \lim_{n\to\infty} B(\hbar_n,\hbar,\varsigma) = 1 \text{ for all } \varsigma > 0\}. \tag{2.2}$$

Definition 2.11 *A SEFbMS is an ordered quadruple $(\mathcal{V},B,\star,\Omega)$ in which $\mathcal{V}$ is a nonempty set, $\star$ is a CTN and B is a fuzzy set on $\mathcal{V}^2 \times (0,\infty)$ so that for all $\hbar,\hbar',\upsilon \in \mathcal{V}$ and $\varsigma, s > 0$,*

(F1) $B(\hbar,\hbar',\varsigma) > 0$;

(F2) $B(\hbar,\hbar',\varsigma) = 1$ if and only if $\hbar = \hbar'$;

(F3) $B(\hbar,\hbar',\varsigma) = B(\hbar',\hbar,\varsigma)$;

(F4) $\Omega[\limsup B(\hbar_n,\hbar',\varsigma)] \leq B(\hbar,\hbar',\varsigma)$ where $\{\hbar_n\} \in \eth(B,\mathcal{V},\hbar)$ and $\Omega : [0,\infty) \to [0,\infty)$ is an unto strictly increasing continuous function with $\Omega^{-1}(\varsigma) \leq \varsigma \leq \Omega(\varsigma)$ for all $0 \leq \varsigma < \infty$;

(F5) $B(\hbar,\hbar',\cdot) : (0,+\infty) \to (0,1]$ is continuous from the left.

Definition 2.12 *Let $(\mathcal{V},B,\star,\Omega)$ be a SEFbMS and $\{\hbar_n\}$ be a sequence in $\mathcal{V}$ and $\hbar \in \mathcal{V}$.*

(i) $\{\hbar_n\}$ is supposed to be convergent and converges to $\hbar$ if $\{\hbar_n\} \in \eth(B,\mathcal{V},\hbar)$.

(ii) $\{\hbar_n\}$ is supposed to be Cauchy if $\lim_{n,m\to\infty} B(\hbar_n,\hbar_m,\varsigma) = 1$ for all $\varsigma > 0$.

(iii) $(\mathcal{V},B,\star,\Omega)$ is called complete if every Cauchy sequence is a convergent sequence.

Definition 2.13 *The SEFbM $(\mathcal{V},B,\star,\Omega)$ is called Ω-convertible whenever,*

$$\frac{1}{\Omega[\limsup B(\hbar_n,\hbar',\varsigma)]} - 1 \leq \Omega[\frac{1}{\limsup B(\hbar_n,\hbar',\varsigma)} - 1].$$

for all $\hbar,\hbar',\upsilon \in \mathcal{V}$, $\varsigma > 0$ and $\hbar_n \in \eth(B,\mathcal{V},\hbar)$.

Remark 2.2 *Notice that $\rho(\hbar,\hbar',\varsigma) = \dfrac{1}{B(\hbar,\hbar',\varsigma)} - 1$ is a SEPbM whenever B is a Ω-convertible SEFbM.*

As an application of Remark 2.2 and the results recognized in Section 3, we can deduce the subsequent results in SEFbMSs.

Theorem 2.5 *Let $(\mathcal{V},B,\star,\Omega)$ be an Ω-convertible complete SEFbMS and $\Upsilon : \mathcal{V} \to \mathcal{V}$ be a mapping so that:*

(i) $\theta\left(\dfrac{1}{B(\Upsilon\hbar,\Upsilon\hbar',\varsigma)} - 1\right) \leq \theta\left[\dfrac{1}{B(\hbar,\hbar',\varsigma)} - 1\right]^{\alpha}$ for all $\hbar,\hbar' \in \mathcal{V}$ and for some $\alpha \in (0,1)$,

(ii) there is $\hbar_0 \in \mathcal{V}$ so that

$$\Delta(B,\Upsilon,\hbar_0) := \sup\left\{\frac{1}{B(\Upsilon^i\hbar_0,\Upsilon^j\hbar_0,\varsigma)} - 1 : i,j = 1,2,\ldots,\ \varsigma > 0\right\} < \infty.$$

Then Υ takes at least one fixed point in $\mathcal{V}$. Furthermore, if $\hbar$ and $\hbar'$ are two fixed points of Υ in $\mathcal{V}$ with $\dfrac{1}{B(\hbar,\hbar',\varsigma)} - 1 < \infty$, then $\hbar = \hbar'$.

Theorem 2.6 *Let $(\mathcal{V}, B, \star, \Omega)$ be a Ω-convertible complete SEFbMS and $\Upsilon : \mathcal{V} \to \mathcal{V}$ such that:*

(i)

$$\theta(\frac{1}{B(\Upsilon\hbar, \Upsilon\hbar', \varsigma)} - 1) \leq \theta\left(\Omega^{-1}\left[\frac{\frac{1}{B(\hbar, \Upsilon\hbar, \varsigma)} - 1 + \frac{1}{B(\hbar', \Upsilon\hbar', \varsigma)} - 1}{2}\right]\right)^{\gamma},$$

for all $\hbar, \hbar' \in \mathcal{V}$ and for some $\gamma \in (0,1)$,

(ii) there is $\hbar_0 \in \mathcal{V}$ such that

$$\Delta(B, \Upsilon, \hbar_0) := \sup\left\{\frac{1}{B(\Upsilon^i\hbar_0, \Upsilon^j\hbar_0, \varsigma)} - 1 : i, j = 1, 2, \ldots, \varsigma > 0\right\} < \infty.$$

Then the Picard iterating sequence $\{\hbar_n\}$, $\hbar_n = \Upsilon^n\hbar_0$ for all $n \in \mathbb{N}$, converges to some $\hbar \in \mathcal{V}$. If $\frac{1}{B(\hbar, \Upsilon\hbar, \varsigma)} - 1 < \infty$, then $\hbar \in \mathcal{V}$ is a fixed point of Υ. Moreover, if $\hbar'$ is a fixed point of Υ in $\mathcal{V}$ such that $\frac{1}{B(\hbar, \hbar', \varsigma)} - 1 < \infty$ and $\frac{1}{B(\hbar', \hbar', \varsigma)} - 1 < \infty$, then $\hbar = \hbar'$.

Theorem 2.7 *Let $(\mathcal{V}, B, \star, \Omega)$ be a Ω-convertible complete SEFbMS and $\Upsilon : \mathcal{V} \to \mathcal{V}$ be a mapping so that:*

(i)

$$\theta(\frac{1}{B(\Upsilon\hbar, \Upsilon\hbar', \varsigma)} - 1) \leq \theta\left(\frac{\left[\frac{1}{B(\hbar, \Upsilon\hbar', \varsigma)} - 1 + \frac{1}{B(\hbar', \Upsilon\hbar, \varsigma)} - 1\right]}{2}\right)^{\beta},$$

for all $\hbar, \hbar' \in \mathcal{V}$, $\varsigma > 0$ and for some $\beta \in (0,1)$,

(ii) there is $\hbar_0 \in \mathcal{V}$ so that

$$\Delta(B, \Upsilon, \hbar_0) := \sup\left\{\frac{1}{B(\Upsilon^i\hbar_0, \Upsilon^j\hbar_0, \varsigma)} - 1 : i, j = 1, 2, \ldots, \varsigma > 0\right\} < \infty.$$

Then the Picard iterating sequence $\{\hbar_n\}$, $\hbar_n = \Upsilon^n\hbar_0$ for all $n \geq 1$, converges to some $\hbar \in \mathcal{V}$. If $\limsup_{n\to\infty} \frac{1}{B(\hbar_n, \Upsilon\hbar, \varsigma)} - 1 < \infty$, then $\hbar \in \mathcal{V}$ is a fixed point of Υ. Also, if $\hbar'$ is a fixed point of Υ in $\mathcal{V}$ such that $\frac{1}{B(\hbar, \hbar', \varsigma)} - 1 < \infty$, then $\hbar = \hbar'$.

2.5 APPLICATION

Let $\mathcal{V} = C[0, T]$ be the set of real continuous functions defined on $[0, T]$ and $\rho : \mathcal{V}^2 \times (0, \infty) \to [0, \infty)$ be defined by:

$$\rho(\hbar, \hbar', \alpha) = \sup_{0 \leq \varsigma \leq T} (e^{-\alpha\varsigma}|\hbar(\varsigma) - \hbar'(\varsigma)|^p) \text{ for all } \hbar, \hbar' \in \Lambda \text{ and all } \varsigma > 0, \quad p \geq 1.$$

Then $(\mathcal{V},\rho)$ is a complete SEPbM space with $\Omega(\varsigma)=2^{p-1}\varsigma$ for all $\varsigma\geq 0$. Now, let us study the integral equation:

$$\hbar(\varsigma)=\mathfrak{h}(\varsigma)+\int_0^T F(\varsigma,s)\mathcal{K}(\varsigma,s,\hbar(s))ds, \tag{2.3}$$

where $\mathfrak{h}:[0,T]\to\mathbb{R}$, $F:[0,T]^2\to[0,\infty)$ and $\mathcal{K}:[0,T]^2\times\mathbb{R}\to\mathbb{R}$ are continuous functions.

Theorem 2.8 *Assume that the subsequent suppositions are fulfilled:*
(i) for all $\varsigma,s\in[0,T]$ *we have*

$$|\mathcal{K}(\varsigma,s,\hbar(s))-\mathcal{K}(\varsigma,s,\hbar'(s))|^p\leq A(e^{-\alpha s}\max_{0\leq s\leq\Upsilon}|\hbar(s)-\hbar'(s)|^p),\;\; p\geq 1, 0\leq A<1,$$

(ii) $\sup_{t\in[0,T]}\left([\int_0^T|F(t,s)|^q ds]^{\frac{1}{q}}\right)\leq 1.$
Then, the integral equation (2.3) *has a unique solution* $u\in\Lambda$.
(iii) there is $\hbar_0\in C[0,T]$ *such that*

$$\sup\left\{\sup_{0\leq\varsigma\leq T}(e^{-\alpha\varsigma}|\Upsilon^i\hbar_0-\Upsilon^j\hbar_0|^p):i,j=1,2,\ldots,\;\varsigma>0\right\}<\infty,$$

where

$$\Upsilon(\hbar_0)(\varsigma)=\mathfrak{h}(\varsigma)+\int_0^T F(\varsigma,s)\mathcal{K}(\varsigma,s,\hbar_0(s))ds,\;\hbar\in\mathcal{V},\;\varsigma,s\in[0,T].$$

Proof. Let us define $\Upsilon:\mathcal{V}\to\mathcal{V}$ by

$$\Upsilon(\hbar)(\varsigma)=\mathfrak{h}(\varsigma)+\int_0^T F(\varsigma,s)\mathcal{K}(\varsigma,s,\hbar(s))ds,\;\hbar\in\mathcal{V},\;\varsigma,s\in[0,T].$$

Then by conditions (i)- (iii), for all $\varphi,\psi\in\mathcal{V}$ we get
$\rho(\Upsilon(\varphi),\Upsilon(\psi),\varsigma)=\sup(e^{-\alpha\varsigma}|\Upsilon(\varphi)(\varsigma)-\Upsilon(\psi)(\varsigma)|^p)$
$=\sup_{\varsigma\in[0,T]}\left[e^{-\alpha\varsigma}|\int_0^T F(\varsigma,s)\{\mathcal{K}(\varsigma,s,\varphi(s))-\mathcal{K}(\varsigma,s,\psi(s))\}ds|^p\right]$
$\leq\sup_{\varsigma\in[0,T]}\left[e^{-\alpha\varsigma}\left([\int_0^T|F(\varsigma,s)|^q ds]^{\frac{1}{q}}[\int_0^T|\mathcal{K}(\varsigma,s,\varphi(s))-\mathcal{K}(\varsigma,s,\psi(s))|^p ds]^{\frac{1}{p}}\right)^p\right]$
$\leq A\left(e^{-\alpha s}\sup_{0\leq s\leq T}\{|\varphi(s)-\psi(s)|^p\}\right)$
$\leq A\rho(\varphi,\psi,\varsigma)$ for all $\varsigma\in[0,T]$, for $A\in(0,1)$ and for all $\varphi,\psi\in\mathcal{V}$.

Hereafter, the circumstances of Theorem 2.2 (with $\theta(\varsigma)=e^{\varsigma}$) are fulfilled, and thus Υ has a unique fixed point in $\mathcal{V}$, namely, the nonlinear integral equation (2.3) has a unique solution in $C[0,T]$. □

For more examples of applications, the readers are referred to the book [11] and the references therein.

Bibliography

1. M. U. Ali, H. Aydi, A. Batool, V. Parvaneh and N. Saleem. Single and multivalued maps on parametric metric spaces endowed with an equivalence relation. *Adv. Math. Phys.*, 2022:1–11, 2022. Article ID 6188108.
2. I. A. Bakhtin. The contraction mapping principle in quasi-metric spaces. *Funct. Anal.*, 30:26–37, 1989.
3. A. E. Bashirov, E. M. Kurplnara and A. Özyapici. Multiplicative calculus and its applications. *J. Math. Anal. Appl.*, 337:36–48, 2008.
4. A. Branciari. A fixed point theorem of Banach-Caccioppoli type on a class of generalized metric spaces. *Publ. Math. Debrecen*, 57:31–37, 2000.
5. S. Czerwik. Contraction mappings in $b-$metric spaces. *Acta Math. Inform. Univ. Ostrav.*, 1:5–11, 1993.
6. P. Debnath and S. A. Mohiuddine. *Soft Computing Techniques in Engineering, Health, Mathematical and Social Sciences*. CRC Press: Boca Raton, FL, 2021.
7. P. Debnath. Some results on Cesaro summability in intuitionistic fuzzy n-normed linear spaces. *Sahand Commun. Math. Anal.*, 19(1): 77–87, 2022.
8. P. Debnath. Results on lacunary difference ideal convergence in intuitionistic fuzzy normed linear spaces. *J. Intell. Fuzzy Syst.*, 28(3): 1299–1306, 2015.
9. P. Debnath. Lacunary ideal convergence in intuitionistic fuzzy normed linear spaces. *Comput. Math. Appl.*, 63(3): 708–715, 2012.
10. P. Debnath. A generalized statistical convergence in intuitionistic fuzzy n-normed linear spaces. *Ann. Fuzzy Math. Inform.*, 12(4): 559–572, 2016.
11. P. Debnath, N. Konwar and S. Radenovic. *Metric Fixed Point Theory: Applications in Science, Engineering and Behavioural Sciences*. Springer: Berlin/Heidelberg, Germany, 2021.
12. J. Fernandez, N. Malviya, A. Savic, M. Paunovic and Z.D. Mitrovic. The extended cone b-metric-like spaces over banach algebra and some applications. *Mathematics*, 10(1):149, 2022.
13. A.D. Filip and A. Petrusel. Fixed point theorems on spaces endowed with vector-valued metrics. *J. Fixed Point Theory Appl.*, 2010:1–15, 2010.
14. S. Hadi Bonab, R. Abazari, A. Bagheri Vakilabad and H. Hosseinzadeh. Generalized metric spaces endowed with vector-valued metrics and matrix equations by tripled fixed point theorems. *J. Inequal. Appl.*, 2014: 1–16, 2020.
15. N. Hussain, S. Khaleghizadeh, P. Salimi and A. A. N. Abdou. A new approach to fixed point results in triangular intuitionistic fuzzy metric spaces. *Abstr. Appl. Anal.*, 2014:1–16, 2014.
16. N. Hussain, P. Salimi and V. Parvaneh. Fixed point results for various contractions in parametric and fuzzy b-metric spaces. *J. Nonlinear Sci. Appl.*, 8:719–739, 2015.
17. M. Jleli and B. Samet. A generalized metric space and related fixed point theorems. *J. Fixed Point Theory Appl.*, 61:1–14, 2015.
18. M. Jleli, E. Karapınar and B. Samet. Further generalization of the Banach contraction principle. *J. Inequal. Appl.*, 439: 1–9, 2014.
19. T. Kamran, M. Samreen and Q.U. Ain. A generalization of $b-$metric space and some fixed point theorems. *Mathematics*, 5, 2 (19):1–7, 2017.
20. A. Karami, S. Sedghi and V. Parvaneh, Sequential extended S-metric spaces and relevant fixed point results with application to nonlinear integral equations. *Adv. Math. Phys.*, 2021:1–11, 2021.

21. N. Konwar and P. Debnath. Continuity and Banach contraction principle in intuitionistic fuzzy n-normed linear spaces. *J. Intell. Fuzzy Syst.*, 33(4): 2363–2373, 2017.
22. N. Konwar and P. Debnath. Intuitionistic fuzzy n-normed algebra and continuous product. *Proyecciones (Antofagasta)*, 37(1): 68–83, 2018.
23. N. Konwar, B. Davvaz and P. Debnath. Approximation of new bounded operators in intuitionistic fuzzy n-Banach spaces. *J. Intell. Fuzzy Syst.*, 35(6): 6301–6312, 2018.
24. N. Konwar and P. Debnath. Some new contractive conditions and related fixed point theorems in intuitionistic fuzzy n-Banach spaces. *J. Intell. Fuzzy Syst.*, 34(1): 361–372, 2018.
25. W. M. Kozlowski. Notes on moduler function spaces. In: M. Dekker (ed.) *Monographs and Textbooks in Pure and Applied Mathematics*, vol. 122. Dekker: New York, 1988.
26. R. Krishnakumar and N. P. Sanatammappa. Fixed point theorems in parametric metric Space. *Int. J. Math. Res.*,8(3):213–220, 2016.
27. Z. Ma, L. Jiang, and H. Sun. C^*–algebra-valued metric spaces and related fixed point theorems. *J. Fixed Point Theory Appl.*, 206: 1–11, 2014.
28. V. Parvaneh, S. Hadi Bonab, H. Hosseinzadeh and H. Aydi. A tripled fixed point theorem in C^*-algebra-valued metric spaces and application in integral equations. *Adv. Math. Phys.*, 2021:1–6, 2021.
29. V. Parvaneh, N. Hussain, M. A. Kutbi and M. Khorshdi. Some fixed point results in extended parametric b-metric spaces with application to integral equations. *J. Math. Anal.*, 10 (5): 14–33, 2019.
30. K. Roy, S. Panja, M. Saha and V. Parvaneh. An extended b-metric-type space and related fixed point theorems with an application to nonlinear integral equations. *Adv. Math. Phys*, 2020:1–7, 2020.
31. B. Schweizer and A. Sklar, Statistical metric spaces. *Pacific J. Math.* 10:314–334, 1960.

3 Analytical Sequel of Rational-Type Fuzzy Contraction in Fuzzy *b*-Metric Spaces

Nabanita Konwar
Birjhora Mahavidyalaya

CONTENTS

3.1 Introduction 29
3.1.1 Background 30
3.1.2 Main Goal 30
3.2 Basic Definitions 30
3.3 Main Results of the Chapter 32
3.3.1 Definition of Rational-Type Fuzzy Contraction in F*b*-MS 32
3.3.2 Related Theorems of Rational-Type Fuzzy Contraction 33
3.3.3 Corollaries 39
3.4 Application of Rational-Type Fuzzy Contraction 40
3.5 Conclusion 42
Bibliography 42

3.1 INTRODUCTION

In mathematical analysis, the study of the existence of fixed point of a function plays a significant role. With the help of fixed point of a function, one can verify the existence of a solution of the function within a metric space. The notion of generalized b-metric spaces has recently contributed significantly to the study of fixed point theory. Such type of generalization can modulate complex situations more effectively for higher order sets and scale down the complexity of modeling systems. It also creates an effective platform for mathematical modeling and designing.

DOI: 10.1201/9781003312017-3

3.1.1 BACKGROUND

In order to model the situations where data or elements are imprecise or vague and to represent a mathematical structure for such types of situations, an extended concept of set theory called fuzzy set theory was established by Zadeh [32] in 1965. Simultaneously, Kaleva and Seikkala [21] initiated the idea of fuzzy metric space. Simultaneously, several mathematicians like Kramosil and Michalek [26], George and Veeramani [14], etc. modified the notion of fuzzy metric space (FMS). The concept of weakly compatible maps was established by Jungck and Rhoads [20] for metric spaces. The development of metric space in multiple ways is an exciting area of research for the mathematicians. By considering a weaker condition, in place of triangular inequality, Bakhtin [4] and Czerwik [7] introduced the notion of b metric space.

Heilpern [18] initiated the study fixed point theory and developed an extended version of the Banach's contraction principle in fuzzy metric spaces. The concept of contraction-type fixed point results in FMS was established by Gregori and Sapena [17]. Some more generalized and extended work in the settings of fuzziness may be found in Refs. [1,3,5,6,8–13,16,22–25,27–31].

3.1.2 MAIN GOAL

The predominant aim of this chapter is to define the notion of rational-type fuzzy contraction in FbMS and establish some new fixed point results. After that the existence and uniqueness of fixed point for rational-type fuzzy contraction in G-complete FbMS is established. We also provide an application in support of the results.

3.2 BASIC DEFINITIONS

Below we discuss a few preliminary definitions which are essential for our main results.

Definition 3.1 *Consider a binary operation* $* : [0,1] \times [0,1] \rightarrow [0,1]$. *Then* $*$ *is known as a continuous* $t-$*norm if it satisfies the condition:*

(i) $*$ *is associative and commutative,*
(ii) $*$ *is continuous,*
(iii) $\alpha * 1 = \alpha$ *for all* $\alpha \in [0,1]$,
(iv) $\alpha * b \leq \beta * d$ *whenever* $\alpha \leq \beta$ *and* $b \leq d$ *and* $\alpha, \beta, c, d \in [0,1]$.

Definition 3.2 *Consider a function* $d : S \times S \longrightarrow \mathbb{R}$, *where* $S \neq \phi$. *Then for all* $s_1, s_2, s_3 \in S$, (S,d) *is called a metric space if it satisfies the following conditions:*

(i) $d(s_1,s_2) \geq 0$ *and* $d(s_1,s_2) = 0$ *iff* $s_1 = s_2$.
(ii) $d(s_1,s_2) = d(s_2,s_1)$.
(iii) $d(s_1,s_3) \leq d(s_1,s_2) + d(s_2,s_3)$.

Definition 3.3 *Suppose X is a classical set, called the universe and $A \in X$. The membership of A is considered as a characteristic function μ_A from X to $\{0,1\}$ such that*

$$\mu_A(x) = \begin{cases} 1 & \text{iff } x \in A \\ 0 & \text{iff } x \notin A. \end{cases}$$

$\{0,1\}$ is called a valuation set. If $\{0,1\}$ is allowed to be $[0,1]$, A is said to be a fuzzy set.

Kramosil and Michalek [26] defined fuzzy metric space as follows:

Definition 3.4 *[26] Consider a set $X \neq \phi$ and a continuous t-norm $*$. Suppose M is a fuzzy set on $X^2 \times \mathbb{R}$. Then for all $a_1, a_2, a_3 \in X$ and $t, s \in \mathbb{R}$, $(X, M, *)$ is called fuzzy metric space if it satisfies the following axioms:*

(i) $M(a_1,a_2,t) = 0 \; \forall \, t \leq 0$.
(ii) $M(a_1,a_2,t) = 1 \; \forall \, t > 0$ *iff* $a_1 = a_2$.
(iii) $M(a_1,a_2,t) = M(a_2,a_1,t)$.
(iv) $M(a_1,a_2,t) * M(a_2,a_3,s) \leq M(a_1,a_3,t+s)$.
(v) $M(a_1,a_2,t) : (0,\infty) \to [0,1]$ *is left continuous.*
(vi) $\lim_{t\to\infty} M(a_1,a_2,t) = 1$.

George and Veeramani [14,15] made an appealing modification of fuzzy metric spaces in the following way:

Definition 3.5 *[14] Consider a set $X \neq \phi$ and a continuous t-norm $*$. Suppose M is a fuzzy set on $X^2 \times (0,\infty)$. Then for all $a_1, a_2, a_3 \in X$ and $t, s \in \mathbb{R}$, $(X, M, *)$ is called fuzzy metric space if it satisfies the following axioms:*

(i) $M(a_1,a_2,t) > 0$.
(ii) $M(a_1,a_2,t) = 1 \; \forall \, t > 0$ *if and only if* $a_1 = a_2$.
(iii) $M(a_1,a_2,t) = M(a_2,a_1,t)$.
(iv) $M(a_1,a_2,t) * M(a_2,a_3,s) \leq M(a_1,a_3,t+s)$.
(v) $M(a_1,a_2,t) : (0,\infty) \to [0,1]$ *is continuous.*

Definition 3.6 *[19] Consider a non-empty set S and a continuous t-norm $*$. Suppose P is a fuzzy set on $S \times S \times (0,\infty)$ such that for all $u, v, w \in S$ and $\alpha, \beta > 0$ following conditions are holds:*

(i) $P(\hbar_1,\hbar_2,\alpha) > 0$,
(ii) $P(\hbar_1,\hbar_2,\alpha) = 1 \iff \hbar_1 = \hbar_2$,
(iii) $P(\hbar_1,\hbar_2,\alpha) = P(\hbar_2,\hbar_1,\alpha)$,
(iv) $P(\hbar_1,\hbar_2,\cdot) : (0,\infty) \to (0,1]$ *is continuous,*
(v) $P(\hbar_1,\hbar_3,\alpha+\beta) \geq *(P(\hbar_1,\hbar_2,\frac{\alpha}{b}), P(\hbar_2,\hbar_3,\frac{\beta}{b}))$

Then $(S,P,*)$ is called a FbMS.

Definition 3.7 *[2] Consider a metric space (Y,d) and a function $T : Y \to Y$. Then T is called a contraction mapping or contraction if there exists a constant α (called constant of contraction), with $0 \leq \alpha < 1$, such that*

$$d(T(y_1),T(y_2)) \leq \alpha d(y_1,y_2), \forall y_1,y_2 \in Y.$$

Definition 3.8 *[17] Let $(U,M_r,*)$ be a FbM-space, $v_1 \in U$ and a sequence (μ_j) in U is fuzzy-contractive if there exists $\alpha \in (0,1)$ such that*

$$\frac{1}{M_r(\mu_j,\mu_{j+1},t)} - 1 \leq \alpha(\frac{1}{M_r(\mu_{j-1},\mu_j,t)} - 1), \textit{for } t > 0,\ j \geq 1$$

Definition 3.9 *[17] Let $(U,M_r,*)$ be a FbM-space. A sequence (μ_j) in U is said to be G-Cauchy if*

$$\lim_j M_r(\mu_j,\mu_{j+p},t) = 1, \textit{for } t > 0 \textit{ and } p > 0.$$

And $(U,M_r,*)$ is called G-complete if every G-Cauchy sequence is convergent.

Definition 3.10 *Let $(U,M_r,*)$ be a FbM-space. Then M_r is said to be triangular if it satisfied the following property*

$$\frac{1}{M_r(\mu_1,\mu^*,t)} - 1 \leq (\frac{1}{M_r(\mu_1,\mu,\frac{t}{b})} - 1) + (\frac{1}{M_r(\mu,\mu_*,\frac{t}{b})} - 1),$$

for all $\mu,\mu_1,\mu^* \in U$, $t > 0$.

Definition 3.11 *[17] Suppose $(U,M_r,*)$ is a FbM-space. Construct a mapping $f : U \to U$. If for all $\mu_1,\mu^* \in U$, $t > 0$, there exists $\alpha \in (0,1)$ such that*

$$\frac{1}{M_r(f(\mu_1),f(\mu^*),t)} - 1 \leq \alpha(\frac{1}{M_r(\mu_1,\mu_*,t)} - 1),$$

Then f is called fuzzy-contractive.

Next we elaborate the results of the chapter.

3.3 MAIN RESULTS OF THE CHAPTER

In this section, we put forward the definition of rational-type fuzzy contraction in F*b*-MS. After defining the main concept, we provide some propositions and related theorems.

3.3.1 DEFINITION OF RATIONAL-TYPE FUZZY CONTRACTION IN F*B*-MS

Definition 3.12 *Consider a FbMS $(U,M_r,*)$ and a function $f : U \to U$. Then f is said to be rational-type fuzzy contraction(RTF-contraction) if there exists $\alpha,\beta \in [0,1)$ such that for all $\mu_1,\mu_* \in U$ and $t > 0$,*

$$\begin{aligned}\frac{1}{M_r(f(\mu_1),f(\mu^*),t)} - 1 \leq& \alpha(\frac{1}{M_r(\mu_1,\mu^*,t)} - 1)\\ &+ \beta(\frac{M_r(\mu_1,\mu^*,t)}{M_r(\mu_1,f(\mu_1),\frac{t}{b}) * M_r(\mu^*,f(\mu_1),\frac{2t}{b})} - 1)\end{aligned}$$

3.3.2 RELATED THEOREMS OF RATIONAL-TYPE FUZZY CONTRACTION

Theorem 3.1 *Consider a G-complete FbMS $(U, M_r, *)$ and a rational-type fuzzy contraction mapping $f : U \to U$ with $\alpha + \beta = 1$. Then in U, f has a unique fixed point.*

Proof. Suppose that $\mu_0 \in U$ is fixed and $\mu_{j+1} = f(\mu_j)$, $j \geq 0$. Then for $t > 0$, $j \geq 1$,

$$
\begin{aligned}
\frac{1}{M_r(\mu_j, \mu_{j+1}, t)} - 1 &= \frac{1}{M_r(f(\mu_{j-1}), f(\mu_j), t)} - 1 \\
&\leq \alpha\left(\frac{1}{M_r(\mu_{j-1}, \mu_j, t)} - 1\right) \\
&\quad + \beta\left(\frac{M_r(\mu_{j-1}, \mu_j, t)}{M_r(\mu_{j-1}, f(\mu_{j-1}), \frac{t}{b}) * M_r(\mu_j, f(\mu_{j-1}), \frac{2t}{b})} - 1\right) \\
&= \alpha\left(\frac{1}{M_r(\mu_{j-1}, \mu_j, t)} - 1\right) \\
&\quad + \beta\left(\frac{M_r(\mu_{j-1}, \mu_j, t)}{M_r(\mu_{j-1}, \mu_j, \frac{t}{b}) * M_r(\mu_j, \mu_j, \frac{2t}{b})} - 1\right)
\end{aligned}
\tag{3.1}
$$

Therefore, for $t > 0$

$$
\frac{1}{M_r(\mu_j, \mu_{j+1}, t)} - 1 \leq \alpha\left(\frac{1}{M_r(\mu_{j-1}, \mu_j, t)} - 1\right) \tag{3.2}
$$

In a similar way we have, for $t > 0$

$$
\frac{1}{M_r(\mu_{j-1}, \mu_j, t)} - 1 \leq \alpha\left(\frac{1}{M_r(\mu_{j-2}, \mu_{j-1}, t)} - 1\right) \tag{3.3}
$$

Therefore, from Eqs. (3.2) and (3.3), we have for $t > 0$,

$$
\begin{aligned}
\frac{1}{M_r(\mu_j, \mu_{j+1}, t)} - 1 &\leq \alpha\left(\frac{1}{M_r(\mu_{j-1}, \mu_j, t)} - 1\right) \\
&\leq \alpha^2\left(\frac{1}{M_r(\mu_{j-2}, \mu_{j-1}, t)} - 1\right) \\
&\leq \cdots \leq \alpha^j\left(\frac{1}{M_r(\mu_0, \mu_1, t)} - 1\right) \\
&\longrightarrow 0, \text{ as } j \longrightarrow \infty.
\end{aligned}
$$

Therefore, (μ_j) is a fuzzy-contractive sequence in U.
Hence for $t > 0$, $\lim_{j\to\infty} M_r(\mu_j, \mu_{j+1}, t) = 1$
Next we have to show that (μ_j) is a G-Cauchy sequence.

Consider a fixed $q \in \mathbb{N}$ and let $j \in \mathbb{N}$ such that

$$\begin{aligned}
M_r(\mu_j, \mu_{j+q}, t) &= M_r(\mu_j, \mu_{j+q}, \underbrace{(\frac{1}{q} + \frac{1}{q} + \cdots + \frac{1}{q})}_{q-times} t) \\
&\geq M_r(\mu_j, \mu_{j+1}, \frac{t}{qb}) * M_r(\mu_{j+1}, \mu_{j+2}, \frac{t}{qb}) \\
&* \cdots * M_r(\mu_{j+q-1}, \mu_{j+q}, \frac{t}{qb}) \\
&\longrightarrow \underbrace{1 * 1 * \cdots * 1}_{q-times} = 1, \text{ as } j \longrightarrow \infty.
\end{aligned}$$

Hence (μ_j) is a G-Cauchy sequence.

Since $(U, M_r, *)$ is G-complete, there exists $v_1 \in U$ such that for $t > 0$, $\mu_j \to v_1$, as $j \longrightarrow \infty$,

$$\lim_{j \to \infty} M_r(\mu_j, v_1, t) = 1$$

As M_r is triangular, for $t > 0$, we have

$$\begin{aligned}
\frac{1}{M_r(v_1, f(v_1), t)} - 1 &\leq (\frac{1}{M_r(v_1, \mu_{j+1}, \frac{t}{b})} - 1) + (\frac{1}{M_r(f(\mu_j), f(v_1), \frac{t}{b})} - 1) \\
&\leq (\frac{1}{M_r(v_1, \mu_{j+1}, \frac{t}{b})} - 1) + \alpha(\frac{1}{M_r(\mu_j, v_1, t)} - 1) \\
&+ \beta(\frac{M_r(\mu_j, v_1, t)}{M_r(\mu_j, f(\mu_j), \frac{t}{b}) * M_r(v_1, f(\mu_j), \frac{2t}{b})} - 1) \\
&= (\frac{1}{M_r(v_1, \mu_{j+1}, \frac{t}{b})} - 1) + \alpha(\frac{1}{M_r(\mu_j, v_1, t)} - 1) \\
&+ \beta(\frac{M_r(\mu_j, v_1, t)}{M_r(\mu_j, \mu_{j+1}, \frac{t}{b}) * M_r(v_1, \mu_{j+1}, \frac{2t}{b})} - 1) \\
&\longrightarrow 0, \text{ as } j \longrightarrow \infty.
\end{aligned}$$

Hence for $t > 0$, $M_r(v_1, f(v_1), t) = 1$ implies $f(v_1) = v_1$

Finally, we have to prove the uniqueness.

Consider that $\exists\, z_1 \in U$ such that $f(z_1) = z_1$ and $f(v_1) = v_1$, then we have

$$\begin{aligned}
\frac{1}{M_r(v_1, z_1, t)} - 1 &= \frac{1}{M_r(f(v_1), f(z_1), t)} - 1 \\
&\leq \alpha(\frac{1}{M_r(v_1, z_1, t)} - 1) \\
&+ \beta(\frac{M_r(v_1, z_1, t)}{M_r(v_1, f(v_1), \frac{t}{b}) * M_r(z_1, f(v_1), \frac{2t}{b})} - 1)
\end{aligned}$$

$$
\begin{aligned}
&\leq \alpha(\frac{1}{M_r(v_1,z_1,t)}-1)\\
&\quad +\beta(\frac{M_r(v_1,z_1,t)}{M_r(v_1,v_1,\frac{t}{b})*M_r(z_1,v_1,\frac{2t}{b})}-1)\\
&=\alpha(\frac{1}{M_r(v_1,z_1,t)}-1)\\
&=\alpha(\frac{1}{M_r(f(v_1),f(z_1),t)}-1)\\
&\leq \alpha^2(\frac{1}{M_r(v_1,z_1,t)}-1)\\
&\leq \cdots \leq \alpha^j(\frac{1}{M_r(v_1,z_1,t)}-1)\\
&\longrightarrow 0,\ \text{as } j\longrightarrow\infty.
\end{aligned}
$$

Therefore, $M_r(v_1,z_1,t)=1$ implies $v_1=z_1$.
Hence f has a unique fixed point. □

Theorem 3.2 *Consider a G-complete FbMS $(U,M_r,*)$ where M_r satisfy the triangular inequality and a mapping $f:U\to U$ with $\alpha+\beta+2\gamma+2\delta<1$ such that for all $\mu_1,\mu^*\in U$, $t>0$, $\alpha,\beta,\gamma,\delta\geq 0$ f satisfies the following property:*

$$
\begin{aligned}
\frac{1}{M_r(f(\mu_1),f(\mu^*),t)}-1\leq&\alpha(\frac{1}{M_r(\mu_1,\mu^*,t)}-1)\\
&+\beta(\frac{M_r(\mu_1,\mu^*,\frac{t}{b})*M_r(\mu^*,f(\mu^*),\frac{t}{b})}{M_r(\mu_1,f(\mu_1),\frac{t}{b})*M_r(\mu_1,f(\mu^*),\frac{t}{b})}-1)\\
&+\gamma(\frac{M_r(\mu_1,f(\mu_1),t)}{M_r(\mu_1,f(\mu^*),\frac{2t}{b})}-1+\frac{M_r(\mu^*,f(\mu^*),t)}{M_r(\mu_1,f(\mu_1),\frac{2t}{b})}-1)\\
&+\delta(\frac{1}{M_r(\mu_1,f(\mu_1),\frac{t}{b})}-1+\frac{1}{M_r(\mu^*,f(\mu^*),\frac{t}{b})}-1)
\end{aligned}
\tag{3.4}
$$

Then f has a unique fixed point in U.

Proof. Consider a fixed $\mu_0\in U$ and $\mu_{j+1}=f(\mu_j)$, $j\geq 0$.
Now for $t>0$, $j\geq 1$

$$
\begin{aligned}
\frac{1}{M_r(\mu_j,\mu_{j+1},t)}-1=&\frac{1}{M_r(f(\mu_{j-1}),f(\mu_j),t)}-1\\
&\leq\alpha(\frac{1}{M_r(\mu_{j-1},\mu_j,t)}-1)
\end{aligned}
$$

$$
\begin{aligned}
&+\beta(\frac{M_r(\mu_{j-1},\mu_j,\frac{t}{b})*M_r(\mu_j,f(\mu_j),\frac{t}{b})}{M_r(\mu_{j-1},f(\mu_{j-1}),\frac{t}{b})*M_r(\mu_{j-1},f(\mu_j),\frac{2t}{b})}-1)\\
&+\gamma(\frac{M_r(\mu_{j-1},f(\mu_{j-1}),t)}{M_r(\mu_{j-1},f(\mu_j),\frac{2t}{b})}-1+\frac{M_r(\mu_j,f(\mu_j),t)}{M_r(\mu_{j-1},f(\mu_j),\frac{2t}{b})}-1)\\
&+\delta(\frac{1}{M_r(\mu_{j-1},f(\mu_{j-1}),\frac{t}{b})}-1+\frac{1}{M_r(\mu_j,f(\mu_j),\frac{t}{b})}-1)\\
=&\alpha(\frac{1}{M_r(\mu_{j-1},\mu_j,t)}-1)\\
&+\beta(\frac{M_r(\mu_{j-1},\mu_j,\frac{t}{b})*M_r(\mu_j,\mu_{j+1},\frac{t}{b})}{M_r(\mu_{j-1},\mu_j,\frac{t}{b})*M_r(\mu_{j-1},\mu_{j+1},\frac{2t}{b})}-1)\\
&+\gamma(\frac{M_r(\mu_{j-1},\mu_j,t)}{M_r(\mu_{j-1},\mu_{j+1},\frac{2t}{b})}-1+\frac{M_r(\mu_j,\mu_{j+1},t)}{M_r(\mu_{j-1},\mu_{j+1},\frac{2t}{b})}-1)\\
&+\delta(\frac{1}{M_r(\mu_{j-1},\mu_j,\frac{t}{b})}-1+\frac{1}{M_r(\mu_j,\mu_{j+1},\frac{t}{b})}-1)
\end{aligned}
$$

Since for $t > 0$ $M_r(\mu_{j-1},\mu_{j+1},2t) \geq M_r(\mu_{j-1},\mu_j,t) * M_r(\mu_j,\mu_{j+1},t)$ we have

$$
\frac{1}{M_r(\mu_j,\mu_{j+1},t)}-1 \leq \lambda(\frac{1}{M_r(\mu_{j-1},\mu_j,t)}-1), \tag{3.5}
$$

where $\lambda = \frac{\alpha+\beta+\gamma+\delta}{1-\gamma-\delta} < 1$

Similarly, for $t > 0$

$$
\frac{1}{M_r(\mu_{j-1},\mu_j,t)}-1 \leq \lambda(\frac{1}{M_r(\mu_{j-2},\mu_{j-1},t)}-1), \tag{3.6}
$$

where $\lambda = \frac{\alpha+\beta+\gamma+\delta}{1-\gamma-\delta} < 1$

Hence from Eqs. (3.5) and (3.6) we have for $t > 0$

$$
\begin{aligned}
\frac{1}{M_r(\mu_j,\mu_{j+1},t)}-1 &\leq \lambda(\frac{1}{M_r(\mu_{j-1},\mu_j,t)}-1)\\
&\leq \lambda^2(\frac{1}{M_r(\mu_{j-2},\mu_{j-1},t)}-1)\\
&\leq \ldots \leq \lambda^j(\frac{1}{M_r(\mu_0,\mu_1,t)}-1)\\
&\longrightarrow 0, \text{ as } j \longrightarrow \infty
\end{aligned}
$$

Therefore, (μ_j) is a rational-type fuzzy-contractive sequence in U.
Hence for $t > 0$, $\lim_{j\to\infty} M_r(\mu_j,\mu_{j+1},t) = 1$
Next we have to show that (μ_j) is a G-Cauchy sequence.

Consider a fixed $q \in \mathbb{N}$ and let $j \in \mathbb{N}$ such that

$$
\begin{aligned}
M_r(\mu_j, \mu_{j+q}, t) &= M_r(\mu_j, \mu_{j+q}, \underbrace{(\frac{1}{q} + \frac{1}{q} + \cdots + \frac{1}{q})t}_{q-times}) \\
&\geq M_r(\mu_j, \mu_{j+1}, \frac{t}{qb}) * M_r(\mu_{j+1}, \mu_{j+2}, \frac{t}{qb}) \\
&* \cdots * M_r(\mu_{j+q-1}, \mu_{j+q}, \frac{t}{qb}) \\
&\longrightarrow \underbrace{1 * 1 * \cdots * 1}_{q-times} = 1, \text{ as } j \longrightarrow \infty.
\end{aligned}
$$

Hence (μ_j) is a G-Cauchy sequence.
Since $(U, M_r, *)$ is G-complete, $\exists\, \nu_1 \in U$ such that for $t > 0$, $\mu_j \to \nu_1$, as $j \longrightarrow \infty$,

$$\lim_{j\to\infty} M_r(\mu_j, \nu_1, t) = 1$$

As M_r is triangular, for $t > 0$, we have

$$\frac{1}{M_r(\nu_1, f(\nu_1), t)} - 1 \leq (\frac{1}{M_r(\nu_1, \mu_{j+1}, \frac{t}{b})} - 1) + (\frac{1}{M_r(\mu_{j+1}, f(\nu_1), \frac{t}{b})} - 1)$$

Hence we have,

$$
\begin{aligned}
\frac{1}{M_r(\mu_{j+1}, f(\nu_1), t)} - 1 &= \frac{1}{M_r(f(\mu_j), f(\nu_1), t)} - 1 \\
&\leq \alpha(\frac{1}{M_r(\mu_j, \nu_1, t)} - 1) \\
&+ \beta(\frac{M_r(\mu_j, \nu_1, \frac{t}{b}) * M_r(\nu_1, f(\nu_1), \frac{t}{b})}{M_r(\mu_j, f(\mu_j), \frac{t}{b}) * M_r(\mu_j, f(\nu_1), \frac{2t}{b})} - 1) \\
&+ \gamma(\frac{M_r(\mu_j, f(\mu_j), t)}{M_r(\mu_j, f(\nu_1), \frac{2t}{b})} - 1 + \frac{M_r(\nu_1, f(\nu_1), t)}{M_r(\mu_j, f(\nu_1), \frac{2t}{b})} - 1) \\
&+ \delta(\frac{1}{M_r(\mu_j, f(\mu_j), \frac{t}{b})} - 1 + \frac{1}{M_r(\nu_1, f(\nu_1), \frac{t}{b})} - 1) \\
&= \alpha(\frac{1}{M_r(\mu_j, \nu_1, t)} - 1) \\
&+ \beta(\frac{M_r(\mu_j, \nu_1, \frac{t}{b}) * M_r(\nu_1, f(\nu_1), \frac{t}{b})}{M_r(\mu_j, \mu_{j+1}, \frac{t}{b}) * M_r(\mu_j, f(\nu_1), \frac{2t}{b})} - 1) \\
&+ \gamma(\frac{M_r(\mu_j, \mu_{j+1}, t)}{M_r(\mu_j, f(\nu_1), \frac{2t}{b})} - 1 + \frac{M_r(\nu_1, f(\nu_1), t)}{M_r(\mu_j, f(\nu_1), \frac{2t}{b})} - 1) \\
&+ \delta(\frac{1}{M_r(\mu_j, \mu_{j+1}, \frac{t}{b})} - 1 + \frac{1}{M_r(\nu_1, f(\nu_1), \frac{t}{b})} - 1)
\end{aligned}
$$

Since for $t > 0$ $M_r(\mu_j, f(v_1), 2t) \geq M_r(\mu_j, v_1, \frac{t}{b}) * M_r(v_1, f(v_1), \frac{t}{b})$ we have

$$\begin{aligned}
\frac{1}{M_r(\mu_{j+1}, f(v_1), t)} - 1 \leq \alpha(&\frac{1}{M_r(\mu_j, v_1, t)} - 1) \\
&+ \beta(\frac{M_r(\mu_j, v_1, \frac{t}{b}) * M_r(v_1, f(v_1), \frac{t}{b})}{M_r(\mu_j, \mu_{j+1}, \frac{t}{b}) * M_r(\mu_j, v_1, \frac{t}{b}) * M_r(v_1, f(v_1), \frac{t}{b})} - 1) \\
&+ \gamma(\frac{M_r(\mu_j, \mu_{j+1}, t)}{M_r(\mu_j, f(v_1), \frac{2t}{b}) * M_r(\mu_j, f(v_1), \frac{2t}{b})} - 1 \\
&+ \frac{M_r(v_1, f(v_1), t)}{M_r(\mu_j, f(v_1), \frac{2t}{b})} - 1) \\
&+ \delta(\frac{1}{M_r(\mu_j, \mu_{j+1}, \frac{t}{b})} - 1 + \frac{1}{M_r(v_1, f(v_1), \frac{t}{b})} - 1) \\
&\longrightarrow (\gamma + \delta)(\frac{1}{M_r(v_1, f(v_1), \frac{t}{b})} - 1), \text{ as } j \longrightarrow \infty
\end{aligned}$$

Hence for $t > 0$,

$$\lim_{j \longrightarrow \infty} \sup(\frac{1}{M_r(\mu_{j+1}, f(v_1), t)} - 1) \leq (\gamma + \delta)(\frac{1}{M_r(v_1, f(v_1), \frac{t}{b})} - 1)$$

Since $j \longrightarrow \infty$, we have for $t > 0$,

$$\frac{1}{M_r(v_1, f(v_1), t)} - 1) \leq (\gamma + \delta)(\frac{1}{M_r(v_1, f(v_1), \frac{t}{b})} - 1)$$

where $(\gamma + \delta) < 1$ and $\alpha + \beta + 2\gamma + 2\delta < 1$.

Hence for $t > 0$,

$$M_r(v_1, f(v_1), t) = 1$$

This implies, $f(v_1) = v_1$.

Next we have to show the uniqueness property.

Consider that there exists $z_1 \in U$ such that $f(z_1) = z_1$ and $f(v_1) = v_1$.

Then for $t > 0$ we have

$$\begin{aligned}
\frac{1}{M_r(v_1, z_1, t)} - 1 &= \frac{1}{M_r(f(v_1), f(z_1), t)} - 1 \\
&\leq \alpha(\frac{1}{M_r(v_1, z_1, t)} - 1)
\end{aligned}$$

$$+\beta(\frac{M_r(v_1,z_1,\frac{t}{b}) * M_r(z_1,f(z_1),\frac{t}{b})}{M_r(v_1,f(v_1),\frac{t}{b}) * M_r(v_1,f(z_1),\frac{2t}{b})} - 1)$$
$$+\gamma(\frac{M_r(v_1,f(v_1),t)}{M_r(v_1,f(z_1),\frac{2t}{b})} - 1 + \frac{M_r(z_1,f(z_1),t)}{M_r(v_1,f(z_1),\frac{2t}{b})} - 1)$$
$$+\delta(\frac{1}{M_r(v_1,f(v_1),\frac{t}{b})} - 1 + \frac{1}{M_r(z_1,f(z_1),\frac{t}{b})} - 1)$$
$$= \alpha(\frac{1}{M_r(v_1,z_1,t)} - 1) + \beta(\frac{M_r(v_1,z_1,\frac{t}{b})}{M_r(v_1,z_1,\frac{2t}{b})} - 1)$$
$$+\gamma(\frac{1}{M_r(v_1,z_1,\frac{2t}{b})} - 1 + \frac{1}{M_r(v_1,z_1,\frac{2t}{b})} - 1)$$
$$= \alpha(\frac{1}{M_r(v_1,z_1,t)} - 1) + \beta(\frac{M_r(v_1,z_1,\frac{t}{b})}{M_r(v_1,z_1,\frac{t}{b^2}) * M_r(z_1,z_1,\frac{t}{b^2})} - 1)$$
$$+\gamma(\frac{1}{M_r(v_1,z_1,\frac{t}{b^2}) * M_r(z_1,z_1,\frac{t}{b^2})} - 1$$
$$+\frac{1}{M_r(v_1,z_1,\frac{t}{b^2}) * M_r(z_1,z_1,\frac{t}{b^2})} - 1)$$
$$= (\alpha + 2\gamma)(\frac{1}{M_r(v_1,z_1,t)} - 1)$$
$$= (\alpha + 2\gamma)(\frac{1}{M_r(f(v_1),f(z_1),t)} - 1)$$
$$\leq (\alpha + 2\gamma)^2(\frac{1}{M_r(v_1,z_1,t)} - 1)$$
$$\leq \ldots \leq (\alpha + 2\gamma)^j(\frac{1}{M_r(v_1,z_1,t)} - 1)$$
$$\longrightarrow 0, \text{ as } j \longrightarrow \infty, \text{ where } (\alpha + 2\gamma) < 1.$$

Therefore, $M_r(v_1,z_1,t) = 1$ which implies that $v_1 = z_1$ for $t > 0$.
Hence f has unique fixed point in U. □

Next we establish some corollaries with the help of the above theorems.

3.3.3 COROLLARIES

Corollary 1 *Consider a G-complete Fb-M space $(U, M_r, *)$ where M_r is triangular. Suppose that $f : U \longrightarrow U$ is a fuzzy contraction mapping satisfying the condition:*

$$\frac{1}{M_r(f(\mu_1),f(\mu^*),t)} - 1 \leq \alpha(\frac{1}{M_r(\mu_1,\mu_*,t)} - 1), \tag{3.7}$$

for all $\mu_1, \mu^* \in U$, $t > 0$.

Then f has a unique fixed point in U.

Corollary 2 *Suppose $(U,M_r,*)$ is a G-complete Fb-M space and M_r is triangular. Consider that for all $\mu_1,\mu^* \in U$, $t>0$, $\alpha,\beta,\delta \geq 0$ and $\alpha+\beta+2\delta<1$, the mapping $f:U \longrightarrow U$ satisfying the condition:*

$$\begin{aligned}\frac{1}{M_r(f(\mu_1),f(\mu^*),t)}-1 \leq &\alpha(\frac{1}{M_r(\mu_1,\mu^*,t)}-1)\\ &+\beta(\frac{M_r(\mu_1,\mu^*,\frac{t}{b})*M_r(\mu^*,f(\mu^*),\frac{t}{b})}{M_r(\mu_1,f(\mu_1),\frac{t}{b})*M_r(\mu_1,f(\mu^*),\frac{2t}{b})}-1)\\ &+\delta(\frac{1}{M_r(\mu_1,f(\mu_1),t)}-1+\frac{1}{M_r(\mu^*,f(\mu^*),t)}-1)\end{aligned}$$

Then in U, f has a unique fixed point.

Corollary 3 *Suppose $(U,M_r,*)$ is a G-complete Fb-M space and M_r is triangular. Consider that for all $\mu_1,\mu^* \in U$, $t>0$, $\alpha,\gamma,\delta \geq 0$ and $\alpha+2\gamma+2\delta<1$, the mapping $f:U \longrightarrow U$ satisfying the condition:*

$$\begin{aligned}\frac{1}{M_r(f(\mu_1),f(\mu^*),t)}-1 \leq &\alpha(\frac{1}{M_r(\mu_1,\mu^*,t)}-1)+\gamma(\frac{M_r(\mu_1,f(\mu_1),t)}{M_r(\mu_1,f(\mu^*),\frac{2t}{b})}-1\\ &+\frac{M_r(\mu^*,f(\mu^*),t)}{M_r(\mu_1,f(\mu^*),\frac{2t}{b})}-1)\\ &+\delta(\frac{1}{M_r(\mu_1,f(\mu_1),t)}-1+\frac{1}{M_r(\mu^*,f(\mu^*),t)}-1)\end{aligned}$$

Then f has a unique fixed point in U.

Corollary 4 *Suppose $(U,M_r,*)$ is a G-complete Fb-M space and M_r is triangular. Consider that for all $\mu_1,\mu^* \in U$, $t>0$, $\alpha,\delta \geq 0$ and $\alpha+2\delta<1$, the mapping $f:U \longrightarrow U$ satisfying the condition:*

$$\begin{aligned}\frac{1}{M_r(f(\mu_1),f(\mu^*),t)}-1 \leq &\alpha(\frac{1}{M_r(\mu_1,\mu^*,t)}-1)\\ &+\delta(\frac{1}{M_r(\mu_1,f(\mu_1),t)}-1+\frac{1}{M_r(\mu^*,f(\mu^*),t)}-1)\end{aligned}$$

Then f has a unique fixed point in U.

3.4 APPLICATION OF RATIONAL-TYPE FUZZY CONTRACTION

In this section, we discuss and elaborate the application of rational-type fuzzy contraction in setting of F*b*M-spaces. We provide an integral-type application of our new results.

Consider the space of all real valued continuous functions $U = C([0,a],\mathbb{R})$ where $0 < a \in \mathbb{R}$ on the interval $[0,a]$.

Consider a mapping $\Im : [0,a] \times [0,a] \times \mathbb{R} \to \mathbb{R}$. Then the equation of nonlinear integral is

$$\mu_1(\tau) = \int_0^\tau \Im(\tau, v, \mu_1(v))dv,$$

for all $\mu_1 \in U$ and $\tau, v \in [0,a]$.

Next we induce a b-metric on U such that

$$d : U^2 \longrightarrow \mathbb{R}$$

defined by

$$\begin{aligned} d(\mu_1,\mu_2) &= \underbrace{\sup}_{\tau\in[0,a]} |\mu_1(\tau) - \mu_2(\tau)| \\ &= \|\mu_1 - \mu_2\| \end{aligned}$$

where $\mu_1, \mu_2 \in C([0,a],\mathbb{R}) = U$.

Next we define the binary operation $*$ such that $\alpha * \lambda = \alpha\lambda$ for all $\alpha, \lambda \in [0,a]$.

Then we construct a standard fuzzy b-metric

$$M_r : U^2 \times (0,\infty) \longrightarrow [0,1]$$

such that

$$M_r(\mu_1,\mu_2,t) = \frac{\frac{t}{b}}{\frac{t}{b} + d(\mu_1,\mu_2)}$$

for all $\mu_1, \mu_2 \in U$ and $t > 0$.

Then M_r is triangular and $(U, M_r, *)$ is a G-complete FbMS.

proposition 3.1 *Consider the nonlinear integral equation*

$$\mu_1(\tau) = \int_0^\tau \Im(\tau, v, \mu_1(v))dv, \tag{3.8}$$

for all $\mu_1 \in U$ and $\tau, v \in [0,a]$.

Then for all $\mu_1, \mu_2 \in U$, there exist $\beta \in (0,1)$ satisfying the condition

$$d(l\mu_1, l\mu_2) \leq \beta N(l, \mu_1, \mu_2)$$

where

$$N(l,\mu_1,\mu_2) = \max \|\mu_1 - \mu_2\|, 2\|\mu_1 - l\mu_2\|$$

Then in U, the integral equation 3.8 has a unique solution.

3.5 CONCLUSION

In this chapter, we put forward the notion of rational-type fuzzy contraction in F*b*MS. We established some fixed point theorems for the newly developed contraction mappings in *G*-complete F*b*MS. With these results, we have provided an application of rational-type fuzzy contraction for finding the solution of nonlinear integral equations. In the future, one can also extend the work in the field of integral as well as differential equations.

Bibliography

1. C. Alaca, D. Turkoglu and C Yildiz. Fixed points in intuitionistic fuzzy metric spaces. *Chaos Solitons Fractals*, 29:1073–1078, 2006.
2. T. M. Apostol *Mathematical Analysis*. Addison-Wesley: Boston, MA, 1974.
3. G. Babu, V. Ravindranadh and D. T. Mosissa Fixed points in b-metric spaces via simulation function. *Novi Sad J. Math.*, 47(2):133–147, 2017.
4. I. A. Bakhtin. The contraction principle in quasimetric spaces. *Funct. Anal.*, 30:26–37, 1989.
5. D. Butnariu. Fixed points for fuzzy mappings. *Fuzzy Sets Syst.*, 7(2):191–207, 1982.
6. I. Cristiana, R. Shahram and S. E. Mohamad. Fixed points of some new contractions on intuitionistic fuzzy metric spaces. *Fixed Point Theory Appl.* DOI: 10.1186/1687-1812-2013-168.
7. S. Czerwik. Contraction mappings in b metric spaces. *Acta Math. Inform. Univ. Ostrav.*, 1(1):5–11, 1993.
8. P. Debnath. Lacunary ideal convergence in intuitionistic fuzzy normed linear spaces. *Comput. Math. Appl.*, 63:708–715, 2012.
9. P. Debnath. Results on lacunary difference ideal convergence in intuitionistic fuzzy normed linear spaces. *J. Intell. Fuzzy Syst.*, 28:1299–1306, 2015.
10. P. Debnath. A generalized statistical convergence in intuitionistic fuzzy n-normed linear spaces. *Ann. Fuzzy Math. Inform.*, 12(4):559–572, 2016.
11. P. Debnath. Some results on cesaro summability in intuitionistic fuzzy n-normed linear spaces. *Sahand-Commun. Math. Anal.*, 19(1):77–87, 2022.
12. P. Debnath, N. Konwar and S. Radenovic. *Metric Fixed Point Theory: Applications in Science, Engineering and Behavioural Sciences*. Springer: Berlin/Heidelberg, Germany, 2021.
13. P. Debnath and S. A. Mohiuddine *Soft Computing Techniques in Engineering, Health, Mathematical and Social Sciences*. CRC Press: Boca Raton, FL, 2021.
14. A. George and P. Veeramani. On some result in fuzzy metric spaces. *Fuzzy Sets Syst.*, 64:359–399, 1994.
15. A. George and P. Veeramani. On some results of analysis for fuzzy metric spaces. *Fuzzy Sets Syst.*, 90:365–368, 1997.
16. M. Grabiec. Fixed points in fuzzy metric spaces. *Fuzzy Sets Syst.*, 27:385–389, 1988.
17. V. Gregori and A. Sapena. On fixed-point theorems in fuzzy metric spaces. *Fuzzy Sets Syst.*, 125 (2):245–252, 2002.
18. S. Heilpern. Fuzzy mappings and fixed point theorem. *J. Math. Anal. Appl.*, 83(2):566–569, 1981.
19. M. Jeyaraman and S. Sowndrarajan. Some common fixed point theorems for (ϕ, φ)-weak contractions in intuitionistic generalized fuzzy cone metric spaces. *Malaya J. Math.*, 1:154–159, 2019.

20. G. Jungck and B. E. Rhoades. Fixed points for setvalued functions without continuity. *Indian J. Pure Appl. Math.*, 29:227–238, 1998.
21. O. Kaleva and S. Seikkala. A banach contraction theorem in fuzzy metric space. *Fuzzy Sets Syst.*, 12:215–229, 1984.
22. N. Konwar, B. Davvaz and P. Debnath. Approximation of new bounded operators in intuitionistic fuzzy n-banach spaces. *J. Intell. Fuzzy Syst.*, 35(6):6301–6312, 2018.
23. N. Konwar and P. Debnath. Continuity and banach contraction principle in intuitionistic fuzzy n-normed linear spaces. *J. Intell. Fuzzy Syst.*, 33(4):2363–2373, 2017.
24. N. Konwar and P. Debnath. Intuitionistic fuzzy n-normed algebra and continuousproduct. *Proyecciones (Antofagasta)*, 37(1):68–83, 2018.
25. N. Konwar and P. Debnath. Some new contractive conditions and related fixed point theorems in intuitionistic fuzzy n-banach spaces. *J. Intell. Fuzzy Syst.*, 35(6):6301–6312, 2018.
26. I. Kramosil and J. Michalek. Fuzzy metric and statistical metric spaces. *Kybernetica*, 11:326–334, 1975.
27. S. Manro and A. Tomar. Faintly compatible maps and existence of common fixed point in fuzzy metric space. *Ann. Fuzzy Math. Inform.*, 8(2):223–230, 2014.
28. D. Rakić, A. Mukheimer, T. Doŝenović, Z. A. Mitrović, and S. Radenović. On some new fixed point results in fuzzy *b* metric spaces. *J. Inequal. Appl.*, 1:1–14, 2020.
29. M. Saheli. A contractive mapping on fuzzy normed linear spaces. *Iran. J. Numer. Anal. Optim.*, 6 (1):121–136, 2016.
30. S. Shukla, D. Gopal, and A. F. R-L-de Hierro. Some fixed point theorems in 1-M-complete fuzzy metric-like spaces. *Int. J. Gen. Syst.*, 2016. DOI: 10.1080/03081079.2016.1153084.
31. T. Suzuki. Basic inequality on a b-metric space and its applications. *J. Inequal. Appl.*, 1:256, 2017.
32. L. A. Zadeh. Fuzzy sets. *Inform. Cont.*, 8:338–353, 1965.

4 Weak-Wardowski Contractions in Generalized Triple-Controlled Modular Metric Spaces and Generalized Triple-Controlled Fuzzy Metric Spaces

Marija V. Paunović
University of Kragujevac

Samira Hadi Bonab and Vahid Parvaneh
Islamic Azad University

CONTENTS

4.1 Introduction 45
4.2 Generalized Triple-Controlled Modular Metric Spaces 48
4.3 Main Results 50
4.4 Weak-Wardowski Contraction 55
4.5 Generalized Triple-Controlled Fuzzy Metric Spaces 59
4.6 Application 62
Bibliography 64

4.1 INTRODUCTION

In this chapter, we present the idea of generalized triple-controlled modular metric spaces and survey some of the fixed point results in generalized triple-controlled fuzzy metric spaces via (χ, δ)-rational F-contractions and weak-Wardowski contractions. Some examples and an application are provided to confirm the results.

DOI: 10.1201/9781003312017-4

Banach's fixed point theorem Banach's fixed point theorem [4] possesses countless applications in numerous disciplines and divisions of mathematics, and many researchers have generalized this theory in nonlinear analysis, such as Cone metric space [12,15], G-metric space [16], vector-valued metric space [13,14], modular metric space [31] extended b-metric space [20,34], double controlled metric space [2], b-rectangular metric space [19,38], partial rectangular b-metric space [29], generalized parametric metric space [43], C^*-algebra-valued metric space [30], c-credibility metric space [33,35], etc.

For more details on fuzzy metric and its generalization, the readers are referred to the articles [7]– [10], [21]– [24], book [6] and the references therein.

Salimi et al. [39], Alsulami et al. [3] and then Stephen et al. [43] used (α,δ)-rational-type contractive mappings. Parvaneh et al. introduced the weak-Wardowski contraction to prove some fixed point theorems. In this chapter, we introduce these concepts in generalized triple-controlled modular metric (GT-CMM) spaces. Also, in the next section, we obtain some fixed point results in the generalized triple-controlled fuzzy metric (GT-CFM) spaces via (χ,δ)-rational F-contractions and weak-Wardowski contractions.

Definition 4.1 *[20] In a nonempty set X, a mapping $d : X^2 \to \mathbb{R}$ is called a b-metric on X, if:*

1. $d(\hbar,\hbar') \geq 0$ *for each* $\hbar,\hbar' \in X$ *and* $d(\hbar,\hbar') = 0$ *if and only if* $\hbar = \hbar'$;
2. $d(\hbar,\hbar') = d(\hbar',\hbar)$ *for each* $\hbar,\hbar' \in X$;
3. $d(\hbar,\hbar') \leq s[d(\hbar,\upsilon) + d(\upsilon,\hbar')]$ *for each* $\hbar,\hbar',\upsilon \in X$,

where $s \geq 1$ is a real number. A set X is termed as a b-metric space whenever it is endowed with a b-metric d and is signified by (X,d).

Definition 4.2 *[20] In a nonempty set X, a function $d_\theta : X^2 \to [0,\infty)$ is called an extended b-metric if for all $\hbar,\hbar',\upsilon \in X$:*

($d_\theta 1$) $d_\theta(\hbar,\hbar') = 0$ if and only if $\hbar = \hbar'$;

($d_\theta 2$) $d_\theta(\hbar,\hbar') = d_\theta(\hbar',\hbar)$;

($d_\theta 3$) $d_\theta(\hbar,\upsilon) \leq \theta(\hbar,\upsilon)[d_\theta(\hbar,\hbar') + d_\theta(\hbar',\upsilon)]$, where $\theta : X^2 \to [1,\infty)$ is a mapping.

The pair (X,d_θ) is called an extended b-metric space.

Definition 4.3 *[2] In a nonempty set X, a function $\rho : X^2 \to [0,\infty)$ is called a double controlled metric if for all $\hbar,\hbar',\upsilon \in X$:*

($\rho 1$) $\rho(\hbar,\hbar') = 0$ if and only if $\hbar = \hbar'$;

($\rho 2$) $\rho(\hbar,\hbar') = \rho(\hbar',\hbar)$;

($\rho 3$) $\rho(\hbar,\upsilon) \leq \theta(\hbar,\hbar')\rho(\hbar,\hbar') + \eta(\hbar',\upsilon)\rho(\hbar',\upsilon)]$, where $\theta,\chi : X^2 \to [1,\infty)$.

The pair (X,ρ) is named a double controlled metric space.

Definition 4.4 *[18] In a nonempty set X, $\omega : (0,+\infty) \times X^2 \to [0,+\infty]$ is said to be a modular metric on X if,*

1. $\hbar = \hbar'$ if and only if $\omega_\lambda(\hbar,\hbar') = 0$ for all $\lambda > 0$;

2. $\omega_\lambda(\hbar,\hbar') = \omega_\lambda(\hbar',\hbar)$ *for all* $\lambda > 0$ *and for all* $\hbar,\hbar' \in X$;
3. $\omega_{\lambda+\mu}(\hbar,\hbar') \leq \omega_\lambda(\hbar,\upsilon) + \omega_\mu(\upsilon,\hbar')$ *for all* $\hbar,\hbar',\upsilon \in X$ *and all* $\lambda,\mu > 0$, *where* $\omega_\lambda(\hbar,\hbar') = \omega(\lambda,\hbar,\hbar')$. *A modular metric space is defined as* (X,ω).

Definition 4.5 *[5] In a nonempty set X, a mapping* $\widehat{\omega} : (0,+\infty) \times X^2 \to [0,+\infty]$ *is said to be a modular b-metric if the following statements hold for all* $\hbar,\hbar',\upsilon \in X$,
(a) $\widehat{\omega}_\lambda(\hbar,\hbar') = 0$ *for all* $\lambda > 0$ *if and only if* $\hbar = \hbar'$;
(b) $\widehat{\omega}_\lambda(\hbar,\hbar') = \widehat{\omega}_\lambda(\hbar',\hbar)$;
(c) $\widehat{\omega}_{\lambda+\mu}(\hbar,\hbar') \leq s(\widehat{\omega}_\lambda(\hbar,\upsilon) + \widehat{\omega}_\mu(\upsilon,\hbar'))$,
where $s \geq 1$ *is a real number.*
Then $(X,\widehat{\omega})$ *is called a modular b-metric space.*

Definition 4.6 *[44] In a metric space* (X,d), *a mapping* $\Sigma : X \to X$ *is said to be an F-contraction if for some* $\tau > 0$ *and for all* $\hbar,\hbar' \in X$,

$$d(\Sigma\hbar,\Sigma\hbar') > 0 \Rightarrow \tau + F(d(\Sigma\hbar,\Sigma\hbar')) \leq F(d(\hbar,\hbar')),$$

where $F : (0,+\infty) \to (-\infty,+\infty)$ *is a mapping so that:*
(F1) F *is strictly increasing,*
(F2)

$$\lim_{n\to\infty} a_n = 0 \Leftrightarrow \lim_{n\to\infty} F(a_n) = -\infty,$$

for any sequence $\{a_n\}$ *of positive real numbers,*
(F3) $\lim_{a\to 0^+} a^k F(a) = 0$ *for some* $k \in (0,1)$.

Definition 4.7 *[40] In a nonempty set X, a mapping* $\Sigma : X \to X$ *is called an* α-*admissible mapping if*

$$\alpha(\hbar,\hbar') \geq 1 \Rightarrow \alpha(\Sigma\hbar,\Sigma\hbar') \geq 1 \text{ for all } \hbar,\hbar' \in X,$$

where $\alpha : X^2 \to [0,\infty)$.

Definition 4.8 *In a nonempty set X, a function* $\omega : (0,\infty) \times X^2 \to [0,\infty]$ *is called a generalized modular metric (GMM) on X if*
(1) $\omega_\lambda(\hbar,\hbar') = 0$ *for all* $\lambda > 0$ *if and only if* $\hbar = \hbar'$;
(2) $\omega_\lambda(\hbar,\hbar') = \omega_\lambda(\hbar',\hbar)$;
(3) $\omega_{\lambda+\mu+\eta}(\hbar,\hbar') \leq \omega_\lambda(\hbar,a) + \omega_\mu(a,b) + \omega_\eta(b,\hbar')$ *for all distinct points* $a,b \in X - \{\hbar,\hbar'\}$.
Then the pair (X,ω) *is called a GMM space.*

In this paper, we will study the new structure of GT-CMM spaces. For more details on generalized metric and modular metric spaces and their extensions, we refer the reader to [17]– [25].

4.2 GENERALIZED TRIPLE-CONTROLLED MODULAR METRIC SPACES

In this section, before beginning the main theorem, we first introduce the concept of GT-CMM space.

Definition 4.9 *In a nonempty set X, if* $\alpha_\lambda, \beta_\lambda, \gamma_\lambda : X^2 \to [1,\infty)$ *and the mapping* $\omega : X^2 \times (0,\infty) \to [0,\infty)$ *be a function satisfying the following properties:*

(ω_1) $\omega_\lambda(\hbar,\hbar') = 0$ *for all* $\lambda > 0$ *implies* $\hbar = \hbar'$;
(ω_2) $\omega_\lambda(\hbar,\hbar') = \omega_\lambda(\hbar',\hbar)$;
(ω_3) $\omega_{\lambda+\mu+\eta}(\hbar,\hbar') \leq \alpha_\lambda(\hbar,a)\omega_\lambda(\hbar,a) + \beta_\mu(a,b)\omega_\mu(a,b) + \gamma_\eta(b,\hbar')\omega_\eta(b,\hbar')$ *for all distinct points* $a,b \in X - \{\hbar,\hbar'\}$,

then, the function ω *is called a GT-CMM on X and* (X,ω) *is called a GT-CMM space.*

Example 4.1 *Let* $X = [0,1]$ *and let d be a generalized metric on X. Define* $\omega : (0,\infty) \times X^2 \to [0,\infty]$ *by*

$$\omega_\lambda(\hbar,\hbar') = \frac{d(\hbar,\hbar')}{\lambda}, \text{ for all } \lambda > 0,$$

and

$$\alpha_\lambda(\hbar,\hbar') = \beta_\mu(\hbar,\hbar') = \gamma_\eta(\hbar,\hbar') = \frac{|\hbar| + |\hbar'|}{\lambda} + 1.$$

For all $\hbar,\hbar' \in X$ *and distinct points* $a,b \in X - \{\hbar,\hbar'\}$, *we have*

$$\begin{aligned}
\omega_{\lambda+\mu+\eta}(\hbar,\hbar') &= \frac{d(\hbar,\hbar')}{\lambda+\mu+\eta} \\
&\leq \frac{d(\hbar,a)}{\lambda+\mu+\eta} + \frac{d(a,b)}{\lambda+\mu+\eta} + \frac{d(b,\hbar')}{\lambda+\mu+\eta} \\
&\leq \omega_\lambda(\hbar,a) + \omega_\mu(a,b) + \omega_\eta(b,\hbar') \\
&\leq \alpha_\lambda(\hbar,a)\omega_\lambda(\hbar,a) + \beta_\mu(a,b)\omega_\mu(a,b) + \gamma_\eta(b,\hbar')\omega_\eta(b,\hbar').
\end{aligned}$$

In the last part of the above inequality, we use the fact that for all $\hbar,\hbar' \in X$ *and distinct points* $a,b \in X - \{\hbar,\hbar'\}$, *we have* $\alpha_\lambda(\hbar,a) \geq 1$, $\beta_\mu(a,b) \geq 1$ *and* $\gamma_\eta(b,\hbar') \geq 1$. *Hence,* ω *is a GT-CMM space.*

Definition 4.10 *In a GT-CMM space* (X,ω),

(i) *a sequence* $\{\hbar_n\}$ *is called* ω*-convergent if and only if there exists* $\hbar \in X$ *such that* $\omega_\lambda(\hbar_n,\hbar)$ *tends to 0 as* $n \to \infty$. *In this case, we write*

$$\lim_{n\to+\infty} \hbar_n = \hbar.$$

(ii) a sequence $\{\hbar_n\}$ *is called* ω*-Cauchy if, for each* $\varepsilon > 0$*, there exists a* $N \in \mathbb{N}$ *such that* $\omega_\lambda(\hbar_n, \hbar_m) < \varepsilon$ *for all* $\lambda > 0$ *and for all* $m, n \geq N$.

Definition 4.11 *The GT-CMM space* (X, ω) *is called complete if, for each* ω*-Cauchy sequence* $\{\hbar_n\}$*, there is* $\hbar \in X$ *such that*

$$\lim_{n \to +\infty} \omega_\lambda(\hbar_n, \hbar) = 0 \text{for all } \lambda > 0.$$

Lemma 4.1 *Let* (X, ω) *be a GT-CMM space with control functions* α_λ*,* β_λ *and* γ_λ *in which* β_λ *and* γ_λ *are necessarily continuous. If there exist sequences* $\{\hbar_n\}$ *and* $\{\hbar'_n\}$ *such that* $\lim_{n\to\infty} \hbar_n = \hbar$ *and* $\lim_{n\to\infty} \hbar'_n = \hbar'$*,* $\hbar \neq \hbar'$*,* $\hbar_n \neq \hbar$ *and* $\hbar'_n \neq \hbar'$ *for all* $n \in \mathbb{N}$*, then*

$$\beta_\lambda^{-1}(\hbar, \hbar')\omega_\lambda(\hbar, \hbar') \leq \limsup_{n \to \infty} \omega_{\frac{\lambda}{3}}(\hbar_n, \hbar'_n)$$

and

$$\limsup_{n \to \infty} \omega_\lambda(\hbar_n, \hbar'_n) \leq \beta_\lambda(\hbar, \hbar')\omega_{\frac{\lambda}{3}}(\hbar, \hbar').$$

Moreover, Suppose that $\{\hbar_n\}$ *is convergent to* $\hbar$*,* $\limsup_{n\to\infty} \omega_\lambda(\hbar_n, \hbar_{n+1}) = 0$ *for all* $\lambda > 0$ *and* $\hbar' \in X$ *is arbitrary. Then, we have*

$$\gamma_\lambda^{-1}(\hbar, \hbar')\omega_\lambda(\hbar, \hbar') \leq \limsup_{n \to \infty} \omega_{\frac{\lambda}{3}}(\hbar_n, \hbar')$$

and

$$\limsup_{n \to \infty} \omega_\lambda(\hbar_n, \hbar') \leq \gamma_\lambda(\hbar, \hbar')\omega_{\frac{\lambda}{3}}(\hbar, \hbar').$$

Proof. a) Using the rectangular inequality, one writes

$$\omega_\lambda(\hbar, \hbar') \leq \alpha_\lambda(\hbar, \hbar_n)\omega_{\frac{\lambda}{3}}(\hbar, \hbar_n) + \beta_\lambda(\hbar_n, \hbar'_n)\omega_{\frac{\lambda}{3}}(\hbar_n, \hbar'_n) + \gamma_\lambda(\hbar'_n, \hbar')\omega_{\frac{\lambda}{3}}(\hbar'_n, \hbar') \tag{4.1}$$

and

$$\omega_\lambda(\hbar_n, \hbar'_n) \leq \alpha_\lambda(\hbar_n, \hbar)\omega_{\frac{\lambda}{3}}(\hbar_n, \hbar) + \beta_\lambda(\hbar, \hbar')\omega_{\frac{\lambda}{3}}(\hbar, \hbar') + \gamma_\lambda(\hbar', \hbar'_n)\omega_{\frac{\lambda}{3}}(\hbar', \hbar'_n). \tag{4.2}$$

Taking the limit as $n \to \infty$ from (4.3) and (4.4), the result is obtained.

b)

$$\omega_\lambda(\hbar, \hbar') \leq \alpha_\lambda(\hbar, \hbar_n)\omega_{\frac{\lambda}{3}}(\hbar, \hbar_n) + \beta_\lambda(\hbar_n, \hbar_{n+1})\omega_{\frac{\lambda}{3}}(\hbar_n, \hbar_{n+1}) + \gamma_\lambda(\hbar_{n+1}, \hbar')\omega_{\frac{\lambda}{3}}(\hbar_{n+1}, \hbar') \tag{4.3}$$

and

$$\omega_\lambda(\hbar_n, \hbar') \leq \alpha_\lambda(\hbar_n, \hbar_{n+1})\omega_{\frac{\lambda}{3}}(\hbar_n, \hbar_{n+1}) + \beta_\lambda(\hbar_{n+1}, \hbar)\omega_{\frac{\lambda}{3}}(\hbar_{n+1}, \hbar) + \gamma_\lambda(\hbar, \hbar')\omega_{\frac{\lambda}{3}}(\hbar, \hbar'). \tag{4.4}$$

□

4.3 MAIN RESULTS

Now, let Δ' be the family of functions $\delta' : [0,\infty) \to [0,\infty)$ such that:
(i) δ' is nondecreasing;
(ii) $\sum_{n=1}^{+\infty} \delta'^{n}(t) < +\infty$, for each $t > 0$.
Note that if $\delta' \in \Delta'$, we have $\delta'(t) < t$ for all $t > 0$ and δ' is continuous at 0.

Definition 4.12 *In a nonempty set X, a mapping $\Sigma : X \to X$ is called an χ-admissible mapping if*

$$\chi_\lambda(\hbar,\hbar') \geq 1 \Rightarrow \chi_\lambda(\Sigma\hbar,\Sigma\hbar') \geq 1 \text{ for all } \hbar,\hbar' \in X \text{ and for all } \lambda > 0,$$

where $\chi : (0,\infty) \times X^2 \to [0,\infty]$.

Definition 4.13 *Suppose that (X,ω) be a GT-CMM space and $\chi : (0,\infty) \times X^2 \to [0,\infty]$. We call the mapping $\Sigma : X \to X$ an (χ,δ')-rational F-contractive mapping of type-I if there is $\tau > 0$ such that*

$$\omega_\lambda(\Sigma\hbar,\Sigma\hbar') > 0 \Rightarrow \tau + F(\beta_\lambda \gamma_\lambda(\Sigma\hbar,\Sigma\hbar')\chi_\lambda(\hbar,\hbar')\omega_\lambda(\Sigma\hbar,\Sigma\hbar')) \leq F(\delta'(\mathcal{M}(\hbar,\hbar'))), \tag{4.5}$$

for all $\lambda > 0$ and for all $\hbar,\hbar' \in X$ where $\delta' \in \Delta'$ and

$$\mathcal{M}(\hbar,\hbar') = \max\{\omega_\lambda(\hbar,\hbar'), \omega_\lambda(\hbar,\Sigma\hbar), \omega_\lambda(\hbar',\Sigma\hbar'), \frac{\omega_\lambda(\hbar,\Sigma\hbar)\omega_\lambda(\hbar',\Sigma\hbar')}{1+\omega_\lambda(\hbar,\hbar')}, \frac{\omega_\lambda(\hbar,\Sigma\hbar)\omega_\lambda(\hbar',\Sigma\hbar')}{1+\omega_\lambda(\Sigma\hbar,\Sigma\hbar')}\}.$$

Note that if $F(t) = \ln(t)$ for all $t > 0$ and $\beta_\lambda\gamma_\lambda(\Sigma\hbar,\Sigma\hbar') = 1$, then we get

$$\chi_\lambda(\hbar,\hbar')\omega_\lambda(\Sigma\hbar,\Sigma\hbar')) \leq e^{-\tau}(\delta'(\omega_\lambda(\hbar,\hbar'))) \leq \delta'(\omega_\lambda(\hbar,\hbar')),\ \lambda > 0.$$

Therefore, Σ is an (χ,δ')-contraction, which will be a generalization of Samet's work [40].

Now, we establish one key result of this chapter as follows.

Theorem 4.2 *Let (X,ω) be a complete GT-CMM space, $\chi : (0,\infty) \times X^2 \to [0,\infty]$, and Σ be an χ-admisible self-mapping on X satisfying*
(i) there is $\hbar_0 \in X$ such that $\chi_\lambda(\hbar_0,\Sigma\hbar_0) \geq 1$ and $\chi_\lambda(\hbar_0,\Sigma^2\hbar_0) \geq 1$;
(ii) Σ is an (χ,δ')-rational F-contractive mapping of type-I.
Then Σ admits a unique fixed point in X.

Proof. Choose an $\hbar_0 \in X$ which satisfies $\chi_\lambda(\hbar_0,\Sigma\hbar_0) \geq 1$ and $\chi_\lambda(\hbar_0,\Sigma^2\hbar_0) \geq 1$, and set

$$\hbar_n = \Sigma\hbar_{n-1},\ n = 1,2,\ldots.$$

As Σ is χ-admissible, $\chi_\lambda(\hbar_0,\Sigma\hbar_0) = \chi_\lambda(\hbar_0,\hbar_1) \geq 1 \Rightarrow \chi_\lambda(\Sigma\hbar_0,\Sigma\hbar_1) = \chi_\lambda(\hbar_1,\hbar_2) \geq 1$. So, by induction we have $\chi_\lambda(\hbar_n,\hbar_{n+1}) \geq 1$ for all $n \geq 0$. Similarly, for

$\chi_\lambda(\hbar_0, \Sigma^2\hbar_0) \geq 1$ we have $\chi_\lambda(\hbar_0, \hbar_2) = \chi_\lambda(\hbar_0, \Sigma^2\hbar_0) \geq 1$ and $\chi_\lambda(\Sigma\hbar_0, \Sigma\hbar_2) = \chi_\lambda(\hbar_1, \hbar_3) \geq 1$. By induction, we get $\chi_\lambda(\hbar_n, \hbar_{n+2}) \geq 1$ for all $n \geq 0$.

By condition (4.5), we get

$$\begin{aligned} F(\omega_\lambda(\hbar_{n+1}, \hbar_{n+2})) &= F(\omega_\lambda(\Sigma(\hbar_n), \Sigma(\hbar_{n+1}))) \\ &\leq F(\beta_\lambda \gamma_\lambda(\hbar_{n+1}, \hbar_{n+2}) \chi_\lambda(\hbar_n, \hbar_{n+1}) \omega_\lambda(\Sigma\hbar_n, \Sigma\hbar_{n+1})) \\ &\leq F(\delta'(\mathcal{M}(\hbar_n, \hbar_{n+1}))) - \tau, \end{aligned}$$

where

$$\begin{aligned} \mathcal{M}(\hbar_n, \hbar_{n+1}) &= \max\Big\{\omega_\lambda(\hbar_n, \hbar_{n+1}), \omega_\lambda(\hbar_n, \Sigma\hbar_n), \omega_\lambda(\hbar_{n+1}, \Sigma\hbar_{n+1}), \\ &\qquad \frac{\omega_\lambda(\hbar_n, \Sigma\hbar_n)\omega_\lambda(\hbar_{n+1}, \Sigma\hbar_{n+1})}{1 + \omega_\lambda(\hbar_n, \hbar_{n+1})}, \frac{\omega_\lambda(\hbar_n, \Sigma\hbar_n)\omega_\lambda(\hbar_{n+1}, \Sigma\hbar_{n+1})}{1 + \omega_\lambda(\Sigma\hbar_n, \Sigma\hbar_{n+1})}\Big\} \\ &= \max\Big\{\omega_\lambda(\hbar_n, \hbar_{n+1}), \omega_\lambda(\hbar_n, \hbar_{n+1}), \omega_\lambda(\hbar_{n+1}, \hbar_{n+2}), \\ &\qquad \frac{\omega_\lambda(\hbar_n, \hbar_{n+1})\omega_\lambda(\hbar_{n+1}, \hbar_{n+2})}{1 + \omega_\lambda(\hbar_n, \hbar_{n+1})}, \frac{\omega_\lambda(\hbar_n, \hbar_{n+1})\omega_\lambda(\hbar_{n+1}, \hbar_{n+2})}{1 + \omega_\lambda(\hbar_{n+1}, \hbar_{n+2})}\Big\} \\ &= \max\big\{\omega_\lambda(\hbar_n, \hbar_{n+1}), \omega_\lambda(\hbar_{n+1}, \hbar_{n+2})\big\}. \end{aligned}$$

If $\mathcal{M}(\hbar_n, \hbar_{n+1}) = \omega_\lambda(\hbar_{n+1}, \hbar_{n+2})$, then we simply see that it is impossible. So, $\mathcal{M}(\hbar_n, \hbar_{n+1}) = \omega_\lambda(\hbar_n, \hbar_{n+1})$ for all $n \in \mathcal{N}$, and

$$F(\omega_\lambda(\hbar_{n+1}, \hbar_{n+2})) \leq F(\delta'(\mathcal{M}(\hbar_n, \hbar_{n+1}))) - \tau = F(\delta'(\omega_\lambda(\hbar_n, \hbar_{n+1}))) - \tau.$$

This implies that

$$\omega_\lambda(\hbar_{n+1}, \hbar_{n+2}) \leq \delta'(\omega_\lambda(\hbar_n, \hbar_{n+1})) < \omega_\lambda(\hbar_n, \hbar_{n+1}).$$

On the other hand

$$\begin{aligned} F(\omega_\lambda(\hbar_{n+1}, \hbar_{n+2})) &\leq F(\omega_\lambda(\hbar_n, \hbar_{n+1})) - \tau \\ &\leq F(\omega_\lambda(\hbar_{n-1}, \hbar_n)) - 2\tau \\ &\ \ \vdots \\ &\leq F(\omega_\lambda(\hbar_0, \hbar_1)) - (n+1)\tau. \end{aligned}$$

Now, by $(F2)$ if $n \to \infty$, then

$$\lim_{n\to\infty} \omega_\lambda(\hbar_{n+1}, \hbar_{n+2}) = 0. \tag{4.6}$$

We will show that $\hbar_n \neq \hbar_m$ for all $n \neq m$. Let $\hbar_n = \hbar_m$ for some $n > m$. So, we have $\hbar_{n+1} = f\hbar_n = f\hbar_m = \hbar_{m+1}$. By continuing this method, we conclude that $\hbar_{n+k} = \hbar_{m+k}$ for all $k \in \mathbb{N}$. Now, the inequality (4.5) yields

$$\begin{aligned} F(\omega_\lambda(\hbar_m, \hbar_{m+1})) &= F(\omega_\lambda(\hbar_n, \hbar_{n+1})) = F(\omega_\lambda(\hbar_n, \Sigma\hbar_n)) = F(\omega_\lambda(\Sigma\hbar_{n-1}, \Sigma\hbar_n)) \\ &\leq F(\beta_\lambda \gamma_\lambda(\Sigma\hbar_{n-1}, \Sigma\hbar_n)\chi_\lambda(\hbar_{n-1}, \hbar_n)\omega_\lambda(\Sigma\hbar_{n-1}, \Sigma\hbar_n)) \\ &\leq F(\delta'(\mathcal{M}(\hbar_{n-1}, \hbar_n))) - \tau, \end{aligned} \tag{4.7}$$

where

$$\begin{aligned}\mathcal{M}(\hbar_{n-1},\hbar_n) &= \max\{\omega_\lambda(\hbar_{n-1},\hbar_n),\omega_\lambda(\hbar_{n-1},\Sigma\hbar_{n-1}),\omega_\lambda(\hbar_n,\Sigma\hbar_n),\\ &\quad \frac{\omega_\lambda(\hbar_{n-1},\Sigma\hbar_{n-1})\omega_\lambda(\hbar_n,\Sigma\hbar_n)}{1+\omega_\lambda(\hbar_{n-1},\hbar_n)},\frac{\omega_\lambda(\hbar_{n-1},\Sigma\hbar_{n-1})\omega_\lambda(\hbar_n,\Sigma\hbar_n)}{1+\omega_\lambda(\Sigma\hbar_{n-1},\Sigma\hbar_n)}\}\\ &= \max\{\omega_\lambda(\hbar_{n-1},\hbar_n),\omega_\lambda(\hbar_{n-1},\hbar_n),\omega_\lambda(\hbar_n,\hbar_{n+1}),\\ &\quad \frac{\omega_\lambda(\hbar_{n-1},\hbar_n)\omega_\lambda(\hbar_n,\hbar_{n+1})}{1+\omega_\lambda(\hbar_{n-1},\hbar_n)},\frac{\omega_\lambda(\hbar_{n-1},\hbar_n)\omega_\lambda(\hbar_n,\hbar_{n+1})}{1+\omega_\lambda(\hbar_n,\hbar_{n+1})}\}\\ &= \max\{\omega_\lambda(\hbar_{n-1},\hbar_n),\omega_\lambda(\hbar_n,\hbar_{n+1})\}.\end{aligned}$$

If $\mathcal{M}(\hbar_{n-1},\hbar_n)=\omega_\lambda(\hbar_n,\hbar_{n+1})$, then

$$\begin{aligned}F(\omega_\lambda(\hbar_m,\hbar_{m+1})) &\le F(\delta'(\omega_\lambda(\hbar_n,\hbar_{n+1})))-\tau\\ &\le F(\delta'^{n-m+1}(\omega_\lambda(\hbar_m,\hbar_{m+1})))-\tau,\end{aligned}$$

which implies that

$$\omega_\lambda(\hbar_m,\hbar_{m+1})\le\delta'^{n-m+1}(\omega_\lambda(\hbar_m,\hbar_{m+1})). \tag{4.8}$$

If $\mathcal{M}(\hbar_{n-1},\hbar_n)=\omega_\lambda(\hbar_{n-1},\hbar_n)$, then

$$\begin{aligned}F(\omega_\lambda(\hbar_m,\hbar_{m+1})) &\le F(\delta'(\omega_\lambda(\hbar_{n-1},\hbar_n)))-\tau\\ &\le F(\delta'^{n-m}(\omega_\lambda(\hbar_m,\hbar_{m+1})))-\tau,\end{aligned}$$

which implies that

$$\omega_\lambda(\hbar_m,\hbar_{m+1}))\le\delta'^{n-m}(\omega_\lambda(\hbar_m,\hbar_{m+1})). \tag{4.9}$$

By (4.8) and (4.9) we have

$$\omega_\lambda(\hbar_m,\hbar_{m+1})<\omega_\lambda(\hbar_m,\hbar_{m+1}),$$

a contradiction. Hence, $a_n\neq a_m$ for all $n\neq m$.

Now, we demonstrate that $\{\hbar_n\}$ is a ω-Cauchy sequence in (X,ω_λ). Let for some $\varepsilon>0$ and for all $i\in\mathbb{N}$ there are m_i,n_i with $i<m_i<n_i$ one has

$$\omega_\lambda(\hbar_{m_i},\hbar_{n_i})\ge\varepsilon,\ for\ all\ \lambda>0, \tag{4.10}$$

where n_i is the least index with the above property, that is,

$$\omega_\lambda(\hbar_{m_i},\hbar_{n_{i-2}})\text{ and }\omega_\lambda(\hbar_{m_i},\hbar_{n_{i-1}})<\varepsilon. \tag{4.11}$$

From Eq. (4.16), we have

$$\begin{aligned}&\varepsilon\le\omega_{3\lambda}(\hbar_{m_i},\hbar_{n_i})\\ &\le\alpha_\lambda(\hbar_{m_i},\hbar_{m_{i+1}})\omega_\lambda(\hbar_{m_i},\hbar_{m_{i+1}})+\beta_\lambda(\hbar_{m_{i+1}},\hbar_{n_{i-1}})\omega_\lambda(\hbar_{m_{i+1}},\hbar_{n_{i-1}}))\\ &\quad+\gamma_\lambda(\hbar_{n_{i-1}},\hbar_{n_i})\omega_\lambda(\hbar_{n_{i-1}},\hbar_{n_i})\\ &\le\beta_\lambda\gamma_\lambda(\hbar_{m_{i+1}},\hbar_{n_{i-1}})\omega_\lambda(\hbar_{m_{i+1}},\hbar_{n_{i-1}})).\end{aligned}$$

On the other hand, we have

$$\begin{aligned}
& F(\beta_\lambda \gamma_\lambda(\hbar_{m_{i+1}},\hbar_{n_{i-1}})\omega_\lambda(\hbar_{m_{i+1}},\hbar_{n_{i-1}}))) \\
& = F(\beta_\lambda \gamma_\lambda(\Sigma\hbar_{m_i},\Sigma\hbar_{n_{i-2}})\omega_\lambda(\Sigma\hbar_{m_i},\Sigma\hbar_{n_i-2}))) \\
& \leq F(\beta_\lambda \gamma_\lambda(\Sigma\hbar_{m_i},\Sigma\hbar_{n_{i-2}})\chi_\lambda(\hbar_{m_i},\hbar_{n_i-2})\omega_\lambda(\Sigma\hbar_{m_i},\Sigma\hbar_{n_i-2}))) \\
& \leq F(\delta'(\mathcal{M}(\hbar_{m_i},\hbar_{n_i-2}))) - \tau, \qquad (4.12)
\end{aligned}$$

where

$$\begin{aligned}
\mathcal{M}(\hbar_{m_i},\hbar_{n_i-2}) = \max\{ & \omega_\lambda(\hbar_{m_i},\hbar_{n_i-2}), \omega_\lambda(\hbar_{m_i},\Sigma\hbar_{m_i}), \omega_\lambda(\hbar_{n_i-2},\Sigma\hbar_{n_i-2}), \\
& \frac{\omega_\lambda((\hbar_{m_i},\Sigma\hbar_{m_i})\omega_\lambda(\hbar_{n_i-2},\Sigma\hbar_{n_i-2})}{1+\omega_\lambda(\hbar_{m_i},\hbar_{n_i-2})}, \frac{\omega_\lambda((\hbar_{m_i},\Sigma\hbar_{m_i})\omega_\lambda(\hbar_{n_i-2},\Sigma\hbar_{n_i-2})}{1+\omega_\lambda(\Sigma\hbar_{m_i},\Sigma\hbar_{n_i-2})}\}.
\end{aligned}$$

Taking the upper limit as $n \to \infty$ and by Eq. (4.6) we have

$$\begin{aligned}
F(\varepsilon) & \leq F(\limsup_{i\to\infty} \beta_\lambda \gamma_\lambda(\Sigma\hbar_{m_i},\Sigma\hbar_{n_{i-2}})\omega_\lambda(\Sigma\hbar_{m_i},\Sigma\hbar_{n_i-2}))) \\
& \leq \limsup_{i\to\infty} F(\delta'(\mathcal{M}(\hbar_{m_i},\hbar_{n_i-2}))) - \tau \\
& \leq F(\delta'(\varepsilon)) - \tau \\
& < F(\varepsilon), \qquad (4.13)
\end{aligned}$$

which is a contradiction. So, $\{\hbar_n\}$ is a Cauchy sequence in X. Since X is complete, then there exists $u \in X$ such that $\hbar_n \to u$, that is,

$$\lim_{n\to\infty} \omega_\lambda(\hbar_n, u) = 0.$$

Now, we demonstrate that u is a fixed point of Σ.

First, assume that Σ be continuous. Then we have

$$u = \lim_{n\to\infty} \hbar_{n+1} = \lim_{n\to\infty} \Sigma\hbar_n = \Sigma u.$$

Let Σ is not continuous. Now, using Lemma 4.1, we have

$$\begin{aligned}
& F(\omega_\lambda(u,\Sigma u)) \\
& \leq F(\beta_\lambda \gamma_\lambda(u,\Sigma u)\chi_\lambda(u,u)\gamma_\lambda^{-1}(u,\Sigma u)\omega_\lambda(u,\Sigma u)) \\
& \leq F(\limsup_{n\to\infty} \beta_\lambda \gamma_\lambda(\Sigma\hbar_n,\Sigma u)\chi_\lambda(\hbar_n,u)\omega_{\frac{\lambda}{3}}(\Sigma\hbar_n,\Sigma u)) \\
& \leq F(\delta'(\limsup_{n\to\infty} \mathcal{M}(\hbar_n,u))) - \tau,
\end{aligned}$$

where

$$\begin{aligned}\mathcal{M}(\hbar_n,u) &= \max\Big\{\omega_{\frac{\lambda}{3}}(\hbar_n,u),\omega_{\frac{\lambda}{3}}(\hbar_n,\Sigma\hbar_n),\omega_{\frac{\lambda}{3}}(u,\Sigma u),\\ &\quad \frac{\omega_{\frac{\lambda}{3}}(\hbar_n,\Sigma\hbar_n)\omega_{\frac{\lambda}{3}}(u,\Sigma u)}{1+\omega_{\frac{\lambda}{3}}(\hbar_n,u)},\frac{\omega_{\frac{\lambda}{3}}(\hbar_n,\Sigma\hbar_n)\omega_{\frac{\lambda}{3}}(u,\Sigma u)}{1+\omega_{\frac{\lambda}{3}}(\Sigma\hbar_n,\Sigma u)}\Big\}\\ &= \max\Big\{\omega_{\frac{\lambda}{3}}(\hbar_n,u),\omega_{\frac{\lambda}{3}}(\hbar_n,\hbar_{n+1}),\omega_{\frac{\lambda}{3}}(u,\Sigma u),\\ &\quad \frac{\omega_{\frac{\lambda}{3}}(\hbar_n,\hbar_{n+1})\omega_{\frac{\lambda}{3}}(u,\Sigma u)}{1+\omega_{\frac{\lambda}{3}}(\hbar_n,u)},\frac{\omega_{\frac{\lambda}{3}}(\hbar_n,\hbar_{n+1})\omega_{\frac{\lambda}{3}}(u,\Sigma u)}{1+\omega_{\frac{\lambda}{3}}(\hbar_{n+1},\Sigma u)}\Big\}.\end{aligned}$$

This gives us, as $n \to \infty$,

$$\begin{aligned}\beta_\lambda\gamma_\lambda(u,\Sigma u)\chi_\lambda(u,u)\gamma_\lambda^{-1}(u,\Sigma u)\omega_\lambda(u,\Sigma u) &\leq \limsup_{n\to\infty}\delta'(\mathcal{M}(\hbar_n,u))\\ &\leq \delta'(\omega_\lambda(u,\Sigma u)) < \omega_\lambda(u,\Sigma u).\end{aligned}$$

a contradiction. Hence, u is a fixed point of Σ. To show the uniqueness, assume that there exists $v \neq u \in X$ such that $\Sigma u = u$ and $\Sigma v = v$. Thus,

$$\begin{aligned}F(\omega_\lambda(u,v)) &= F(\omega_\lambda(\Sigma u,\Sigma v))\\ &\leq F(\beta_\lambda\gamma_\lambda(\Sigma u,\Sigma v)\chi_\lambda(u,v)\omega_\lambda(\Sigma u,\Sigma v))\\ &\leq F(\delta'(\mathcal{M}(u,v))) - \tau\\ &\leq F(\delta'(\omega_\lambda(u,v))) - \tau\\ &< F(\omega_\lambda(u,v)) - \tau,\end{aligned}$$

because

$$\begin{aligned}\mathcal{M}(u,v) &= \max\Big\{\omega_\lambda(u,v),\omega_\lambda(u,\Sigma u),\omega_\lambda(v,\Sigma v),\\ &\quad \frac{\omega_\lambda(u,\Sigma u)\omega_\lambda(v,\Sigma v)}{1+\omega_\lambda(u,v)},\frac{\omega_\lambda(u,\Sigma u)\omega_\lambda(v,\Sigma v)}{1+\omega_\lambda(\Sigma u,\Sigma v)}\Big\}\\ &= \max\Big\{\omega_\lambda(u,v),\omega_\lambda(u,u),\omega_\lambda(v,v),\\ &\quad \frac{\omega_\lambda(u,u)\omega_\lambda(v,v)}{1+\omega_\lambda(u,v)},\frac{\omega_\lambda(u,u)\omega_\lambda(v,v)}{1+\omega_\lambda(u,v)}\Big\}\\ &= \omega_\lambda(u,v),\end{aligned}$$

which leads us to a contradiction, then $u = v$. Therefore the fixed point of Σ is unique. □

Example 4.2 *Let $X = [0,1]$. Consider the modular metric space as in Example* (4.1) *and the functions α_λ, β_λ and γ_λ by $\alpha_\lambda = \beta_\lambda = \gamma_\lambda = |\frac{\hbar}{6\lambda} - \frac{\hbar'}{6\lambda}| + 1$. Choose*

$$\Sigma\hbar = \begin{cases}\frac{\hbar}{6} & \text{if } \hbar \in [0,\frac{1}{2});\\ \frac{\hbar}{12} & \text{if } \hbar \in [\frac{1}{2},1].\end{cases}$$

Also, let $\delta(t) = \frac{t}{2}$, $F(\hbar) = \ln \hbar$, $\tau = \frac{1}{2}$ *and* $\chi_\lambda(\hbar, \hbar') = 1$.

Consider the following cases:

(1) Let $\hbar, \hbar' \in [0, \frac{1}{2})$. *Then, we have*

$$\begin{aligned}\tau + F(\beta_\lambda \gamma_\lambda(\Sigma\hbar, \Sigma\hbar')\chi_\lambda(\hbar,\hbar')\omega_\lambda(\Sigma\hbar,\Sigma\hbar')) &= \frac{1}{2} + \ln(|\frac{\hbar}{6\lambda} - \frac{\hbar'}{6\lambda}| + 1)^2 + \ln(|\frac{\hbar - \hbar'}{6\lambda}|)\\ &\leq \ln[\frac{1}{2\lambda}|\hbar - \hbar'|]\\ &= F(\delta'(\omega_\lambda(\hbar,\hbar')))\\ &\leq F(\delta'(\mathcal{M}(\hbar,\hbar'))).\end{aligned}$$

(2) Let $\hbar, \hbar' \in [\frac{1}{2}, 1]$. *Then we have*

$$\begin{aligned}\tau + F(\beta_\lambda \gamma_\lambda(\Sigma\hbar, \Sigma\hbar')\chi_\lambda(\hbar,\hbar')\omega_\lambda(\Sigma\hbar,\Sigma\hbar')) &= \frac{1}{2} + \ln(|\frac{\hbar}{12\lambda} - \frac{\hbar'}{12\lambda}| + 1)^2 + \ln(|\frac{\hbar - \hbar'}{12\lambda}|)\\ &\leq \ln[\frac{1}{2\lambda}|\hbar - \hbar'|]\\ &= F(\delta'(\omega_\lambda(\hbar,\hbar')))\\ &\leq F(\delta'(\mathcal{M}(\hbar,\hbar'))).\end{aligned}$$

(3) Let $\hbar' \in [0, \frac{1}{2})$ *and* $\hbar \in [\frac{1}{2}, 1]$, *clearly we have*

$$\begin{aligned}\tau + F(\beta_\lambda \gamma_\lambda(\Sigma\hbar, \Sigma\hbar')\chi_\lambda(\hbar,\hbar')\omega_\lambda(\Sigma\hbar,\Sigma\hbar')) &= \frac{1}{2} + \ln(|\frac{\hbar}{6\lambda} - \frac{\hbar'}{12\lambda}| + 1)^2\\ &\quad + \ln(|\frac{\frac{\hbar}{6\lambda} - \frac{\hbar'}{12\lambda}}{\lambda}|)\\ &\leq \ln[\frac{1}{2\lambda}|\hbar - \hbar'|]\\ &= F(\delta'(\omega_\lambda(\hbar,\hbar')))\\ &\leq F(\delta'(\mathcal{M}(\hbar,\hbar'))).\end{aligned}$$

As a result, all suppositions of Theorem 4.2 are fulfilled, and Σ *enjoys from having a unique fixed point.*

4.4 WEAK-WARDOWSKI CONTRACTION

Let **F** be the set of all functions $F : \mathbb{R}^+ \to \mathbb{R}$ such that

$(F1)$ F is a continuous and strictly increasing mapping,

$(F2)$ $\lim \mu_n = 0$ if and only if $\lim F(\mu_n) = -\infty$, for each sequence $\{\mu_n\}$ in $(0, +\infty)$.

Let Δ be the collection of all functions $\delta : \mathbb{R} \to (0, +\infty)$ such that

(i) δ is continuous;

(ii) $\sum_{n=1}^{\infty} \delta(t_n) = \infty$ and $\liminf_{n\to\infty} \delta(t_n) > 0$ for all $\{t_n\} \subseteq \mathbb{R}$.

Definition 4.14 *In a GT-CMM space (X,ω), we call the mapping $\Sigma : X \to X$ a weak-Wardowski contraction if there are $\delta \in \Delta$ and $F \in \mathbf{F}$ such that*

$$F(\beta_\lambda \gamma_\lambda(\Sigma\hbar,\Sigma\hbar')\omega_\lambda(\Sigma\hbar,\Sigma\hbar')) \le F(\omega_\lambda(\hbar,\hbar')) - \delta(F(\omega_\lambda(\hbar,\hbar'))),\ \lambda > 0, \quad (4.14)$$

for all $\hbar,\hbar' \in X$ with $\Sigma\hbar \neq \Sigma\hbar'$.

Theorem 4.3 *In a complete GT-CMM space (X,ω), any weak-Wardowski contraction $\Sigma : X \to X$ admits a unique fixed point.*

Proof. We choose an $\hbar_0 \in X$, and set

$$\hbar_n = \Sigma(\hbar_{n-1}),\ n = 1,2,\ldots.$$

By condition (4.14), we get

$$\begin{aligned} F(\omega_\lambda(\hbar_{n+1},\hbar_{n+2})) &= F(\omega_\lambda(\Sigma\hbar_n,\Sigma\hbar_{n+1})) \\ &\le F(\beta_\lambda \gamma_\lambda(\Sigma\hbar_n,\Sigma\hbar_{n+1})\omega_\lambda(\Sigma\hbar_n,\Sigma\hbar_{n+1})) \\ &\le F(\omega_\lambda(\hbar_n,\hbar_{n+1})) - \delta(F(\omega_\lambda(\hbar_n,\hbar_{n+1}))) \\ &\le F(\omega_\lambda(\hbar_{n-1},\hbar_n)) - \delta(F(\omega_\lambda(\hbar_{n-1},\hbar_n))) - \delta(F(\omega_\lambda(\hbar_n,\hbar_{n+1}))) \\ &\ \vdots \\ &\le F(\omega_\lambda(\hbar_0,\hbar_1)) - \sum_{i=0}^{n} \delta(F(\omega_\lambda(\hbar_i,\hbar_{i+1}))) \to -\infty,\ (as\ n \to \infty). \end{aligned}$$

We infer from $(F2)$ that,

$$\omega_\lambda(\hbar_{n+1},\hbar_{n+2}) \to 0^+, \quad (4.15)$$

as $n \to \infty$.

Now, we illustrate that $\{\hbar_n\}$ is a ω-Cauchy sequence in (X,ω_λ). Let for an $\varepsilon > 0$ and for all $i \in \mathbb{N}$ there are m_i, n_i with $i < m_i < n_i$ one has

$$\omega_\lambda(\hbar_{m_i},\hbar_{n_i}) \ge \varepsilon,\ for\ all\ \lambda > 0, \quad (4.16)$$

that is,

$$\omega_\lambda(\hbar_{m_i},\hbar_{n_{i-2}}) \text{ and } \omega_\lambda(\hbar_{m_i},\hbar_{n_{i-1}}) < \varepsilon. \quad (4.17)$$

From eq. (4.16), we have

$$\begin{aligned} \varepsilon \le \omega_{3\lambda}(\hbar_{m_i},\hbar_{n_i}) &\le \alpha_\lambda(\hbar_{m_i},\hbar_{m_{i+1}})\omega_\lambda(\hbar_{m_i},\hbar_{m_{i+1}}) + \beta_\lambda(\hbar_{m_{i+1}},\hbar_{n_{i-1}})\omega_\lambda(\hbar_{m_{i+1}},\hbar_{n_{i-1}})) \\ &\quad + \gamma_\lambda(\hbar_{n_{i-1}},\hbar_{n_i})\omega_\lambda(\hbar_{n_{i-1}},\hbar_{n_i}) \\ &\le \beta_\lambda \gamma_\lambda(\hbar_{m_{i+1}},\hbar_{n_{i-1}})\omega_\lambda(\hbar_{m_{i+1}},\hbar_{n_{i-1}})). \end{aligned}$$

Letting $i \to \infty$ and using (4.15), we get

$$\varepsilon \le \limsup_{i\to\infty} \beta_\lambda \gamma_\lambda(\hbar_{m_{i+1}},\hbar_{n_{i-1}})\omega_\lambda(\hbar_{m_{i+1}},\hbar_{n_{i-1}})). \quad (4.18)$$

On the other hand, we have

$$\begin{aligned} F(\beta_\lambda \gamma_\lambda(\hbar_{m_{i+1}},\hbar_{n_{i-1}})\omega_\lambda(\hbar_{m_{i+1}},\hbar_{n_{i-1}}))) &= F(\beta_\lambda \gamma_\lambda(\Sigma\hbar_{m_i},\Sigma\hbar_{n_{i-2}})\omega_\lambda(\Sigma\hbar_{m_i},\Sigma\hbar_{n_{i-2}}))) \\ &\le F(\omega_\lambda(\hbar_{m_i},\hbar_{n_{i-2}})) - \delta(F(\omega_\lambda(\hbar_{m_i},\hbar_{n_{i-2}})). \end{aligned} \tag{4.19}$$

Taking the upper limit as $n \to \infty$ we have

$$\begin{aligned} F(\varepsilon) &\le \limsup_{i\to\infty} F(\beta_\lambda \gamma_\lambda(\hbar_{m_{i+1}},\hbar_{n_{i-1}})\omega_\lambda(\hbar_{m_{i+1}},\hbar_{n_{i-1}}))) \\ &\le \limsup_{i\to\infty} F(\omega_\lambda(\hbar_{m_i},\hbar_{n_{i-2}})) - \liminf_{i\to\infty} \delta(F(\omega_\lambda(\hbar_{m_i},\hbar_{n_{i-2}}))) \\ &\le F(\varepsilon) - \liminf_{i\to\infty} \delta(F(\omega_\lambda(\hbar_{m_i},\hbar_{n_{i-2}}))) \\ &< F(\varepsilon), \end{aligned} \tag{4.20}$$

which is a contradiction. So, $\{\hbar_n\}$ is a ω-Cauchy sequence in X. Since X is complete, then there is $u \in X$ such that $\hbar_n \to u$, that is,

$$\lim_{n\to\infty} \omega_\lambda(\hbar_n,u) = 0.$$

It will be displayed that u is a fixed point of Σ.

First, let Σ be continuous. Then we have

$$u = \lim_{n\to\infty} \hbar_{n+1} = \lim_{n\to\infty} \Sigma\hbar_n = \Sigma u.$$

Let Σ be not continuous. Now, using Lemma 4.1, we have

$$\begin{aligned} &F(\omega_\lambda(u,\Sigma u)) \\ &= F(\gamma_\lambda(u,\Sigma u)\gamma_\lambda^{-1}(u,\Sigma u)\omega_\lambda(u,\Sigma u)) \\ &\le F(\beta_\lambda \gamma_\lambda(u,\Sigma u)\gamma_\lambda^{-1}(u,\Sigma u)\omega_\lambda(u,\Sigma u)) \\ &\le \limsup_{n\to\infty} F(\gamma_\lambda(\Sigma\hbar_n,\Sigma u)\omega_{\frac{\lambda}{3}}(\Sigma\hbar_n,\Sigma u)) \\ &\le \limsup_{n\to\infty} F(\omega_{\frac{\lambda}{3}}(\hbar_n,u)) - \liminf_{n\to\infty} \delta(F(\omega_{\frac{\lambda}{3}}(\hbar_n,u))) \\ &< \limsup_{n\to\infty} F(\omega_{\frac{\lambda}{3}}(\hbar_n,u)), \end{aligned}$$

so,

$$\omega_\lambda(u,\Sigma u) \le \lim\sup_{n\to\infty} \omega_{\frac{\lambda}{3}}(\hbar_n,u) = \omega_{\frac{\lambda}{3}}(u,u) = 0.$$

Hence, u is a fixed point of Σ. To show the uniqueness, assume that there exists $v \neq u \in X$ such that $\Sigma u = u$ and $\Sigma v = v$. Thus,

$$\begin{aligned} F(\omega_\lambda(u,v)) &= F(\omega_\lambda(\Sigma u,\Sigma v)) \\ &\le F(\beta_\lambda \gamma_\lambda(\Sigma u,\Sigma v)\omega_\lambda(\Sigma u,\Sigma v)) \\ &\le F(\omega_\lambda(u,v)) - \delta(F(\omega_\lambda(u,v))) \\ &< F(\omega_\lambda(u,v)), \end{aligned}$$

which leads us to a contradiction. Then $u = v$. Therefore, the fixed point of Σ is unique. □

Example 4.3 *According to the assumptions of Example 4.2, we consider the following: choose*

$$\Sigma x = \begin{cases} \frac{\sinh^{-1} x}{6} & \text{if } x \in [0, \frac{1}{2}); \\ \frac{\sinh^{-1} x}{12} & \text{if } x \in [\frac{1}{2}, 1]. \end{cases}$$

Consider the following cases:

(1) Let $\hbar, \hbar' \in [0, \frac{1}{2})$. Then, according to the mean value theorem we have

$$\begin{aligned} &F(\beta_\lambda \gamma_\lambda(\Sigma\hbar, \Sigma\hbar')\omega_\lambda(\Sigma\hbar, \Sigma\hbar')) \\ &= \ln(|\frac{\sinh^{-1}\hbar}{6\lambda} - \frac{\sinh^{-1}\hbar'}{6\lambda}| + 1)^2 + \ln(|\frac{\sinh^{-1}\hbar - \sinh^{-1}\hbar'}{6\lambda}|) \\ &\leq \frac{1}{2}\ln[\frac{|\hbar - \hbar'|}{\lambda}] \\ &\leq \frac{1}{2}F(\omega_\lambda(\hbar, \hbar')) \leq \ln[\omega_\lambda(\hbar, \hbar')] - \frac{1}{2}\ln[\omega_\lambda(\hbar, \hbar')] \\ &\leq F(\omega_\lambda(\hbar, \hbar')) - \delta(F(\omega_\lambda(\hbar, \hbar'))). \end{aligned}$$

(2) Let $\hbar, \hbar' \in [\frac{1}{2}, 1]$. Then we have

$$\begin{aligned} F(\beta_\lambda \gamma_\lambda(\Sigma\hbar, \Sigma\hbar')\omega_\lambda(\Sigma\hbar, \Sigma\hbar')) &= \ln(|\frac{\sinh^{-1}\hbar}{12\lambda} - \frac{\sinh^{-1}\hbar'}{12\lambda}| + 1)^2 \\ &\quad + \ln(|\frac{\sinh^{-1}\hbar - \sinh^{-1}\hbar'}{12\lambda}|) \\ &\leq \frac{1}{2}\ln[\frac{|\hbar - \hbar'|}{\lambda}] \\ &\leq \frac{1}{2}F(\omega_\lambda(\hbar, \hbar')) \leq \ln[\omega_\lambda(\hbar, \hbar')] - \frac{1}{2}\ln[\omega_\lambda(\hbar, \hbar')] \\ &\leq F(\omega_\lambda(\hbar, \hbar')) - \delta(F(\omega_\lambda(\hbar, \hbar'))). \end{aligned}$$

(3) Let $\hbar' \in [0, \frac{1}{2})$ and $\hbar \in [\frac{1}{2}, 1]$, clearly we have

$$\begin{aligned} F(\beta_\lambda \gamma_\lambda(\Sigma\hbar, \Sigma\hbar')\omega_\lambda(\Sigma\hbar, \Sigma\hbar')) &= \ln(|\frac{\sinh^{-1}\hbar}{6\lambda} - \frac{\sinh^{-1}\hbar'}{12\lambda}| + 1)^2 \\ &\quad + \ln(|\frac{\frac{\sinh^{-1}\hbar}{6\lambda} - \frac{\sinh^{-1}\hbar'}{12\lambda}}{\lambda}|) \\ &\leq \frac{1}{2}\ln[\frac{|\hbar - \hbar'|}{\lambda}] \\ &\leq \frac{1}{2}F(\omega_\lambda(\hbar, \hbar')) \leq \ln[\omega_\lambda(\hbar, \hbar')] - \frac{1}{2}\ln[\omega_\lambda(\hbar, \hbar')] \\ &\leq F(\omega_\lambda(\hbar, \hbar')) - \delta(F(\omega_\lambda(\hbar, \hbar'))). \end{aligned}$$

Consequently, all propositions of Theorem 4.3 are fulfilled, and Σ possesses a unique fixed point.

Taking $\delta(t) = \tau$ and $\beta_\lambda(\Sigma\hbar, \Sigma\hbar') = 1 = \gamma_\lambda(\Sigma\hbar, \Sigma\hbar')$, we have:

Corollary 5 *In a complete GT-CMM space (X, ω), let $\Sigma : X \to X$ be a self-mapping such that*

$$\tau + F(\omega_\lambda(\Sigma\hbar, \Sigma\hbar')) \leq F(\omega_\lambda(\hbar, \hbar')),\ \lambda > 0, \tag{4.21}$$

for all $\hbar, \hbar' \in X$ with $\Sigma\hbar \neq \Sigma\hbar'$. Then, Σ possesses a unique fixed point in X.

If in the above corollary we define $F(t) = \ln t$, then we have:

Corollary 6 *In a complete GT-CMM space (X, ω), if $\Sigma : X \to X$ be a self-mapping such that for some $0 \leq k < 1$*

$$\omega_\lambda(\Sigma\hbar, \Sigma\hbar') \leq k\omega_\lambda(\hbar, \hbar'),\ \lambda > 0, \tag{4.22}$$

for all $\hbar, \hbar' \in X$ with $\Sigma\hbar \neq \Sigma\hbar'$, then, Σ possesses a unique fixed point in X.

Taking $\delta(t) = \tau + \sum_{i=1}^{\infty} t^{2i}$ and $\beta_\lambda(\Sigma\hbar, \Sigma\hbar') = 1 = \gamma_\lambda(\Sigma\hbar, \Sigma\hbar')$, we have:

Corollary 7 *In a complete GT-CMM space (X, ω), if $\Sigma : X \to X$ be a self-mapping such that*

$$F(\omega_\lambda(\Sigma\hbar, \Sigma\hbar')) \leq F(\omega_\lambda(\hbar, \hbar')) - \tau - \sum_{i=1}^{\infty} F(\omega_\lambda(\hbar, \hbar'))^{2i},\ \lambda > 0, \tag{4.23}$$

for all $\hbar, \hbar' \in X$ with $\Sigma\hbar \neq \Sigma\hbar'$, then Σ possesses a unique fixed point in X.

4.5 GENERALIZED TRIPLE-CONTROLLED FUZZY METRIC SPACES

In this section, we introduce the concept of a GT-CFM space. We create a relationship between GT-CMM and GT-CFM and present some new fixed point results in GT-CFM spaces. For more details on fuzzy metric spaces and fixed point results, the readers are referred to [1], [26]– [28], [42].

Definition 4.15 *[41] A commutative, associative and continuous binary operation $\bullet : [0,1] \times [0,1] \to [0,1]$ is called a continuous t-norm (CTN) if for all $a, b, c, d \in [0,1]$:*

(T1) $a \bullet 1 = a$ for all $a \in [0,1]$;
(T2) $a \bullet b \leq c \bullet d$ where $a \leq c$ and $b \leq d$.

Definition 4.16 *[32] A 3-tuple $(\mathcal{U}, \mathcal{V}, \bullet)$ is said to be a fuzzy metric space if $\mathcal{U}$ is an arbitrary set, $\bullet$ is a CTN and $\mathcal{V}$ is a fuzzy set on $\mathcal{U}^2 \times (0, \infty)$ so that for all $\hbar, \hbar', \upsilon \in \mathcal{U}$ and $t, s > 0$,*

(i) $\mathcal{V}(\hbar, \hbar', t) > 0$;
(ii) $\mathcal{V}(\hbar, \hbar', t) = 1$ for all $t > 0$ if and only if $\hbar = \hbar'$;
(iii) $\mathcal{V}(\hbar, \hbar', t) = \mathcal{V}(\hbar', \hbar, t)$;
(iv) $\mathcal{V}(\hbar, \hbar', t) \bullet \mathcal{V}(\hbar', \upsilon, s) \leq \mathcal{V}(\hbar, \upsilon, t+s)$;
(v) $\mathcal{V}(\hbar, \hbar', \cdot) : (0, \infty) \to [0,1]$ is continuous.

The function $\mathcal{V}(\hbar, \hbar', t)$ represents the degree of closeness among $\hbar$ and $\hbar'$ with respect to t.

Definition 4.17 *[43] A generalized fuzzy metric is an ordered triple* $(\mathcal{U},\mathcal{V},\bullet)$ *such that* $\mathcal{U}$ *is a nonempty set,* $\bullet$ *is a CTN and* $\mathcal{V}$ *is a fuzzy set on* $\mathcal{U}^2\times(0,\infty)$ *so that for all* $\hbar,\hbar'\in\mathcal{U}$*, distinct points* $a,b\in\mathcal{U}-\{\hbar,\hbar'\}$ *and* $t,s,r>0$*,*

(F1) $\mathcal{V}(\hbar,\hbar',t)>0$*;*

(F2) $\mathcal{V}(\hbar,\hbar',t)=1$ *if and only if* $\hbar=\hbar'$*;*

(F3) $\mathcal{V}(\hbar,\hbar',t)=\mathcal{V}(\hbar',\hbar,t)$*;*

(F4) $\mathcal{V}(\hbar,a,t)\bullet\mathcal{V}(a,b,s)\bullet\mathcal{V}(b,\hbar',r)\leq\mathcal{V}(\hbar,\hbar',t+s+r)$*;*

(F5) $\mathcal{V}(\hbar,\hbar',\cdot):(0,+\infty)\to(0,1]$ *is left continuous.*

Definition 4.18 *A GT-CFM space is an ordered triple* $(\mathcal{U},\mathcal{V},\bullet)$ *such that* $\mathcal{U}$ *is a nonempty set,* $\bullet$ *is a CTN and* $\mathcal{V}$ *is a fuzzy set on* $\mathcal{U}^2\times(0,\infty)$ *so that for all* $\hbar,\hbar'\in\mathcal{U}$*, for all distinct points* $a,b\in\mathcal{U}-\{\hbar,\hbar'\}$*, for all* $t,s,r>0$ *there are* $\alpha,\beta,\gamma:\mathcal{U}^2\times(0,\infty)\to[1,\infty)$ *and*

(F1) $\mathcal{V}(\hbar,\hbar',t)>0$*;*

(F2) $\mathcal{V}(\hbar,\hbar',t)=1$ *if and only if* $\hbar=\hbar'$*;*

(F3) $\mathcal{V}(\hbar,a,t)\bullet\mathcal{V}(a,b,s)\bullet\mathcal{V}(b,\hbar',r)\leq\mathcal{V}(\hbar,\hbar',\alpha(\hbar,a,\lambda)t+\beta(a,b,\mu)s$
$+\gamma(b,\hbar',\eta)r)$*;*

(F5) $\mathcal{V}(\hbar,\hbar',\cdot):(0,+\infty)\to(0,1]$ *is left continuous.*

Definition 4.19 *In a GT-CFM space* $(\mathcal{U},\mathcal{V},\bullet)$*, if* $\{a_n\}$ *be a sequence in* $\mathcal{U}$ *and* $a\in\mathcal{U}$*, then*

(i) $\{a_n\}$ *is said to be converges to a if* $\lim\mathcal{V}(a_n,a,t)=1$ *for all* $t>0$*.*

(ii) $\{a_n\}$ *is said to be a Cauchy sequence if and only if for all* $\varepsilon\in(0,1)$ *and* $t>0$*, there exists* n_0 *such that* $\mathcal{V}(a_n,a_m,t)>1-\varepsilon$ *for all* $m,n\geq n_0$*.*

(iii) $(\mathcal{U},\mathcal{V},\bullet)$ *is said to be complete if every Cauchy sequence is a convergent sequence.*

Definition 4.20 *The GT-CFM space* $(\mathcal{U},\mathcal{V},\bullet)$ *is called rectangular if,*

$$\frac{1}{\mathcal{V}(\hbar,\hbar',t)}-1\leq\alpha(\hbar,a,t)\frac{1}{\mathcal{V}(\hbar,a,t)}-1+\beta(a,b,t)\frac{1}{\mathcal{V}(a,b,t)}-1$$
$$+\gamma(b,\hbar',t)\frac{1}{\mathcal{V}(b,\hbar',t)}-1.$$

for all $\hbar,\hbar'\in\mathcal{U}$*, for all distinct points* $a,b\in\mathcal{U}-\{\hbar,\hbar'\}$ *and for all* $t>0$*.*

Example 4.4 *In a generalized metric space* $(\mathcal{U},d)$*, let* $\mathcal{V}:\mathcal{U}^2\times(0,\infty)\to[0,\infty)$ *such that*

$$\mathcal{V}(\hbar,\hbar',t)=\frac{t}{t+d(\hbar,\hbar')}.$$

Also, suppose that $p\bullet q=p.q$ *and* $\alpha(\hbar,\hbar',t),\beta(\hbar,\hbar',t),\gamma(\hbar,\hbar',t)=|\hbar|+|\hbar'|+1$*. Then* $(\mathcal{U},\mathcal{V},\bullet)$ *is a GT-CFM space.*

Proof. We check only (F3). Let $\hbar,\hbar' \in \mathcal{U}$, distinct points $a,b \in \mathcal{U}-\{\hbar,\hbar'\}$ and $t,s,r > 0$. We have

$$\begin{aligned}
\mathcal{V}(\hbar,a,t)\bullet\mathcal{V}(a,b,s)\bullet\mathcal{V}(b,\hbar',r) &= \frac{t}{t+d(\hbar,a)}\cdot\frac{s}{s+d(a,b)}\cdot\frac{r}{r+d(b,\hbar')}\\
&= \frac{1}{1+\frac{d(\hbar,a)}{t}}\cdot\frac{1}{1+\frac{d(a,b)}{s}}\cdot\frac{1}{1+\frac{d(b,\hbar')}{r}}\\
&\leq \frac{1}{1+\frac{d(\hbar,a)}{t+s+r}}\cdot\frac{1}{1+\frac{d(a,b)}{t+s+r}}\cdot\frac{1}{1+\frac{d(b,\hbar')}{t+s+r}}\\
&\leq \frac{1}{1+\frac{d(\hbar,a)+d(a,b)+d(b,\hbar')}{t+s+r}}\\
&\leq \frac{1}{1+\frac{d(\hbar,\hbar')}{\alpha(\hbar,a,t)t+\beta(a,b,t)s+\gamma(b,\hbar',t)r}}\\
&= \frac{\alpha(\hbar,a,t)t+\beta(a,b,t)s+\gamma(b,\hbar',t)r}{\alpha(\hbar,a,t)t+\beta,t(a,b)s+\gamma(b,\hbar',t)r+d(\hbar,\hbar')}\\
&= \mathcal{V}(\hbar,\hbar',\alpha(\hbar,a,t)t+\beta(a,b,t)s+\gamma(b,\hbar',t)r),
\end{aligned}$$

which is true. □

Remark 4.1 *Notice that* $\omega_\lambda(\hbar,\hbar') = \frac{1}{\mathcal{V}(\hbar,\hbar',\lambda)} - 1$ *is a GT-CMM space, whenever* $\mathcal{V}$ *is a rectangular triple-controlled fuzzy metric.*

Definition 4.21 *Suppose that* $(\mathcal{U},\mathcal{V},\bullet)$ *be a rectangular GT-CFM space, and* $\chi : (0,\infty)\times\mathcal{U}^2 \to [0,\infty]$. *We call the mapping* $\Sigma : \mathcal{U}\to\mathcal{U}$ *an* (χ,δ')*-rational fuzzy F-contractive mapping of type-I if for all* $\hbar,\hbar' \in \mathcal{U}$ *there exist a function* $\delta' \in \Delta'$ *and a positive value* $\tau > 0$ *such that*

$$\tau + F(\beta_\lambda\gamma_\lambda(\Sigma\hbar,\Sigma\hbar')\chi_\lambda(\hbar,\hbar')[\frac{1}{\mathcal{V}(\Sigma\hbar,\Sigma\hbar',t)}-1]) \leq F(\delta'(\mathcal{M}(\hbar,\hbar'))),\ t>0, \tag{4.24}$$

where

$$\begin{aligned}
\mathcal{M}(\hbar,\hbar') = \max\{&\frac{1}{\mathcal{V}(\hbar,\hbar',t)}-1, \frac{1}{\mathcal{V}(\hbar,\Sigma\hbar,t)}-1, \frac{1}{\mathcal{V}(\hbar',\Sigma\hbar',t)}-1,\\
&\frac{(\frac{1}{\mathcal{V}(\hbar,\Sigma\hbar,t)}-1)(\frac{1}{\mathcal{V}(\hbar',\Sigma\hbar',t)}-1)}{\frac{1}{\mathcal{V}(\hbar,\hbar',t)}},\\
&\frac{(\frac{1}{\mathcal{V}(\hbar,\Sigma\hbar,t)}-1)(\frac{1}{\mathcal{V}(\hbar',\Sigma\hbar',t)}-1)}{\frac{1}{\mathcal{V}(\Sigma\hbar,\Sigma\hbar',t)}}\}.
\end{aligned}$$

Theorem 4.4 *Let* $(\mathcal{U},\mathcal{V},\bullet)$ *be a complete rectangular GT-CFM space,* $\chi : (0,\infty)\times\mathcal{U}^2 \to [0,\infty]$ *and let* Σ *be an* η*-admissible self-mapping on* $\mathcal{U}$*, satisfying*

(i) there is $\hbar_0 \in \mathcal{U}$ *such that* $\chi_\lambda(\hbar_0, \Sigma\hbar_0) \geq 1$ *and* $\chi_\lambda(\hbar_0, \Sigma^2\hbar_0) \geq 1$*;*
(ii) Σ *is an* (χ, δ')*-rational fuzzy* F*-contractive mapping of type-I.*
Then Σ *possesses a unique fixed point in* $\mathcal{U}$*.*

Definition 4.22 *Suppose that* $(\mathcal{U}, \mathcal{V}, \bullet)$ *be a rectangular GT-CFM space. We call the mapping* $\Sigma : \mathcal{U} \to \mathcal{U}$ *a weak-Wardowski fuzzy contraction if there are* $\delta \in \Delta$ *and* $F \in \mathbf{F}$ *such that*

$$F(\beta_\lambda \gamma_\lambda(\Sigma\hbar, \Sigma\hbar')[\frac{1}{\mathcal{V}(\Sigma\hbar, \Sigma\hbar', t)} - 1]) \leq F(\frac{1}{\mathcal{V}(\hbar, \hbar', t)} - 1) - \delta(F(\frac{1}{\mathcal{V}(\hbar, \hbar', t)} - 1)), \tag{4.25}$$

.

for all $\hbar, \hbar' \in \mathcal{U}$ *with* $\Sigma\hbar \neq \Sigma\hbar'$*.*

Theorem 4.5 *Suppose that* $(\mathcal{U}, \mathcal{V}, \bullet)$ *be a complete rectangular GT-CFM space. Then, any weak-Wardowski fuzzy contraction* $\Sigma : \mathcal{U} \to \mathcal{U}$ *possesses a unique fixed point.*

Corollary 8 *Let* $(\mathcal{U}, \mathcal{V}, \bullet)$ *be a complete rectangular GT-CFM space so that*

$$\tau + F(\frac{1}{\mathcal{V}(\Sigma\hbar, \Sigma\hbar', t)} - 1) \leq F(\frac{1}{\mathcal{V}(\hbar, \hbar', t)} - 1), \tag{4.26}$$

for all $\hbar, \hbar' \in \mathcal{U}$ *with* $\Sigma\hbar \neq \Sigma\hbar'$*. Then,* Σ *possesses a unique fixed point in* $\mathcal{U}$*.*

Corollary 9 *Let* $(\mathcal{U}, \mathcal{V}, \bullet)$ *be a complete rectangular GT-CFM space so that for some* $k \in [0, 1)$

$$\frac{1}{\mathcal{V}(\Sigma\hbar, \Sigma\hbar', t)} - 1 \leq k\frac{1}{\mathcal{V}(\hbar, \hbar', t)} - 1, \tag{4.27}$$

for all $\hbar, \hbar' \in \mathcal{U}$ *with* $\Sigma\hbar \neq \Sigma\hbar'$*. Then,* Σ *possesses a unique fixed point in* $\mathcal{U}$*.*

Corollary 10 *Let* $(\mathcal{U}, \mathcal{V}, \bullet)$ *be a complete rectangular GT-CFM space so that*

$$F(\frac{1}{\mathcal{V}(\Sigma\hbar, \Sigma\hbar', t)} - 1) \leq F(\frac{1}{\mathcal{V}(\hbar, \hbar', t)} - 1) - \tau - \sum_{i=1}^{\infty} F(\frac{1}{\mathcal{V}(\hbar, \hbar', t)} - 1)^{2i}, \tag{4.28}$$

for all $\hbar, \hbar' \in \mathcal{U}$ *with* $\Sigma\hbar \neq \Sigma\hbar'$*. Then,* Σ *admits a unique fixed point in* $\mathcal{U}$*.*

4.6 APPLICATION

In $\mathcal{U} = C([a, b], (-\infty, +\infty))$ which is the set of real continuous functions defined on $[a, b]$, consider the following Fredholm integral equation:

$$\hbar(t) = \int_a^b f(t, s, \hbar(s))ds + g(t), \tag{4.29}$$

for all $s,t \in [a,b]$, where $f : [a,b]^2 \times (-\infty,+\infty) \to (-\infty,+\infty)$ and $g : [a,b] \to (-\infty,+\infty)$. Define $\omega_\lambda : \mathcal{U}^2 \times (0,+\infty) \to [0,+\infty)$ by:

$$\omega_\lambda(\hbar,\hbar') = \sup_{t\in[a,b]} \frac{|\hbar(t)-\hbar'(t)|}{\lambda} = \sup \frac{\|\hbar-\hbar'\|}{\lambda}$$

for all $\hbar,\hbar' \in \mathcal{U}$ and $\lambda > 0$. Now, define the mappings $\alpha_\lambda, \beta_\lambda, \gamma_\lambda : \mathcal{U}^3 \to [1,\infty)$ by

$$\alpha_\lambda(\hbar,\hbar') = (\hbar,\hbar') = \gamma_\lambda(\hbar,\hbar') = \frac{|\hbar(t)|+|\hbar'(t)|}{\lambda} + 1.$$

Then $(\mathcal{U},\omega_\lambda)$ is a complete GT-CMM space. Now we consider the following assumption:

For all $\hbar,\hbar' \in \mathcal{U}$ and for all $\lambda > 0$:

$$F\Big(\frac{(|\int_a^b f(t,s,\hbar(s))ds+g(t)| + |\int_a^b f(t,s,\hbar'(s))ds+g(t)|+1)^2}{\lambda}\int_a^b |f(t,s,\hbar(s)) - f(t,s,\hbar'(s))|ds\Big) \le F\big(\delta'\big(\frac{|\hbar(t)-\hbar'(t)|}{\lambda}\big)\big) - \tau.$$

Theorem 4.6 *The integral equation (4.29) possesses a unique solution in $\mathcal{U}$ provided that the above assumptions hold.*

Proof. We define $\Sigma : \mathcal{U} \to \mathcal{U}$ by

$$\Sigma\hbar(t) = \int_a^b f(t,s,\hbar(s))ds + g(t), \quad \forall s,t \in [a,b].$$

Then, for every $\hbar,\hbar' \in \mathcal{U}$ and $\lambda > 0$, we have

$$\begin{aligned}
&F\big((|\Sigma\hbar|+|\Sigma\hbar'|+1)^2 \sup_{t\in[a,b]} \frac{|\Sigma\hbar(t)-\Sigma\hbar'(t)|}{\lambda}\big)\\
&= F\big(\frac{(|\Sigma\hbar|+|\Sigma\hbar'|+1)^2}{\lambda}\big(\sup_{t\in[a,b]} \big|\int_a^b [f(t,s,\hbar(s)) - f(t,s,\hbar'(s))]ds\big|\big)\\
&\le F\big(\frac{(|\Sigma\hbar|+|\Sigma\hbar'|+1)^2}{\lambda} \sup_{t\in[a,b]} \int_a^b |f(t,s,\hbar(s)) - f(t,s,\hbar'(s))|ds\big)\\
&\le F\big(\delta'(\max \frac{|\hbar(t)-\hbar'(t)|}{\lambda})\big) - \tau\\
&= [F(\delta'(\omega_\lambda(\hbar,\hbar'))) - \tau],
\end{aligned}$$

for $\lambda > 0$. This via taking the supremum on $[a,b]$, implies that

$$F(\beta_\lambda\gamma_\lambda(\Sigma\hbar,\Sigma\hbar')\chi_\lambda(\hbar,\hbar')\omega_\lambda(\Sigma\hbar,\Sigma\hbar')) \le F(\delta'(\mathcal{M}(\hbar,\hbar'))) - \tau.$$

Consequently, it is understandable that the mapping Σ possesses all the circumstances of Theorem 4.2. Hereafter, the Fredholm integral Equation (4.29) admits a unique solution, that is, Σ admits a unique fixed point. □

For more examples of applications, the readers are referred to the book [11] and the references therein. In addition, the future work of authors will be the application of the fuzzy metric spaces in image noise removal, segmentation, etc. (see for example [36,37]).

Bibliography

1. M. Abbas, N. Saleem and K. Sohail. Optimal coincidence best approximation solution in B-fuzzy metric spaces. *Commun. Nonlinear Anal.*, 6:1–12, 2019.
2. T. Abdeljawad, N. Mlaiki, H. Aydi and N. Souayah. Double controlled metric type spaces and some fixed point results. *Mathematics*, 6(12):1–10, 2018.
3. H. H. Alsulami, S. Chandok, M. Aziz Taoudi and I. M. Erhan. Some fixed point theorems for (α, ψ)-rational type contractive mappings. *Fixed Point Theory Appl.*, 97:1–12, 2015.
4. S. Banach. Sur les opérations dans les ensembles abstraits et leur application aux équations intégrales. *Fund. Math.*, 3:133–181, 1922.
5. M. E. Ege and C. Alaca. Some results for modular b-metric spaces and an application to system of linear equations. *Azerb. J. Math.*, 8:3–14, 2018.
6. P. Debnath and S. A. Mohiuddine. *Soft Computing Techniques in Engineering, Health, Mathematical and Social Sciences*. CRC Press: Boca Raton, FL, 2021.
7. P. Debnath. Some results on Cesaro summability in intuitionistic fuzzy n-normed linear spaces. *Sahand Commun. Math. Anal.*, 19(1):77–87, 2022.
8. P. Debnath. Results on lacunary difference ideal convergence in intuitionistic fuzzy normed linear spaces. *J. Intell. Fuzzy Syst.*, 28(3):1299–1306, 2015.
9. P. Debnath. Lacunary ideal convergence in intuitionistic fuzzy normed linear spaces. *Comput. Math. Appl.*, 63(3):708–715, 2012.
10. P. Debnath. A generalized statistical convergence in intuitionistic fuzzy n-normed linear spaces. *Ann. Fuzzy Math. Inform.*, 12(4):559–572, 2016.
11. P. Debnath, N. Konwar and S. Radenovic. *Metric Fixed Point Theory: Applications in Science, Engineering and Behavioural Sciences*. Springer: Berlin/Heidelberg, Germany, 2021.
12. J. Fernandez, N. Malviya, A. Savic, M. Paunovic and Z. D. Mitrovic. The extended cone b-metric-like spaces over Banach Algebra and some applications. *Mathematics*, 10(1):149, 2022.
13. A. D. Filip and A. Petrusel. Fixed point theorems on spaces endowed with vector-valued metrics. *Fixed Point Theory Appl.*, 2010:1–15, 2010.
14. S. Hadi Bonab, R. Abazari, A. Bagheri Vakilabad and H. Hosseinzadeh. Generalized metric spaces endowed with vector-valued metrics and matrix equations by tripled fixed point theorems. *J. Inequal. Appl.*, 2020(204):1–16, 2020.
15. S. Hadi Bonab, R. Abazari and A. Bagheri Vakilabad. Partially ordered cone metric spaces and coupled fixed point theorems via α-series. *Math. Anal. Contemp. Appl.*, 1(1):50–61, 2019.
16. S. Hadi Bonab, R. Abazari, A. Bagheri Vakilabad and H. Hosseinzadeh. Coupled fixed point theorems on G-metric spaces via α-series. *Global Anal. Discrete Math.*, 6(1):1–12, 2021.

17. H. Hosseinzadeh and V. Parvaneh. Meir–Keeler type contractive mappings in modular and partial modular metric spaces. *Asian-Eur. J. Math.*, 13(05):1–20, 2020.
18. N. Hussain, S. Khaleghizadeh, P. Salimi and A. A. N. Abdou. A new approach to fixed point results in triangular intuitionistic fuzzy metric spaces. *Abstr. Appl. Anal.*, 2014:1–16, 2014.
19. N. Hussain, V. Parvaneh, B. A. S. Alamri and Z. Kadelburg. F-HR-type contractions on (α,η)-complete rectangular b-metric spaces. *J. Nonlinear Sci. Appl.*, 10:1030–1043, 2017.
20. T. Kamran, M. Samreen and Q. U. Ain. A generalization of $b-$metric space and some fixed point theorems. *Mathematics*, 5(19):1–7, 2017.
21. N. Konwar and P. Debnath. Continuity and Banach contraction principle in intuitionistic fuzzy n-normed linear spaces. *J. Intell. Fuzzy Syst.*, 33(4):2363–2373, 2017.
22. N. Konwar, B. Davvaz and P. Debnath. Approximation of new bounded operators in intuitionistic fuzzy n-Banach spaces. *J. Intell. Fuzzy Syst.*, 35(6):6301–6312, 2018.
23. N. Konwar and P. Debnath. Some new contractive conditions and related fixed point theorems in intuitionistic fuzzy n-Banach spaces. *J. Intell. Fuzzy Syst.*, 34(1):361–372, 2018.
24. N. Konwar and P. Debnath. Intuitionistic fuzzy n-normed algebra and continuous product. *Proyecciones (Antofagasta)*, 37(1):68–83, 2018.
25. Z. Mustafa, V. Parvaneh, M. M. M. Jaradat and Z. Kadelburg. Extended rectangular b-metric spaces and some fixed point theorems for contractive mappings. *Symmetry*, 11(4):1–17, 2019.
26. S. Naeem, M. Abbas and Z. Raza. Fixed fuzzy point results of generalized Suzuki type F-contraction mappings in ordered metric spaces. *Georgian Math. J.*, 27(2):307–320, 2020.
27. S. Naeem, I. Iqbal, B. Iqbal and S. Radenovíc. Coincidence and fixed points of multivalued F-contractions in generalized metric space with application. *J. Fixed Point Theory Appl.*, 22(4):1-24, 2020.
28. S. Naeem, M. Abbas and Z. Raza. Optimal coincidence best approximation solution in non-Archimedean Fuzzy Metric Spaces. *Iran. J. Fuzzy Syst.*, 13(3):113–124, 2016.
29. V. Parvaneh, F. Golkarmanesh and R. George. Fixed points of Wardowski-ciric-Presic type contractive mappings in a partial rectangular b-metric space. *J. Math. Anal.*, 8(1):183–201, 2017.
30. V. Parvaneh, S. Hadi Bonab, H. Hosseinzadeh and H. Aydi. A tripled fixed point theorem in C^*-algebra-valued metric spaces and application in integral equations. *Adv. Math. Phys.*, 2021:1–6, 2021.
31. V. Parvaneh, N. Hussain, M. Khorshidi, N. Mlaiki and H. Aydi. Fixed point results for generalized F-contractions in modular b-metric spaces with applications. *Mathematics*, 7(10):1–16, 2019.
32. V. Parvaneh, N. Hussain, M. A. Kutbi and M. Khorshdi. Some fixed point results in extended modular b-metric spaces with application to integral equations. *J. Math. Anal.*, 10(5):14–33, 2019.
33. M. Paunović, N. Ralević and V. Gajović. Application of the C-credibility measure. *Tehnicki vjesnik*, 27(1):237–242, 2020.
34. D. Rakic, A. Mukheimer, T. Dosenovic, Z. D. Mitrovic and S. Radenovic. On some new fixed point results in fuzzy b-metric spaces. *J. Inequal. Appl.*, 2020:99, 2020.
35. N. Ralević and M. Paunović. c-credibility measure. *Filomat*, 33(9):2571–2582, 2019.
36. N. M. Ralević and M. Paunović. Applications of the Fuzzy metrics in image denoising and segmentation. *Tehnicki vjesnik - Technical Gazette*, 28(3):819–826, 2021.

37. N. M. Ralević, M. Paunović and B. Iričanin. Fuzzy metric spaces and applications in image processing. *Math. Montisnigri*, 48(XLVIII):103–117, 2020.
38. J. R. Roshan, V. Parvaneh, Z. Kadelburg and N. Hussain. New fixed point results in *b*-rectangular metric spaces. *Nonlinear Anal. Model. Control*, 21(5):614–634, 2016.
39. P. Salimi, A. Latif and N. Hussain. Modified $\alpha - \psi$-contractive mappings with applications. *Fixed Point Theory Appl.*, 2013(151):1–19, 2013.
40. B. Samet, C. Vetro and P. Vetro. Fixed point theorems for $\alpha - \psi$-contractive type mapping. *Nonlinear Anal.*, 75:2154–2165, 2012.
41. B. Schweizer and A. Sklar. Statistical metric spaces. *Pacific J. Math.* 10:314–334, 1960.
42. M. D. L. Sen, M. Abbas and N. Saleem, N. On optimal fuzzy best proximity coincidence points of proximal contractions involving cyclic mappings in non-Archimedean fuzzy metric spaces. *Mathematics*, 5(2):22, 2017.
43. T. Stephen, Y. Rohen, N. Mlaiki, M. Bina, N. Hussain and D. Rizk. On fixed points of rational contractions in generalized parametric metric and fuzzy metric spaces. *J. Inequal. Appl.*, 125:1–15, 2021.
44. D. Wardowski, Fixed points of a new type of contractive mappings in complete metric spaces. *Fixed Point Theory Appl.*, 2012(94):1–6, 2012.

5 Some First-Order-Like Methods for Solving Systems of Nonlinear Equations

Sani Aji
King Mongkut's University of Technology Thonburi (KMUTT)
Gombe State University

Poom Kumam
King Mongkut's University of Technology Thonburi (KMUTT)

Wiyada Kumam
Rajamangala University of Technology Thanyaburi (RMUTT)

CONTENTS

5.1 Introduction 67
5.2 Algorithms and Convergence Analysis 70
  5.2.1 Modified CD Method 70
  5.2.2 A Spectral DY-Type Method 75
5.3 Numerical Experiments 82
5.4 Conclusion 84
Bibliography 85

5.1 INTRODUCTION

Systems of nonlinear equations deal with finding a solution vector u such that:

$$J(u) = 0, \tag{5.1}$$

where $J : \mathbb{R}^n \to \mathbb{R}^n$ is a vector-valued continuous function. When the solution is restricted to be from a closed and convex set $C \subseteq \mathbb{R}^n$, then, Eq. (10.1) is called a convex-constrained system of nonlinear equations. In addition, when the mapping J is monotone, that is, if

$$\langle J(u) - J(v),\, u - v\rangle \geq 0 \quad \text{for all} \quad u, v \in \mathbb{R}^n,$$

then, Eq. (10.1) is called system of nonlinear monotone equations.

DOI: 10.1201/9781003312017-5

Recently, soft computing techniques have been applicable in many branches of science and engineering, including image and signal-processing problems, power flow equations, and chemical equilibrium systems, among others. Most of these problems can be formulated as systems of nonlinear equations (see, for example [1–3,11,13,18,25,31,32]).

Some classical methods for solving Eq. (10.1) include Newton [19,36] and quasi-Newton methods [6,10]. These methods generate approximations using the procedure:

$$u_{k+1} = u_k + \Delta_k d_k, \tag{5.2}$$

where Δ_k is called a step size which is obtained using some line search procedures, and d_k is a search direction. One of the advantages of these classical methods is that they have fast convergence from good initial points. However, computing their search direction involves solving linear system using a Jacobian matrix or an approximation to it at every iteration. As a result, these methods are not suitable to handle large-scale problems.

First-order approaches such as conjugate and spectral gradient methods are popular for solving minimization problems of the form:

$$\min_{u \in \mathbb{R}^n} j(u), \tag{5.3}$$

where $j : \mathbb{R}^n \to \mathbb{R}$ is a continuous differentiable function. Unlike the classical methods, these gradient methods do not require computation of any Jacobian matrix or its approximation. They are attractive due to their low storage requirement, global convergence properties and simplicity in implementation.

Hestenes and Stiefel [17] proposed conjugate gradient method to solve linear systems, and later on, Fletcher and Reeves [14] extended the method and proposed nonlinear conjugate gradient method for unconstrained optimization.

In conjugate gradient methods, the search direction d_k is computed using the following formula:

$$d_k = \begin{cases} -g_k, & \text{if } k = 0, \\ -g_k + \beta_k d_{k-1}, & \text{if } k \geq 1, \end{cases} \tag{5.4}$$

where $g_k := \nabla j(u_k)$. Different conjugate gradient methods are developed using different choices of the parameter β_k.

A lot of choices for the parameter β_k have been proposed in literature, some of which include the Fletcher and Reeves (FR) [15], Dai-Yuan (DY) [9], Conjugate Descent (CD) [14], Hestenes and Stiefel (HS) [17], Polak–Ribière–Polyak (PRP) [26] and Liu-Storey method (LS) [24]. The definition of each of these β_k is given as follows:

$$\beta_k^{FR} = \frac{\|g_k\|^2}{\|g_{k-1}\|^2}, \quad \beta_k^{DY} = \frac{\|g_k\|^2}{v_{k-1}^T d_{k-1}}, \quad \beta_k^{CD} = \frac{\|g_k\|^2}{-g_{k-1}^T d_{k-1}}$$

$$\beta_k^{HS} = \frac{g_k^T v_{k-1}}{v_{k-1}^T d_{k-1}}, \quad \beta_k^{PRP} = \frac{g_k^T v_{k-1}}{\|g_{k-1}\|^2}, \quad \beta_k^{LS} = \frac{g_k^T v_{k-1}}{-g_{k-1}^T d_{k-1}}.$$

These parameters can be categorized into two groups; the FR, DY, and CD, while the second category includes the HS, PRP, and LS. The methods in the first category have some good convergence behavior, and those in the second category are known for their good numerical performance [29].

Spectral gradient method was proposed by Barzilai and Borwein (BB) [4] to solve Eq. (5.3). They proved the global convergence of the method for two-dimensional quadratic case. Raydan [27] presented a generalization of the BB method and established its convergence for all n. In Ref. [8], an extension of the spectral gradient method to solve the system of nonlinear equations was proposed by La Cruz and Raydan. The search direction d_k in the spectral gradient method is defined as:

$$d_k = \begin{cases} -g_k, & \text{if } k = 0, \\ -\tau_k g_k, & \text{if } k \geq 1, \end{cases} \tag{5.5}$$

where the parameter τ_k is called the spectral parameter.

In spectral conjugate gradient method, the search direction uses a combination of Eqs. (5.4) and (5.5) as follows:

$$d_k = \begin{cases} -g_k, & \text{if } k = 0, \\ -\tau_k g_k + \beta_k g_k, & \text{if } k \geq 1. \end{cases} \tag{5.6}$$

Following the successful work of La Cruz and Raydan [8], these first-order methods are extended to solve systems of nonlinear equations. Hence, the directions (5.4), (5.5) and (5.6) respectively becomes:

$$d_k = \begin{cases} -J(u_k), & \text{if } k = 0, \\ -J(u_k) + \beta_k d_{k-1}, & \text{if } k \geq 1, \end{cases} \tag{5.7}$$

$$d_k = \begin{cases} -J(u_k), & \text{if } k = 0, \\ -\tau_k J(u_k), & \text{if } k \geq 1, \end{cases} \tag{5.8}$$

and

$$d_k = \begin{cases} -J(u_k), & \text{if } k = 0, \\ -\tau_k J(u_k) + \beta_k d_{k-1}, & \text{if } k \geq 1. \end{cases} \tag{5.9}$$

For example, Cheng [7] combined the projection technique proposed by Solodov and Svaiter [30] with the Polak–Ribière–Polyak (PRP) method [26,27] to propose a conjugate gradient projection-based method for solving nonlinear monotone equations. Xiao and Zhou [33] extended the popular descent conjugate gradient method (CG˙Descent) [16] from solving problem (5.3) to solve (10.1). This was achieved using the combination of the CG˙Descent with the projection technique in Ref. [30]. They established the global convergence of the method and performed some numerical experiments. Liu and Li [22] proposed a modification of Ref. [33], which is another extension of the CG˙descent method to solve Eq. (10.1). Later on, a multivariate spectral DY-type method was proposed by Liu and Li [23] to solve Eq. (10.1).

In the work, the search direction combines the DY conjugate gradient method and the multivariate spectral gradient method. Global convergence of the method was proved, and numerical experiments were presented to show the effectiveness of the method. Inspired by the work of Liu and Li [23], Liu and Feng [21] proposed a spectral conjugate gradient method for solving Eq. (10.1). They established both the global and linear convergence of the method under some suitable assumptions.

In Yuan et al. [35], a modified LS-like conjugate gradient method for solving Eq. (10.1) was proposed. The search direction combined the steepest descent with a modified LS method. The global convergence of the method was proved, and numerical experiments were presented to show its effectiveness in solving Eq. (10.1).

In this chapter, we discuss two algorithms for solving Eq. (10.1). The first algorithm is based on the conjugate gradient method, and the second algorithm is a spectral conjugate gradient-like method. We showed the global convergence of the methods and performed some numerical experiments to compare their performance.

5.2 ALGORITHMS AND CONVERGENCE ANALYSIS

Definition 5.1 *Consider a nonempty set $C \subset \mathbb{R}^n$ which is closed and convex. For any $u \in \mathbb{R}^n$, its projection onto C, is defined by*

$$P_C(u) = \arg\min\{\|u-v\| \ : v \in C\}.$$

The projection operator P_C has the properties

$$\|P_C(u) - P_C(v)\| \leq \|u-v\|, \quad \forall u, v \in \mathbb{R}^n, \tag{5.10}$$

and

$$\|P_C(u) - v\| \leq \|u-v\|, \quad \forall v \in C. \tag{5.11}$$

To establish the global convergence of the algorithms, we consider the following assumption.

Assumption 1 *We assumed that:*

(A_1) The mapping J is monotone.

(A_2) The mapping J is Lipschitz continuous, that is there exists a positive constant L such that

$$\|J(u) - J(v)\| \leq L\|u-v\|, \forall u, v \in \mathbb{R}^n.$$

(A_3) The solution set of (10.1), denoted by C, is nonempty.

5.2.1 MODIFIED CD METHOD

In the work of Yuan et al. [35], the search direction is given as:

$$d_k = \begin{cases} -J(u_k), \text{ if } k=0, \\ -\rho_k J(u_k) + (1-\rho_k)\frac{J(u_k)^T v_{k-1} d_{k-1} - d_{k-1}^T J(u_k) v_{k-1}}{\max\{2\delta\|d_{k-1}\|\|v_{k-1}\|, -d_{k-1}^T J(u_{k-1})\}}, \text{ if } k \geq 1, \end{cases} \tag{5.12}$$

where $\delta \in (0,1)$, $\rho_k = \frac{v_k^T v_k}{v_k^T \hat{s_k}}$ and $\hat{s_k} = s_k + (\max\{0, \frac{-s_k^T v_k}{\|v_k\|^2} + 1\})v_k$, $s_k = u_{k+1} - u_k$ and $v_k = J(u_{k+1}) - J(u_k)$. The term ρ_k has the following property

$$v_k^T \hat{s_k} \geq \max\{v_k^T s_k, \|v_k\|^2\} \geq \|v_k\|^2 > 0,$$

Thus, $\rho_k \in (0,1)$.

To establish a more effective method, we modified the search direction (5.12) and proposed algorithm with d_k defined as:

$$d_k = \begin{cases} -J(u_k), \text{ if } k = 0, \\ -\rho_k J(u_k) + (1-\rho_k)\frac{\|J(u_k)\|^2 d_{k-1} - J(u_k)^T d_{k-1} J(u_k)}{\max\{2\delta\|d_{k-1}\|\|J(u_k)\|, -d_{k-1}^T J(u_{k-1})\}}, \text{ if } k \geq 1. \end{cases} \tag{5.13}$$

Algorithm 1 (H) *Modified CD Method (MCDPM)*
Choose initial point $u_0 \in C$, $\eta \in (0,2)$, $\sigma > 0$, β, $\delta \in (0,1)$ *and* $\varepsilon > 0$. *Set* $k := 0$.
Step 1: *If* $\|J(u_k)\| \leq \varepsilon$, *stop, otherwise proceed with* ***Step 2***.
Step 2: *Compute* d_k *using (5.13).*
Step 3: *Compute* $\alpha_k = \max\{\beta^i : i = 0,1,2,\cdots\}$ *such that*

$$-J(u_k + \beta^i d_k)^T d_k \geq \sigma \beta^i \|d_k\|^2. \tag{5.14}$$

Step 4: *Set* $t_k = u_k + \alpha_k d_k$. *If* $\|J(t_k)\| = 0$ *stop. Else compute*

$$u_{k+1} = P_C[u_k - \eta \zeta_k J(t_k)],$$

where

$$\zeta_k = \frac{J(t_k)^T (u_k - t_k)}{\|J(t_k)\|^2}.$$

Step 5: *Let* $k = k+1$ *and go to* ***Step 1***.

Lemma 5.1 *Let* $\{d_k\}$ *be given by Eq. (5.13). Then there exists* $c > 0$ *such that* $J(u_k)^T d_k \leq -c\|J(u_k)\|^2$.

Proof. Using Eq. (5.13), if $k = 0$, $d_0 = -J(u_0)$ and so we have $J(u_0)^T d_0 = -\|J(u_0)\|^2$. When $k \neq 0$,

$$\begin{aligned} J(u_k)^T d_k &= -\rho_k \|J(u_k)\|^2 + (1-\rho_k)\frac{\|J(u_k)\|^2 J(u_k)^T d_{k-1} - \|J(u_k)\|^2 J(u_k)^T d_{k-1}}{\max\{2\delta\|d_{k-1}\|\|J(u_k)\|, -d_{k-1}^T J(u_{k-1})\}} \\ &= -\rho_k \|J(u_k)\|^2. \end{aligned}$$

Taking $\rho_k = c \in (0,1)$ fixed, we have

$$J(u_k)^T d_k = -c\|J(u_k)\|^2. \tag{5.15}$$

□

Lemma 5.2 *Let $\{u_k\}$ and $\{t_k\}$ be produced by the MCDPM algorithm. Then*

$$\alpha_k \geq \max\left\{1, \frac{c\beta\|J(u_k)\|^2}{(L+\sigma)\|d_k\|^2}\right\}. \tag{5.16}$$

Proof. If $\alpha_k \neq 1$, then $\alpha_k' = \alpha_k\beta^{-1}$ which violates Eq. (5.14), implying,

$$-J(u_k+\alpha_k' d_k)^T d_k < \sigma\alpha_k'\|d_k\|^2.$$

From Lemma 5.1 and by the assumption that J is Lipschitz continuous, we have

$$\begin{aligned}
c\|J(u_k)\|^2 &= -J(u_k)^T d_k \\
&= (J(u_k+\alpha_k' d_k) - J(u_k))^T d_k - J(u_k+\alpha_k' d_k)^T d_k \\
&\leq \|J(u_k+\alpha_k' d_k) - J(u_k)\|\|d_k\| + \sigma\alpha_k'\|d_k\|^2 \\
&\leq L\|u_k+\alpha_k' d_k - u_k\|\|d_k\| + \sigma\alpha_k'\|d_k\|^2 \\
&\leq \alpha_k'(L+\sigma)\|d_k\|^2.
\end{aligned}$$

Solving for α_k' completes the proof. □

Lemma 5.3 *Suppose that Assumption 1 hold, then the sequences $\{u_k\}$ and $\{t_k\}$ produced by the MCDPM algorithm are bounded. In addition,*

$$\lim_{k\to\infty}\|u_k - t_k\| = \lim_{k\to\infty}\alpha_k\|d_k\| = 0, \tag{5.17}$$

and

$$\lim_{k\to\infty}\|u_{k+1} - u_k\| = 0. \tag{5.18}$$

Proof. Let $\bar{u}$ be a solution of problem (10.1), since J is monotone, we have

$$\begin{aligned}
\langle J(t_k),\, u_k - \bar{u}\rangle &= \langle J(t_k),\, u_k - t_k + t_k - \bar{u}\rangle \\
&= \langle J(t_k),\, u_k - t_k\rangle + \langle J(t_k) - J(\bar{u}),\, t_k - \bar{u}\rangle \\
&\geq \langle J(t_k),\, u_k - t_k\rangle.
\end{aligned} \tag{5.19}$$

Now, to prove $\{u_k\}$ and $\{t_k\}$ are bounded, from Eq. (5.11), the definition of u_{k+1} and Eq. (5.19) we have

$$\begin{aligned}
\|u_{k+1}-\bar{u}\|^2 &= \|P_C[u_k-\eta\zeta_k J(t_k)]-\bar{u}\|^2 \\
&\leq \|u_k-\eta\zeta_k J(t_k)-\bar{u}\|^2 \\
&= \|u_k-\bar{u}\|^2-2\eta\zeta_k J(t_k)^T(u_k-\bar{u})+\eta^2\zeta_k^2\|J(t_k)\|^2 \\
&= \|u_k-\bar{u}\|^2-2\eta\frac{J(t_k)^T(u_k-t_k)}{\|J(t_k)\|^2}J(t_k)^T(u_k-\bar{u})+\eta^2\left(\frac{J(t_k)^T(u_k-t_k)}{\|J(t_k)\|}\right)^2 \\
&\leq \|u_k-\bar{u}\|^2-2\eta\frac{J(t_k)^T(u_k-t_k)}{\|J(t_k)\|^2}J(t_k)^T(u_k-t_k)+\eta^2\left(\frac{J(t_k)^T(u_k-t_k)}{\|J(t_k)\|}\right)^2 \\
&= \|u_k-\bar{u}\|^2-\eta(2-\eta)\left(\frac{J(t_k)^T(u_k-t_k)}{\|J(t_k)\|}\right)^2 \\
&\leq \|u_k-\bar{u}\|^2-\eta(2-\eta)\frac{\sigma^2\|u_k-t_k\|^4}{\|J(t_k)\|^2}.
\end{aligned} \tag{5.20}$$

This implies that $\{\|u_k-\bar{u}\|\}$ is a decreasing, hence, $\{u_k\}$ is bounded. Moreover, using this, together with the Lipschitz continuity assumption of the mapping J, we can find $c_1 \geq 0$ such that $\|J(u_k)\| \leq c_1$. Since $(J(u_k)-J(t_k))^T(u_k-t_k) \geq 0$, applying Cauchy-Schwarz inequality and using Eq. (5.14), we have

$$\begin{aligned}
\|J(u_k)\|\|u_k-t_k\| \geq J(u_k)^T(u_k-t_k) \geq J(t_k)^T(u_k-t_k) &= -\alpha_k J(t_k)^T d_k \geq \sigma\alpha_k^2\|d_k\|^2 \\
&= \sigma\|u_k-t_k\|^2.
\end{aligned}$$

Therefore,

$$\sigma\|u_k-t_k\| \leq \|J(u_k)\| \leq c_1,$$

showing that $\{t_k\}$ is bounded.
Also, applying Lipschitz continuity assumption, there exists constant $c_2 \geq 0$ such that $\|J(t_k)\| \leq c_2$ for all $k \geq 0$. using this and Eq. (5.20) we have

$$\eta(2-\eta)\frac{\sigma^2}{c_2^2}\|u_k-t_k\|^4 \leq \|u_k-\bar{u}\|^2-\|u_{k+1}-\bar{u}\|^2, \tag{5.21}$$

adding Eq. (5.21) for $k = 0, 1, 2, \ldots$, we have

$$\eta(2-\eta)\frac{\sigma^2}{c_2^2}\sum_{k=0}^{\infty}\|u_k-t_k\|^4 \leq \sum_{k=0}^{\infty}(\|u_k-\bar{u}\|^2-\|u_{k+1}-\bar{u}\|^2) \leq \|u_0-\bar{u}\|^2, \tag{5.22}$$

which implies

$$\lim_{k\to\infty}\|u_k-t_k\| = 0.$$

Note that using the projection in **Step 4,** we have

$$
\begin{aligned}
\lim_{k\to\infty} \|u_{k+1} - u_k\| &= \lim_{k\to\infty} \left\| P_C \left[u_k - \eta \frac{\langle J(t_k),\, u_k - t_k\rangle}{\|J(t_k)\|^2} J(t_k) \right] - u_k \right\| \\
&\leq \lim_{k\to\infty} \left\| u_k - \eta \frac{\langle J(t_k),\, u_k - t_k\rangle}{\|J(t_k)\|^2} J(t_k) - u_k \right\| \\
&\leq \eta \lim_{k\to\infty} \|u_k - t_k\| \\
&= 0.
\end{aligned} \tag{5.23}
$$

□

Lemma 5.4 *The search direction given by Eq. (5.13) is bounded.*

Proof. Observe from Eq. (5.13), if $k = 0$, then $\|d_0\| = \|J(u_0)\| \leq c_1$. If $k \neq 0$ and since

$$\max\{2\delta\|d_{k-1}\|\|J(u_k)\|, -d_{k-1}^T J(u_{k-1})\} \geq 2\delta\|d_{k-1}\|\|J(u_k)\|,$$

then we have

$$\|d_k\| = \left\| -\rho_k J(u_k) + (1-\rho_k)\frac{\|J(u_k)\|^2 d_{k-1} - J(u_k)^T d_{k-1} J(u_k)}{\max\{2\delta\|d_{k-1}\|\|J(u_k)\|, -d_{k-1}^T J(u_{k-1})\}} \right\|.$$

Applying triangular inequality, we have

$$
\begin{aligned}
\|d_k\| &\leq \rho_k\|J(u_k)\| + (1-\rho_k)\frac{\|J(u_k)\|^2\|d_{k-1}\| + |J(u_k)^T d_{k-1}|\|J(u_k)\|}{\max\{2\delta\|d_{k-1}\|\|J(u_k)\|, -d_{k-1}^T J(u_{k-1})\}} \\
&\leq \rho_k\|J(u_k)\| + (1-\rho_k)\|\frac{\|J(u_k)\|^2\|d_{k-1}\| + |J(u_k)^T d_{k-1}|\|J(u_k)\|}{2\delta\|d_{k-1}\|\|J(u_k)\|}.
\end{aligned}
$$

By applying Cauchy-Schwarz on $|J(u_k)^T d_{k-1}|$ we get

$$
\begin{aligned}
\|d_k\| &\leq \rho_k\|J(u_k)\| + (1-\rho_k)\|\frac{\|J(u_k)\|^2\|d_{k-1}\| + \|J(u_k)\|^2\|d_{k-1}\|}{2\delta\|d_{k-1}\|\|J(u_k)\|} \\
&\leq \rho_k\|J(u_k)\| + (1-\rho_k)\frac{\|J(u_k)\|}{\delta} \\
&\leq \left(\rho_k + \frac{(1-\rho_k)}{\delta}\right)\|J(u_k)\| \\
&\leq \left(\rho_k + \frac{(1-\rho_k)}{\delta}\right)c_1.
\end{aligned} \tag{5.24}
$$

Letting $\omega = \min\{\rho_k + \frac{(1-\rho_k)}{\delta}, 1\}$ and $M = \omega c_1$, then

$$\|d_k\| \leq M. \tag{5.25}$$

□

Theorem 5.5 *Suppose that Assumption 1 holds and let the sequence $\{u_k\}$ be produced by the MCDPM algorithm, then*

$$\liminf_{k\to\infty} \|J(u_k)\| = 0. \tag{5.26}$$

Proof. Suppose (5.26) does not hold, then we can find a constant r_1 such that $\forall k \geq 0$,

$$\|J(u_k)\| \geq r_1. \tag{5.27}$$

By the relations (5.15) and (5.27), we have that $\forall k \geq 0$,

$$\|d_k\| \geq cr_1. \tag{5.28}$$

From (5.16), multiplying $\|d_k\|$ on both sides, and using (5.25) together with (5.27), we get

$$\begin{aligned} \alpha_k \|d_k\| &\geq \max\left\{1, \frac{c\beta\|J(u_k)\|^2}{(L+\sigma)\|d_k\|^2}\right\}\|d_k\| \\ &\geq \max\left\{cr_1 \,, \frac{c\beta r_1^2}{(L+\sigma)M}\right\}. \end{aligned} \tag{5.29}$$

This contradicts (10.4). Thus, we have (5.26) hold. □

5.2.2 A SPECTRAL DY-TYPE METHOD

Inspired by the work of Liu and Feng [21], and to further popularize the DY method and expand its application, we proposed a new algorithm for solving Eq. (10.1). The search direction here combines the DY conjugate gradient method and a modified CD parameter as follows:

$$d_k = \begin{cases} -J(u_k), & \text{if } k = 0, \\ -\lambda_k J(u_k) + [(1-\theta_k)\beta_k^{DY} + \theta_k \tilde{\beta}_k] d_{k-1}, & \text{if } k \geq 1, \end{cases} \tag{5.30}$$

where

$$\lambda_k = \frac{s_{k-1}^T s_{k-1}}{s_{k-1}^T v_{k-1}}, \; v_{k-1} = J(u_k) - J(u_{k-1}) + rs_{k-1}, \; s_{k-1} = u_k - u_{k-1}, \tag{5.31}$$

β_k^{DY} is defined as

$$\beta_k^{DY} = \frac{\|J(u_k)\|^2}{v_{k-1}^T d_{k-1}}, \tag{5.32}$$

$\tilde{\beta}_k = \frac{\|J(u_k)\|^2}{\max\{-J(u_k)^T d_{k-1}, \gamma\|d_{k-1}\|\}}$ and $\theta_k \in (0,1)$. Substituting the value of β_k^{DY} and $\tilde{\beta}_k$ in Eq. (5.30) we get

$$d_k = \begin{cases} -J(u_k), & \text{if } k = 0 \\ -\lambda_k J(u_k) + \left[(1-\theta_k)\frac{\|J(u_k)\|^2}{v_{k-1}^T d_{k-1}} + \theta_k \frac{\|J(u_k)\|^2}{\max\{-J(u_k)^T d_{k-1}, \gamma\|d_{k-1}\|\}}\right] d_{k-1} & \text{if } k \geq 1. \end{cases} \tag{5.33}$$

Algorithm 2 (H) **: A Spectral DY-type Method (MDY)**

Choose initial point $u_0 \in C$, $\theta_k \in (0,1)$, $\kappa \in (0,1]$, $\phi \in (0,1)$ $\eta > 1$, $\sigma, \gamma > 0$, $\delta \in (0,2)$, ***and*** $\varepsilon > 0$. ***Set*** $k := 0$. **Step 1: If** $\|J(u_k)\| \leq \varepsilon$**, stop, otherwise go to Step 2. Step 2: Compute** $d_k = -J(u_k)$, $k = 0$ **and**

$$d_k = \begin{cases} -\lambda_k J(u_k), \text{ if } v_{k-1}^T d_{k-1} \leq \eta \|J(u_k)\| \|d_{k-1}\|, \\ -\lambda_k J(u_k) + \left[(1-\theta_k) \frac{\|J(u_k)\|^2}{v_{k-1}^T d_{k-1}} + \theta_k \frac{\|J(u_k)\|^2}{\max\{-J(u_k)^T d_{k-1}, \gamma \|d_{k-1}\|\}} \right] d_{k-1}, \text{ otherwise.} \end{cases} \tag{5.34}$$

Step 3: Compute $\Lambda_k = \max\{\kappa\phi^i \ : i = 0, 1, 2, \ldots\}$ **such that**

$$-\langle J(u_k + \kappa\phi^i d_k), d_k \rangle \geq \sigma\kappa\phi^i \|d_k\|^2 \min\left\{1, \ \|J(u_k + \kappa\phi^i d_k)\|^{\frac{1}{c}}\right\}, \quad c \geq 1. \tag{5.35}$$

Step 4: Set $t_k = u_k + \Lambda_k d_k$**. If** $\|J(t_k)\| = 0$ **stop. Else compute**

$$u_{k+1} = P_C \left[u_k - \delta \frac{J(t_k)^T (u_k - t_k)}{\|J(t_k)\|^2} J(t_k) \right].$$

Step 5: Let $k = k + 1$.

Remark 5.1 *Note that if* $v_{k-1}^T d_{k-1} \leq \eta \|J(u_k)\| \|d_{k-1}\|$*, the direction* (5.34) *becomes similar to the one proposed by Yu et al. [34]. Therefore, we can state that this work is an extension of [34].*

Lemma 5.6 *The parameter* λ_k *defined by Eq.* (5.31) *is well defined, and* d_k *satisfies*

$$J(u_k)^T d_k \leq -\tau \|J(u_k)\|^2, \ \forall k \geq 0. \tag{5.36}$$

Proof. Since J is monotone, then

$$\langle J(u_k) - J(u_{k-1}), u_k - u_{k-1} \rangle \geq 0,$$

which yields

$$\langle v_{k-1}, s_{k-1} \rangle \geq r \|s_{k-1}\|^2. \tag{5.37}$$

Again, by Lipschitz continuity, we have

$$\langle v_{k-1}, s_{k-1} \rangle = \langle J(u_k) - J(u_{k-1}), s_{k-1} \rangle + r \|s_{k-1}\|^2 \leq (L + r) \|s_{k-1}\|^2. \tag{5.38}$$

From Eqs. (5.37) and (5.38) we get

$$\frac{1}{(L+r)} \leq \lambda_k \leq \frac{1}{r}. \tag{5.39}$$

Now, to show Eq. (5.36), for $k = 0$, $J(u_k)^T d_k = -\|J(u_k)\|^2$, thus Eq. (5.36) holds with $\tau = 1$. When $k \neq 0$, If $v_{k-1}^T d_{k-1} \leq \eta \|J(u_k)\| \|d_{k-1}\|$, then from Eq. (5.34),

$$J(u_k)^T d_k = -\lambda_k \|J(u_k)\|^2,$$

using Eq. (5.39), we have

$$J(u_k)^T d_k \leq -\frac{1}{(L+r)}\|J(u_k)\|^2,$$

and taking $\tau = \frac{1}{L+r}$ we have Eq. (5.36).

However, if $v_{k-1}^T d_{k-1} > \eta\|J(u_k)\|\|d_{k-1}\|$, multiplying Eq. (5.34) by $J(u_k)^T$ we obtain

$$\begin{aligned}
J(u_k)^T d_k =& -\lambda_k\|J(u_k)\|^2 \\
&+ \left[(1-\theta_k)\frac{\|J(u_k)\|^2}{v_{k-1}^T d_{k-1}} + \theta_k\frac{\|J(u_k)\|^2}{\max\{-J(u_k)^T d_{k-1}, \gamma\|d_{k-1}\|\}}\right] J(u_k)^T d_{k-1} \\
&\leq -\lambda_k\|J(u_k)\|^2 + (1-\theta_k)\frac{\|J(u_k)\|^2}{v_{k-1}^T d_{k-1}} J(u_k)^T d_{k-1} + \theta_k\frac{\|J(u_k)\|^2 J(u_k)^T d_{k-1}}{-J(u_k)^T d_{k-1}} \\
&= -\lambda_k\|J(u_k)\|^2 + (1-\theta_k)\frac{\|J(u_k)\|^2}{v_{k-1}^T d_{k-1}} J(u_k)^T d_{k-1} - \theta_k\|J(u_k)\|^2 \\
&\leq -\lambda_k\|J(u_k)\|^2 + (1-\theta_k)\frac{\|J(u_k)\|^2}{v_{k-1}^T d_{k-1}} J(u_k)^T d_{k-1} \\
&\leq -\lambda_k\|J(u_k)\|^2 + \frac{\|J(u_k)\|^2}{v_{k-1}^T d_{k-1}} J(u_k)^T d_{k-1} \\
&= -\lambda_k\|J(u_k)\|^2 + \frac{J(u_k)^T d_{k-1}}{v_{k-1}^T d_{k-1}}]\|J(u_k)\|^2 \\
&\leq -\lambda_k\|J(u_k)\|^2 + \frac{\|J(u_k)\|\|d_{k-1}\|}{v_{k-1}^T d_{k-1}}\|J(u_k)\|^2 (\text{by Cauchy-Schwarz inequality}) \\
&< -\lambda_k\|J(u_k)\|^2 + \frac{\|J(u_k)\|\|d_{k-1}\|}{\eta\|J(u_k)\|\|d_{k-1}\|}\|J(u_k)\|^2 \\
&\leq -\left[\frac{1}{(L+r)} - \frac{1}{\eta}\right]\|J(u_k)\|^2.
\end{aligned} \tag{5.40}$$

The last inequality is obtained from Eq. (5.39). And letting $\tau = (\frac{1}{L+r} - \frac{1}{\eta}) > 0$ give us the desired result. □

Lemma 5.7 *Let $\{d_k\}$ be given by Eq. (5.34), then there are some constants $p_1 > 0$, $m_1 > 0$ and $m_2 > 0$ for which*

$$\|d_k\| \leq \begin{cases} p_1\|J(u_k)\|, & \text{if } v_{k-1}^T d_{k-1} \leq \eta\|J(u_k)\|\|d_{k-1}\|, \\ m_1\|J(u_k)\| + m_2\|J(u_k)\|^2, & \text{otherwise}. \end{cases} \tag{5.41}$$

Proof. If $v_{k-1}^T d_{k-1} \leq \eta\|J(u_k)\|\|d_{k-1}\|$,

$$\|d_k\| = \lambda_k\|J(u_k)\|.$$

Using Eq. (5.39), we have

$$\|d_k\| \leq p_1 \|J(u_k)\|,$$

where $p_1 = \dfrac{1}{r}$. However, if $v_{k-1}^T d_{k-1} > \eta \|J(u_k)\| \|d_{k-1}\|$, then

$$\begin{aligned}
\|d_k\| &= \lambda_k \|J(u_k)\| + (1-\theta_k)\frac{\|J(u_k)\|^2 \|d_{k-1}\|}{|v_{k-1}^T d_{k-1}|} + \theta_k \frac{\|J(u_k)\|^2 \|d_{k-1}\|}{\max\{-J(u_k)^T d_{k-1}, \gamma \|d_{k-1}\|\}} \\
&\leq \lambda_k \|J(u_k)\| + \frac{\|J(u_k)\|^2 \|d_{k-1}\|}{|v_{k-1}^T d_{k-1}|} + \frac{\|J(u_k)\|^2 \|d_{k-1}\|}{\gamma \|d_{k-1}\|} \\
&\leq \lambda_k \|J(u_k)\| + \frac{\|J(u_k)\|^2 \|d_{k-1}\|}{\eta \|J(u_k)\| \|d_{k-1}\|} + \frac{\|J(u_k)\|^2}{\gamma} \\
&\leq (\lambda_k + \frac{1}{\eta}) \|J(u_k)\| + \frac{1}{\gamma} \|J(u_k)\|^2 \\
&\leq (p_1 + \frac{1}{\eta}) \|J(u_k)\| + \frac{1}{\gamma} \|J(u_k)\|^2 \\
&\leq m_1 \|J(u_k)\| + m_2 \|J(u_k)\|^2,
\end{aligned} \tag{5.42}$$

where $m_1 = p_1 + \frac{1}{\eta}$, $p_1 = \frac{1}{r}$ and $m_2 = \frac{1}{\gamma}$. □

Lemma 5.8 *Suppose that Assumption 1 hold, then the sequences* $\{u_k\}$ *and* $\{t_k\}$ *generated by Algorithm 2 are bounded. Also,*

$$\lim_{k \to \infty} \Lambda_k \|d_k\| = 0, \tag{5.43}$$

and

$$\lim_{k \to \infty} \|u_{k+1} - u_k\| = 0. \tag{5.44}$$

Proof. Suppose $\tilde{u}$ is a solution of Eq. (10.1), from Assumption (A_1) we have

$$\begin{aligned}
\langle J(t_k),\, u_k - \tilde{u} \rangle &= \langle J(t_k),\, u_k - t_k + t_k - \tilde{u} \rangle \\
&= \langle J(t_k),\, u_k - t_k \rangle + \langle J(t_k) - J(\tilde{u}),\, t_k - \tilde{u} \rangle \\
&\geq \langle J(t_k),\, u_k - t_k \rangle.
\end{aligned} \tag{5.45}$$

Using the above equation (5.45) and u_{k+1}, we obtain

$$\begin{aligned}
\|u_{k+1}-\tilde{u}\|^2 &= \left\| P_C\left[u_k - \delta\frac{\langle J(t_k),\, u_k - t_k\rangle}{\|J(t_k)\|^2}J(t_k)\right] - \tilde{u}\right\|^2\\
&\le \left\| u_k - \tilde{u} - \delta\frac{\langle J(t_k),\, u_k - t_k\rangle}{\|J(t_k)\|^2}J(t_k)\right\|^2\\
&= \|u_k-\tilde{u}\|^2 - 2\delta\frac{\langle J(t_k),\, u_k - t_k\rangle}{\|J(t_k)\|^2}\langle J(t_k),\, u_k-\tilde{u}\rangle + \delta^2\frac{\langle J(t_k),\, u_k - t_k\rangle^2}{\|J(t_k)\|^2}\\
&\le \|u_k-\tilde{u}\|^2 - 2\delta\frac{\langle J(t_k),\, u_k - t_k\rangle}{\|J(t_k)\|^2}\langle J(t_k),\, u_k-t_k\rangle + \delta^2\frac{\langle J(t_k),\, u_k - t_k\rangle^2}{\|J(t_k)\|^2}\\
&= \|u_k-\tilde{u}\|^2 - \delta(2-\delta)\frac{\langle J(t_k),\, u_k - t_k\rangle^2}{\|J(t_k)\|^2} \qquad (5.46)\\
&\le \|u_k-\tilde{u}\|^2.
\end{aligned}$$

Showing that $\|u_k-\tilde{u}\| \le \|u_0-\tilde{u}\|$ for all k and hence $\{u_k\}$ is bounded and $\lim_{k\to\infty}\|u_k-\tilde{u}\|$ exists. Since $\{u_k\}$is bounded, and J is Lipschitz continuous,

$$\|J(u_k)\| \le p, p > 0. \tag{5.47}$$

Using this and Eq. (5.41), we have

$$\|d_k\| \le \begin{cases} n1, & \text{if } v_{k-1}^T d_{k-1} \le \eta\|J(u_k)\|\|d_{k-1}\|,\\ n2 & \text{otherwise,}\end{cases} \tag{5.48}$$

where $n_1 = p1p$ and $n2 = m_1p + m_2p^2$ and taking $M = min(n1, n2)$, we have

$$\|d_k\| \le M, M > 0. \tag{5.49}$$

Now, to show $\{t_k\}$ is bounded, remember

$$t_k - u_k = \Lambda_k d_k,$$

and we have shown that d_k is bounded. Thus, $\{t_k\}$ is also bounded. Using Lipschitz continuity assumption,

$$\|J(t_k)\| \le n, n > 0. \tag{5.50}$$

Now from Eq. (5.35), $\min\{1,\ \|J(u_k+\kappa\phi^i d_k)\|^{\frac{1}{c}}\} \le 1$, squaring from both sides of Eq. (5.35) we get

$$\sigma^2\Lambda_k^4\|d_k\|^4 \le \langle J(t_k),\, \Lambda_k d_k\rangle^2. \tag{5.51}$$

Also, since $0 < \delta < 2$, then from Eq. (5.46) we have

$$\langle J(t_k),\, u_k - t_k\rangle^2 \le \frac{\|J(t_k)\|^2(\|u_k-\tilde{u}\|^2 - \|u_{k+1}-\tilde{u}\|^2)}{\delta(2-\delta)}. \tag{5.52}$$

This together with Eq. (5.51) gives

$$\sigma^2\Lambda_k^4\|d_k\|^4 \leq \frac{\|J(t_k)\|^2(\|u_k-\tilde{u}\|^2-\|u_{k+1}-\tilde{u}\|^2)}{\delta(2-\delta)}. \tag{5.53}$$

We know $\lim_{k\to\infty}\|u_k-\tilde{u}\|$ exists, and $\|J(t_k)\|\leq n$, taking the limit as $k\to\infty$ gives

$$\sigma^2\lim_{k\to\infty}\Lambda_k^4\|d_k\|^4 = 0, \tag{5.54}$$

therefore,

$$\lim_{k\to\infty}\Lambda_k\|d_k\| = 0. \tag{5.55}$$

Using this and the definition t_k, we obtain

$$\lim_{k\to\infty}\|t_k-u_k\| = 0. \tag{5.56}$$

From the definition of projection operator, we get

$$\begin{aligned}\lim_{k\to\infty}\|u_{k+1}-u_k\| &= \lim_{k\to\infty}\left\|P_C\left[u_k-\delta\frac{\langle J(t_k),\, u_k-t_k\rangle}{\|J(t_k)\|^2}J(t_k)\right]-u_k\right\|\\ &\leq \lim_{k\to\infty}\left\|u_k-\delta\frac{\langle J(t_k),\, u_k-t_k\rangle}{\|J(t_k)\|^2}J(t_k)-u_k\right\|\\ &\leq \delta\lim_{k\to\infty}\|u_k-t_k\|\\ &= 0.\end{aligned} \tag{5.57}$$

□

Lemma 5.9 *Suppose* $\{u_k\}$ *and* $\{t_k\}$ *generated by Algorithm 2. Then*

$$\Lambda_K \geq \max\left\{\kappa, \frac{\tau\phi\|J(u_k)\|^2}{(L+\sigma)\|d_k\|^2}\right\}. \tag{5.58}$$

Proof. Consider (5.35), if $\Lambda_k\neq\kappa$, then $\tilde{\Lambda_k}=\Lambda_k\phi^{-1}$ which violates (5.35), that is,

$$-\langle J(u_k+\tilde{\Lambda}_k d_k), d_k\rangle < \sigma\|d_k\|^2\tilde{\Lambda}_k\min\{1, \|J(u_k+\tilde{\Lambda}_k d_k)\|^{\frac{1}{c}}\}.$$

Since $\min\{1, \|J(u_k+\tilde{\Lambda}_k d_k)\|^{\frac{1}{c}}\}\leq 1$. Using Eq. (5.36) and Lipschitz continuity, we have

$$\begin{aligned}\tau\|J(u_k)\|^2 &\leq -J(u_k)^T d_k\\ &= (J(u_k+\widehat{\Lambda}_k d_k)-J(u_k))^T d_k - \langle J(u_k+\widehat{\Lambda}_k d_k), d_k\rangle\\ &\leq \|J(u_k+\widehat{\Lambda}_k d_k)-J(u_k)\|\|d_k\| - \langle J(u_k+\widehat{\Lambda}_k d_k), d_k\rangle\\ &\leq L\|u_k+\widehat{\Lambda}_k d_k-u_k\|\|d_k\| + \sigma\widehat{\Lambda}_k\|d_k\|^2\\ &\leq \widehat{\Lambda}_k L\|d_k\|^2+\sigma\widehat{\Lambda}_k\|d_k\|^2\\ &\leq \widehat{\Lambda}_k(L+\sigma)\|d_k\|^2.\end{aligned}$$

Therefore,

$$\widehat{\Lambda}_k \geq \frac{\tau\|J(u_k)\|^2}{(L+\sigma)\|d_k\|^2}, \tag{5.59}$$

substituting $\tilde{\Lambda}_k = \Lambda_k \phi^{-1}$ we get

$$\Lambda_k \geq \frac{\tau\phi\|J(u_k)\|^2}{(L+\sigma)\|d_k\|^2}. \tag{5.60}$$

Thus, we have

$$\Lambda_K \geq \max\left\{\kappa, \frac{\tau\phi\|J(u_k)\|^2}{(L+\sigma)\|d_k\|^2}\right\}. \tag{5.61}$$

□

Theorem 5.10 *Suppose that Assumption 1 hold and let the sequence $\{u_k\}$ be generated by Algorithm 2, then*

$$\liminf_{k\to\infty} \|J(u_k)\| = 0. \tag{5.62}$$

Proof. Suppose (5.62) does not hold, then there exist $\alpha > 0$ such that $\forall k \geq 0$,

$$\|J(u_k)\| \geq \alpha. \tag{5.63}$$

Equation (5.36) and (5.63) gives $\forall k \geq 0$,

$$\|d_k\| \geq \tau\alpha. \tag{5.64}$$

Multiplying both sides of (5.58) by $\|d_k\|$, and from Eqs. (5.49) and (5.63), we have

$$\begin{aligned}\Lambda_k\|d_k\| &\geq \max\left\{\kappa, \frac{\tau\phi\|J(u_k)\|^2}{(L+\sigma)\|d_k\|^2}\right\}\|d_k\| \\ &\geq \max\left\{\kappa\tau\alpha, \frac{\tau\phi\alpha^2}{(L+\sigma)M}\right\}.\end{aligned} \tag{5.65}$$

Taking limit on both sides as $k \to \infty$ gives

$$\lim_{k\to\infty} \Lambda_k\|d_k\| > 0, \tag{5.66}$$

which contradicts equation (5.55). Therefore,

$$\liminf_{k\to\infty} \|J(u_k)\| = 0. \tag{5.67}$$

□

5.3 NUMERICAL EXPERIMENTS

In this section, we present the numerical experiments of the two algorithms (MCDPM and MDY). All codes are written on Matlab R2019b and are run on a PC of corei3-4005U processor, 4 GB RAM, and 1.70 GHz CPU.

For MCDPM, we choose $\sigma = 0.0001$, $\beta = 0.6$, $\eta = 1.8$ and $\delta = 0.1$. In MDY, the parameters are chosen as follows: $r = 0.001$, $\theta_k = 1/(k+1)$, $\eta = 1.9$, $\gamma = 0.9$, $\kappa = 1$, $\sigma = 0.02$, $c = 2$, $\phi = 0.70$ and $\delta = 1.1$. We perform the experiments on seven test problems with eight initial points. These problems are tested on five different dimensions: $n = 1,000$, $n = 5,000$, $n = 10,000$, $n = 50,000$ and $n = 100,000$. We used $\|J(u_k)\| \leq 10^{-5}$ as a stopping criteria. We now state the test problems considered for the experiment, where the function J is taken as $J(u) = (j_1(u),\ j_2(u),\ \ldots,\ j_n(u))^T$.

Problem 1 Exponential Function.

$$j_1(u) = e^{u_1} - 1,$$
$$j_i(u) = e^{u_i} + u_i - 1, \text{ for } i = 2,3,\ldots,n,$$
$$\text{and } C = \mathbb{R}^n_+.$$

Problem 2 [20] Modified Logarithmic Function.

$$j_i(u) = \ln(u_i + 1) - \frac{u_i}{n}, \text{ for } i = 2,3,\ldots,n,$$
$$\text{and } C = \{u \in \mathbb{R}^n : \sum_{i=1}^{n} u_i \leq n, u_i > -1, i = 1,2,\ldots,n\}.$$

Problem 3 [37] Nonsmooth Function.

$$j_i(u) = 2u_i - \sin|u_i|,\ i = 1,2,3,\ldots,n,$$
$$\text{and } C = \{u \in \mathbb{R}^n : \sum_{i=1}^{n} u_i \leq n, u_i \geq 0, i = 1,2,\ldots,n\}.$$

Problem 4 [20] Strictly Convex Function I.

$$j_i(u) = e^{u_i} - 1, \text{ for } i = 1,2,\ldots,n,$$
$$\text{and } C = \mathbb{R}^n_+.$$

Problem 5 [5] Tridiagonal Exponential Function.

$$j_1(u) = u_1 - e^{\cos(h(u_1+u_2))},$$
$$j_i(u) = u_i - e^{\cos(h(u_{i-1}+u_i+u_{i+1}))}, \text{ for } i = 2,\ldots,n-1,$$
$$j_n(u) = u_n - e^{\cos(h(u_{n-1}+u_n))},$$
$$h = \frac{1}{n+1} \text{ and } C = \mathbb{R}^n_+.$$

Problem 6

$$j_i(u) = e^{{u_i}^2} + \frac{3}{2}\sin(2u_i) - 1, \text{ for } i = 1,2,\ldots,n,$$
$$\text{and } C = \mathbb{R}^n_+.$$

Problem 7:

$$\begin{aligned}
j_1(u) &= 2u_1 - u_2 + e^{u_1} - 1, \\
j_i(u) &= -u_{i-1} + 2u_i - u_{i+1} + e^{u_i} - 1, \text{ for } i = 1,2,...,n, \\
j_n(u) &= u_{n-1} + 2u_n + e^{u_n} - 1 \text{ and} \\
C &= \mathbb{R}^n_+.
\end{aligned}$$

The experiment can be found tabulated in the link: https://github.com/sani-aji/MCDPM-experiment/blob/main/mcdpmmdy.xlsx. From the tables, ITER denotes the number of iterations, FVAL denotes the number of function evaluations, TIME denotes the CPU time, and NORM denotes the norm of the function when an approximate solution is achieved. It can be observed that both the MCDPM and MDY algorithms solved the seven test problems considered. However, the MDY algorithm has some advantages of solving some of the problems with less number of iterations and function evaluations.

We also used the Dolan and Morè performance profile [12] to visualize the performance of the algorithms graphically. The performance is shown in Figures 5.3-1–5.3-3. From these figures, it can be observed that both the methods solved the problems considered; however, MDY is reported to be better in terms of the number of iterations and the number of function evaluations. This can be observed from Figures 5.3-1 and 5.3-2 where the MDY solved around 56% and 85% of the problems with less number of iterations and function evaluations, respectively. On the other hand, Figure 5.3-3 vividly shows that MCDPM is better than the MDY algorithm in terms of CPU time.

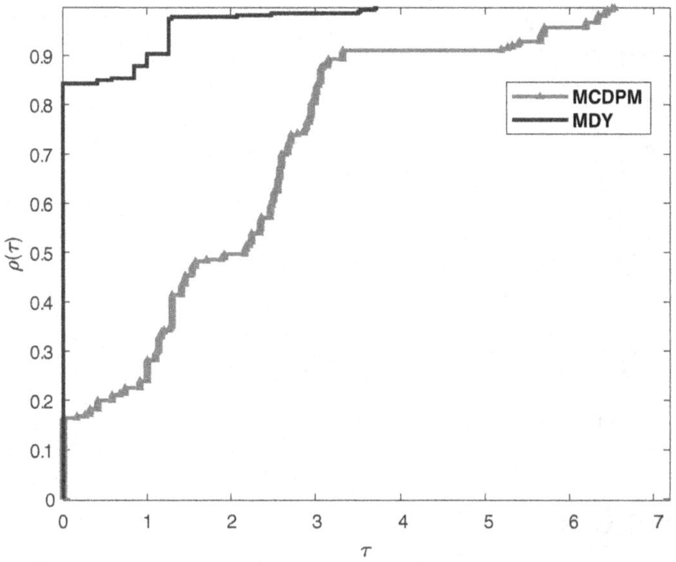

Figure 5.3-1 Number of iterations.

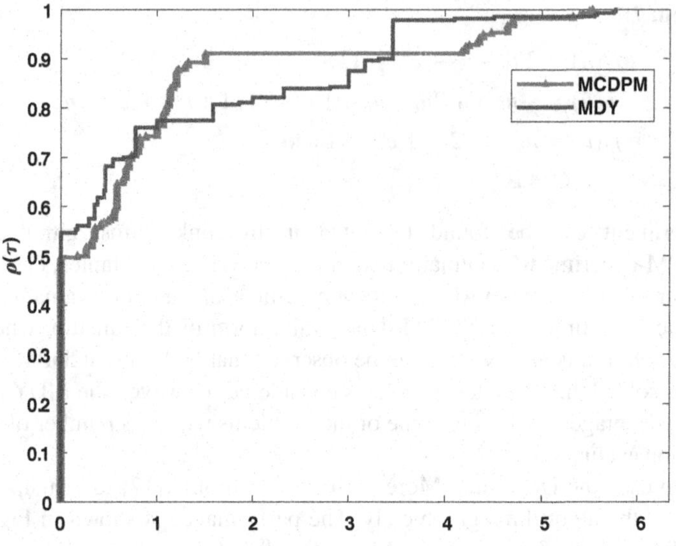

Figure 5.3-2 Function evaluations.

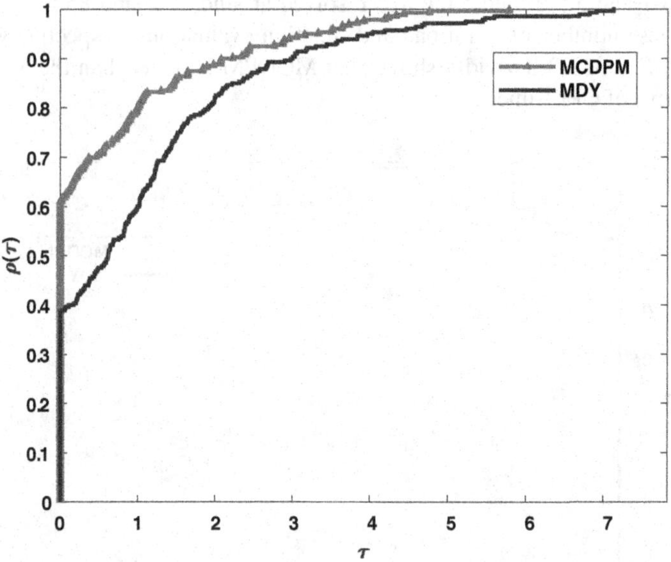

Figure 5.3-3 CPU time.

5.4 CONCLUSION

In this chapter, we studied some conjugate and spectral gradient-like algorithms for solving systems of nonlinear equations with convex constraint. We showed the global convergence of the methods under Lipschitz continuity and monotonicity assumptions of the underlined operator. We also performed numerical experiments on some test problems to show the efficiency of the algorithms. Our numerical experiments depicted that both the methods are efficient in their own capacity. However, in terms of the number of iterations and the number of function evaluations, the spectral conjugate gradient-like method is reported to be more efficient as opposed to the conjugate gradient-like method with better CPU time.

Bibliography

1. A. B. Abubakar, P. Kumam, H. Mohammad, and A. M. Awwal. A barzilai-borwein gradient projection method for sparse signal and blurred image restoration. *J. Franklin Inst.*, 357(11):7266–7285, 2020.
2. S. Aji, P. Kumam, A. M. Awwal, M. M. Yahaya, and W. Kumam. Two hybrid spectral methods with inertial effect for solving system of nonlinear monotone equations with application in robotics. *IEEE Access*, 9:30918–30928, 2021.
3. A. M. Awwal, P. Kumam, L. Wang, S. Huang, and W. Kumam. Inertial-based derivative-free method for system of monotone nonlinear equations and application. *IEEE Access*, 8:226921–226930, 2020.
4. J. Barzilai and J. M. Borwein. Two-point step size gradient methods. *IMA J. Numer. Anal.*, 8(1):141–148, 1988.
5. Y. Bing and G. Lin. An efficient implementation of merrills method for sparse or partially separable systems of nonlinear equations. *SIAM J. Optim.*, 1(2):206–221, 1991.
6. C. G. Broyden. A class of methods for solving nonlinear simultaneous equations. *Math. Comput.* , 19(92):577–593, 1965.
7. W. Cheng. A prp type method for systems of monotone equations. *Math. Comput. Modell.*, 50(1–2):15–20, 2009.
8. W. La Cruz and M. Raydan. Nonmonotone spectral methods for large-scale nonlinear systems. *Optim. Methods Softw.* , 18(5):583–599, 2003.
9. Y.-H. Dai and Y. Yuan. A nonlinear conjugate gradient method with a strong global convergence property. *SIAM J. Optim.*, 10(1):177–182, 1999.
10. J. E. Dennis and J. J. Moré. A characterization of superlinear convergence and its application to quasi-newton methods. *Math. Comput.*, 28(126):549–560, 1974.
11. S. Dirkse and M. Ferris. A collection of nonlinear mixed complementarity problems. *Optim. Methods Softw.*, 5:319–345, 1995.
12. E. D. Dolan and J. J. Moré. Benchmarking optimization software with performance profiles. *Math. Program.*, 91(2):201–213, 2002.
13. M. A. Figueiredo, R. D. Nowak, and S. J. Wright. Gradient projection for sparse reconstruction: Application to compressed sensing and other inverse problems. *IEEE J. Sel. Top. Signal Process*, 1(4):586–597, 2007.
14. R. Fletcher. *Practical Methods of Optimization: Vol. 1 Unconstrained Optimization*. John Wiley & Sons: Hoboken, NJ, 1980.
15. R. Fletcher and C. M. Reeves. Function minimization by conjugate gradients. *Comput. J.*, 7(2):149–154, 1964.
16. W. W. Hager and H. Zhang. A new conjugate gradient method with guaranteed descent and an efficient line search. *SIAM J. Optim.*, 16(1):170–192, 2005.
17. M. R. Hestenes, E. Stiefel, et al. Methods of conjugate gradients for solving linear systems. *J. Res. Natl. Bur. Stand. (U. S.)*, 49(6):409–436, 1952.

18. N. A. Iusem and V. M. Solodov. Newton-type methods with generalized distances for constrained optimization. *Optimization*, 41(3):257–278, 1997.
19. C. T. Kelley. *Iterative Methods for Linear and Nonlinear Equations*. SIAM: Thailand, 1995.
20. W. La Cruz, J. Martínez, and M. Raydan. Spectral residual method without gradient information for solving large-scale nonlinear systems of equations. *Math. Comput.*, 75(255):1429–1448, 2006.
21. J. Liu and Y. Feng. A derivative-free iterative method for nonlinear monotone equations with convex constraints. *Numer. Algorithms*, 82(1):245–262, 2019.
22. J. Liu and S. Li. A projection method for convex constrained monotone nonlinear equations with applications. *Comput. Math. Appl.*, 70(10):2442–2453, 2015.
23. J. Liu and S. Li. Multivariate spectral dy-type projection method for convex constrained nonlinear monotone equations. *J. Ind. Manag. Optim.*, 13(1):283, 2017.
24. Y. Liu and C. Storey. Efficient generalized conjugate gradient algorithms, part 1: Theory. *J. Optim. Theory Appl.*, 69(1):129–137, 1991.
25. K. Meintjes and A. P. Morgan. A methodology for solving chemical equilibrium systems. *Appl. Math. Comput.*, 22(4):333–361, 1987.
26. E. Polak and G. Ribiere. Note sur la convergence de méthodes de directions conjuguées. *ESAIM: Math. Model. Numer. Anal.*, 3(R1):35–43, 1969.
27. B. T. Polyak. The conjugate gradient method in extremal problems. *Comput. Math. Math. Phys.*, 9(4):94–112, 1969.
28. M. Raydan. On the barzilai and borwein choice of steplength for the gradient method. *IMA J. Numer. Anal.*, 13(3):321–326, 1993.
29. R. Shan, G. Wang, W. Huang, J. Zhao, and W. Liu. A new spectral conjugate gradient method and arima combined forecasting model and application. *J. Algorithms Comput. Technol.*, 12(3):245–252, 2018.
30. M. V. Solodov and B. F. Svaiter. A globally convergent inexact newton method for systems of monotone equations. In: M. Fukushima and L. Qi (eds.), *Reformulation: Nonsmooth, Piecewise Smooth, Semismooth and Smoothing Methods*, pp 355–369. Springer: Berlin/Heidelberg, Germany, 1998.
31. A. J. Wood, B. F. Wollenberg, and G. B. Sheblé. *Power Generation, Operation, and Control*. John Wiley & Sons: Hoboken, NJ, 2013.
32. Y. Xiao, Q. Wang, and Q. Hu. Non-smooth equations based method for ℓ_1-norm problems with applications to compressed sensing. *Nonlinear Anal. Theory Methods Appl.*, 74(11):3570–3577, 2011.
33. Y. Xiao and H. Zhu. A conjugate gradient method to solve convex constrained monotone equations with applications in compressive sensing. *J. Math. Anal*, 405(1):310–319, 2013.
34. Z. Yu, J. Lin, J. Sun, Y. Xiao, L. Liu, and Z. Li. Spectral gradient projection method for monotone nonlinear equations with convex constraints. *Appl. Numer. Math.*, 59(10):2416–2423, 2009.
35. G. Yuan, T. Li, and W. Hu. A conjugate gradient algorithm for large-scale nonlinear equations and image restoration problems. *Appl. Numer. Math.*, 147:129–141, 2020.
36. G. Zhou and K.-C. Toh. Superlinear convergence of a newton-type algorithm for monotone equations. *J. Optim. Theory Appl.*, 125(1):205–221, 2005.
37. W. J. Zhou and D. H. Li. A globally convergent BFGS method for nonlinear monotone equations without any merit functions. *Math. Comput.*, 77(264):2231–2240, 2008.

6 Cubic Inverse Soft Set

Srinivasan Vijayabalaji
University College of Engineering Panruti (A Constituent College of Anna University)

Kaliyaperumal Punniyamoorthy
Rajalakshmi Engineering College (Autonomous)

CONTENTS

6.1 Introduction 87
6.2 Preliminaries 88
6.3 Inverse Interval-Valued Fuzzy Soft ($i.v.\mathcal{F}.so.$) set 89
6.4 Cubic Inverse Soft Set 90
6.5 $\mathbb{P}, \mathbb{R}$- Union and Intersection of Cubic Inverse Soft Sets 93
6.6 Conclusion 94
Bibliography 94

6.1 INTRODUCTION

Zadeh [10] initiated a remarkable way to study uncertainty using fuzzy set theory. Recently, Molodtsov [8] presented another innovative tool to deal with uncertainty and named it as soft set. Cağman et al. [2] provided the idea of decision-making concepts on soft sets. Turksen [7] and Chetia et al. [3] hosted the perception of interval-valued fuzzy sets and interval-valued fuzzy soft ($i.v.\mathcal{F}.so.$) sets, respectively. Vijayabalaji et al. [9] defined and established the theory of interval-valued fuzzy n-normed linear space. For recent results, one may refer Debnath ([4] and [5]). Bayramov et al. [1] and Khalil et al. [6] extended the idea of soft set to inverse fuzzy soft ($i.\mathcal{F}.so.$) set. The thought of cubic set was dealt by Jun et al. [7]. The notion of a theoretical approach of cubic set to linear space was provided by Vijayabalaji et al. [8].

Further, Jun et al. [7] introduced various operations on cubic sets namely $\mathbb{P}$ and $\mathbb{R}$ operations on cubic sets. They gave excellent results exhibiting about the operations on cubic sets. Recent development on cubic set and cubic soft set ($\mathfrak{Cu}.so.$) can be viewed in the papers [7,8].

Our idea focuses on the introduction of inverse soft set in interval setting. We then extend it to cubic set theory. Basic definitions are given in Section 6.2. In particular, we discuss the notion of cubic soft sets with suitable examples in the same section. In Section 6.3, we define a new idea namely inverse interval-valued soft set and give the example on it. In Section 6.4, we introduce cubic inverse soft set with example

DOI: 10.1201/9781003312017-6

and present some operations on them, namely union, intersection, and complement. In Section 6.5, we give two new operations on cubic inverse soft sets namely $\mathbb{P},\mathbb{R}$-union and intersection. We provide interesting theorems and examples to support our new operations. This chapter provides conclusion and direction for future research in Section 6.6.

6.2 PRELIMINARIES

This section recollects some basic definitions which are requisite in the growth of our chapter. Also we use $\mathbb{U}$ and $\mathbb{E}$ to denote universe and parameter set, respectively, $\mathcal{P}(\mathbb{E})$ being the power set of $\mathbb{E}$.

Definition 6.1 *[10] A fuzzy set over $\mathbb{U}$ is the function $\Psi : \mathbb{U} \to \mathbb{I}$, where $\mathbb{I} = [0,1]$.*

Definition 6.2 *[8] A soft set means a pair $(\mathcal{F},\mathbb{E})$ under the function $\mathcal{F} : \mathbb{E} \to \mathcal{P}(\mathbb{U})$.*

Definition 6.3 *[6] A fuzzy soft set is a pair $(\hat{\mathcal{F}},\mathbb{E})$ under the function $\hat{\mathcal{F}} : \mathbb{E} \to \mathbb{I}^{\mathbb{U}}$, where $\mathbb{I}^{\mathbb{U}}$ is a collections of all fuzzy sets.*

Definition 6.4 *[6] An inverse soft set is a pair $(\check{\mathcal{F}},\mathbb{E})$ over $\mathbb{E}$ under the function $\check{\mathcal{F}} : \mathbb{U} \to \mathcal{P}(\mathbb{E})$.*
That is, an inverse soft set is $\left\{\left(\varphi_i, \check{\mathcal{F}}(\varphi_i)\right) : \varphi_i \in \mathbb{U}, \check{\mathcal{F}}(\varphi_i) \in \mathcal{P}(\mathbb{E})\right\}$.

Definition 6.5 *[6] Suppose that $\mathbb{U} = \{\varphi_1, \varphi_2, \varphi_3, \varphi_4\}$ and $\mathbb{E} = \{\rho_1, \rho_2, \rho_3, \rho_4, \rho_5\}$ are being the universe and parameter set respectively. If $\check{\mathcal{F}} : \mathbb{U} \to \mathcal{P}(\mathbb{E})$ and $\check{\mathcal{F}}(\varphi_1) = \{\rho_2, \rho_5\}, \check{\mathcal{F}}(\varphi_2) = \{\rho_4\}, \check{\mathcal{F}}(\varphi_3) = \{\rho_1, \rho_3, \rho_5\}, \check{\mathcal{F}}(\varphi_4) = \mathbb{E}$ then the inverse soft set is $\{(\varphi_1, \{\rho_2, \rho_5\}), (\varphi_2, \{\rho_4\}), (\varphi_3, \{\rho_1, \rho_3, \rho_5\}), (\varphi_4, \mathbb{E})\}$.*

Definition 6.6 *[6] An inverse fuzzy soft (i.$\mathcal{F}$.so.) set is a pair $(\tilde{\mathcal{F}},\mathbb{E})$ under the function $\tilde{\mathcal{F}} : \mathbb{U} \to \mathbb{I}^{\mathbb{E}}$*

Example 6.1 *[6] Suppose that $\mathbb{U} = \{\varphi_1, \varphi_2, \varphi_3, \varphi_4\}$ and $\mathbb{E} = \{\rho_1, \rho_2, \rho_3, \rho_4, \rho_5\}$ are the universe and parameter set. Then the i.$\mathfrak{F}$.so. set is*
$\tilde{\mathcal{F}}(\rho_1) = \{\varphi_1/0.1, \varphi_2/0, \varphi_3/0.4, \varphi_4/0.5\}$
$\tilde{\mathcal{F}}(\rho_2) = \{\varphi_1/0.6, \varphi_2/0.1, \varphi_3/0.3, \varphi_4/0.2\}$
$\tilde{\mathcal{F}}(\rho_3) = \{\varphi_1/0.5, \varphi_2/0.2, \varphi_3/0.3, \varphi_4/1\}$
$\tilde{\mathcal{F}}(\rho_4) = \{\varphi_1/0, \varphi_2/0.3, \varphi_3/0.1, \varphi_4/0\}$
$\tilde{\mathcal{F}}(\rho_5) = \{\varphi_1/0, \varphi_2/1, \varphi_3/0.2, \varphi_4/0.9\}$

Definition 6.7 *[9] An interval-valued fuzzy set $\aleph$ is the function $\aleph : \mathbb{U} \to \imath nt[0,1]$, where $\imath nt[0,1]$ means a collections of all closed subintervals of $[0,1]$.*

Definition 6.8 *[9] An interval-valued fuzzy soft (i.$\mathcal{F}$.so.) set is a pair $(\check{\aleph},\mathbb{E})$ under the function $\check{\aleph} : \mathbb{E} \to \mathcal{B}(\mathbb{U})$, where $\mathcal{B}(\mathbb{U}) = \left[\check{\aleph}_E^-, \check{\aleph}_E^+\right]$ is a collections of all interval-valued fuzzy sets.*

Example 6.2 *[9] Suppose that* $\mathbb{U} = \{\varphi_1, \varphi_2, \varphi_3, \varphi_4\}$ *and* $\mathbb{E} = \{\rho_1, \rho_2, \rho_3, \rho_4, \rho_5\}$ *are the universe and parameter set. Then the i.v.$\mathcal{F}$.so. set is*
$\check{\aleph}(\rho_1) = \{\varphi_1/[0.1,0.4], \varphi_2/[0.3,0.5], \varphi_3/[0.2,0.9], \varphi_4/[0.1,0.7]\}$
$\check{\aleph}(\rho_2) = \{\varphi_1/[0.2,0.3], \varphi_2/[0.5,0.7], \varphi_3/[0.1,0.4], \varphi_4/[0.2,0.5]\}$
$\check{\aleph}(\rho_3) = \{\varphi_1/[0.4,0.6], \varphi_2/[0.8,1], \varphi_3/[0.1,0.3], \varphi_4/[0.3,0.8]\}$
$\check{\aleph}(\rho_4) = \{\varphi_1/[0.3,0.4], \varphi_2/[0,0.5], \varphi_3/[0.3,0.8], \varphi_4/[0.2,0.6]\}$
$\check{\aleph}(\rho_5) = \{\varphi_1/[0.1,0.3], \varphi_2/[0.2,0.5], \varphi_3/[0.5,0.7], \varphi_4/[0,0.9]\}$

Definition 6.9 *[7] The cubic set is* $\mathfrak{C} = \{\langle \tau, \aleph(\tau), \Psi(\tau)\rangle : \tau \in X \subset \mathbb{U}\}$.

Definition 6.10 *[5] The cubic soft ($\mathfrak{C}$u.so.) set is* $\check{\mathfrak{C}} = \{\langle \rho, \check{\aleph}(\rho), \hat{\mathcal{F}}(\rho)\rangle : \rho \in \mathbb{E}\}$ *where* $\check{\aleph}(\rho) = \left[\check{\aleph}^-_{\mathbb{E}}, \check{\aleph}^+_{\mathbb{E}}\right]$.

Example 6.3 *[5] Suppose that* $\mathbb{U} = \{\varphi_1, \varphi_2, \varphi_3, \varphi_4\}$ *and* $\mathbb{E} = \{\rho_1, \rho_2, \rho_3, \rho_4, \rho_5\}$ *are the universe and parameter set. Then the $\mathfrak{C}$u.so. set is*

$$\begin{aligned}
\check{\mathfrak{C}}(\rho_1) = \{&\varphi_1/\langle[0.2,0.5],0.1\rangle, \varphi_2/\langle[0.1,0.8],0.7\rangle,\\
&\varphi_3/\langle[0,0.4],0.5\rangle, \varphi_4/\langle[0.3,0.7],0\rangle\}\\
\check{\mathfrak{C}}(\rho_2) = \{&\varphi_1/\langle[0.3,0.4],0.8\rangle, \varphi_2/\langle[0.1,0],1\rangle,\\
&\varphi_3/\langle[0.2,0.5],0.4\rangle, \varphi_4/\langle[0.7,0.8],0.9\rangle\}\\
\check{\mathfrak{C}}(\rho_3) = \{&\varphi_1/\langle[0.7,0.9],0.2\rangle, \varphi_2/\langle[0.2,0.4],0.5\rangle,\\
&\varphi_3/\langle[0.8,0.9],0\rangle, \varphi_4/\langle[0.4,0.6],0.1\rangle\}\\
\check{\mathfrak{C}}(\rho_4) = \{&\varphi_1/\langle[0.2,0.3],0.1\rangle, \varphi_2/\langle[0.4,0.5],0.3\rangle,\\
&\varphi_3/\langle[0.7,0.8],0.9\rangle, \varphi_4/\langle[0.1,0.9],1\rangle\}\\
\check{\mathfrak{C}}(\rho_5) = \{&\varphi_1/\langle[0.2,0.6],1\rangle, \varphi_2/\langle[0.6,0.9],0.1\rangle,\\
&\varphi_3/\langle[0.2,0.5],0.9\rangle, \varphi_4/\langle[0.2,0.4],0.3\rangle\}.
\end{aligned}$$

Remark 6.1 *[5] Let* $\check{\mathfrak{C}}_1 = \{\langle \rho, \check{\aleph}(\rho), \hat{\mathcal{F}}(\rho)\rangle : \rho \in \mathbb{E}\}$ *and* $\check{\mathfrak{C}}_2 = \{\langle \iota, \check{\aleph}(\iota), \hat{\mathcal{F}}(\iota)\rangle : \iota \in \mathbb{E}\}$ *be two cubic soft sets.*
The union of $\check{\mathfrak{C}}$u.so. sets $\check{\mathfrak{C}}_1$ *and* $\check{\mathfrak{C}}_2$ *is* $\check{\mathfrak{C}}_1 \sqcup \check{\mathfrak{C}}_2 = \{\langle \ell, \check{\aleph}(\ell), \hat{\mathcal{F}}(\ell)\rangle : \ell \in \mathbb{E}\}$ *where* $\check{\aleph}(\ell) = \left[min\{\check{\aleph}^-_{\mathbb{E}}(\rho), \check{\aleph}^-_{\mathbb{E}}(\iota)\}, max\{\check{\aleph}^+_{\mathbb{E}}(\rho), \check{\aleph}^+_{\mathbb{E}}(\iota)\}\right], \hat{\mathcal{F}}(\ell) = max\{\hat{\mathcal{F}}(\rho), \hat{\mathcal{F}}(\iota)\}$ *for all* $\rho, \iota \in \mathbb{E}$.

The intersection of $\check{\mathfrak{C}}$u.so. sets $\check{\mathfrak{C}}_1$ *and* $\check{\mathfrak{C}}_2$ *is* $\check{\mathfrak{C}}_1 \sqcap \check{\mathfrak{C}}_2 = \{\langle \ell, \check{\aleph}(\ell), \hat{\mathcal{F}}(\ell)\rangle : \ell \in \mathbb{E}\}$ *where* $\check{\aleph}(\ell) = \left[min\{\check{\aleph}^-_{\mathbb{E}}(\rho), \check{\aleph}^-_{\mathbb{E}}(\iota)\}, max\{\check{\aleph}^+_{\mathbb{E}}(\rho), \check{\aleph}^+_{\mathbb{E}}(\iota)\}\right], \hat{\mathcal{F}}(\ell) = min\{\hat{\mathcal{F}}(\rho), \hat{\mathcal{F}}(\iota)\}$ *for all* $\rho, \iota \in \mathbb{E}$.

The complement of the $\mathfrak{C}$u.so. set $\check{\mathfrak{C}}_1$ *is* $\check{\mathfrak{C}}^c_1 = \{\langle \rho, [1 - \check{\aleph}^+_{\mathbb{E}}(\rho), 1 - \check{\aleph}^-_{\mathbb{E}}(\rho)], 1 - \hat{\mathcal{F}}(\rho)\rangle : \rho \in \mathbb{E}\}$ *for all* $\rho \in \mathbb{E}$.

6.3 INVERSE INTERVAL-VALUED FUZZY SOFT (*I.V.$\mathcal{F}$.SO.*) SET

We define the inverse *i.v.$\mathcal{F}$.so.* set with example as follows.

Definition 6.11 *An inverse interval-valued fuzzy soft (i.v.$\mathcal{F}$.so.) set is a pair* $(\tilde{\aleph}, \mathcal{B}(\mathbb{U}))$ *under the transformation* $\tilde{\aleph} : \mathcal{B}(\mathbb{U}) \to \mathbb{I}^{\mathbb{E}}$.

Example 6.4 *Suppose that* $\mathbb{U} = \{\varphi_1, \varphi_2, \varphi_3, \varphi_4\}$ *and* $\mathbb{E} = \{\rho_1, \rho_2, \rho_3, \rho_4, \rho_5\}$ *are the universe and parameter set. Then the inverse i.v.*$\mathcal{F}$*.so. set is*
$\tilde{\aleph}(\varphi_1) = \{\rho_1/[0.2,0.5], \rho_2/[0.1,0.8], \rho_3/[0,0.4], \rho_4/[0.3,0.7], \rho_5/[0.2,0.6]\}$
$\tilde{\aleph}(\varphi_2) = \{\rho_1/[0.3,0.4], \rho_2/[0.1,0.3], \rho_3/[0.2,0.5], \rho_4/[0.7,0.8], \rho_5/[0.8,0.9]\}$
$\tilde{\aleph}(\varphi_3) = \{\rho_1/[0.7,0.9], \rho_2/[0.2,0.4], \rho_3/[0.8,0.9], \rho_4/[0.4,0.6], \rho_5/[0.2,0.5]\}$
$\tilde{\aleph}(\varphi_4) = \{\rho_1/[0.2,0.3], \rho_2/[0.4,0.5], \rho_3/[0.7,0.8], \rho_4/[0.1,0.9], \rho_5/[0,0.1]\}$.

6.4 CUBIC INVERSE SOFT SET

We coin the definition of cubic inverse soft set with examples and operations on it in this section.

Definition 6.12 *The cubic inverse soft set is defined as* $\tilde{\mathfrak{C}}in_s = \{\langle \varphi, \tilde{\aleph}(\varphi), \tilde{\mathcal{F}}(\varphi) \rangle : \varphi \in \mathbb{U}\}$ *and it is denoted by* $\langle \tilde{\aleph}, \tilde{\mathcal{F}} \rangle$*, where* $\tilde{\aleph}(\varphi) = [\tilde{\aleph}^-_{\mathbb{U}}, \tilde{\aleph}^+_{\mathbb{U}}]$ *and* $\tilde{\mathcal{F}} : \mathbb{U} \to \mathbb{I}^{\mathbb{E}}$.

Example 6.5 *Suppose that* $\mathbb{U} = \{\varphi_1, \varphi_2, \varphi_3, \varphi_4\}$ *and* $\mathbb{E} = \{\rho_1, \rho_2, \rho_3, \rho_4, \rho_5\}$ *are the universe and parameter set. Then the cubic inverse soft set is*

$$\begin{aligned}
\tilde{\mathfrak{C}}in_s(\varphi_1) &= \{\rho_1/\langle[0.2,0.5],0.1\rangle, \rho_2/\langle[0.1,0.8],0.7\rangle,\\
&\quad \rho_3/\langle[0,0.4],0.5\rangle, \rho_4/\langle[0.3,0.7],0\rangle, \rho_5/\langle[0.2,0.6],1\rangle\}\\
\tilde{\mathfrak{C}}in_s(\varphi_2) &= \{\rho_1/\langle[0.3,0.4],0.8\rangle, \rho_2/\langle[0.1,0],1\rangle,\\
&\quad \rho_3/\langle[0.2,0.5],0.4\rangle, \rho_4/\langle[0.7,0.8],0.9\rangle, \rho_5/\langle[0.6,0.9],0.1\rangle\}\\
\tilde{\mathfrak{C}}in_s(\varphi_3) &= \{\rho_1/\langle[0.7,0.9],0.2\rangle, \rho_2/\langle[0.2,0.4],0.5\rangle,\\
&\quad \rho_3/\langle[0.8,0.9],0\rangle, \rho_4/\langle[0.4,0.6],0.2\rangle, \rho_5/\langle[0.2,0.5],0.5\rangle\}\\
\tilde{\mathfrak{C}}in_s(\varphi_4) &= \{\rho_1/\langle[0.2,0.3],0.1\rangle, \rho_2/\langle[0.4,0.5],0.3\rangle,\\
&\quad \rho_3/\langle[0.7,0.8],0.9\rangle, \rho_4/\langle[0.1,0.9],1\rangle, \rho_5/\langle[0,0.1],0.6\rangle\}.
\end{aligned}$$

Definition 6.13 *Let* $\tilde{\mathfrak{C}}in_{s_1} = \{\langle \varphi, \tilde{\aleph}(\varphi), \tilde{\mathcal{F}}(\varphi) \rangle : \upsilon \in \mathbb{U}\}$ *and* $\tilde{\mathfrak{C}}in_{s_2} = \{\langle \vartheta, \tilde{\aleph}(\vartheta), \tilde{\mathcal{F}}(\vartheta) \rangle : \vartheta \in \mathbb{U}\}$ *be cubic inverse soft sets.*
The union between $\tilde{\mathfrak{C}}in_{s_1}$ *and* $\tilde{\mathfrak{C}}in_{s_2}$ *is*

$$\tilde{\mathfrak{C}}in_{s_1} \Cup \tilde{\mathfrak{C}}in_{s_2} = \{\langle \varpi, \tilde{\aleph}(\varpi), \tilde{\mathcal{F}}(\varpi) \rangle : \varpi \in \mathbb{U}\}$$
where $\tilde{\aleph}(\varpi) = \left[min\{\tilde{\aleph}^-_{\mathbb{U}}(\upsilon), \tilde{\aleph}^-_{\mathbb{U}}(\vartheta)\}, max\{\tilde{\aleph}^+_{\mathbb{U}}(\varphi), \tilde{\aleph}^+_{\mathbb{U}}(\vartheta)\}\right], \tilde{F}(\varpi)$
$= max\{\tilde{\mathcal{F}}(\varphi), \tilde{\mathcal{F}}(\vartheta)\}$ *for all* $\varphi, \vartheta \in \mathbb{U}$.

Example 6.6 *Let*

$$\begin{aligned}
\tilde{\mathfrak{C}}in_s(\varphi_1) &= \{\rho_1/\langle[0.2,0.5],0.1\rangle, \rho_2/\langle[0.1,0.8],0.7\rangle,\\
&\quad \rho_3/\langle[0,0.4],0.5\rangle, \rho_4/\langle[0.3,0.7],0\rangle, \rho_5/\langle[0.2,0.6],1\rangle\}\\
\tilde{\mathfrak{C}}in_s(\varphi_2) &= \{\rho_1/\langle[0.3,0.4],0.8\rangle, \rho_2/\langle[0.1,0],1\rangle,\\
&\quad \rho_3/\langle[0.2,0.5],0.4\rangle, \rho_4/\langle[0.7,0.8],0.9\rangle, \rho_5/\langle[0.6,0.9],0.1\rangle\}.
\end{aligned}$$

Then

$$\tilde{\mathfrak{C}}in_s(\varphi_1) \Cup \tilde{\mathfrak{C}}in_s(\varphi_2) = \{\rho_1/\langle[0.2,0.5],0.8\rangle, \rho_2/\langle[0.1,0.8],1\rangle, \rho_3/\langle[0,0.5],0.5\rangle, \rho_4/\langle[0.3,0.8],0.9\rangle, \rho_5/\langle[0.2,0.9],1\rangle\}.$$

Definition 6.14 *Let* $\tilde{\mathfrak{C}}in_{s_1} = \{\langle \varphi, \tilde{\aleph}(\varphi), \tilde{\mathcal{F}}(\varphi)\rangle : \varphi \in \mathbb{U}\}$ *and* $\tilde{\mathfrak{C}}in_{s_2} = \{\langle \vartheta, \tilde{\aleph}(\vartheta), \tilde{\mathcal{F}}(\vartheta)\rangle : \vartheta \in \mathbb{U}\}$ *be cubic inverse soft sets.*
The intersection between $\tilde{\mathfrak{C}}in_{s_1}$ *and* $\tilde{\mathfrak{C}}in_{s_2}$ *is*

$$\tilde{\mathfrak{C}}in_{s_1} \Cap \tilde{\mathfrak{C}}in_{s_2} = \{\langle \varpi, \tilde{\aleph}(\varpi), \tilde{\mathcal{F}}(\varpi)\rangle : \varpi \in \mathbb{U}\}$$
where $\tilde{\aleph}(\varpi) = \left[min\{\tilde{\aleph}^{-}_{\mathbb{U}}(\varphi), \tilde{\aleph}^{-}_{\mathbb{U}}(\vartheta)\}, max\{\tilde{\aleph}^{+}_{\mathbb{U}}(\varphi), \tilde{\aleph}^{+}_{\mathbb{U}}(\vartheta)\}\right], \tilde{\mathcal{F}}(\varpi)$
$= min\{\tilde{\mathcal{F}}(\varphi), \tilde{\mathcal{F}}(\vartheta)\}$ *for all* $\upsilon, \vartheta \in \mathbb{U}$.

Example 6.7 *Let*

$$\tilde{\mathfrak{C}}in_s(\varphi_1) = \{\rho_1/\langle[0.2,0.5],0.1\rangle, \rho_2/\langle[0.1,0.8],0.7\rangle, \rho_3/\langle[0,0.4],0.5\rangle, \rho_4/\langle[0.3,0.7],0\rangle, \rho_5/\langle[0.2,0.6],1\rangle\}$$
$$\tilde{\mathfrak{C}}in_s(\varphi_2) = \{\rho_1/\langle[0.3,0.4],0.8\rangle, \rho_2/\langle[0.1,0],1\rangle, \rho_3/\langle[0.2,0.5],0.4\rangle, \rho_4/\langle[0.7,0.8],0.9\rangle, \rho_5/\langle[0.6,0.9],0.1\rangle\}.$$

Then

$$\tilde{\mathfrak{C}}in_s(\varphi_1) \Cap \tilde{\mathfrak{C}}in_s(\varphi_2) = \{\rho_1/\langle[0.2,0.5],0.1\rangle, \rho_2/\langle[0.1,0.8],0.7\rangle, \rho_3/\langle[0,0.5],0.4\rangle, \rho_4/\langle[0.3,0.8],0\rangle, \rho_5/\langle[0.2,0.9],0.1\rangle\}$$

Definition 6.15 *Let* $\tilde{\mathfrak{C}}in_{s_1} = \{\langle \varphi, \tilde{\aleph}(\varphi), \tilde{\mathcal{F}}(\varphi)\rangle : \varphi \in \mathbb{U}\}$ *be the cubic inverse soft set.*
The complement of $\tilde{\mathfrak{C}}in_{s_1}$ *is*
$\tilde{\mathfrak{C}}in^{c}_{s_1} = \{\varpi, [1 - \tilde{\aleph}^{+}_{\mathbb{U}}(\varphi), 1 - \tilde{\aleph}^{-}_{\mathbb{U}}(\varphi)], 1 - \tilde{\mathcal{F}}(\varphi)\}$ *for all* $\varpi \in \mathbb{U}$.

Example 6.8

$$Let \tilde{\mathfrak{C}}in_s(\varphi_1) = \{\rho_1/\langle[0.2,0.5],0.1\rangle, \rho_2/\langle[0.1,0.8],0.7\rangle, \rho_3/\langle[0,0.4],0.5\rangle, \rho_4/\langle[0.3,0.7],0\rangle, \rho_5/\langle[0.2,0.6],1\rangle\}.$$

Then

$$\tilde{\mathfrak{C}}in^{c}_s(\varphi_1) = \{\rho_1/\langle[0.5,0.8],0.9\rangle, \rho_2/\langle[0.2,0.9],0.3\rangle, \rho_3/\langle[0.5,1],0.6\rangle, \rho_4/\langle[0.2,0.7],1\rangle, \rho_5/\langle[0.1,0.8],0.9\rangle\}.$$

Theorem 6.1 *Let* $\tilde{\mathfrak{C}}in_{s_1}$ *and* $\tilde{\mathfrak{C}}in_{s_2}$ *be cubic inverse soft sets. Then the following results are associated to the operations holds.*

1. $\tilde{\mathfrak{C}}in_{s_1} \Cup \tilde{\mathfrak{C}}in_{s_2} = \tilde{\mathfrak{C}}in_{s_2} \Cup \tilde{\mathfrak{C}}in_{s_1}$
2. $\tilde{\mathfrak{C}}in_{s_1} \Cap \tilde{\mathfrak{C}}in_{s_2} = \tilde{\mathfrak{C}}in_{s_2} \Cap \tilde{\mathfrak{C}}in_{s_1}$

3. $\left(\tilde{\mathfrak{C}}in_{s_1} \Cup \tilde{\mathfrak{C}}in_{s_2}\right)^c = \tilde{\mathfrak{C}}in^c_{s_1} \Cap \tilde{\mathfrak{C}}in^c_{s_2}$
4. $\left(\tilde{\mathfrak{C}}in_{s_1} \Cap \tilde{\mathfrak{C}}in_{s_2}\right)^c = \tilde{\mathfrak{C}}in^c_{s_1} \Cup \tilde{\mathfrak{C}}in^c_{s_2}$

Proof. Let $\tilde{\mathfrak{C}}in_{s_1} = \{\langle \varphi, \tilde{\aleph}(\varphi), \tilde{\mathcal{F}}(\varphi)\rangle : \varphi \in \mathbb{U}\}$ and $\tilde{\mathfrak{C}}in_{s_2} = \{\langle \vartheta, \aleph(\vartheta), \tilde{\mathcal{F}}(\vartheta)\rangle : \vartheta \in \mathbb{U}\}$ be cubic inverse soft sets.

$$
\begin{aligned}
1.\tilde{\mathfrak{C}}in_{s_1} \Cup \tilde{\mathfrak{C}}in_{s_2} &= \{\langle \varphi, \tilde{\aleph}(\varphi), \tilde{\mathcal{F}}(\varphi)\rangle : \varphi \in \mathbb{U}\} \Cup \{\langle \vartheta, \tilde{\aleph}(\vartheta), \tilde{\mathcal{F}}(\vartheta)\rangle : \vartheta \in \mathbb{U}\} \\
&= \{\langle \varphi, [\tilde{\aleph}^-_{\mathbb{U}}(\varphi), \tilde{\aleph}^+_{\mathbb{U}}(\varphi)], \tilde{\mathcal{F}}(\varphi)\rangle : \varphi \in \mathbb{U}\} \\
&\quad \Cup \{\langle \vartheta, [\tilde{\aleph}^-_{\mathbb{U}}(\vartheta), \aleph^+_{\mathbb{U}}(\vartheta)], \tilde{\mathcal{F}}(\vartheta)\rangle : \vartheta \in \mathbb{U}\} \\
&= \{\langle \varpi, [\tilde{\aleph}^-_{\mathbb{U}}(\upsilon), \tilde{\aleph}^+_{\mathbb{U}}(\upsilon)] \cup [\tilde{\aleph}^-_{\mathbb{U}}(\vartheta), \tilde{\aleph}^+_{\mathbb{U}}(\vartheta)], max\{\tilde{\mathcal{F}}(\varphi), \tilde{\mathcal{F}}(\vartheta)\}\rangle : \varpi \in \mathbb{U}\} \\
&= \{\langle \varpi, [min\{\tilde{\aleph}^-_{\mathbb{U}}(\varphi), \tilde{\aleph}^-_{\mathbb{U}}(\vartheta)\}, max\{\tilde{\aleph}^+_{\mathbb{U}}(\upsilon), \tilde{\aleph}^+_{\mathbb{U}}(\vartheta)\}], \\
&\quad max\{\tilde{\mathcal{F}}(\varphi), \tilde{\mathcal{F}}(\vartheta)\}\rangle : \varpi \in \mathbb{U}\} \\
&= \{\langle \varpi, [min\{\tilde{\aleph}^-_{\mathbb{U}}(\vartheta), \tilde{\aleph}^-_{\mathbb{U}}(\varphi)\}, max\{\tilde{\aleph}^+_{\mathbb{U}}(\vartheta), \tilde{\aleph}^+_{\mathbb{U}}(\varphi)\}], \\
&\quad max\{\tilde{\mathcal{F}}(\vartheta), \tilde{\mathcal{F}}(\varphi)\}\rangle : \varpi \in \mathbb{U}\} \\
&= \{\langle \varpi, [\tilde{\aleph}^-_{\mathbb{U}}(\vartheta), \tilde{\aleph}^+_{\mathbb{U}}(\vartheta)] \Cup [\tilde{\aleph}^-_{\mathbb{U}}(\varphi), \tilde{\aleph}^+_{\mathbb{U}}(\varphi)], max\{\tilde{\mathcal{F}}(\vartheta), \tilde{\mathcal{F}}(\varphi)\}\rangle : \varpi \in \mathbb{U}\} \\
&= \{\langle \vartheta, \tilde{\aleph}(\vartheta), \tilde{\mathcal{F}}(\vartheta)\rangle : \vartheta \in \mathbb{U}\} \Cup \{\langle \varphi, \tilde{\aleph}(\varphi), \tilde{\mathcal{F}}(\upsilon)\rangle : \varphi \in \mathbb{U}\} \\
\tilde{\mathfrak{C}}in_{s_1} \Cup \tilde{\mathfrak{C}}in_{s_2} &= \tilde{\mathfrak{C}}in_{s_2} \Cup \tilde{\mathfrak{C}}in_{s_1}.
\end{aligned}
$$

2. $\tilde{\mathfrak{C}}in_{s_1} \Cap \tilde{\mathfrak{C}}in_{s_2} = \tilde{\mathfrak{C}}in_{s_2} \Cap \tilde{\mathfrak{C}}in_{s_1}$
Proof is similar to 1.

$$
\begin{aligned}
3. \left(\tilde{\mathfrak{C}}in_{s_1} \Cup \tilde{\mathfrak{C}}in_{s_2}\right)^c &= \left(\{\langle \varphi, \tilde{\aleph}(\varphi), \tilde{\mathcal{F}}(\varphi)\rangle : \varphi \in \mathbb{U}\} \Cup \{\langle \vartheta, \tilde{\aleph}(\vartheta), \tilde{\mathcal{F}}(\vartheta)\rangle : \vartheta \in \mathbb{U}\}\right)^c \\
&= \left(\{\langle \varphi, [\tilde{\aleph}^-_{\mathbb{U}}(\varphi), \tilde{\aleph}^+_{\mathbb{U}}(\varphi)], \tilde{\mathcal{F}}(\varphi)\rangle : \varphi \in \mathbb{U}\}\right. \\
&\quad \left.\Cup \{\langle \vartheta, [\tilde{\aleph}^-_{\mathbb{U}}(\vartheta), \tilde{\aleph}^+_{\mathbb{U}}(\vartheta)], \tilde{\mathcal{F}}(\vartheta)\rangle : \vartheta \in \mathbb{U}\}\right)^c \\
&= \left(\langle \varphi, [\tilde{\aleph}^-_{\mathbb{U}}(\varphi), \tilde{\aleph}^+_{\mathbb{U}}(\varphi)], \tilde{\mathcal{F}}(\varphi)\rangle : \varphi \in \mathbb{U}\right)^c \\
&\quad \Cap \left(\langle \vartheta, [\tilde{\aleph}^-_{\mathbb{U}}(\vartheta), \tilde{\aleph}^+_{\mathbb{U}}(\vartheta)], \tilde{\mathcal{F}}(\vartheta)\rangle : \vartheta \in \mathbb{U}\right)^c \\
&= \left(\langle \varphi^c, [1 - \tilde{\aleph}^+_{\mathbb{U}}(\varphi), 1 - \tilde{\aleph}^-_{\mathbb{U}}(\varphi)], 1 - \tilde{\mathcal{F}}(\varphi)\rangle : \varphi \in \mathbb{U}\right) \\
&\quad \Cap \left(\langle \vartheta^c, [1 - \tilde{\aleph}^+_{\mathbb{U}}(\vartheta), 1 - \tilde{\aleph}^-_{\mathbb{U}}(\vartheta)], 1 - \tilde{\mathcal{F}}(\vartheta)\rangle : \vartheta \in \mathbb{U}\right) \\
&= \{\langle \varpi, [min\{1 - \tilde{\aleph}^-_{\mathbb{U}}(\varphi), 1 - \tilde{\aleph}^-_{\mathbb{U}}(\vartheta)\}, max\{1 - \tilde{\aleph}^+_{\mathbb{U}}(\varphi), 1 - \tilde{\aleph}^+_{\mathbb{U}}(\vartheta)\}] \\
&\quad min\{1 - \tilde{\mathcal{F}}(\varphi), 1 - \tilde{\mathcal{F}}(\vartheta)\}\rangle : \varpi \in \mathbb{U}\} \\
&= \{\langle \varpi, [1 - \tilde{\aleph}^+_{\mathbb{U}}(\varphi), 1 - \tilde{\aleph}^-_{\mathbb{U}}(\varphi)] \Cap [1 - \tilde{\aleph}^+_{\mathbb{U}}(\vartheta), 1 - \tilde{\aleph}^-_{\mathbb{U}}(\vartheta)], \\
&\quad min\{1 - \tilde{\mathcal{F}}(\varphi), 1 - \tilde{\mathcal{F}}(\vartheta)\}\rangle : \varpi \in \mathbb{U}\} \\
&= \{\langle \varphi[1 - \tilde{\aleph}^+_{\mathbb{U}}(\varphi), 1 - \tilde{\aleph}^-_{\mathbb{U}}(\varphi)], 1 - \tilde{\mathcal{F}}(\varphi)\rangle : \varphi \in \mathbb{U}\} \\
&\quad \Cap \{\langle \vartheta, [1 - \tilde{\aleph}^+_{\mathbb{U}}(\vartheta), 1 - \tilde{\aleph}^-_{\mathbb{U}}(\vartheta)], 1 - \tilde{\mathcal{F}}(\vartheta)\rangle : \vartheta \in \mathbb{U}\} \\
\left(\tilde{\mathfrak{C}}in_{s_1} \Cup \tilde{\mathfrak{C}}in_{s_2}\right)^c &= \tilde{\mathfrak{C}}in^c_{s_1} \Cap \tilde{\mathfrak{C}}in^c_{s_2}.
\end{aligned}
$$

4. $\left(\tilde{\mathfrak{C}}in_{s_1} \Cap \tilde{\mathfrak{C}}in_{s_2}\right)^c = \tilde{\mathfrak{C}}in^c_{s_1} \Cup \tilde{\mathfrak{C}}in^c_{s_2}$
Proof is similar to 3. □

Theorem 6.2 *Let* $\tilde{\mathfrak{C}}in_{s_1} = \{\langle \varphi, \tilde{\aleph}(\varphi), \tilde{\mathcal{F}}(\varphi)\rangle : \varphi \in \mathbb{U}\}$ *be cubic inverse soft set. Then* $\left(\tilde{\mathfrak{C}}in^c_{s_1}\right)^c = \tilde{\mathfrak{C}}in_{s_1}$.

Proof. Since $\tilde{\mathfrak{C}}in^c_{s_1} = \{\langle \varpi, [1 - \aleph^+_U(\varphi), 1 - \aleph^-_U(\varphi)], 1 - \tilde{\mathcal{F}}(\varphi)\rangle\}$ for all $\varpi \in \mathbb{U}$.

$$\begin{aligned}
\left(\tilde{\mathfrak{C}}in^c_{s_1}\right)^c &= \left(\{\langle \varpi, [1 - \tilde{\aleph}^+_{\mathbb{U}}(\varphi), 1 - \tilde{\aleph}^-_{\mathbb{U}}(\varphi)], 1 - \tilde{\mathcal{F}}(\varphi)\rangle\}\right)^c forall \varpi \in \mathbb{U} \\
&= \{\langle \varpi, [1 - (1 - \tilde{\aleph}^-_{\mathbb{U}}(\varphi)), 1 - (1 - \tilde{\aleph}^+_{\mathbb{U}}(\varphi))], 1 - (1 - \tilde{\mathcal{F}}(\varphi))\rangle : \varphi \in \mathbb{U}\} \\
&= \{\langle \varphi, [\tilde{\aleph}^-_{\mathbb{U}}(\varphi), \tilde{\aleph}^+_{\mathbb{U}}(\varphi)], \tilde{\mathcal{F}}(\varphi)\rangle : \varphi \in \mathbb{U}\} \\
&= \{\langle \varphi, \aleph(\varphi), \tilde{\mathcal{F}}(\varphi)\rangle : \varphi \in \mathbb{U}\} \\
\left(\tilde{\mathfrak{C}}in^c_{s_1}\right)^c &= \tilde{\mathfrak{C}}in_{s_1}.
\end{aligned}$$

□

6.5 $\mathbb{P}, \mathbb{R}$- UNION AND INTERSECTION OF CUBIC INVERSE SOFT SETS

In this section, we discuss the $\mathbb{P}, \mathbb{R}$- union and intersection of cubic inverse soft sets. We also consider three cubic inverse soft sets namely $\tilde{\mathfrak{C}}in_{s_1} = \{\langle \varphi, \tilde{\aleph}(\varphi), \tilde{\mathcal{F}}(\varphi)\rangle : \varphi \in \mathbb{U}\}, \tilde{\mathfrak{C}}in_{s_2} = \{\langle \vartheta, \tilde{\aleph}(\vartheta), \tilde{\mathcal{F}}(\vartheta)\rangle : \vartheta \in \mathbb{U}\}$ and $\tilde{\mathfrak{C}}in_{s_3} = \{\langle \varsigma, \aleph(\varsigma), \tilde{\mathcal{F}}(\varsigma)\rangle : \varsigma \in \mathbb{U}\}$ and study some of their properties.

Definition 6.16 *We define*

1. *(Equality)* $\tilde{\mathfrak{C}}in_{s_1} = \tilde{\mathfrak{C}}in_{s_2} \Leftrightarrow \tilde{\aleph}(\varphi) = \tilde{\aleph}(\vartheta) and \tilde{\mathcal{F}}(\varphi) = \tilde{\mathcal{F}}(\vartheta)$
2. *($\mathbb{P}$-order)* $\tilde{\mathfrak{C}}in_{s_1} \subseteq_{\mathbb{P}} \tilde{\mathfrak{C}}in_{s_2} \Leftrightarrow \tilde{\aleph}(\varphi) \subseteq \tilde{\aleph}(\vartheta) and \tilde{\mathcal{F}}(\varphi) \leq \tilde{\mathcal{F}}(\vartheta)$
3. *($\mathbb{R}$-order)* $\tilde{\mathfrak{C}}in_{s_1} \subseteq_{\mathbb{R}} \tilde{\mathfrak{C}}in_{s_2} \Leftrightarrow \tilde{\aleph}(\varphi) \subseteq \tilde{\aleph}(\vartheta) and \tilde{\mathcal{F}}(\varphi) \geq \tilde{\mathcal{F}}(\vartheta)$

Definition 6.17 *The $\mathbb{P}$-union between* $\tilde{\mathfrak{C}}in_{s_1}$ *and* $\tilde{\mathfrak{C}}in_{s_2}$ *is*
$\tilde{\mathfrak{C}}in_{s_1} \Cup_{\mathbb{P}} \tilde{\mathfrak{C}}in_{s_2} = \{\langle \varpi_{\mathbb{P}}, \tilde{\aleph}_{\mathbb{P}}(\varpi), \tilde{\mathcal{F}}_{\mathbb{P}}(\varpi)\rangle : \varpi \in \mathbb{U}\}$
where $\aleph_{\mathbb{P}}(\varpi) = \Cup_{\mathbb{P}}\{[\tilde{\aleph}^-_U(\varphi), \tilde{\aleph}^+_{\mathbb{U}}(\varphi)], [\tilde{\aleph}^-_{\mathbb{U}}(\vartheta), \tilde{\aleph}^+_{\mathbb{U}}(\vartheta)]\}, \tilde{\mathcal{F}}_{\mathbb{P}}(\varpi) = max\{\tilde{\mathcal{F}}(\varphi), \tilde{\mathcal{F}}(\vartheta)\}$
for all $\varphi, \vartheta \in \mathbb{U}$.

Definition 6.18 *The $\mathbb{P}$-intersection between* $\tilde{\mathfrak{C}}in_{s_1}$ *and* $\tilde{\mathfrak{C}}in_{s_2}$ *is*
$\tilde{\mathfrak{C}}in_{s_1} \Cap \tilde{\mathfrak{C}}in_{s_2} = \{\langle \varpi_{\mathbb{P}}, \tilde{\aleph}_{\mathbb{P}}(\varpi), \tilde{\mathcal{F}}_{\mathbb{P}}(\varpi)\rangle : \varpi \in \mathbb{U}\}$
where $\tilde{\aleph}_{\mathbb{P}}(\varpi) = \Cap_{\mathbb{P}}\{[\tilde{\aleph}^-_{\mathbb{U}}(\varphi), \tilde{\aleph}^+_{\mathbb{U}}(\varphi)], [\tilde{\aleph}^-_{\mathbb{U}}(\vartheta), \tilde{\aleph}^+_{\mathbb{U}}(\vartheta)]\}, \tilde{\mathcal{F}}_{\mathbb{P}}(\varpi) = min\{\tilde{\mathcal{F}}(\varphi), \tilde{\mathcal{F}}(\vartheta)\}$
for all $\varphi, \vartheta \in \mathbb{U}$.

Definition 6.19 *The R-union between* $\tilde{\mathfrak{C}}in_{s_1}$ *and* $\tilde{\mathfrak{C}}in_{s_2}$ *is*
$\tilde{\mathfrak{C}}in_{s_1} \Cup_{\mathbb{R}} \tilde{\mathfrak{C}}in_{s_2} = \{\langle \varpi_{\mathbb{R}}, \tilde{\aleph}_{\mathbb{R}}(\varpi), \tilde{\mathcal{F}}_{\mathbb{R}}(\varpi)\rangle : \varpi \in \mathbb{U}\}$
where $\tilde{\aleph}_{\mathbb{R}}(\varpi) = \Cup_{\mathbb{R}}\{[\tilde{\aleph}^-_{\mathbb{U}}(\varphi), \tilde{\aleph}^+_{\mathbb{U}}(\varphi)], [\tilde{\aleph}^-_{\mathbb{U}}(\vartheta), \tilde{\aleph}^+_{\mathbb{U}}(\vartheta)]\}, \tilde{\mathcal{F}}_R(\varpi) = min\{\tilde{\mathcal{F}}(\varphi), \tilde{\mathcal{F}}(\vartheta)\}$
for all $\varphi, \vartheta \in \mathbb{U}$.

Definition 6.20 *The R-intersection between* $\tilde{\mathfrak{C}}in_{s_1}$ *and* $\tilde{\mathfrak{C}}in_{s_2}$ *is*
$\tilde{\mathfrak{C}}in_{s_1} \Cap_{\mathbb{R}} \tilde{\mathfrak{C}}in_{s_2} = \{\langle \varpi_{\mathbb{R}}, \tilde{\aleph}_{\mathbb{R}}(\varpi), \tilde{\mathcal{F}}_{\mathbb{R}}(\varpi)\rangle : \varpi \in \mathbb{U}\}$
where $\tilde{\aleph}_{\mathbb{R}}(\varpi) = \Cap_{\mathbb{R}}\{[\tilde{\aleph}^-_{\mathbb{U}}(\varphi), \tilde{\aleph}^+_{\mathbb{U}}(\varphi)], [\tilde{\aleph}^-_{\mathbb{U}}(\vartheta), \tilde{\aleph}^+_{\mathbb{U}}(\vartheta)]\}, \tilde{\mathcal{F}}_{\mathbb{R}}(\varpi) = max\{\tilde{\mathcal{F}}(\varphi), \tilde{\mathcal{F}}(\vartheta)\}$
for all $\varphi, \vartheta \in \mathbb{U}$.

Theorem 6.3 *Let $\tilde{\mathfrak{C}}in_{s_1}$ and $\tilde{\mathfrak{C}}in_{s_2}$ be cubic inverse soft sets. Then the following results are associated to the operations holds.*

1. $\tilde{\mathfrak{C}}in_{s_1} \Cup_{\mathbb{P}} \tilde{\mathfrak{C}}in_{s_2} = \tilde{\mathfrak{C}}in_{s_2} \Cup_{\mathbb{P}} \tilde{\mathfrak{C}}in_{s_1}$
2. $\tilde{\mathfrak{C}}in_{s_1} \Cap_{\mathbb{P}} \tilde{\mathfrak{C}}in_{s_2} = \tilde{\mathfrak{C}}in_{s_2} \Cap_{\mathbb{P}} \tilde{\mathfrak{C}}in_{s_1}$
3. $\left(\tilde{\mathfrak{C}}in_{s_1} \Cup_{\mathbb{P}} \tilde{\mathfrak{C}}in_{s_2}\right)^c = \tilde{\mathfrak{C}}in^c_{s_1} \Cap_{\mathbb{P}} \tilde{\mathfrak{C}}in^c_{s_2}$
4. $\left(\tilde{\mathfrak{C}}in_{s_1} \Cap_{\mathbb{P}} \tilde{\mathfrak{C}}in_{s_2}\right)^c = \tilde{\mathfrak{C}}in^c_{s_1} \Cup_{\mathbb{P}} \tilde{\mathfrak{C}}in^c_{s_2}$

Proof. Straightforward. □

Theorem 6.4 *Let $\tilde{\mathfrak{C}}in_{s_1}, \tilde{\mathfrak{C}}in_{s_2}$ and $\tilde{\mathfrak{C}}in_{s_3}$ be cubic inverse soft sets. Then the following results are associated to the operations holds.*

1. $\tilde{\mathfrak{C}}in_{s_1} \Cup_{\mathbb{P}} (\tilde{\mathfrak{C}}in_{s_2} \Cup_{\mathbb{P}} \tilde{\mathfrak{C}}in_{s_3}) = (\tilde{\mathfrak{C}}in_{s_1} \Cup_{\mathbb{P}} \tilde{\mathfrak{C}}in_{s_2}) \Cup_{\mathbb{P}} \tilde{\mathfrak{C}}in_{s_3}$
2. $\tilde{\mathfrak{C}}in_{s_1} \Cap_{\mathbb{P}} (\tilde{\mathfrak{C}}in_{s_2} \Cap_{\mathbb{P}} \tilde{\mathfrak{C}}in_{s_3}) = (\tilde{\mathfrak{C}}in_{s_1} \Cap_{\mathbb{P}} \tilde{\mathfrak{C}}in_{s_2}) \Cap_{\mathbb{P}} \tilde{\mathfrak{C}}in_{s_3}$
3. $\tilde{\mathfrak{C}}in_{s_1} \Cup_{\mathbb{P}} (\tilde{\mathfrak{C}}in_{s_2} \Cap_{\mathbb{P}} \tilde{\mathfrak{C}}in_{s_3}) = (\tilde{\mathfrak{C}}in_{s_1} \Cup_{\mathbb{P}} \tilde{\mathfrak{C}}in_{s_2}) \Cap_{\mathbb{P}} (\tilde{\mathfrak{C}}in_{s_1} \Cup_{\mathbb{P}} \tilde{\mathfrak{C}}in_{s_3})$
4. $\tilde{\mathfrak{C}}in_{s_1} \Cap_{\mathbb{P}} (\tilde{\mathfrak{C}}in_{s_2} \Cup_{\mathbb{P}} \tilde{\mathfrak{C}}in_{s_3}) = (\tilde{\mathfrak{C}}in_{s_1} \Cap_{\mathbb{P}} \tilde{\mathfrak{C}}in_{s_2}) \Cup_{\mathbb{P}} (\tilde{\mathfrak{C}}in_{s_1} \Cap_{\mathbb{P}} \tilde{\mathfrak{C}}in_{s_3})$

Proof. Straightforward. □

Remark 6.2 *Theorems 6.3 and 6.4 are also hold good under the operations $\mathbb{R}$-union and $\mathbb{R}$-intersection of cubic inverse soft sets $\tilde{\mathfrak{C}}in_{s_1}, \tilde{\mathfrak{C}}in_{s_2}$ and $\tilde{\mathfrak{C}}in_{s_3}$.*

6.6 CONCLUSION

In this chapter, we have defined inverse $i.v.\mathcal{F}.so.$ set, cubic inverse soft set with suitable examples. We have provided some operations between cubic inverse soft sets namely union, intersection, and complement. The operations namely $\mathbb{P}$,$\mathbb{R}$-union and intersection between the cubic inverse soft sets were also discussed. Motivated by our new notion namely cubic inverse soft set, we plan to provide a real-time application on it by using multi-criteria decision-making technique along with the appropriate decision tools.

Bibliography

1. Bayramov, S., Gunduz, C., & Yazar, M. I. (2012). Inverse system of fuzzy soft modules. *Ann. Fuzzy Math. Inform., 4*(2), 349–363.
2. Cağman, N., & Enginoğlu, S. (2010). Soft set theory and uni-int decision making. *Eur. J. Oper. Res., 207*(2), 848–855.
3. Chetia, B., & Das, P. K. (2010). An application of interval-valued fuzzy soft. *Int. J. Contemp. Math. Sci., 5*(38), 1887–1894.
4. Debnath, P. (2022). Some results on Cesáro summability in Intuitionistic Fuzzy *n*-normed linear spaces. *Sahand Commun. Math. Anal., 19*(1), 77–87.
5. Debnath, P. (2016). A generalized statistical convergence in intuitionistic fuzzy n-normed linear spaces. *Ann. Fuzzy Math. Inform., 12*(4), 559–572.
6. Jun, Y. B., Kim, C. S. & Yang, K. O.(2012). Cubic sets, *Ann. Fuzzy Math. Inform., 4*(1), 83–98.

7. Khalil, A. M., & Hassan, N. (2019). Inverse fuzzy soft set and its application in decision making. *Int. J. Inf. Decis. Sci., 11*(1), 73–92.
8. Molodtsov, D. (1999). Soft set theory-first results. *Comput. Math. Appl., 37*(4–5), 19–31.
9. Turksen, I. B. (1986). Interval valued fuzzy sets based on normal forms. *Fuzzy Sets Syst., 20*(2), 191–210.
10. Vijayabalaji, S., Shanthi, S. A., & Thillaigovindan, N. (2008). Interval valued Fuzzy n-normed linear space. *Mal. J. Fund. Appl. Sci., 4*(1), 287–297.

7 Inverse Soft-Rough Matrices

Srinivasan Vijayabalaji
University College of Engineering Panruti (A Constituent College of Anna University)

CONTENTS

7.1 Introduction 97
7.2 Preliminaries 98
7.3 Inverse Soft-Rough ($\mathcal{S}.\mathcal{R}.$) Set and Inverse Soft-Rough ($\mathcal{S}.\mathcal{R}.$) Matrix 99
7.4 MCDM on Inverse $\mathcal{S}.\mathcal{R}.$ Matrix 101
7.4.1 Algorithm 101
7.5 Conclusion 104
Bibliography 105

7.1 INTRODUCTION

Molodtsov [6] introduced an innovative tool to deal with uncertainty namely soft set. Inspired by this theory numerous researchers namely Pawlak [7], Bustince et al. [1] and Riaz et al. [10] discussed the theory of rough set, vague set, and soft-rough $\mathcal{S}.\mathcal{R}.$ sets. They also provided multi-criteria decision-making problems (MCDM) on them. Cağman et al. [2] provided the matrix form of soft sets. Vijayabalaji et al. [12], [13] used the novel idea of soft matrix and rough matrix and dealt with multi-criteria decision-making. Vijayabalaji ([14], [15]) introduced $\mathcal{S}.\mathcal{R}.$ matrices and generalized $\mathcal{S}.\mathcal{R}.$ matrices. Kamacı et al. [4] and Petchimuthu et al. [8] built the inverse soft set and constructed the inverse soft matrices in multi-criteria decision-making problems. Demirtas et al. [3] initiated the idea of inverse $\mathcal{S}.\mathcal{R}.$ set with decision-making problems.

Analytic Hierarchy Process (AHP) technique provides good results in complex decision-making situations. Saaty [11] was the first person to introduce and develop the idea of AHP technique. Maji et al. [5] assigned weights using the AHP technique and solved group decision problems for soft matrices. Later Razak et al. [9] took the task of improving their work and applied the same idea on house selection problem.

In this chapter, we provide the basic definitions in Section 7.2. In Section 7.3 we introduce inverse $\mathcal{S}.\mathcal{R}.$ set and $\mathcal{S}.\mathcal{R}.$ matrix with example and provide various operations on it. Section 7.4 delivers a MCDM on inverse soft-rough matrices using the AHP technique. The concluding part and direction for the future research are presented in Section 7.5.

DOI: 10.1201/9781003312017-7

7.2 PRELIMINARIES

This section remembers some basic definitions which will be required in the development of the subsequent sections. We represent the universe set and parameter set as $\mathbb{U}$ and $\mathbb{E}$, respectively.

Definition 7.1 *[6] A soft set over* $\mathbb{U}$ *is a pair* $(\mathcal{F},\mathbb{A})$, *where* $\mathcal{F}:\mathbb{A}\to\mathcal{P}(\mathbb{U})$, $\mathcal{P}(\mathbb{U})$ *is the power set of* $\mathbb{U}$ *and* $\mathbb{A}\subset\mathbb{U}$.

Definition 7.2 *[15] Let* $\mathcal{T}=(\mathcal{F},\mathbb{A})$ *be a soft set. Let a soft approximation space be* $\mathcal{S}=(\mathbb{U},\mathcal{T})$. *Then we define two different operations based on* $\mathcal{S}$ *as follows:*

$$\underline{apr_{\mathcal{S}}}(\mathcal{X})=\{\upsilon\in\mathbb{U}:\exists a\in\mathbb{A},\upsilon\in f(a),f(a)\subseteq\mathcal{X}\}$$
$$\overline{apr_{\mathcal{S}}}(\mathcal{X})=\{\upsilon\in\mathbb{U}:\exists a\in\mathbb{A},\upsilon\in f(a),f(a)\cap\mathcal{X}\neq\phi\}.$$

Allocating to each $\mathcal{X}\subseteq\mathbb{U}$, *two sets lower and upper* $\mathcal{S.R.}$ *approximations of* $\mathcal{X}$ *in* $\mathcal{S}$ *are denotes* $\underline{apr_{\mathcal{S}}}(\mathcal{X})$ *and* $\overline{apr_{\mathcal{S}}}(\mathcal{X})$, *respectively. Furthermore, the soft positive, soft negative and soft boundary areas of* $\mathcal{X}$ *are*
$Pos_{\mathcal{S}}(\mathcal{X})=\underline{apr_{\mathcal{S}}}(\mathcal{X})$
$Neg_{\mathcal{S}}(\mathcal{X})=\mathbb{U}-\overline{apr_{\mathcal{S}}}(\mathcal{X})$
$Bnd_{\mathcal{S}}(\mathcal{X})=\overline{apr_{\mathcal{S}}}(\mathcal{X})-\underline{apr_{\mathcal{S}}}(\mathcal{X})$, *respectively.*
If $\overline{apr_{\mathcal{S}}}(\mathcal{X})\neq\underline{apr_{\mathcal{S}}}(\mathcal{X})$, $\mathcal{X}$ *is said to be soft-rough* ($\mathcal{S.R.}$) *set, otherwise it is called soft definable.*

Definition 7.3 *[15] Let* $\mathcal{T}=(\mathcal{F},\mathbb{A})$ *be a soft set with the soft approximation space* $\mathcal{S}=(\mathbb{U},\mathcal{T})$. *Let* $\mathcal{X}$ *be a* $\mathcal{S.R.}$ *set with the soft positive* ($Pos_{\mathcal{S}}(\mathcal{X})$), *soft negative* ($Neg_{\mathcal{S}}(\mathcal{X})$) *and soft boundary* ($Bnd_{\mathcal{S}}(\mathcal{X})$) *areas of* $\mathcal{X}$, *respectively. We now define a special function* $C_{Sr}:\mathbb{U}\to\{0,0.5,1\}$ *in this* $\mathcal{S.R.}$ *set as follows:*

$$C_{Sr}=\begin{cases}1, & if\ \upsilon\in Pos_{\mathcal{S}}(\mathcal{X})\\ 0, & if\ \upsilon\in Neg_{\mathcal{S}}(\mathcal{X})\\ 0.5, & if\ \upsilon\in Bnd_{\mathcal{S}}(\mathcal{X})\end{cases}$$

The elements of $\mathcal{S.R.}$ *matrix is a elements of* C_{Sr}.

Definition 7.4 *[4] Let* $\mathbb{U}=\{\upsilon_1,\ldots,\upsilon_n\}$ *and* $\mathbb{E}=\{e_1,\ldots,e_m\}$ *be the universe and the parameter set, respectively. The set of ordered pairs* $\{(\upsilon_i,\tilde{\mathcal{F}}(\upsilon_i)):\upsilon_i\in\mathbb{U},\tilde{\mathcal{F}}(\upsilon_i)\in\mathcal{P}(\mathbb{E})\}$ *is called an inverse soft set on* $\mathbb{U}$ *where* $\tilde{\mathcal{F}}:\mathbb{U}\to\mathcal{P}(\mathbb{E})$.

Definition 7.5 *[3] Let an inverse soft approximation space be* $i.\mathcal{S}=(\mathcal{T}_1,\mathbb{U})$. *Then we define two different operations based on* $i.\mathcal{S}$ *as follows:*

$$\underline{apr_{i.\mathcal{S}}}(\mathcal{X})=\{a\in\tilde{\mathcal{F}}:\exists\upsilon\in\mathbb{U},\mathcal{E}\in\tilde{\mathcal{F}}(\upsilon),\tilde{\mathcal{F}}(\upsilon)\subseteq\mathcal{X}\}$$
$$\overline{apr_{i.\mathcal{S}}}(\mathcal{X})=\{a\in\tilde{\mathcal{F}}:\exists\upsilon\in\mathbb{U},\mathcal{E}\in\tilde{\mathcal{F}}(\upsilon),\tilde{\mathcal{F}}(\upsilon)\cap\mathcal{X}\neq\phi\}\ where\ \mathcal{E}\in\mathcal{P}(\mathbb{E}).$$

Allocating to each $\mathcal{X}\subseteq\mathcal{P}(\mathbb{E})$, *two sets lower and upper inverse* $\mathcal{S.R.}$ *approximations of* $\mathcal{X}$ *in* $\mathcal{S}$ *are denotes* $\underline{apr_{i.\mathcal{S}}}(\mathcal{X})$ *and* $\overline{apr_{i.\mathcal{S}}}(\mathcal{X})$, *respectively. Furthermore, the inverse soft positive, inverse soft negative and inverse soft boundary areas of* $\mathcal{X}$ *are*

$Pos_{i.\mathcal{S}}(\mathcal{X}) = \underline{apr_{i.\mathcal{S}}}(\mathcal{X})$
$Neg_{i.\mathcal{S}}(\mathcal{X}) = \mathcal{P}(\mathbb{E}) - \overline{apr_{i.\mathcal{S}}}(\mathcal{X})$
$Bnd_{i.\mathcal{S}}(\mathcal{X}) = \overline{apr_{i.\mathcal{S}}}(\mathcal{X}) - \underline{apr_{i.\mathcal{S}}}(\mathcal{X})$, *respectively.*
If $\overline{apr_{i.\mathcal{S}}}(\mathcal{X}) \neq \underline{apr_{i.\mathcal{S}}}(\mathcal{X})$, $\mathcal{X}$ *is said to be inverse* $\mathcal{S.R.}$ *set, otherwise it is called inverse soft definable.*

7.3 INVERSE SOFT-ROUGH ($\mathcal{S.R.}$) SET AND INVERSE SOFT-ROUGH ($\mathcal{S.R.}$) MATRIX

In this section, we define the notion of an inverse $\mathcal{S.R.}$ set, inverse $\mathcal{S.R.}$ matrix and provide various operations on them with suitable examples.

Definition 7.6 *Let* $\mathcal{X}$ *be an inverse* $\mathcal{S.R.}$ *set. Now we define a special function* $C_{in.Sr} : \mathcal{P}(\mathbb{E}) \to \{0, 0.5, 1\}$ *in this inverse* $\mathcal{S.R.}$ *set as follows:*

$$C_{in.Sr} = \begin{cases} 1, & if\ \mathcal{E} \in Pos_{i.\mathcal{S}}(\mathcal{X}) \\ 0, & if\ \mathcal{E} \in Neg_{i.\mathcal{S}}(\mathcal{X}) \\ 0.5, & if\ \mathcal{E} \in Bnd_{i.\mathcal{S}}(\mathcal{X}) \end{cases}$$

The elements of an inverse $\mathcal{S.R.}$ *matrix is a elements of* $C_{in.Sr}$*(inverse soft-rough set).*

$$\text{That is,} C_{in.Sr} = \begin{bmatrix} c_{11} & \cdots & c_{1n} \\ \vdots & \vdots & \vdots \\ c_{m1} & \cdots & c_{mn} \end{bmatrix}, \text{where} c_{ij} \in C_{in.Sr}.$$

Example 7.1 *Let* $\mathbb{U} = \{\upsilon_1, \upsilon_2, \upsilon_3, \upsilon_4\}$ *and* $\mathbb{E} = \{e_1, e_2, e_3\}$ *be the universe and parameter set, respectively.*
Let $\mathcal{X} = \{\{e_1\}, \{e_2\}, \{e_1, e_2\}, \{e_2, e_3\}, \{e_1, e_2, e_3\}\} \subset \mathcal{P}(\mathbb{E})$, *we have*
$\underline{apr_{i.\mathcal{S}}}(\mathcal{X}) = \{\{e_2\}, \{e_1, e_2\}\}$ *and* $\overline{apr_{i.\mathcal{S}}}(\mathcal{X}) = \{\{e_2\}, \{e_1, e_2\}, \{e_1, e_2, e_3\}\}$.
Also, $Pos_{i.\mathcal{S}}(\mathcal{X}) = \{\{e_2\}, \{e_1, e_2\}\}$
$Neg_{i.\mathcal{S}}(\mathcal{X}) = \{\{e_1\}, \{e_3\}, \{e_1, e_3\}, \{e_2, e_3\}\phi\}$
$Bnd_{i.\mathcal{S}}(\mathcal{X}) = \{\{e_1, e_2, e_3\}\}$.
Therefore, an inverse $\mathcal{S.R.}$ *matrix is*

$$[C_{in.Sr}] = [c_{ij}] = \begin{bmatrix} 0 & 1 & 0 & 1 & 0 & 0 & 0.5 & 0 \\ 0 & 1 & 0 & 1 & 0 & 0 & 0.5 & 0 \\ 0 & 1 & 0 & 1 & 0 & 0 & 0.5 & 0 \\ 0 & 1 & 0 & 1 & 0 & 0 & 0.5 & 0 \end{bmatrix}.$$

Definition 7.7 *Let* $[C_{in.Sr}] = (c_{ij})_{m \times n}$ *and* $[D_{in.Sr}] = (d_{ij})_{m \times n}$ *be inverse* $\mathcal{S.R.}$ *matrices of same order.*
Then the AND operation of inverse $\mathcal{S.R.}$ *matrices is defined by,*
$[C_{in.Sr}] AND [D_{in.Sr}] = [b_{ij}]$ *where* $b_{ij} = min\{c_{ij}, d_{ij}\}$ *for all i and j.*

Example 7.2 *Let* $\mathbb{U} = \{\upsilon_1, \upsilon_2, \upsilon_3, \upsilon_4\}$ *and* $\mathbb{E} = \{e_1, e_2, e_3\}$ *are the universe and parameter set, respectively. Consider two inverse* $\mathcal{S.R.}$ *matrices*

$$[C_{in.Sr}] = \begin{bmatrix} 0 & 1 & 0 & 1 & 0 & 0 & 0.5 & 0 \\ 0 & 1 & 0 & 1 & 0 & 0 & 0.5 & 0 \\ 0 & 1 & 0 & 1 & 0 & 0 & 0.5 & 0 \\ 0 & 1 & 0 & 1 & 0 & 0 & 0.5 & 0 \end{bmatrix} \text{ and}$$

$$[D_{in.Sr}] = \begin{bmatrix} 0.5 & 1 & 0 & 0.5 & 1 & 0 & 0.5 & 0 \\ 0.5 & 1 & 0 & 0.5 & 1 & 0 & 0.5 & 0 \\ 0.5 & 1 & 0 & 0.5 & 1 & 0 & 0.5 & 0 \\ 0.5 & 1 & 0 & 0.5 & 1 & 0 & 0.5 & 0 \end{bmatrix}$$

$$\text{Then } [C_{in.Sr}]AND[D_{in.Sr}] = \begin{bmatrix} 0 & 1 & 0 & 0.5 & 0 & 0 & 0.5 & 0 \\ 0 & 1 & 0 & 0.5 & 0 & 0 & 0.5 & 0 \\ 0 & 1 & 0 & 0.5 & 0 & 0 & 0.5 & 0 \\ 0 & 1 & 0 & 0.5 & 0 & 0 & 0.5 & 0 \end{bmatrix}.$$

Definition 7.8 *Let $[C_{in.Sr}] = (c_{ij})_{m\times n}$ and $[D_{in.Sr}] = (d_{ij})_{m\times n}$ be inverse $\mathcal{S}.\mathcal{R}.$ matrices of same order.*
Then the OR operation of inverse $\mathcal{S}.\mathcal{R}.$ matrices is defined by,
$[C_{in.Sr}]OR[D_{in.Sr}] = [b_{ij}]$ where $b_{ij} = max\{c_{ij}, d_{ij}\}$ for all i and j.

Example 7.3 *Let $\mathbb{U} = \{\upsilon_1, \upsilon_2, \upsilon_3, \upsilon_4\}$ and $\mathbb{E} = \{e_1, e_2, e_3\}$ be the universe and parameter set, respectively. Consider two inverse $\mathcal{S}.\mathcal{R}.$ matrices*

$$[C_{in.Sr}] = \begin{bmatrix} 0 & 1 & 0 & 1 & 0 & 0 & 0.5 & 0 \\ 0 & 1 & 0 & 1 & 0 & 0 & 0.5 & 0 \\ 0 & 1 & 0 & 1 & 0 & 0 & 0.5 & 0 \\ 0 & 1 & 0 & 1 & 0 & 0 & 0.5 & 0 \end{bmatrix} \text{ and}$$

$$[D_{in.Sr}] = \begin{bmatrix} 0.5 & 1 & 0 & 0.5 & 1 & 0 & 0.5 & 0 \\ 0.5 & 1 & 0 & 0.5 & 1 & 0 & 0.5 & 0 \\ 0.5 & 1 & 0 & 0.5 & 1 & 0 & 0.5 & 0 \\ 0.5 & 1 & 0 & 0.5 & 1 & 0 & 0.5 & 0 \end{bmatrix}$$

$$\text{Then } [C_{in.Sr}]OR[D_{in.Sr}] = \begin{bmatrix} 0.5 & 1 & 0 & 1 & 1 & 0 & 0.5 & 0 \\ 0.5 & 1 & 0 & 1 & 1 & 0 & 0.5 & 0 \\ 0.5 & 1 & 0 & 1 & 1 & 0 & 0.5 & 0 \\ 0.5 & 1 & 0 & 1 & 1 & 0 & 0.5 & 0 \end{bmatrix}.$$

Definition 7.9 *Let $[C_{in.Sr}] = (c_{ij})_{m\times n}$ be inverse $\mathcal{S}.\mathcal{R}.$ matrix. The complement of an inverse $\mathcal{S}.\mathcal{R}.$ matrix $[C_{in.Sr}]$ is $[C_{in.Sr}]^c = [b_{ij}]$ where $b_{ij} = 1 - c_{ij}$ for all i and j.*

Example 7.4 *Let $\mathbb{U} = \{\upsilon_1, \upsilon_2, \upsilon_3, \upsilon_4\}$ and $\mathbb{E} = \{e_1, e_2, e_3\}$ be the universe and parameter set, respectively. Consider the inverse $\mathcal{S}.\mathcal{R}.$ matrix*

$$C_{in.Sr} = \begin{bmatrix} 0 & 1 & 0 & 1 & 0 & 0 & 0.5 & 0 \\ 0 & 1 & 0 & 1 & 0 & 0 & 0.5 & 0 \\ 0 & 1 & 0 & 1 & 0 & 0 & 0.5 & 0 \\ 0 & 1 & 0 & 1 & 0 & 0 & 0.5 & 0 \end{bmatrix}$$

$$Then\ [C_{in.Sr}]^c = \begin{bmatrix} 1 & 0 & 0 & 0 & 1 & 1 & 0.5 & 1 \\ 1 & 0 & 0 & 0 & 1 & 1 & 0.5 & 1 \\ 1 & 0 & 0 & 0 & 1 & 1 & 0.5 & 1 \\ 1 & 0 & 0 & 0 & 1 & 1 & 0.5 & 1 \end{bmatrix}.$$

7.4 MCDM ON INVERSE $\mathcal{S}.\mathcal{R}.$ MATRIX

This section begins with an algorithm for making multi-criteria decision for $\mathcal{S}.\mathcal{R}.$ matrices using the AHP technique. The algorithm is explained by a suitable example.

7.4.1 ALGORITHM

Decision-making model in inverse $\mathcal{S}.\mathcal{R}.$ matrices using the notion of the Max-Min decision-making algorithm is as follows:

Step 1: Making the comparison matrices in AHP.
Step 2: Identify the possible subsets of the parameter set and also inverse soft set.
Step 3: Produce $\overline{apr_{i.\mathcal{S}}}(\mathcal{X})$ *and* $\underline{apr_{i.\mathcal{S}}}(\mathcal{X})$.
Step 4: Compute $Pos_{i.\mathcal{S}}(\mathcal{X}), Neg_{i.\mathcal{S}}(\mathcal{X})$ *and* $Bnd_{i.\mathcal{S}}(\mathcal{X})$.
Step 5: Find the inverse $\mathcal{S}.\mathcal{R}.$ matrices.
Step 6: Using the AHP procedure, calculate the weightiness of criteria by each decision creator.
Step 7: With the help of weightiness of criteria, calculate the values for every alternative and build the inverse $\mathcal{S}.\mathcal{R}.$ matrices.
Step 8: Obtain the Max-Min decision matrix.
Step 9: Determine the optimal set of $\mathcal{P}(\mathbb{E})$.

Example 7.5 *Let* $U = \{\upsilon_1, \upsilon_2, \upsilon_3, \upsilon_4, \upsilon_5, \upsilon_6, \upsilon_7, \upsilon_8\}$ *be the set of satellites launched from different countries in the entire world for gathering information in various domains of the corresponding countries to Moon. Observations of satellites consist of parameters, given by*
$\mathbb{E} = \{weather, security, web\} = \{e_1, e_2, e_3\}$.
The parameter set is given by
$\mathcal{P}(\mathbb{E}) = \{\phi, \{e_1\}, \{e_2\}, \{e_3\}, \{e_1, e_2\}, \{e_2, e_3\}, \{e_1, e_3\}, \{e_1, e_2, e_3\}\}$.

Step 1: *Using Saaty's nine-point scale, the decision makers A, B and C have to evaluate matrix for each criterion and they are constructed via pairwise comparison given below.*

$$A = \begin{bmatrix} 1 & 1/3 & 1/5 & 6 & 1/8 & 3 & 1/4 & 1/9 \\ 3 & 1 & 2 & 2 & 1/3 & 1/6 & 1/6 & 7 \\ 5 & 1/2 & 1 & 1/9 & 4 & 1/5 & 2 & 3 \\ 1/6 & 1/2 & 9 & 1 & 3 & 3 & 1/7 & 1/5 \\ 8 & 3 & 1/4 & 1/3 & 1 & 2 & 9 & 1/6 \\ 1/3 & 6 & 5 & 1/3 & 1/2 & 1 & 3 & 7 \\ 4 & 6 & 1/2 & 7 & 1/9 & 1/3 & 1 & 8 \\ 9 & 1/7 & 1/3 & 5 & 6 & 1/7 & 1/8 & 1 \end{bmatrix}$$

$$B = \begin{bmatrix} 1 & 9 & 1/4 & 1/2 & 6 & 7 & 7 & 4 \\ 1/9 & 1 & 1/2 & 3 & 1/5 & 1/3 & 1/2 & 1/6 \\ 4 & 2 & 1 & 7 & 3 & 1/5 & 1/8 & 9 \\ 2 & 1/3 & 1/7 & 1 & 1/6 & 9 & 7 & 1/3 \\ 1/6 & 5 & 1/3 & 6 & 1 & 1/5 & 1/4 & 2 \\ 1/7 & 3 & 5 & 1/9 & 5 & 1 & 1/2 & 7 \\ 1/7 & 2 & 8 & 1/7 & 4 & 2 & 1 & 8 \\ 1/4 & 6 & 1/9 & 3 & 1/2 & 1/7 & 1/8 & 1 \end{bmatrix}$$

$$\text{and } C = \begin{bmatrix} 1 & 2 & 2 & 1/3 & 1/3 & 4 & 7 & 3 \\ 1/2 & 1 & 3 & 5 & 1/7 & 1/2 & 1/4 & 8 \\ 1/2 & 1/3 & 1 & 2 & 6 & 6 & 1/3 & 1/5 \\ 3 & 1/5 & 1/2 & 1 & 1/4 & 1/5 & 5 & 5 \\ 3 & 7 & 1/6 & 4 & 1 & 2 & 2 & 1/7 \\ 1/4 & 2 & 1/6 & 5 & 1/2 & 1 & 4 & 1/8 \\ 1/7 & 4 & 3 & 1/5 & 1/2 & 1/4 & 1 & 9 \\ 1/3 & 1/8 & 5 & 1/5 & 7 & 8 & 1/9 & 1 \end{bmatrix}$$

Step 2: *Suppose the countries $\mathcal{X}$, $\mathcal{Y}$ and $\mathcal{Z}$ together receives message regarding parameters from satellite. $A \subseteq \mathcal{P}(\mathbb{E}), B \subseteq \mathcal{P}(\mathbb{E}) and C \subseteq \mathcal{P}(\mathbb{E})$. Let the inverse soft sets $(\tilde{\mathcal{F}},A),(\tilde{\mathcal{F}},B) and (\tilde{\mathcal{F}},C)$ be the evaluations of countries $\mathcal{X}$, $\mathcal{Y}$ and $\mathcal{Z}$.*

Step 3: *For $\mathcal{X} = \{\{e_1\},\{e_2\},\{e_1,e_2\},\{e_2,e_3\},\{e_1,e_2,e_3\}\} \subset \mathcal{P}(\mathbb{E})$, we have $\underline{apr_{i.\mathcal{S}}}(\mathcal{X}) = \{\{e_2\},\{e_1,e_2\}\}$ and $\overline{apr_{i.\mathcal{S}}}(\mathcal{X}) = \{\{e_2\},\{e_1,e_2\},\{e_1,e_2,e_3\}\}$.*
For $\mathcal{Y} = \{\{e_2\},\{e_3\},\{e_1,e_2\},\{e_1,e_3\},\{e_1,e_2,e_3\}\} \subset \mathcal{P}(\mathbb{E})$, we have $\underline{apr_{i.\mathcal{S}}}(\mathcal{Y}) = \{e_1,e_3\}\}$ and $\overline{apr_{i.\mathcal{S}}}(\mathcal{Y}) = \{\{e_3\},\{e_1,e_3\},\{e_1,e_2,e_3\}\}$.
For $\mathcal{Z} = \{\{e_1\},\{e_2\},\{e_1,e_2\},\{e_2,e_3\},\{e_1,e_3\},\{e_1,e_2,e_3\}\} \subset \mathcal{P}(\mathbb{E})$, we have $\underline{apr_{i.\mathcal{S}}}(\mathcal{Z}) = \{\{e_3\},\{e_2,e_3\}\}$ and $\overline{apr_{i.\mathcal{S}}}(\mathcal{Z}) = \{\{e_1\},\{e_2\},\{e_3\},\{e_2,e_3\},\{e_1,e_2,e_3\}\}$.

Step 4: *We have, $Pos_{i.\mathcal{S}}(\mathcal{X}) = \{\{e_2\},\{e_1,e_2\}\}$*
$Neg_{i.\mathcal{S}}(\mathcal{X}) = \{\{e_1\},\{e_3\},\{e_1,e_3\},\{e_2,e_3\},\phi\}$
and $Bnd_{i.\mathcal{S}}(\mathcal{X}) = \{\{e_1,e_2,e_3\}\}$.
Similarly, $Pos_{i.\mathcal{S}}(\mathcal{Y}) = \{\{e_1,e_3\}\}$
$Neg_{i.\mathcal{S}}\mathcal{Y} = \{\{e_1\},\{e_2\},\{e_1,e_2\},\{e_2,e_3\},\phi\}$
and $Bnd_{i.\mathcal{S}}(\mathcal{Y}) = \{\{e_3\},\{e_1,e_2,e_3\}\}$.
$Pos_{i.\mathcal{S}}(\mathcal{Z}) = \{\{e_3\},\{e_1,e_3\}\}$
$Neg_{i.\mathcal{S}}(\mathcal{Z}) = \{\{e_1,e_2\},\{e_1,e_3\},\phi\}$

and $Bnd_{i.\mathcal{S}}(\mathcal{Z}) = \{\{e_1\},\{e_2\},\{e_1,e_2,e_3\}\}$.

Step 5: *The inverse soft-rough matrices of* $(\tilde{\mathcal{F}},A),(\tilde{\mathcal{F}},B)$*and*$(\tilde{\mathcal{F}},C)$ *are*

$$A_{in.Sr} = [a_{ij}] = \begin{bmatrix} 0 & 1 & 0 & 1 & 0 & 0 & 0.5 & 0 \\ 0 & 1 & 0 & 1 & 0 & 0 & 0.5 & 0 \\ 0 & 1 & 0 & 1 & 0 & 0 & 0.5 & 0 \\ 0 & 1 & 0 & 1 & 0 & 0 & 0.5 & 0 \\ 0 & 1 & 0 & 1 & 0 & 0 & 0.5 & 0 \\ 0 & 1 & 0 & 1 & 0 & 0 & 0.5 & 0 \\ 0 & 1 & 0 & 1 & 0 & 0 & 0.5 & 0 \\ 0 & 1 & 0 & 1 & 0 & 0 & 0.5 & 0 \end{bmatrix}$$

$$B_{in.Sr} = [b_{ij}] = \begin{bmatrix} 0 & 0 & 0.5 & 0 & 0 & 1 & 0.5 & 0 \\ 0 & 0 & 0.5 & 0 & 0 & 1 & 0.5 & 0 \\ 0 & 0 & 0.5 & 0 & 0 & 1 & 0.5 & 0 \\ 0 & 0 & 0.5 & 0 & 0 & 1 & 0.5 & 0 \\ 0 & 0 & 0.5 & 0 & 0 & 1 & 0.5 & 0 \\ 0 & 0 & 0.5 & 0 & 0 & 1 & 0.5 & 0 \\ 0 & 0 & 0.5 & 0 & 0 & 1 & 0.5 & 0 \\ 0 & 0 & 0.5 & 0 & 0 & 1 & 0.5 & 0 \end{bmatrix}$$

$$C_{in.Sr} = [c_{ij}] = \begin{bmatrix} 0.5 & 0.5 & 0 & 0 & 1 & 0 & 0.5 & 0 \\ 0.5 & 0.5 & 0 & 0 & 1 & 0 & 0.5 & 0 \\ 0.5 & 0.5 & 0 & 0 & 1 & 0 & 0.5 & 0 \\ 0.5 & 0.5 & 0 & 0 & 1 & 0 & 0.5 & 0 \\ 0.5 & 0.5 & 0 & 0 & 1 & 0 & 0.5 & 0 \\ 0.5 & 0.5 & 0 & 0 & 1 & 0 & 0.5 & 0 \\ 0.5 & 0.5 & 0 & 0 & 1 & 0 & 0.5 & 0 \\ 0.5 & 0.5 & 0 & 0 & 1 & 0 & 0.5 & 0 \end{bmatrix}$$

Step 6: *Using the AHP tool, the weight of each criterion is obtained as:*
$[\mathcal{W}_A] = \{0.0838, 0.0903, 0.1006, 0.1941, 0.1443, 0.1452, 0.1143, 0.1274\}^T$
$[\mathcal{W}_B] = \{0.2114, 0.0361, 0.1799, 0.1527, 0.0810, 0.1263, 0.1542, 0.0584\}^T$
$[\mathcal{W}_C] = \{0.1326, 0.1185, 0.1171, 0.1142, 0.1578, 0.0909, 0.1130, 0.1559\}^T$

Step 7: Multiplying each parameter with weightiness of criterion for each decision creator, we have

$$[[A_{in.Sr}] \times [\mathcal{W}_A]] = [\widehat{a}_{ij}] = \begin{bmatrix} 0 & 0.0838 & 0 & 0.0838 & 0 & 0 & 0.0419 & 0 \\ 0 & 0.0903 & 0 & 0.0903 & 0 & 0 & 0.0451 & 0 \\ 0 & 0.1006 & 0 & 0.1006 & 0 & 0 & 0.0503 & 0 \\ 0 & 0.1941 & 0 & 0.1941 & 0 & 0 & 0.0971 & 0 \\ 0 & 0.1443 & 0 & 0.1443 & 0 & 0 & 0.0722 & 0 \\ 0 & 0.1452 & 0 & 0.1452 & 0 & 0 & 0.0726 & 0 \\ 0 & 0.1143 & 0 & 0.1143 & 0 & 0 & 0.0571 & 0 \\ 0 & 0.1274 & 0 & 0.1274 & 0 & 0 & 0.0637 & 0 \end{bmatrix}$$

$$[[B_{in.Sr}] \times [\mathcal{W}_B]] = [\widehat{b}_{ij}] = \begin{bmatrix} 0 & 0 & 0.1057 & 0 & 0 & 0.2114 & 0.1057 & 0 \\ 0 & 0 & 0.0181 & 0 & 0 & 0.0361 & 0.0181 & 0 \\ 0 & 0 & 0.0900 & 0 & 0 & 0.1799 & 0.0900 & 0 \\ 0 & 0 & 0.0763 & 0 & 0 & 0.1527 & 0.0763 & 0 \\ 0 & 0 & 0.0405 & 0 & 0 & 0.0810 & 0.0405 & 0 \\ 0 & 0 & 0.0631 & 0 & 0 & 0.1263 & 0.0631 & 0 \\ 0 & 0 & 0.0771 & 0 & 0 & 0.1542 & 0.0771 & 0 \\ 0 & 0 & 0.0292 & 0 & 0 & 0.0584 & 0.0292 & 0 \end{bmatrix}$$

$$[[C_{in.Sr}] \times [\mathcal{W}_C]] = [\widehat{c}_{ij}] = \begin{bmatrix} 0.0663 & 0.0663 & 0.1326 & 0 & 0.1326 & 0 & 0.0663 & 0 \\ 0.0593 & 0.0593 & 0.1185 & 0 & 0.1185 & 0 & 0.0593 & 0 \\ 0.0586 & 0.0586 & 0.1171 & 0 & 0.1171 & 0 & 0.0586 & 0 \\ 0.0571 & 0.0571 & 0.1142 & 0 & 0.1142 & 0 & 0.0571 & 0 \\ 0.0789 & 0.0789 & 0.1578 & 0 & 0.1578 & 0 & 0.0789 & 0 \\ 0.0454 & 0.0454 & 0.0909 & 0 & 0.0909 & 0 & 0.0454 & 0 \\ 0.0565 & 0.0565 & 0.1130 & 0 & 0.1130 & 0 & 0.0565 & 0 \\ 0.0779 & 0.0779 & 0.1559 & 0 & 0.1559 & 0 & 0.0779 & 0 \end{bmatrix}$$

Step 8: *Computation of Max-Min decision matrix is as follows:*

$$min\{[\widehat{a}_{ij}], [\widehat{b}_{ij}][\widehat{c}_{ij}]\} = \begin{bmatrix} 0 & 0 & 0 & 0 & 0 & 0 & 0.0419 & 0 \\ 0 & 0 & 0 & 0 & 0 & 0 & 0.0181 & 0 \\ 0 & 0 & 0 & 0 & 0 & 0 & 0.0503 & 0 \\ 0 & 0 & 0 & 0 & 0 & 0 & 0.0571 & 0 \\ 0 & 0 & 0 & 0 & 0 & 0 & 0.0405 & 0 \\ 0 & 0 & 0 & 0 & 0 & 0 & 0.0454 & 0 \\ 0 & 0 & 0 & 0 & 0 & 0 & 0.0565 & 0 \\ 0 & 0 & 0 & 0 & 0 & 0 & 0.0292 & 0 \end{bmatrix}$$

$$Max\left\{min\{[\widehat{a}_{ij}], [\widehat{b}_{ij}], [\widehat{c}_{ij}]\}\right\} = \{\{e_1, e_2, e_3\}\}.$$

Step 9: *Finally the optimal choice of the countries $\mathcal{X}$, $\mathcal{Y}$ and $\mathcal{Z}$ together receives the messages from all satellites regarding all the parameters like weather, security, web details. Since all the countries are expected to take the preventive measure for individual growth.*

7.5 CONCLUSION

As an inspiration received from inverse soft set and inverse $\mathcal{S}.\mathcal{R}.$ set, we have introduced the novel ideal of inverse $\mathcal{S}.\mathcal{R}.$ matrix theory with suitable examples. We have developed various operations between inverse soft-rough matrices like AND, OR, and complement operations. We have also provided the decision theory on inverse $\mathcal{S}.\mathcal{R}.$ matrix using the AHP technique. Keeping future research directions in mind, we further plan to extend this idea to fuzzy setting and neutrosophic setting.

Bibliography

1. Bustince, H., & Burillo, P. (1996). Vague sets are intuitionistic fuzzy sets. *Fuzzy Sets Syst., 79*(3), 403–405.
2. Cağman, N., & Enginoğlu, S. (2010). Soft matrix theory and its decision-making. *Comput. Math. Appl., 59*(10), 3308–3314.
3. Demirtas, N., Hussain, S., & Dalkilic, O. (2020). New approaches of inverse soft rough sets and their applications in a decision making problem. *J. Appl. Math. Inform., 38*(3–4), 335–349.
4. Kamacı, H., Saltık, K., Fulya Akız, H., & Osman Atagun, A. (2018). Cardinality inverse soft matrix theory and its applications in multicriteria group decision making. *J. Intell. Fuzzy Syst., 34*(3), 2031–2049.
5. Maji, P. K., Roy, A. R., & Biswas, R. (2002). An application of soft sets in a decision making problem. *Comput. Math. Appl., 44*(8–9), 1077–1083.
6. Molodtsov, D. (1999). Soft set theory—first results. *Comput. Math. Appl., 37*(4–5), 19–31.
7. Pawlak, Z. (1982). Rough sets. *Int. J. Inf. Sci. Comput., 11*(5), 341–356.
8. Petchimuthu, S., & Kamacı, H. (2019). The row-products of inverse soft matrices in multicriteria decision making. *J. Intell. Fuzzy Syst., 36*(6), 6425–6441.
9. Razak, S. A., & Mohamad, D. (2011). A soft set based group decision making method with criteria weight. *Int. J. Math. Comput. Sci., 5*(10), 1641–1646.
10. Riaz, M., Davvaz, B., Firdous, A., & Fakhar, A. (2019). Novel concepts of soft rough set topology with applications. *J. Intell. Fuzzy Syst., 36*(4), 3579–3590.
11. Saaty, T. L. (2008). Decision making with the analytic hierarchy process. *Int. J. Serv. Sci., 1*(1), 83–98.
12. Vijayabalaji, S., & Ramesh, A. (2013). A new decision making theory in soft matrices. *Int. J. Pure. Appl. Math., 86*(6), 927–939.
13. Vijayabalaji, S., & Balaji, P. (2013). Rough matrix theory and its decision making. *Int. J. Pure. Appl. Math., 87*(6), 845–853.
14. Vijayabalaji, S. (2013). Soft-rough matrices and its applications in decision making. *Abstract Published in the Proceedings of the International Conference on Facets of Uncertainties and Applications*, December 5–7, India.
15. Vijayabalaji, S. (2014). Multi decision making in generalized soft-rough matrices. *Math. Sci. Int. Res. J., 3*(1), 19–24.

8 New Observations on Lacunary $\mathcal{I}$-Invariant Convergence for Sequences in Fuzzy Cone Normed Spaces

Ömer Kisi
Bartın University

Mehmet Gürdal
Suleyman Demirel University

Erhan Güler
Bartın University

CONTENTS

8.1 Introduction 107
8.1.1 Background 108
8.1.2 Main Goal 109
8.2 Basic Definitions 109
8.3 Prime Results of the Chapter 110
8.3.1 Essential Definitions 111
8.3.2 Main Results 112
8.4 Conclusion 122
Bibliography 122

8.1 INTRODUCTION

In mathematical analysis, the notion of fuzzy cone normed linear space (FCNS in short) is introduced in a different approach, which generalizes the concept of fuzzy normed linear space. It has been observed that fuzzy normed linear space is a special case of FCNS. In FCNS, the range of fuzzy cone norm is considered for ordering fuzzy real numbers determined on a real fuzzy Banach space. It is seen that Felbin's

DOI: 10.1201/9781003312017-8

type (max, min) fuzzy normed linear space is a particular case of fuzzy cone normed linear space. There is a wide scope of development in future in the field of fuzzy functional analysis.

8.1.1 BACKGROUND

Fuzzy set theory is an advancement on the mathematical foundations of the classical set theory, initiated by Zadeh [52] in 1965. Fuzziness can be utilized in a comprehensive variety of real life problems. Since the inception of fuzzy sets, researchers have worked on this and developed new concepts in the context of topology and analysis. The concept of a fuzzy norm (FN) on a linear space was presented by Katsaras [19]. Felbin [12] proposed the concept of a fuzzy norm whose associated metric is of Kaleva and Seikkala [17] type.

The idea of cone metric space which is a generalization of metric space was investigated by Huang and Zhang [29] by replacing the range of metric with an ordered real Banach space. They obtained some fixed point theorems on contractive mappings on such spaces. The notion of FCNS was studied by Bag [1] which generalizes the corresponding notion of Felbin [12] type FN. Meaningful results on this topic were examined in Ref. [3,31,38]. In the study [48], the concept of FCNS was introduced with a different approach, and some significant results on finite dimensional FCNS were established.

Güler [15] generalized FN by taking ordered Banach space in place of $\mathbb{R}^+$ in the description of FN which was investigated by Lael and Nourouzi [28]. In Ref. [15], the notions of $\mathcal{I}$-convergence and $\mathcal{I}^*$-convergence in FCNS were worked. Also, $\mathcal{I}$-cluster points and $\mathcal{I}$-limit points of sequences in FCNS were examined.

The notion of statistical convergence was studied initially by Fast [11]. Some significant works on this can be found in Refs. [19,32,39–41,43]. Fridy and Orhan [13] gave the definition of lacunary statistical convergence by using lacunary sequence. The notion of $\mathcal{I}$-convergence as a generalization of the usual convergence was established in Ref. [24]. In addition, Kostyrko et al. [24] investigated $\mathcal{I}$-limit points and $\mathcal{I}$-cluster points of sequences and obtained some topological features of these concepts.

Nabiev et al. [36] presented the idea of $\mathcal{I}$-Cauchy and $\mathcal{I}^*$-Cauchy sequence. Ideal convergence in fuzzy normed spaces was first examined by Kumar and Kumar [25]. $\mathcal{I}$-convergence for sequences of fuzzy numbers was investigated by Kumar and Kumar [26]. Moreover, the concept of $\mathcal{I}$-convergence of sequences was studied in 2-normed linear spaces by Gürdal [26] and in intuitionistic fuzzy normed spaces by Kumar and Kumar [28]. Yamancı and Gürdal [51] examined lacunary ideal convergence in random n-normed space. Later on, Tripathy et al. [49] worked $\mathcal{I}$-lacunary convergent sequences. For further information on sequence spaces and fuzzy valued sequences, readers should refer to the monographs [2] and [35], as well as recent publications [4–10,16,20,21–23,45–47].

Following the works of [33,38,49], invariant convergence became a notable topic in mathematical analysis. Nuray et al. [37] investigated $\mathcal{I}_\sigma$-convergence with the aid of σ-uniform density. Mursaleen [34] presented the opinion of strongly σ-convergence. Savas and Nuray [42] put forward to σ-statistical convergence and lacunary σ-statistical convergence. Nuray and Ulusu [50] examined lacunary $\mathcal{I}$-invariant convergence and lacunary $\mathcal{I}$-invariant Cauchy sequence.

This chapter consists of two sections with the new conclusions in Section 8.2. In Section 8.2, the notions of lacunary invariant convergence, lacunary $\mathcal{I}$-invariant convergence, $\mathcal{I}$-invariant statistical convergence, lacunary $\mathcal{I}$-invariant statistical convergence of sequences in FNCS, $\mathcal{I}_{\sigma\theta}$-limit points and $\mathcal{I}_{\sigma\theta}$-cluster points of sequences in FCNS are examined. In addition, $\mathcal{I}_{\sigma\theta}$-Cauchy and $\mathcal{I}^*_{\sigma\theta}$-Cauchy sequences in FCNS are presented, and their fundamental features are worked.

8.1.2 MAIN GOAL

The main goal of this chapter is to examine some recent developments in FCNS and its applications. More recently, features of FCNS and some convergence types for ordinary (single) sequences in FCNS have been carried out. First, we introduce the concepts of lacunary $\mathcal{I}$-invariant convergence, $\mathcal{I}$-invariant statistical convergence, lacunary $\mathcal{I}$-invariant statistical convergence for sequences in FCNS. Then, $\mathcal{I}_{\sigma\theta}$-limit points and $\mathcal{I}_{\sigma\theta}$-cluster points of sequences in FCNS are examined. In addition, $\mathcal{I}_{\sigma\theta}$-Cauchy and $\mathcal{I}^*_{\sigma\theta}$-Cauchy sequences in FCNS are presented. In FCNS, we establish several properties of new types of convergences and prove some related theorems.

8.2 BASIC DEFINITIONS

This section covers some fundamental and important definitions that will be used throughout the chapter.

Definition 8.1 *[16] Suppose that E is a real Banach space and $P \subseteq E$. Then, P is called a cone provided that*

(a) $P \neq \{\theta_E\}$, P is non-empty and closed;
(b) $u,v \in R$, $u,v > 0$, $t,w \in P \Rightarrow ut + vw \in P$;
(c) $t \in P$, $-t \in P \Rightarrow t = \theta_E$.

For a cone $P \subseteq E$, a partial ordering $\preceq$ in the context of P is determined by $q \preceq r$ iff $r - q \in P$, $q \prec r$ will stand for $q \preceq r$ and $q \neq r$ while $q \ll r$ will stand for $r - q \in \operatorname{int}(P)$, where $int(P)$ symbolizes the set of the interior points of P.

The sets of the form $[q,r]$ are named order-intervals and are identified as the subsequent:

$$[q,r] = \{z \in E : q \preceq z \preceq r\}.$$

It is emphasized that *order-intervals* are convex. If $[q,r] \subset A$ when $q,r \in A$ and $q \preceq r$, then $A \subset E$ is named *order-convex.* When ordered topological vector space (E,P) has a neighborhoods' base of θ that consist of *order-convex* sets then, it is order-convex. At this point, the cone P is known as a normal cone. Contemplating the normed space, this situation comes to mean that the unit ball is *order-convex,* it is identical to the situation that $\exists K$ such that $q,r \in E$ and $\theta \preceq q \preceq r \Rightarrow \|q\| \leq K\|r\|$.

If K is the smallest constant, it is known as normal constant of P. When each one of the increasing bounded sequence is convergent, then we describe P as a regular cone. Namely, when there is a sequence $\{q_n\}$ such that

$$q_1 \preceq q_2 \preceq \ldots \preceq q_n \preceq \ldots \preceq r,$$

for some $r \in E$, then $\exists q \in E$ such that $\lim_{n\to\infty} \|q_n - q\| = 0$. Identically the cone P is regular if each decreasing sequence which is bounded from below is convergent. We know that if P is regular cone then it is normal cone. In this chapter, we presume that all cones have non-empty interior.

Triangular norms (t-norms) (TN) were investigated by Menger [30]. In metric space concepts, TNs are used to generalize with the probability distribution of triangle inequality. Triangular conorms (t-conorms) (TC) identified as dual operations of TNs. TNs and TCs are significant for fuzzy operations.

Definition 8.2 *[48] Take V as a linear space over the field K and assume that E be a real Banach space with cone P. Let $*$ be a t-norm. Then, a fuzzy subset $N_C : V \times E \to [0,1]$ is called to be a FCN, if*

$(FCN1)$ $\forall\, z \in E$ with $z \preceq \theta_E, N_C(t,z) = 0$;
$(FCN2)$ $\forall\, \theta_E \prec z, N_C(t,z) = 1 \Leftrightarrow t = \theta_V$ (θ_V shows the zero element of V)
$(FCN3)$ $\forall\, \theta_E \prec z, N_C(kt,z) = N_C\left(t, \frac{z}{|k|}\right)$ for all $0 \neq k \in K$;
$(FCN4)$ $\forall\, t,p \in V$ and $z,q \in E, N_C(t,z) * N_C(p,q) \leq N_C(t+p, z+q)$;
$(FCN5)$ $\lim_{\|z\|\to\infty} N_C(t,z) = 1$.

Then, $(V, N_C, *)$ is called to be a fuzzy cone normed linear space with regards to (w.r.t.) E.

Definition 8.3 *[48] Let $(V, N_C, *)$ be a FCNS, $\eta \in V$ and (t_w) be a sequence in V. Then, (t_w) is named to be convergent to η, if for any $z \in E$ with $\theta_E \prec z$ and $\xi \in (0,1)$, $\exists$ a $w_0 \in \mathbb{N}$ such that*

$$N_C(t_w - \eta, z) > 1 - \xi,$$

$\forall w > w_0$ and $\theta_E \prec z$. We indicate this by $N_C - \lim_{w\to\infty} t_w = \xi$.

Definition 8.4 *[48] The sequence (t_w) is known as a Cauchy sequence, provided that for any $z \in E$ with $\theta_E \prec z$ and $\xi \in (0,1)$, $\exists$ a $w_0 \in \mathbb{N}$ such that*

$$N_C(t_{w+p} - t_w, m) > 1 - \xi, \ \forall w > w_0,\ p = 1, 2, \ldots.$$

Definition 8.5 *[15] For any $z \succeq \theta$, $\eta \in V$ and $\xi \in (0,1)$,*

$$B_{N_C}(z, \eta, \xi) = \{t \in V : N_C(t - \eta, z) > 1 - \xi\}$$

is named open ball with center η and radius ξ with regards to z.

8.3 PRIME RESULTS OF THE CHAPTER

This section includes the discussion of the main results for this chapter. Initially, we establish some essential definitions in the area of FCNS.

8.3.1 ESSENTIAL DEFINITIONS

Definition 8.6 *A sequence (t_n) in V is named to be lacunary invariant convergent to $\eta \in V$ w.r.t FCN on V, provided that for each $\xi \in (0,1)$ and for any $z \in E$ with $\theta_E \prec z$, there is a $r_1 \in \mathbb{N}$ such that*

$$\frac{1}{h_r}\sum_{n\in I_r} N_C\left(t_{\sigma^n(w)} - \eta, z\right) > 1 - \xi$$

for all $r \geq r_1$ uniformly in w. We write V_σ^θ-$\lim t_n = \eta\,(N_C)$.

Definition 8.7 *A sequence (t_n) is named to be lacunary $\mathcal{I}$-invariant convergent to $\eta \in V$ w.r.t FCN ($\mathcal{I}_{\sigma\theta}$-FCN), provided that for each $\xi \in (0,1)$ and for any $z \in E$ with $\theta_E \prec z$ the set*

$$H(\xi, z) = \{n \in \mathbb{N} : N_C(t_n - \eta, z) \leq 1 - \xi\} \in \mathcal{I}_{\sigma\theta},$$

namely, $V_\theta(H(\xi, z)) = 0$. We write $t_n \to \eta\left(\mathcal{I}_{\sigma\theta}^{N_C}\right)$.

Definition 8.8 *A sequence (t_n) is named to be $\mathcal{I}$-invariant statistical convergent to $\eta \in V$ w.r.t FCN provided that for each $\xi \in (0,1)$, $\gamma > 0$ and for any $z \in E$ with $\theta_E \prec z$ the set*

$$\left\{k \in \mathbb{N} : \frac{1}{k}|\{n \leq k : N_C(t_n - \eta, z) \leq 1 - \xi\}| \geq \gamma\right\} \in \mathcal{I}_\sigma.$$

We write $t_n \to \eta\,(S_{\mathcal{I}_\sigma}(N_C))$.

Definition 8.9 *A sequence (t_n) is named to be lacunary $\mathcal{I}$-invariant statistical convergent to $\eta \in V$ w.r.t FCN provided that for each $\xi \in (0,1)$, $\gamma > 0$ and for any $z \in E$ with $\theta_E \prec z$ the set*

$$\left\{r \in \mathbb{N} : \frac{1}{h_r}|\{n \in I_r : N_C(t_n - \eta, z) \leq 1 - \xi\}| \geq \gamma\right\} \in \mathcal{I}_{\sigma\theta}.$$

We write $t_n \to \eta\left(S_{\mathcal{I}_{\sigma\theta}}(N_C)\right)$.

Definition 8.10 *The sequence (t_n) is named to be $\mathcal{I}_{\sigma\theta}^*$-convergent to η provided that there is a subset*

$$J = \{k_n : k_1 < k_2 < \ldots < k_n < \ldots\} \in \mathcal{F}(\mathcal{I}_{\sigma\theta})$$

such that $N_C - \lim_{n\to\infty} t_{k_n} = \eta\,(N_C)$ for each $z \in E$ with $\theta_E \prec z$. In that case, we denote $\mathcal{I}_{\sigma\theta}^* - \lim t_n = \eta\,(N_C)$.

Definition 8.11 *Let V be an FCNS and take $t = (t_n)$ in V.*
(a) An element $\eta \in V$ is named to be $\mathcal{I}_{\sigma\theta}$-limit point of $t = (t_n)$ if there is set $J = \{p_1 < p_2 < \ldots < p_n < ..\} \subset \mathbb{N}$ such that the set

$$J' = \{r \in \mathbb{N} : p_n \in I_r\} \notin \mathcal{I}_{\sigma\theta}$$

and $N_C - \lim t_{p_n} = \eta\,(N_C)$ *for all* $z \in E$ *with* $\theta_E \prec z$.
(*b*) *An element* $\eta \in V$ *is called to be* $\mathcal{I}_{\sigma\theta}$*-cluster point of* $t = (t_n)$ *if, for any* $z \in E$ *with* $\theta_E \prec z$ *and* $\xi \in (0,1)$, *we get*

$$\{n \in \mathbb{N} : N_C(t_n - \eta, z) > 1 - \xi\} \notin \mathcal{I}_{\sigma\theta}.$$

Definition 8.12 *A sequence* $t = (t_n)$ *is named to be* $\mathcal{I}_{\sigma\theta}$*-Cauchy w.r.t FCN on* V, *provided that, for each* $\xi \in (0,1)$ *and for any* $z \in E$ *with* $\theta_E \prec z$, *there is a* $s = s(\xi) \in \mathbb{N}$ *providing*

$$\{n \in \mathbb{N} : N_C(t_n - t_s, z) \leq 1 - \xi\} \in \mathcal{I}_{\sigma\theta}.$$

Definition 8.13 *A sequence* $t = (t_n)$ *is named to be* $\mathcal{I}^*_{\sigma\theta}$*-Cauchy w.r.t FCN on* V, *provided that there is a subset*

$$J = \left\{k = (k_j) : k_j < k_{j+1},\ j \in \mathbb{N}\right\} \in \mathcal{F}(\mathcal{I}_{\sigma\theta})$$

such that $\lim_{m,l\to\infty} N_C\left(t_{k_m} - t_{k_l}, z\right) = 0$.

Definition 8.14 *A sequence* (t_n) *is named to be lacunary invariant statistical convergent or* $S^\theta_\sigma(N_C)$*-convergent to* η, *provided that for all* $\xi \in (0,1)$, $\gamma > 0$ *and for any* $z \in E$ *with* $\theta_E \prec z$

$$\lim_{r\to\infty} \frac{1}{h_r}\left|\left\{k \in I_r : N_C\left(t_{\sigma^n(w)} - \eta, z\right) \leq 1 - \xi\right\}\right| = 0$$

uniformly in w. *In that case, we indicate* $S^\theta_\sigma - \lim t_n = \eta\,(N_C)$.

8.3.2 MAIN RESULTS

Theorem 8.1 *Let* V *be a FCNS,* $\eta \in V$ *and* (t_n) *be a sequence in* V. *Then,* V^θ_σ*-*$\lim t_n = \eta\,(N_C)$ *supplies iff*

$$\lim_{r\to\infty} \frac{1}{h_r} \sum_{n\in I_r} N_C\left(t_{\sigma^n(w)} - \eta, z\right) = 1, \text{ uniformly in } w,$$

for $\forall z \in E$ *with* $\theta_E \prec z$.

Proof. Assume that V^θ_σ-$\lim t_n = \eta\,(N_C)$. At that time, for any $z \in E$ with $\theta_E \prec z$ and $\xi \in (0,1)$, $\exists$ a $r_1 \in \mathbb{N}$ such that

$$\frac{1}{h_r} \sum_{n\in I_r} N_C\left(t_{\sigma^n(w)} - \eta, z\right) > 1 - \xi$$

for all $r \geq r_1$ uniformly in w. As ξ is arbitrary, it claims that

$$\lim_{r\to\infty} \frac{1}{h_r} \sum_{n\in I_r} N_C\left(t_{\sigma^n(w)} - \eta, z\right) = 1, \forall z \in E \text{ with } \theta_E \prec z.$$

Conversely, presume that

$$\lim_{r\to\infty}\frac{1}{h_r}\sum_{n\in I_r} N_C\left(t_{\sigma^n(w)}-\eta,z\right)=1,\ \forall z\in E \text{ with } \theta_E\prec z.$$

Then, for each $\xi\in(0,1)$, $z\in E$ with $\theta_E\prec z$, $\exists$ a $r_1\in\mathbb{N}$ such that

$$\frac{1}{h_r}\sum_{n\in I_r} N_C\left(t_{\sigma^n(w)}-\eta,z\right)>1-\xi$$

for all $r\geq r_1$ uniformly in w. Thus, V_σ^θ-$\lim t_n=\eta\,(N_C)$. □

Theorem 8.2 *Limit of a lacunary invariant convergent sequence in a FCNS* $(V,N_C,*)$ *is unique, provided* $*$ *is continuous at* $(1,1)$.

Proof. Assume that (t_n) be a lacunary invariant convergent sequence in $(V,N_C,*)$ and $*$ is continuous at $(1,1)$. Presume that V_σ^θ-$\lim t_n=\eta_1\,(N_C)$ and V_σ^θ-$\lim t_n=\eta_2\,(N_C)$, where $\eta_1\neq\eta_2$. Then

$$\lim_{r\to\infty}\frac{1}{h_r}\sum_{n\in I_r} N_C\left(t_{\sigma^n(w)}-\eta_1,z_1\right)=1,\ \forall z_1\in E \text{ with } \theta_E\prec z_1$$

and

$$\lim_{r\to\infty}\frac{1}{h_r}\sum_{n\in I_r} N_C\left(t_{\sigma^n(w)}-\eta_2,z_2\right)=1,\ \forall z_2\in E \text{ with } \theta_E\prec z_2,$$

uniformly in w. Now,

$$\begin{aligned} N_C(\eta_1-\eta_2,z_1+z_2) &= N_C\left(\eta_1-t_{\sigma^n(w)}+t_{\sigma^n(w)}-\eta_2,z_1+z_2\right)\\ &\geq N_C\left(\eta_1-t_{\sigma^n(w)},z_1\right)*N_C\left(t_{\sigma^n(w)}-\eta_2,z_2\right)\\ &= N_C\left(t_{\sigma^n(w)}-\eta_1,z_1\right)*N_C\left(t_{\sigma^n(w)}-\eta_2,z_2\right)\end{aligned}$$

So, we write

$$N_C(\eta_1-\eta_2,z_1+z_2)\geq\frac{1}{h_r}\sum_{n\in I_r} N_C\left(t_{\sigma^n(w)}-\eta_1,z_1\right)*\frac{1}{h_r}\sum_{n\in I_r} N_C\left(t_{\sigma^n(w)}-\eta_2,z_2\right).$$

Taking limit as $r\to\infty$, we get

$$\begin{aligned}&N_C(\eta_1-\eta_2,z_1+z_2)\\ &\geq \lim_{r\to\infty}\tfrac{1}{h_r}\sum_{n\in I_r} N_C\left(t_{\sigma^n(w)}-\eta_1,z_1\right)*\lim_{r\to\infty}\tfrac{1}{h_r}\sum_{n\in I_r} N_C\left(t_{\sigma^n(w)}-\eta_2,z_2\right)\\ &=1*1=1.\end{aligned}$$

Thus, we obtain

$$N_C(\eta_1-\eta_2,z_1+z_2)=1,\ \forall z_1,z_2\in E \text{ with } \theta_E\prec z_1,\theta_E\prec z_2.$$

So $\eta_1-\eta_2=\theta_V$, by (FCN2) (θ_V indicates the zero element of V). Hence, $\eta_1=\eta_2$. □

Theorem 8.3 *Presume that (t_n) be sequences in FCNS $(V, N_C, *)$.*
(a) If $\mathcal{I}_{\sigma\theta} - \lim_{n\to\infty} t_n = \eta\,(N_C)$ and $\mathcal{I}_{\sigma\theta} - \lim_{n\to\infty} t_n = \lambda\,(N_C)$, then $\eta = \lambda$.
(b) $\mathcal{I}_{\sigma\theta} - \lim_{n\to\infty} t_n = \eta\,(N_C)$ iff $\mathcal{I}_{\sigma\theta} - \lim_{n\to\infty} N_C(t_n - \eta, z) = 1$.

Proof. (b) Presume that $\mathcal{I}_{\sigma\theta} - \lim_{n\to\infty} t_n = \eta\,(N_C)$. For all $\xi \in (0,1)$ and $z \in E$ with $\theta_E \prec z$, we get

$$\begin{aligned}\{n \in \mathbb{N} : |N_C(t_n - \eta, z) - 1| \geq \xi\} &= \{n \in \mathbb{N} : N_C(t_n - \eta, z) \geq 1 + \xi\} \\ &\cup \{n \in \mathbb{N} : N_C(t_n - \eta, z) \leq 1 - \xi\}.\end{aligned}$$

It is obvious that

$$\{n \in \mathbb{N} : N_C(t_n - \eta, z) \geq 1 + \xi\} = \emptyset \in \mathcal{I}_{\sigma\theta}.$$

According to the hypothesis,

$$\{n \in \mathbb{N} : N_C(t_n - \eta, z) \leq 1 - \xi\} \in \mathcal{I}_{\sigma\theta}.$$

Hence, we acquire $\mathcal{I}_{\sigma\theta} - \lim_{n\to\infty} N_C(t_n - \eta, z) = 1$. When $\mathcal{I}_{\sigma\theta} - \lim_{n\to\infty} N_C(t_n - \eta, z) = 1$, it is clear that $\mathcal{I}_{\sigma\theta} - \lim_{n\to\infty} t_n = \eta\,(N_C)$. □

Theorem 8.4 *Let (t_n) and (p_n) be sequences in FCNS $(V, N_C, *)$. Then*
(a) If $\mathcal{I}_{\sigma\theta} - \lim t_n = \eta\,(N_C)$ and $\mathcal{I}_{\sigma\theta} - \lim p_n = \lambda\,(N_C)$, then $\mathcal{I}_{\sigma\theta} - \lim(t_n + p_n) = \eta + \lambda\,(N_C)$.
(b) If $\mathcal{I}_{\sigma\theta} - \lim t_n = \eta\,(N_C)$ and $q \in \mathbb{R}$, then $\mathcal{I}_{\sigma\theta} - \lim q t_n = q\eta\,(N_C)$.

Proof. (a) Let $\xi \in (0,1)$. By Remark 1.6 in [14], we can select $\xi_0 \in (0,1)$ such that

$$(1 - \xi_0) * (1 - \xi_0) > 1 - \xi. \tag{8.1}$$

For $z \in E$ with $\theta_E \prec z$, contemplate

$$\begin{aligned}A(\xi, z) &= \{n \in \mathbb{N} : N_C(t_n + p_n - (\eta + \lambda), z) \leq 1 - \xi\}, \\ K_1(\xi_0, z) &= \{n \in \mathbb{N} : N_C(t_n - \eta, z) \leq 1 - \xi_0\}, \\ K_2(\xi_0, z) &= \{n \in \mathbb{N} : N_C(p_n - \lambda, z) \leq 1 - \xi_0\}.\end{aligned}$$

By presumption $K_1(\xi_0, z) \in \mathcal{I}_{\sigma\theta}$ and $K_2(\xi_0, z) \in \mathcal{I}_{\sigma\theta}$. We acquire $K(\xi, z) = K_1(\xi_0, z) \cup K_2(\xi_0, z) \in \mathcal{I}_{\sigma\theta}$ and $K^c(\xi, z) \in \mathcal{F}(\mathcal{I}_{\sigma\theta})$. We have to indicate that $K^c(\xi, z) \subseteq A^c(\xi, z)$. Let $w \in K^c(\xi, z)$. Then, we acquire

$$N_C\left(t_w - \eta, \frac{z}{2}\right) > 1 - \xi_0 \text{ and } N_C\left(p_w - \lambda, \frac{z}{2}\right) > 1 - \xi_0.$$

As N_C is a FCN and by Eq. (9.1),

$$\begin{aligned}&N_C(t_w + p_w - (\eta + \lambda), m) \\ &\quad \geq N_C\left(t_w - \eta, \tfrac{z}{2}\right) * N_C\left(p_w - \lambda, \tfrac{m}{2}\right) \\ &\quad > (1 - \xi_0) * (1 - \xi_0) \\ &\quad > 1 - \xi.\end{aligned}$$

Then, we acquire $w \in A^c(\xi, z)$. Since $K^c(\xi, z) \in \mathcal{F}(\mathcal{I}_{\sigma\theta})$, we get $A^c(\xi, z) \in \mathcal{F}(\mathcal{I}_{\sigma\theta})$. Therefore, $\mathcal{I}_{\sigma\theta} - \lim(t_n + p_n) = \eta + \lambda(N_C)$.

(b) Case-(1) $q = 0$, then it is clear.

Case-(2) $|q| \geq 1$: For $z \in E$ with $\theta_E \prec z$, take

$$A(\xi, z) = \{n \in \mathbb{N} : N_C(t_n - \eta, z) \leq 1 - \xi\},$$
$$B(\xi, z) = \{n \in \mathbb{N} : N_C(q(t_n - \eta), z) \leq 1 - \xi\}.$$

Considering that N_C is a FCN,

$$N_C(q(t_n - \eta), z) = N_C\left(t_n - \eta, \frac{z}{|q|}\right) \tag{8.2}$$

As N_C is an non-decreasing function and $\frac{z}{|q|} \leq z$ for $|q| \geq 1$,

$$N_C\left(t_n - \eta, \frac{z}{|q|}\right) \leq N_C(t_n - \eta, z) \tag{8.3}$$

As $\mathcal{I}_{\sigma\theta} - \lim t_n = \eta(N_C)$, $A(\xi, z) \in \mathcal{I}_{\sigma\theta}$. By Eqs. (9.2) and (8.3), it follows that $B(\xi, z) \subseteq A(\xi, z)$. Then, we acquire $B(\xi, z) \in \mathcal{I}_{\sigma\theta}$.

Case-(3) $|q| < 1$ and $q \neq 0$: For all $\xi > 0$ and $z \in E$,

$$K(\xi, z) = \{n \in \mathbb{N} : N_C(t_n - \eta, z) > 1 - \xi\},$$
$$M(\xi, z) = \{n \in \mathbb{N} : N_C(q(t_n - \eta), z) > 1 - \xi\}.$$

Since N_C is a FCN, we get

$$N_C\left(t_n - \eta, \frac{z}{|q|}\right) \geq N_C(t_n - \eta, z) * N_C\left(0, \frac{z}{|q|} - z\right) = N_C(t_n - \eta, z) \tag{8.4}$$

In view of the fact that $\mathcal{I}_{\sigma\theta} - \lim t_n = \eta(N_C)$, $K(\xi, z) \in \mathcal{F}(\mathcal{I}_{\sigma\theta})$. In accordance with Eqs. (9.2) and (8.4), it claims that $K(\xi, z) \subseteq M(\xi, z)$. Then, we have $M(\xi, z) \in \mathcal{F}(\mathcal{I}_{\sigma\theta})$. □

Theorem 8.5 *Take $\mathcal{I}$ as an admissible ideal and assume that (t_n) be a sequence in FCNS $(V, N_C, *)$. If all subsequence of (t_n) is $\mathcal{I}_{\sigma\theta}$-convergent to η w.r.t. FCN on V, then (t_n) is $\mathcal{I}_{\sigma\theta}$-convergent to η.*

Proof. Presume that $t_n \nrightarrow \eta\left(\mathcal{I}_{\sigma\theta}^{N_C}\right)$. Then, there is $\xi \in (0,1)$ and $z \in E$ with $\theta_E \prec z$ such that

$$A(\xi, z) = \{n \in \mathbb{N} : N_C(t_n - \eta, z) \geq 1 - \xi\} \notin \mathcal{I}_{\sigma\theta}.$$

As $\mathcal{I}$ is an admissible ideal, $A(\xi, z)$ have to be an infinite set. Take $A(\xi, z) = \{n_1 < n_2 < ... < n_k < ...\}$. Let $y_k = t_{n_k}$ for $k \in \mathbb{N}$ that is not $\mathcal{I}_{\sigma\theta}$-convergent to η. This causes a contradiction. □

The subsequent example indicates that the converse of Theorem 8.5 might not be true.

Example 8.1 *Let $E=\mathbb{R}^2$. Then, $P=\{(b_1,b_2):b_1,b_2\geq 0\}\subset E$ is a normal cone. Let $V=\mathbb{R}$, $u*v=uv$ and $N_C:V\times E\to[0,1]$ contemplated by $N(t,z)=e^{-\frac{|t|}{\|z\|}}$ for all $t\in V$ and $z\in E$ with $\theta_E\prec z$. Let $\mathcal{I}_{\sigma\theta}$=$\{A\subseteq\mathbb{N}:\delta(A)=0\}$. Identify a sequence (t_n) in V*

$$t_n=\begin{cases}1, & \text{if } p=n^2,\\ 0, & \text{otherwise.}\end{cases}$$

Then, for each $\xi\in(0,1)$ and $z\in E$ with $\theta_E\prec z$, the set

$$A(\xi,z)=\{n\in\mathbb{N}:N_C(t_n-0,z)\leq 1-\xi\}$$

will be a finite set. Consequently $A(\xi,z)\in\mathcal{I}_{\sigma\theta}$, i.e., $\mathcal{I}_{\sigma\theta}-\lim t_n=0(N_C)$. But $(t_{p_m})=(1)$, subsequence of (t_n) is not $\mathcal{I}_{\sigma\theta}$-convergent to 0.

Theorem 8.6 *Assume that $\mathcal{I}_{\sigma\theta}$ be an admissible ideal with the feature (AP) and take (t_n) as a sequence in FCNS $(V,N_C,*)$. $t_n\to\eta\left(\mathcal{I}_{\sigma\theta}^{N_C}\right)$ iff there exists a N_C-convergent sequence (s_n) such that $\{n\in\mathbb{N}:t_n\neq s_n\}\in\mathcal{I}_{\sigma\theta}$.*

Proof. Presume that $\mathcal{I}_\theta-\lim t_n=\eta\,(N_C)$. For each $r\in\mathbb{N}$ and $z\in E$ with $\theta_E\prec z$, we take

$$Q_r=\left\{n\in\mathbb{N}:N_C(t_n-\eta,z)\geq\frac{1}{r}\right\}.$$

Then $Q_r\in\mathcal{F}(\mathcal{I}_{\sigma\theta})$ for $r\in\mathbb{N}$. Utilizing the feature (AP) of $\mathcal{I}_{\sigma\theta}$, we see that there is a $Q\subset\mathbb{N}$ such that $Q\in\mathcal{F}(\mathcal{I}_{\sigma\theta})$ and $Q\backslash Q_r$ is finite for each $r\in\mathbb{N}$. We can observe that $t_n\to_Q\eta$ i.e. for all $\xi>0$, $z\in E$ with $\theta_E\prec z$, there is a $n_0>0$ such that $N_C(t_n-\eta,z)>1-\xi$ for all $n>n_0$ and $n\in Q$. Identify a sequence $(t_n)\in V$

$$s_n=\begin{cases}t_n, & \text{for } n\in Q,\\ \eta, & \text{for } n\in\mathbb{N}\backslash Q.\end{cases}$$

Also, (s_n) is N_C-converges to η. Hence, we acquire $\{n\in\mathbb{N}:t_n\neq s_n\}\in\mathcal{I}_{\sigma\theta}$.
At the same time, we presume that $\{n\in\mathbb{N}:t_n\neq s_n\}\in\mathcal{I}_{\sigma\theta}$ and $N_C-\lim_{n\to\infty}s_n=\eta$. Then, for each $\xi>0$, $z\in E$ with $\theta_E\prec z$, we obtain

$$\begin{aligned}\{n\in\mathbb{N}:N_C(t_n-\eta,z)\leq 1-\xi\}\ &\subseteq\{n\in\mathbb{N}:t_n\neq s_n\}\\ &\cup\{n\in\mathbb{N}:N_C(s_n-\eta,z)\leq 1-\xi\}.\end{aligned}$$

If we consider that $\mathcal{I}_{\sigma\theta}$ is an admissible ideal and as stated in hypothesis one acquires

$$\{n\in\mathbb{N}:N_C(s_n-\eta,z)\leq 1-\xi\}\in\mathcal{I}_{\sigma\theta}.$$

According to the definition of ideal, we have

$$\{n\in\mathbb{N}:N_C(t_n-\eta,z)\leq 1-\xi\}\in\mathcal{I}_{\sigma\theta}.$$

So, we get $t_n\to\eta\left(\mathcal{I}_{\sigma\theta}^{N_C}\right)$. □

Theorem 8.7 *If there is an $\mathcal{I}_{\sigma\theta}$-convergent sequence (t_n) in FCNS $(V, N_C, *)$ such that $\{n \in \mathbb{N} : t_n \neq s_n\} \in \mathcal{I}_{\sigma\theta}$, then (s_n) is also $\mathcal{I}_{\sigma\theta}$-convergent in V.*

Proof. Presume that $\mathcal{I}_{\sigma\theta} - \lim t_n = \eta\,(N_C)$ and $\{n \in \mathbb{N} : t_n \neq s_n\} \in \mathcal{I}_{\sigma\theta}$. Then, for each $\xi \in (0,1)$ and $z \in E$ with $\theta_E \prec z$

$$\{n \in \mathbb{N} : N_C\,(t_n - \eta, z) \leq 1 - \xi\} \in \mathcal{I}_{\sigma\theta}.$$

For all $\xi \in (0,1)$ and $z \in E$ with $\theta_E \prec z$, we get

$$\{n \in \mathbb{N} : N_C\,(s_n - \eta, z) \leq 1 - \xi\} \subseteq \{n \in \mathbb{N} : t_n \neq s_n\} \cup \{n \in \mathbb{N} : N_C\,(t_n - \eta, z) \leq 1 - \xi\}.$$

As a consequence of the hypothesis, we get

$$\{n \in \mathbb{N} : t_n \neq s_n\} \cup \{n \in \mathbb{N} : N_C\,(t_n - \eta, z) \leq 1 - \xi\} \in \mathcal{I}_{\sigma\theta},$$

therefore we acquire

$$\{n \in \mathbb{N} : N_C\,(s_n - \eta, z) \leq 1 - \xi\} \in \mathcal{I}_{\sigma\theta}.$$

Hence, $\mathcal{I}_{\sigma\theta} - \lim s_n = \eta\,(N_C)$. □

Theorem 8.8 *If $\mathcal{I}^*_{\sigma\theta} - \lim t_n = \eta\,(N_C)$, then $\mathcal{I}_{\sigma\theta} - \lim t_n = \eta\,(N_C)$.*

Proof. Presume that $\mathcal{I}^*_{\sigma\theta} - \lim t_n = \eta\,(N_C)$. Then, there is a set $P \in \mathcal{I}_{\sigma\theta}$ such that for

$$J = \mathbb{N} \setminus P = \{k_n : k_1 < k_2 < ... < k_n < ...\} \in \mathcal{F}\,(\mathcal{I}_{\sigma\theta})$$

we acquire $N_C - \lim_{n\to\infty} t_{k_n} = \eta\,(N_C)$. So, there is a $k_0 \in \mathbb{N}$ such that $|t_{k_n} - \eta| < \rho$ for all $k > k_0$. In addition, it is clear that for all $\rho > 0$

$$W\,(\rho, z) = \{n \in \mathbb{N} : N_C\,(t_n - \eta, z) \leq 1 - \xi\} \subset P \cup \{k_n : k_1 < k_2 < ... < k_{n_0}\}.$$

As $\mathcal{I}_{\sigma\theta}$ is an admissible ideal, $P \cup \{k_1 < k_2 < ... < k_{n_0}\} \in \mathcal{I}_{\sigma\theta}$. We obtain that $W\,(\rho, z) \in \mathcal{I}_{\sigma\theta}$. Therefore, we get $\mathcal{I}_{\theta} - \lim t_n = \eta\,(N_C)$. □

The set of $\mathcal{I}_{\sigma\theta}$-limit points of (t_n) is indicated by $\mathcal{L}_{N_C}^{\mathcal{I}_{\sigma\theta}}\,(t)$ and the set of $\mathcal{I}_{\sigma\theta}$-cluster points of (t_n) is indicated by $Cl_{N_C}^{\mathcal{I}_{\sigma\theta}}\,(t)$ in $(V, N_C, *)$.

Theorem 8.9 *For all sequence $t = (t_n)$ in FCNS, we get $\mathcal{L}_{N_C}^{\mathcal{I}_{\sigma\theta}}\,(t) \subseteq Cl_{N_C}^{\mathcal{I}_{\sigma\theta}}\,(t)$.*

Proof. Let $\eta \in \mathcal{L}_{N_C}^{\mathcal{I}_{\theta}}\,(t)$. Then, there is a set $J = \{p_1 < p_2 < ... < p_n < ..\} \subset \mathbb{N}$ such that the set

$$J' = \{r \in \mathbb{N} : p_n \in I_r\} \notin \mathcal{I}_{\sigma\theta}$$

and $N_C - \lim t_{p_n} = \eta\,(N_C)$ for all $z \in E$ with $\theta_E \prec z$.

Let $\xi \in (0,1)$ and $z \in E$. As stated in the hypothesis, there is an $n_0 \in \mathbb{N}$ such that

$$N_C(t_{p_n} - \eta, z) > 1 - \xi$$

for all $n \geq n_0$. Thus, we get

$$H = \{n \in \mathbb{N} : N_C(t_n - \eta, z) > 1 - \xi\} \supseteq J' \setminus \{p_1, p_2, ..., p_{n_0}\}.$$

Now, with $\mathcal{I}$ being admissible, we have

$$J' \setminus \{p_1, p_2, ..., p_{n_0}\} \notin \mathcal{I}_{\sigma\theta}$$

and in essence

$$H = \{n \in \mathbb{N} : N_C(t_n - \eta, z) > 1 - \xi\} \notin \mathcal{I}_{\sigma\theta}.$$

Hence, $\eta \in Cl_{N_C}^{\mathcal{I}_{\sigma\theta}}(t)$. □

Theorem 8.10 *If $\mathcal{I}_{\sigma\theta} - \lim t_n = \eta\ (N_C)$, then $\mathcal{L}_{N_C}^{\mathcal{I}_{\sigma\theta}}(t_n) = Cl_{N_C}^{\mathcal{I}_{\sigma\theta}}(t_n) = \{\eta\}$.*

Proof. Presume that $\mathcal{I}_{\sigma\theta} - \lim t_n = \eta\ (N_C)$. Then, for each $\xi \in (0,1)$ and $z \in E$ with $\theta_E \prec z$, the set

$$A = \{n \in \mathbb{N} : N_C(t_n - \eta, m) \leq 1 - \xi\} \in \mathcal{I}_{\sigma\theta}$$

and so

$$A^c = \{n \in \mathbb{N} : N_C(t_n - \eta, m) > 1 - \xi\} \notin \mathcal{I}_{\sigma\theta}.$$

and $\eta \in Cl_{N_C}^{\mathcal{I}_{\sigma\theta}}(t_n)$. We suppose that $Cl_{N_C}^{\mathcal{I}_{\sigma\theta}}(t_n) = \{\gamma\}$ where $\eta \neq \gamma$. In accordance with Definition 8.11, for all $\xi \in (0,1)$ and $z \in E$ with $\theta_E \prec z$, the sets

$$P = \{n \in \mathbb{N} : N_C(t_n - \eta, z) > 1 - \xi\} \notin \mathcal{I}_{\sigma\theta}.$$
$$R = \{n \in \mathbb{N} : N_C(t_n - \gamma, z) > 1 - \xi\} \notin \mathcal{I}_{\sigma\theta}.$$

For $\eta \neq \gamma$, we get $P \cap R = \emptyset$. By hypothesis,

$$P^c = \{n \in \mathbb{N} : N_C(t_n - \eta, z) \leq 1 - \xi\} \in \mathcal{I}_{\sigma\theta}$$

so we acquire $R \in \mathcal{I}_{\sigma\theta}$, which contradictions to $P \notin \mathcal{I}_{\sigma\theta}$. Therefore, $Cl_{N_C}^{\mathcal{I}_{\sigma\theta}}(t_n) = \{\eta\}$.

At the same time, by hypothesis, Theorem 8.9 and Definition 8.11, we obtain $\eta \in \mathcal{L}_{N_C}^{\mathcal{I}_{\sigma\theta}}(t_n)$. According to Theorem 10, we get $\mathcal{L}_{N_C}^{\mathcal{I}_{\sigma\theta}}(t_n) = Cl_{N_C}^{\mathcal{I}_{\sigma\theta}}(t_n) = \{\eta\}$. □

Theorem 8.11 *Let $t = (t_n)$ be a sequence in FCNS $(V, N_C, *)$. The subsequent situations are equivalent.*
(a) $\eta \in \mathcal{L}_{N_C}^{\mathcal{I}_{\sigma\theta}}(t_n)$.
(b) There are two sequences $w = (w_n)$ and $q = (q_n)$ in V such that $t = w + q$ and V_σ^θ-$\lim w = \xi$ and

$$\{r \in \mathbb{N} : n \in I_r,\ q_n \neq \theta\} \in \mathcal{I}_{\sigma\theta},$$

where θ indicates the zero element of V.

Proof. Presume that (a) supplies. Then, there are J and J' such that $J' \notin \mathcal{I}$ and V_σ^θ-$\lim t_{p_n} = \eta$. Itendify the sequences w and q as follows:

$$w_n = \begin{cases} t_n, & \text{if } n \in I_r \text{ such that } r \in J' \\ \eta, & \text{otherwise} \end{cases}$$

and

$$q_n = \begin{cases} \theta, & \text{if } n \in I_r \text{ such that } r \in J' \\ t_n - \eta, & \text{otherwise.} \end{cases}$$

It suffices to think the case $n \in I_r$ such that $r \in \mathbb{N} \backslash J'$. Then, for each $\xi \in (0,1)$, for any $z \in E$ with $\theta_E \prec z$, we have

$$\frac{1}{h_r} \sum_{n \in I_r} N_C \left(t_{\sigma^n(w)} - \eta, z \right) > 1 - \xi, \text{ uniformly in } w.$$

Hence, $V_\sigma^\theta - \lim w_n = \eta$. Now,

$$\{r \in \mathbb{N} : n \in I_r,\ q_n \neq \theta\} \subset \mathbb{N} \backslash J'.$$

Then, $\mathbb{N} \backslash J' \in \mathcal{I}$, and so

$$\{r \in \mathbb{N} : n \in I_r,\ q_n \neq \theta\} \in \mathcal{I}_{\sigma\theta}.$$

Now, assume that (b) supplies. Take $J' = \{r \in \mathbb{N} : n \in I_r,\ q_n = \theta\}$. Then, obviously $J' \in \mathcal{F}(\mathcal{I}_{\sigma\theta})$ and so it is an infinite set. Create the set $J = \{p_1 < p_2 < ... < p_n < ...\} \subset \mathbb{N}$ such that $p_n \in I_r$ and $q_{p_n} = \theta$. Since $t_{p_n} = w_{p_n}$ and $V_\sigma^\theta - \lim w_n = \eta$ we get $V_\sigma^\theta - \lim t_{p_n} = \eta$. This finalizes the proof. □

Theorem 8.12 *Take $\mathcal{I}$ as an admissible ideal. For each sequence $t = (t_n)$ in FCNS, the set $Cl_{N_C}^{\mathcal{I}_{\sigma\theta}}(t_n)$ is closed in V with regards to the topology induced by the FCN N_C.*

Proof. Take $q \in \overline{Cl_{N_C}^{\mathcal{I}_{\sigma\theta}}(t_n)}$. Then, we acquire $B(q,r,z) \cap Cl_{N_C}^{\mathcal{I}_{\sigma\theta}}(t_n) \neq \emptyset$ where $z \in E$ with $\theta_E \prec z$ and $r \in (0,1)$. Let $p \in B(q,r,z) \cap Cl_{N_C}^{\mathcal{I}_{\sigma\theta}}(t_n)$. Select $r_0 \in (0,1)$ such that $B(p,r_0,z) \subset B(q,r,z)$. We get

$$\begin{aligned} G &= \{n \in \mathbb{N} : N_C(t_n - q, z) > 1 - r\} \\ &\supseteq \{n \in \mathbb{N} : N_C(t_n - p, m) > 1 - r_0\} = H. \end{aligned}$$

Since $p \in Cl_{N_C}^{\mathcal{I}_{\sigma\theta}}(t_n)$, $H \notin \mathcal{I}$, and so $G \notin \mathcal{I}$. Hence, $q \in Cl_{N_C}^{\mathcal{I}_{\sigma\theta}}(t_n)$. □

Theorem 8.13 *If $t_n \to \eta \left(\mathcal{I}_{\sigma\theta}^{N_C}\right)$, then (t_n) is $\mathcal{I}_{\sigma\theta}$-Cauchy w.r.t FCN on V.*

Proof. Presume that $t_n \to \eta \left(\mathcal{I}_{\sigma\theta}^{N_C}\right)$. Then, for all $\xi \in (0,1)$ and for any $z \in E$ with $\theta_E \prec z$

$$P(\xi, z) = \{n \in \mathbb{N} : N_C(t_n - \eta, z) \leq 1 - \xi\} \in \mathcal{I}_{\sigma\theta}.$$

As $\mathcal{I}_{\sigma\theta}$ is an admissible ideal, then there is $n_0 \in \mathbb{N}$ with the consequence that $n_0 \notin P(\xi,z)$. Now, assume that

$$R(\xi,z) = \left\{n \in \mathbb{N} : N_C\left(t_n - t_{n_0}, z\right) \leq 1 - 2\xi\right\}.$$

Contemplating the inequality

$$\begin{aligned} N_C\left(t_n - t_{n_0}, z\right) &= N_C\left(t_n - \eta + \eta - t_{n_0}, z\right) \\ &\geq N_C\left(t_n - \eta, z\right) * N_C\left(\eta - t_{n_0}, z\right) \\ &= N_C\left(t_n - \eta, z\right) * N_C\left(t_{n_0} - \eta, z\right) \end{aligned}$$

Observe that if $n \in R(\xi,z)$, therefore

$$N_C\left(t_n - \eta, z\right) * N_C\left(t_{n_0} - \eta, z\right) \leq 1 - 2\xi.$$

From another standpoint, since $n_0 \notin P(\xi,z)$, we obtain $N_C\left(t_{n_0} - \eta, z\right) > 1 - \xi$. We reach that

$$N_C\left(t_n - \eta, z\right) \leq 1 - \xi.$$

Hence, $n \in P(\xi,z)$. This gives that $R(\xi,z) \subset P(\xi,z) \in \mathcal{I}_{\sigma\theta}$ for every $\xi \in (0,1)$ and for any $z \in E$ with $\theta_E \prec z$. So, $R(\xi,z) \in \mathcal{I}_{\sigma\theta}$, so (t_n) is $\mathcal{I}_{\sigma\theta}$-Cauchy w.r.t FCN on V. □

Theorem 8.14 *Let $\mathcal{I}$ be an admissible ideal. If a sequence (t_n) is $\mathcal{I}^*_{\sigma\theta}$-Cauchy sequence, then (t_n) is $\mathcal{I}_{\sigma\theta}$-Cauchy sequence w.r.t FCN on V.*

Proof. Assume that sequence (t_n) is $\mathcal{I}^*_{\sigma\theta}$-Cauchy w.r.t FCN on V. Then, for any $z \in E$ with $\theta_E \prec z$ and for each $\xi \in (0,1)$, there is $R \in \mathcal{F}(\mathcal{I}_{\sigma\theta})$, where $R = \left\{p = (p_j) : p_j < p_{j+1}, j \in \mathbb{N}\right\}$ such that

$$N_C\left(t_{p_k} - t_{p_l}, z\right) \leq 1 - \xi,$$

Take $N = N(\xi) = p_{k_0+1}$. So, for each $\xi \in (0,1)$, one gets

$$N_C\left(t_{p_k} - t_N, z\right) \leq 1 - \xi,$$

for all $k > k_0$. Now, consider that $H = \mathbb{N} \setminus R$. Clearly, $H \in \mathcal{I}_{\sigma\theta}$ and

$$\begin{aligned} Q(\xi,z) &= \{k \in \mathbb{N} : N_C(t_k - t_N, z) \leq 1 - \xi\} \\ &\subset H \cup \left\{p_1, p_2, \ldots, p_{k_0}\right\} \in \mathcal{I}_{\sigma\theta}. \end{aligned}$$

As a consequence, for each $\xi \in (0,1)$ and for any $z \in E$ with $\theta_E \prec z$, one can select $N = N(\xi)$ such that $Q(\xi,z) \in \mathcal{I}_{\sigma\theta}$, namely, the sequence (t_n) is $\mathcal{I}_{\sigma\theta}$-Cauchy w.r.t FCN on V. □

Theorem 8.15 *If $N_C - \lim t_n = \eta$, then $\mathcal{I}_{\sigma\theta} - \lim t_n = \eta\ (N_C)$.*

The converse of Theorem 8.15 is not true in general, which can be examined from the subsequent example.

Example 8.2 *Take $E = \mathbb{R}$. Here, $P = [0,\infty) \subset E$ is a normal cone. Consider $V = \mathbb{R}^2$, $u * v = uv$ and $N_C : V \times E \to [0,1]$ contemplated by $N_C(t,m) = \frac{z}{z+\|t\|}$ for all $t \in V$ and $z \in E$ with $\theta_E \prec z$. We take a sequence (t_k) by*

$$t_k = \begin{cases} k, & \text{if } n - \left[\sqrt{h_r}\right] + 1 \le k \le n,\ r \in \mathbb{N}, \\ 0, & \text{otherwise.} \end{cases}$$

Think

$$K_r(\xi,z) := \{k \in I_r : N_C(t_k,z) \le 1-\xi\}$$

for every $\xi \in (0,1)$ and $z \in E$ with $\theta_E \prec z$. Then, we get

$$\begin{aligned} K_r(\xi,z) &= \left\{k \in I_r : \tfrac{z}{z+\|t_k\|} \le 1-\xi\right\} \\ &= \left\{k \in I_r : \|t_k\| \ge \tfrac{z\xi}{1-\xi} > 0\right\} \\ &\subseteq \{k \in I_r : t_k = k\} \end{aligned}$$

Thus,

$$\left\{r \in \mathbb{N} : \frac{1}{h_r}\left|\{n \in \mathbb{N} : N_C(t_n - 0,z) \le 1-\xi\}\right| \ge \gamma\right\} \in \mathcal{I}_{\sigma\theta}.$$

Therefore, $\mathcal{I}_{\sigma\theta} - \lim t_k = 0(N_C)$. But the sequence (t_n) is not convergent w.r.t FCN.

Theorem 8.16 *Take an FCNS V. Then, $\mathcal{I}_{\sigma\theta} - \lim t_n = \eta\ (N_C)$ iff there is an increasing index sequence $K = \{n_i\}$ of $\mathbb{N}$ such that $K \in \mathcal{F}(\mathcal{I}_{\sigma\theta})$ and $N_C - \lim t_{n_i} = \eta$.*

Theorem 8.17 *Take an FCNS V. Then $\mathcal{I}_{\sigma\theta} - \lim t_n = \eta\ (N_C)$ iff there is a sequence $s = (s_n)$ such that $N_C - \lim s_n = \eta$ and $\{n \in \mathbb{N} : t_n = s_n\} \in \mathcal{F}(\mathcal{I}_{\sigma\theta})$.*

Proof. Let $\mathcal{I}_{\sigma\theta} - \lim t_n = \eta\ (N_C)$. By Theorem 8.16, we have an increasing index sequence $K = \{n_i\}$ of $\mathbb{N}$ such that $K \in \mathcal{F}(\mathcal{I}_{\sigma\theta})$ and $N_C - \lim t_{n_i} = \eta$. Think the sequence $s = (s_n)$ given by

$$s_n = \begin{cases} t_n, & \text{if } n \in K, \\ \eta, & \text{otherwise.} \end{cases}$$

Then, s serves our purpose.

Conversely presume that t and s are sequences such that

$$N_C - \lim s_n = \eta \text{ and } \{n \in \mathbb{N} : t_n = s_n\} \in \mathcal{F}(\mathcal{I}_{\sigma\theta}).$$

Then, for all $\xi \in (0,1)$ and $z \in E$ with $\theta_E \prec z$, we get

$$\begin{aligned} &\{n \in \mathbb{N} : N_C(t_n - \eta,z) \le 1-\xi\} \\ &\quad \subseteq \{n \in \mathbb{N} : N_C(s_n - \eta,z) \le 1-\xi\} \cup \{n \in \mathbb{N} : t_n \ne s_n\}. \end{aligned}$$

Since $N_C - \lim s_n = \eta$, so the set $\{n \in \mathbb{N} : N_C(s_n - \eta,z) \le 1-\xi\}$ involves at most finitely many terms. Also by supposition,

$$\{n \in \mathbb{N} : t_n \ne s_n\} \in \mathcal{I}_{\sigma\theta}.$$

Hence

$$\{n \in \mathbb{N} : N_C(t_n - \eta, z) \leq 1 - \xi\} \in \mathcal{I}_{\sigma\theta}.$$

Hence, we obtain $\mathcal{I}_{\sigma\theta} - \lim t_n = \eta\ (N_C)$. □

Theorem 8.18 *A sequence* (t_n) *is* $S_\sigma^\theta\ (N_C)$*-convergent to* η *iff it is* $\mathcal{I}_{\sigma\theta}^{(N_C)}$*-convergent to* η.

8.4 CONCLUSION

In this chapter, we established the concepts of lacunary $\mathcal{I}$-invariant convergence, $\mathcal{I}$-invariant statistical convergence, lacunary $\mathcal{I}$-invariant statistical convergence for sequences in FCNS, which are generalizations of analogous concepts in fuzzy normed linear space. By utilizing these concepts, some fundamental results on finite-dimensional FCNS are established. Since fuzzy mathematics along with the classical ones is constantly developing, the concept of fuzzy cone normed linear spaces will also play a significant role in the new evolution of fuzzy functional analysis.

Bibliography

1. T. Bag. Finite dimensional fuzzy cone normed linear spaces. *Int. J. Math. Sci. Comput.*, 3(1):9–14, 2013.
2. F. Basar. *Summability Theory and Its Applications*. CRC Press/Taylor & Francis Group: Boca Raton, FL, 2022.
3. S. B. Choudhury and P. Das. A new contraction mapping principle in partially ordered fuzzy metric spaces. *Ann. Fuzzy Math. Inform.*, 8(6):889–901, 2014.
4. P. Debnath. Lacunary ideal convergence in intuitionistic fuzzy normed linear spaces. *Comput. Math. Appl.*, 63:708–715, 2012.
5. P. Debnath. Results on lacunary difference ideal convergence in intuitionistic fuzzy normed linear spaces. *J. Intell. Fuzzy Syst.*, 28(3):1299–1306, 2015.
6. P. Debnath. A generalised statistical convergence in intuitionistic fuzzy n-normed linear spaces. *Ann. Fuzzy Math. Inform.*, 12(4):559–572, 2016.
7. P. Debnath. A new type of convergence in intuitionistic fuzzy normed linear spaces. *J. New Theory*, 15:19–25, 2017.
8. P. Debnath. Some results on Cesàro summability in intuitionistic fuzzy n-normed linear spaces. *Sahand Commun. Math. Anal.*, 19(1):77–87, 2022.
9. P. Debnath and M. Sen. Some completeness results in terms of infinite series and quotient spaces in intuitionistic fuzzy n-normed linear spaces. *J. Intell. Fuzzy Syst.*, 26(6):975–982, 2014.
10. P. Debnath and M. Sen. Some results of calculus for functions having values in an intuitionistic fuzzy n-normed linear space. *J. Intell. Fuzzy Syst.*, 26(2):2983–2991, 2014.
11. H. Fast. Sur la convergence statistique. *Colloq. Math.*, 2:241–244, 1951.
12. C. Felbin. Finite dimensional fuzzy normed linear space. *Fuzzy Sets Syst.*, 48(2):239–248, 1992.
13. J. A. Fridy and C. Orhan. Lacunary statistical convergence. *Pacific J. Math.*, 160(1):43–51, 1993.
14. A. George and P. Veeramani. On some results in fuzzy metric spaces. *Fuzzy Sets Syst.*, 64:395–399, 1994.

15. A. C. Güler. $\mathcal{I}$-convergence in fuzzy cone normed spaces. *Sahand Commun. Math.*, 18(4):45–57, 2021.
16. U. Kadak and F. Basar. Power series with real or fuzzy coefficients. *Filomat*, 25(3):519–528, 2012.
17. O. Kaleva and S. Seikkala. On fuzzy metric spaces. *Fuzzy Sets Syst.*, 12:215–229, 1984.
18. S. Karakus, K. Demirci, and O. Duman. Statistical convergence on intuitionistic fuzzy normed spaces. *Chaos, Solitons Fractals*, 35:763–769, 2008.
19. A. K. Katsaras. Fuzzy topological vector spaces. *Fuzzy Sets Syst.*, 12:143–154, 1984.
20. N. Konwar and P. Debnath. $\mathcal{I}_\lambda$-convergence in intuitionistic fuzzy n-normed linear space. *Ann. Fuzzy Math. Inform.*, 13(1):91–107, 2017.
21. N. Konwar and P. Debnath. Some new contractive conditions and related fixed point theorems in intuitionistic fuzzy n-Banach spaces. *J. Intell. Fuzzy Syst.*, 34(1):361–372, 2018.
22. N. Konwar, B. Davvaz, and P. Debnath. Approximation of new bounded operators in intuitionistic fuzzy n-Banach spaces. *J. Intell. Fuzzy Syst.*, 35(6):6301–6312, 2018.
23. N. Konwar, B. Davvaz, and P. Debnath. Results on generalized intuitionistic fuzzy hypergroupoids. *J. Intell. Fuzzy Syst.*, 36(3):2571–2580, 2019.
24. P. Kostyrko, T. Šalát, and W. Wilczynski. $\mathcal{I}$-convergence. *Real Anal. Exch.*, 26(2):669–686, 2000.
25. K. Kumar and V. Kumar. On the $\mathcal{I}$ and $\mathcal{I}^*$-convergence of sequences in fuzzy normed spaces. *Adv. Fuzzy Syst.*, 3:341–365, 2008.
26. K. Kumar and V. Kumar. On the ideal convergence of sequences of fuzzy numbers. *Inf. Sci.*, 178:4670–4678, 2008.
27. K. Kumar and V. Kumar. On the ideal convergence of sequences in intuitionistic fuzzy normed spaces. *Selcuk J. Math.*, 10(2):27–41, 2009.
28. F. Lael and K. Nourouzi. Some results on the if-normed spaces. *Chaos, Solitions Fractals*, 37:931–939, 2008.
29. H. Long-Guang and Z. Xian. Cone metric spaces and fixed point theorems of contractive mappings. *J. Math. Anal. Appl.*, 332:1468–1476, 2007.
30. K. Menger. Statistical metrics. *Proc. Nat. Acad. Sci.*, 28(12):535–537, 1942.
31. S. Mohinta and T. K. Samanta. Coupled fixed point theorems in partially ordered non-Archimedean complete fuzzy metric spaces. *Ann. Fuzzy Math. Inform.*, 11(5):829–840, 2016.
32. S. A. Mohiuddine and Q. M. D Lohani. On generalized statistical convergence in intuitionistic fuzzy normed space. *Chaos, Soliton's Fractals*, 42:1731–1737, 2009.
33. M. Mursaleen. On finite matrices and invariant means. *Indian J. Pure Appl. Math.*, 10:457–460: 1979.
34. M. Mursaleen. Matrix transformation between some new sequence spaces. *Houst. J. Math.*, 9:505–509, 1983.
35. M. Mursaleen and F. Basar. *Sequence Spaces: Topics in Modern Summability Theory*, Series: Mathematics and Its Applications. CRC Press, Taylor & Francis Group: Boca Raton, FL, London, New York, 2020.
36. A. Nabiev, S. Pehlivan, and M. Gürdal. On $\mathcal{I}$-Cauchy sequence. *Taiwanese J. Math.*, 11(2):569–576, 2007.
37. F. Nuray, H. Gök, and U. Ulusu. $\mathcal{I}_\sigma$-convergence. *Math. Commun.*, 16:531–538, 2011.
38. R. A. Raimi. Invariant means and invariant matrix methods of summability. *Duke Math. J.*, 30:81–94, 1963.

39. E. Savas and M. Gürdal. Certain summability methods in intuitionistic fuzzy normed spaces. *J. Intell. Fuzzy Syst.*, 27(4):1621–1629, 2014.
40. E. Savas and M. Gürdal. Generalized statistically convergent sequences of functions in fuzzy 2-normed spaces. *J. Intell. Fuzzy Syst.*, 27(4):2067–2075, 2014.
41. E. Savas and M. Gürdal. A generalized statistical convergence in intuitionistic fuzzy normed spaces. *Sci. Asia*, 41:289–294, 2015.
42. E. Savas and F. Nuray. On σ-statistically convergence and lacunary σ-statistically convergence. *Math. Slovaca*, 43(3):309–315, 1993.
43. A. Sahiner, M. Gürdal, and T. Yigit. Ideal convergence characterization of the completion of linear n-normed spaces. *Comput. Math. Appl.*, 61(3):683–689, 2011.
44. R. M. Somasundaram and T. Beaula. Some aspects of 2-fuzzy 2-normed linear spaces. *Bull. Malays. Math. Soc.*, 32:211–221, 2009.
45. Ö. Talo and F. Basar. On the space $bv_p(F)$ of sequences of p-bounded variation of fuzzy numbers. *Acta Math. Sin. Eng. Ser.*, 24(7):1205–1212, 2008.
46. Ö. Talo and F. Basar. Certain spaces of sequences of fuzzy numbers defined by a modulus function. *Demonstratio Math.*, 43(1):139–149, 2010.
47. Ö. Talo and F. Basar. Quasilinearity of the classical sets of sequences of fuzzy numbers and some related results. *Taiwanese J. Math.*, 14(5):1799–1819, 2010.
48. P. Tamang and T. Bag. Some results on finite dimensional fuzzy cone normed linear space. *Ann. Fuzzy Math. Inform.*, 13(1):123–134, 2017.
49. P. Schaefer. Infinite matrices and invariant means. *Proc. Am. Math. Soc.*, 36:104–110, 1972.
50. U. Ulusu and F. Nuray. Lacunary $\mathcal{I}$-invariant convergence. *Cumhuriyet Sci. J.*, 41(3):617–624, 2020.
51. U. Yamancı and M. Gürdal. On lacunary ideal convergence in random n-normed space. *J. Math.*, 2013:1–8, 2013.
52. L. A. Zadeh. Fuzzy sets. *Inform. Control*, 8:338–353, 1965.

9 Some Convergent Sequence Spaces of Fuzzy Star-Shaped Numbers

Erhan Güler and Ömer Kisi
Bartın University

CONTENTS

9.1 Introduction 125
9.1.1 Background 125
9.1.2 Main Goal 126
9.2 Basic Definitions 126
9.3 Prime Results of the Chapter 128
9.3.1 Essential Definitions 128
9.3.2 Theorems for Main Result 129
9.4 Conclusion 138
Bibliography 138

9.1 INTRODUCTION

The convexity of a set in the n-dimensional Euclidean space $\mathbb{R}^n$, or more general in a Banach space, is a very significant notion. It plays an important role in optimization theory. Convex optimization research and star-shapedness have been attracting the attention of mathematicians for decades, see Refs. [2,36] for details.

In classical convex analysis, in the practical applications, we need the convex fuzzy set (star-shaped fuzzy set relative to a point) satisfying more conditions such as normality, upper semi-continuity, and the compactness of the support set, called a fuzzy number (star-shaped fuzzy number relative to the point, respectively). Since fuzzy number plays an enormous role in applications of fuzzy mathematics, many authors recently investigated star-shaped fuzzy numbers and obtained significant features of them.

9.1.1 BACKGROUND

Theory of fuzzy sets (FSs) was initially introduced by Zadeh [45] as an extension of crisp set theory. Diamond and Kloeden were mainly interested in the convexity

DOI: 10.1201/9781003312017-9

property of FSs because of its importance in metric definitions and their topological properties [12]– [15]. FSs have been widely implemented in different disciplines and technologies. The theory of FSs cannot always cope with the lack of knowledge of membership degrees. That is why Atanassov [1] investigated the theory of intuitionistic fuzzy set, which is the extension of the theory of FSs. Katsaras [18] presented fuzzy norm in fuzzy topological vector spaces by utilizing fuzzy set with norm processors. Felbin [16] introduced the notion of fuzzy normed space.

After the work of the ideal convergence introduced by Kostyrko et al. [27], there have been valuable research studies to discover summability works of the classical theories. Ideal convergence in fuzzy normed spaces was firstly examined by Kumar and Kumar [28]. $\mathcal{I}$-convergence for sequences of fuzzy numbers was investigated by Kumar and Kumar [29]. Moreover, the concept of $\mathcal{I}$-convergence of sequences in 2-normed linear spaces was studied by Gürdal [30] and in intuitionistic fuzzy normed spaces by Kumar and Kumar [31]. For further information on sequence spaces and on the classical sets of fuzzy valued sequences and related topics, the readers should also consult the recent papers [3]– [10], [22]– [26], [32]– [34], [37]– [40], [41,42].

Due to the significance of the convexity and the star-shapedness can be seen as a natural extension to this feature, it has been examined in various ways, see [17,21,35,43,44,46,47]. The notion of fuzzy star-shaped numbers (FSSN) was initially introduced by Diamond [11]. Diamond [11] introduced the conceptualization of FSSN and examined the properties of L_p-metric for $p \geq 1$ on the same.

9.1.2 MAIN GOAL

The intention of this chapter is to survey some recent developments of FSSN and its applications. We investigate the notions of convergent, Cauchy, bounded double sequences of FSSN in $\mathbb{R}^n$ with regard to L_p-metric and examine some features of these concepts. Also, we acquire new sequence spaces by using ideal for double sequences of FSSN. We examine some algebraic and topological features of the new corresponding spaces as well. In support of our results, we provide several examples of these new resulting sequences.

9.2 BASIC DEFINITIONS

This section covers some fundamental definitions that will be used throughout this chapter.

$q : \mathbb{R}^n \to [0,1]$ is a FS supplying the following situations:
(i) there is a $t_0 \in \mathbb{R}^n$ so that $q(t_0) = 1$, i.e., q is a normal,
(ii) q is upper semi-continuous,
(iii) $\text{supp}q = cl\{t \in \mathbb{R}^n : q(t) > 0\}$ is compact,
(iv) q is FSS w.r.t. $t \in \mathbb{R}^n$ so that, for any $p \in \mathbb{R}^n$ and $\nu \in [0,1]$,

$$q(\nu p + (1-\nu)t) \geq q(p).$$

For all $\alpha \in (0,1]$, the α-level set

$$\emptyset \neq [q]^{\alpha} = \begin{cases} \{m \in \mathbb{R}^n : q(m) \geq \alpha\}, & \text{if } \alpha \in (0,1] \\ \text{supp} q & \text{if } \alpha = 0 \end{cases}$$

is a compact FSS subset of $\mathbb{R}^n$. By means of S^n, we symbolize the space of FSSN. For all $p \geq 1$, and every $q, \varpi \in S^n$, one determines a metric

$$\rho_p(q,\varpi) = \left(\int_0^1 \rho_H\left([q]^{\alpha}, [\varpi]^{\alpha}\right)^p d\alpha \right)^{\frac{1}{p}},$$

where ρ_H is the Hausdorff metric. Then, ρ_p is named the L_p-metric on S^n. Hence, (S^n, ρ_p) is known as the Hausdorff metric space [46]. Additional details on L_p-metric can be seen in [17,21,47].

Some definitions of FSSN can be seen in [19,20].

Definition 9.1 *[19] A sequence $q = (q_r) \in w^*(S^n)$ is named to be convergent to FSSN q_0 provided that there is a $M = M(\eta)$ so that*

$$\rho_p(q_r, q_0) < \eta \text{ for } \forall r \geq M.$$

We indicate the spaces of all null convergent and convergent sequences of FSSN in $\mathbb{R}^n$ as $c_0(S^n)$, $c(S^n)$, respectively.

Definition 9.2 *[19] A sequence $q = (q_r) \in w^*(S^n)$ is named to be bounded provided that there is a $N \in \mathbb{N}$, so that*

$$\rho_p\left(q_r, \overline{0}\right) \leq N \text{ for } \forall r \in \mathbb{N}.$$

We indicate the space of bounded sequences of FSSN as $l_\infty(S^n)$ and characterized as

$$l_\infty(S^n) = \left\{ q = (q_r) \in w^*(S^n) : \sup_r \rho_p\left(q_r, \overline{0}\right) < \infty \right\}.$$

Definition 9.3 *[19] A sequence $q = (q_r) \in w^*(S^n)$ is stated to be Cauchy provided that for each $\eta > 0$, there is a $M = M(\eta)$ so that*

$$\rho_p(q_r, q_s) < \eta \text{ for } \forall r, s \geq M.$$

Definition 9.4 *[19] Contemplate the metric space (S^n, ρ_p). The open ball with center at q and radius $\kappa > 0$ is determined as*

$$\mathcal{B}_{\rho_p}(q,\kappa) = \{\varpi \in S^n : \rho_p(\varpi, q) < \kappa\}$$

for all $(q_r) \in w^*(S^n)$.

Definition 9.5 *[37])A sequence space Ψ_{S^n} is stated to be normal (or solid) provided that for $(q_r) \in \Psi_{S^n}$ and $|\beta_r| \leq 1$, we get $(\beta_r q_r) \in \Psi_{S^n}$.*

Definition 9.6 *[37] Ψ_{S^n} is named to monotone, provided that for all infinite $K \subseteq \mathbb{N}$ and $(q_r) \in \Psi_{S^n}$ the sequence $(\beta_r q_r)$, where*

$$\beta_r = \begin{cases} 1, & r \in K \\ 0, & otherwise \end{cases}$$

belongs to Ψ_{S^n}.

Definition 9.7 *[37] Ψ_{S^n} is said to be symmetric, when $(q_r) \in \Psi_{S^n}$. Then $\left(q_{\pi(r)}\right) \in \Psi_{S^n}$, where π is a permutation of $\mathbb{N}$.*

Lemma 9.1 *([37]) When a sequence space is solid, then it is monotone.*

Lemma 9.2 *[37] For a maximal ideal $\mathcal{I}$ and all subset K of $\mathbb{N}$, either $K \in \mathcal{I}$ or $\mathbb{N} \setminus K \in \mathcal{I}$.*

We aim to investigate the notions of convergent, Cauchy, bounded double sequences of FSSN in $\mathbb{R}^n$ w.r.t. L_p-metric. Also, we acquire new sequence spaces by utilizing ideal for double sequence of FSSN. We examine several algebraic and topological features of the new corresponding spaces as well. We also provide several examples of these new resulting sequences.

In the chapter, we determine the set of all double sequences $q = (q_{rs})$ of the FSSN in $\mathbb{R}^n$ by $w^*\left(S_2^n\right)$.

9.3 PRIME RESULTS OF THE CHAPTER

This section includes the discussion of the main results for the chapter. Initially, we establish some essential definitions in the area of FSSN.

9.3.1 ESSENTIAL DEFINITIONS

Definition 9.8 *A sequence $q = (q_{rs}) \in w^*\left(S_2^n\right)$ is convergent to $q_0 \in w^*\left(S_2^n\right)$ if there exists a positive integer $M = M(\eta)$ so that*

$$\rho_p\left(q_{rs}, q_0\right) < \eta \; for \; \forall r, s \geq M.$$

In this case, we write $\lim_{r,s \to \infty} \rho_p\left(q_{rs}, q_0\right) = 0$ and q_0 is called the limit of the sequence (q_{rs}). We define $c\left(S_2^n\right)$ as the space of all convergent double sequences of FSSN in $\mathbb{R}^n$.

Definition 9.9 *A sequence $q = (q_{rs}) \in w^*\left(S^n\right)$ is named to be bounded provided that there is a $M = M(\eta) \in \mathbb{N}$ so that*

$$\rho_p\left(q_{rs}, \overline{0}\right) \leq M \; for \; \forall r, s \in \mathbb{N}.$$

We define $l_\infty^2\left(S_2^n\right)$ as the space of all bounded double sequences of FSSN in $\mathbb{R}^n$.

Definition 9.10 *A sequence $q = (q_{rs}) \in w^*(S^n)$ is a Cauchy sequence if, for each $\eta > 0$, there is a $M = M(\eta)$ so that*

$$\rho_p\left(q_{rs}^{(i,j)}, q_{rs}^{(k,l)}\right) < \eta \text{ for } \forall i,j,k,l \geq M.$$

Definition 9.11 *Contemplate the metric space (S_2^n, ρ_p). For $q = (q_{rs}) \in S_2^n$ the open ball with center at q and radius $\kappa > 0$ is determined as*

$$\mathcal{B}_{\rho_p}(q,\kappa) = \{\varpi = (\varpi_{rs}) \in S_2^n : \rho_p(\varpi, q) < \kappa\}.$$

Definition 9.12 *A sequence space $E_{S_2^n}$ is said to be solid (or normal) if for $(q_{rs}) \in E_{S_2^n}$ and $|\beta_{rs}| \leq 1$, we have $(q_{rs}\beta_{rs}) \in E_{S_2^n}$.*

Definition 9.13 *$E_{S_2^n}$ is said to be monotone, if for all infinite $K \subset \mathbb{N} \times \mathbb{N}$, and $(q_{rs}) \in E_{S_2^n}$ the sequence $(\beta_{rs}q_{rs})$, where*

$$\beta_{rs} = \begin{cases} 1, & (r,s) \in K \\ 0, & \text{otherwise,} \end{cases}$$

belongs to $E_{S_2^n}$.

Definition 9.14 *Take $\mathcal{I}_2$ as a strongly admissible ideal. A sequence $q = (q_{rs})$ is called to be $\mathcal{I}_2$-Cauchy provided that for all $\eta > 0$ there exist $Y = Y(\eta) \in \mathbb{N}$, $Z = Z(\eta) \in \mathbb{N}$ such that*

$$W(\eta) = \{(r,s) \in \mathbb{N} \times \mathbb{N} : \rho_p(q_{rs}, q_{YZ}) \geq \eta\} \in \mathcal{I}_2.$$

9.3.2 THEOREMS FOR MAIN RESULT

Theorem 9.3 *The space of every FSSN S_2^n with L_p-metric is a Hausdorff metric space.*

Proof. Consider the metric space (S_2^n, ρ_p), and let $q = (q_{rs}) \in S_2^n$, $\varpi = (\varpi_{rs}) \in S_2^n$ such that $q \neq \varpi$. Let $\kappa = \rho_p(q,\varpi)$, $\Psi = \mathcal{B}_{\rho_p}\left(q, \frac{\kappa}{2}\right)$ and $\Theta = \mathcal{B}_{\rho_p}\left(\varpi, \frac{\kappa}{2}\right)$ such that $q \in \Psi$ and $\varpi \in \Theta$. We have to demonstrate that $\Psi \cap \Theta = \emptyset$. Let on contrary $\varkappa \in \Psi \cap \Theta$, this gives that $\rho_p(q,\varkappa) < \frac{\kappa}{2}$ and $\rho_p(\varpi,\varkappa) < \frac{\kappa}{2}$. By triangle inequality

$$\kappa = \rho_p(q,\varpi) \leq \rho_p(q,\varkappa) + \rho_p(\varkappa,\varpi) < \frac{\kappa}{2} + \frac{\kappa}{2} = \kappa,$$

which is a contradiction. So, $\Psi \cap \Theta = \emptyset$. □

Corollary 11 *A double convergent sequence $(q_{rs}) \in w^*(S_2^n)$ has a unique limit.*

Theorem 9.4 *Each open ball in the metric space (S_2^n, ρ_p) is an open set.*

Proof. Contemplate $\mathcal{B}_{\rho_p}(q,\kappa)$ to be an open ball. Take $\kappa_1 = \kappa - \rho_p(q,\varpi)$. To demonstrate that $\mathcal{B}_{\rho_p}(\varpi,\kappa_1) \subseteq \mathcal{B}_{\rho_p}(q,\kappa)$, let $\varkappa \in \mathcal{B}_{\rho_p}(\varpi,\kappa_1)$, this gives the following

$$\begin{aligned} \mathcal{B}_{\rho_p}(\varkappa,\varpi) < \kappa_1 = \kappa - \rho_p(q,\varpi) &\Rightarrow \rho_p(q,\varpi) + \rho_p(\varpi,\varkappa) < \kappa \\ &\Rightarrow \rho_p(q,\varkappa) < \kappa \Rightarrow \varkappa \in \mathcal{B}_{\rho_p}(q,\kappa). \end{aligned}$$

Hence, $\mathcal{B}_{\rho_p}(q,\kappa)$ is an open set. □

Theorem 9.5 *A convergent sequence $q = (q_{rs})$ of FSSN is bounded but converse is not true.*

Proof. Assume that $\lim_{r,s\to\infty} \rho_p(q_{rs}, q_0) = 0$ and $\Theta = \{(q_{rs}) : r, s = 1, 2, ...\}$. Let $\eta = 1$. Thus, there is a $M = M(\eta) \in \mathbb{N}$ such that $\rho_p(q_{rs}, q_0) < 1$ for all $r, s \geq M$. Presume that

$$\beta = \max\{\rho_p(q_{11}, q_0), \rho_p(q_{22}, q_0), ..., \rho_p(q_{rs}, q_0), 1\}.$$

Then, $\rho_p(q_{rs}, q_0) < \beta$ for any $r, s \in \mathbb{N}$. Since ρ_p is a metric on S_2^n, by triangle inequality, we obtain

$$\rho_p(q_{rs}, q_{kl}) \leq \rho_p(q_{rs}, q_0) + \rho_p(q_0, q_{kl}) < 2\beta.$$

This gives $\beta(\Theta) \leq 2\beta$, i.e., the sequence (q_{rs}) is bounded. We create the subsequent counter-example to prove our claim. □

Example 9.1 *Contemplate the sequence of FSSN $q_{rs}(m) : \mathbb{R} \to [0, 1]$ defined by*

$$q_{rs}(m) = \begin{cases} \frac{3m}{2}, & 0 \leq m \leq \frac{2}{3}, \\ 1, & \frac{2}{3} \leq m \leq \frac{4}{3}, \\ \frac{-3}{2}(m-2), & \frac{4}{3} \leq m \leq 2, \\ 0, & otherwise. \end{cases}$$

So, $(q_{rs}) \in c(S_2^n)$. Assume that P be the collection of all finite subsets of $\mathbb{N}$, then there is a set $Q \subseteq \mathbb{N}$ such that $Q \notin P$ and $\mathbb{N} \backslash Q \notin P$, define $\varpi = (\varpi_{rs})$ by

$$\varpi_{rs} = \begin{cases} q_{rs}, & (r, s) \in Q \\ 0, & otherwise. \end{cases}$$

Then, the sequence $(\varpi_{rs}) \in l_\infty(S_2^n)$ but $(\varpi_{rs}) \notin c(S_2^n)$.

Theorem 9.6 *When $(q_{rs}) \in w^*(S_2^n)$ is convergent to q_0, then any subsequence of (q_{rs}) also converges to the same limit.*

Proof. Presume that $\lim_{r,s\to\infty} \rho_p(q_{rs}, q_0) = 0$, then we demonstrate that for any subsequence $(q_{r_i s_j})$ of (q_{rs}),

$$\lim_{i,j\to\infty} \rho_p(q_{r_i s_j}, q_0) = 0,$$

namely, for each $\eta > 0$, there is $M_0 \in \mathbb{N}$ so that $(q_{r_i s_j}) \in \mathcal{B}_{\rho_p}(q_0, \eta)$ for all $i, j \geq M_0$. As $\lim_{r,s\to\infty} \rho_p(q_{rs}, q_0) = 0$, there is a $M \in \mathbb{N}$ so that $(q_{rs}) \in \mathcal{B}_{\rho_p}(q_0, \eta)$ for all $r, s \geq M$. Also, since (r_i) and (s_j) are increasing sequences of $\mathbb{N}^+$ there is a $M_0 \in \mathbb{N}$ such that $r_i, s_j \geq M$ whenever $i, j \geq M_0$. As a result, $(q_{r_i s_j}) \in \mathcal{B}_{\rho_p}(q_0, \eta)$. □

Theorem 9.7 *The space $l_\infty(S_2^n)$ is a complete metric space with the metric ρ defined by*

$$\rho(q, \varpi) = \sup_{r,s} \rho_p(q_{rs}, \varpi_{rs}).$$

Proof. Let $\left(q_{rs}^{(i,j)}\right)$ for $i,j=1,2,\dots$ be a Cauchy sequence in $l_\infty\left(S_2^n\right)$. Then, for each $\eta>0$ there is a $M\in\mathbb{N}$ such that

$$\rho\left(q_{rs}^{(i,j)},q_{rs}^{(k,l)}\right)<\eta$$

for all $i,j,k,l\geq M$. Then, we write

$$\rho_p\left(q_{rs}^{(i,j)},q_{rs}^{(k,l)}\right)<\eta^{rs}. \tag{9.1}$$

So, for all $r,s\in\mathbb{N}$, we acquire

$$\rho_p\left(q_{rs}^{(i,j)},q_{rs}\right)<\eta,$$

i.e., $\left(q_{rs}^{(i,j)}\right)$ is convergent to (q_{rs}). But, according to (9.1), we conclude that

$$\rho\left(q_{rs}^{(i,j)},q_{rs}\right)<\eta \text{ as } k,l\to\infty.$$

We have to demonstrate that $(q_{rs})\in l_\infty\left(S_2^n\right)$. For this

$$\rho_p\left(q_{rs},\overline{0}\right)\leq\rho_p\left(q_{rs},q_{rs}^{(i,j)}\right)+\rho_p\left(q_{rs}^{(i,j)},\overline{0}\right)\leq\rho_p\left(q_{rs}^{(i,j)},\overline{0}\right)+\eta.$$

Since $\left(q_{rs}^{(i,j)}\right)$ is a Cauchy sequence in $l_\infty\left(S_2^n\right)$, so $\rho_p\left(q_{rs}^{(i,j)},\overline{0}\right)\leq H$. This gives that

$$\rho_p\left(q_{rs},\overline{0}\right)\leq H+\eta=H'.$$

□

Theorem 9.8 *The space $c\left(S_2^n\right)\cap l_\infty^2\left(S_2^n\right)$ is a closed subset of the complete metric space $l_\infty^2\left(S_2^n\right)$.*

Proof. Assume that $\left(q_{rs}^{(i,j)}\right)$ be a Cauchy sequence in $c\left(S_2^n\right)\cap l_\infty^2\left(S_2^n\right)$ and $q_{rs}^{(i,j)}\to q_{rs}$ in $l_\infty^2\left(S_2^n\right)$. As $\left(q_{rs}^{(i,j)}\right)\in c\left(S_2^n\right)\cap l_\infty^2\left(S_2^n\right)$, so, there is a FSSN $\left(\varpi^{(i,j)}\right)$ so that $\lim_{r,s\to\infty}q_{rs}^{(i,j)}=\varpi^{(i,j)}$. Since $\left(q_{rs}^{(i,j)}\right)$ is a Cauchy sequence which means that there is a $M>0$ so that

$$\rho\left(q_{rs}^{(k,l)},q_{rs}^{(i,j)}\right)<\frac{\eta}{3}$$

for $k,l,i,j\geq M$. Also $\lim_{r,s\to\infty}q_{rs}^{(k,l)}=\varpi^{(k,l)}$. Then, we get

$$\rho\left(\varpi^{(k,l)},\varpi^{(i,j)}\right)\leq\rho\left(q_{rs}^{(k,l)},\varpi^{(k,l)}\right)+\rho\left(q_{rs}^{(k,l)},q_{rs}^{(i,j)}\right)+\rho\left(q_{rs}^{(i,j)},\varpi^{(i,j)}\right)\leq\frac{\eta}{3}+\frac{\eta}{3}+\frac{\eta}{3}=\eta.$$

This denotes that $\left(\varpi^{(i,j)}\right)$ is a Cauchy sequence in $l_\infty^2\left(S_2^n\right)$, and so convergent to ϖ, namely,

$$\lim\varpi^{(i,j)}=\varpi. \tag{9.2}$$

Now, we denote that (q_{rs}) is convergent to ϖ. As $\left(q_{rs}^{(i,j)}\right) \to q_{rs}$, so for all $\eta > 0$, there is a $M_0 \in \mathbb{N}$ so that

$$\rho\left(q_{rs}^{(i,j)}, q_{rs}\right) < \frac{\eta}{3}$$

for all $i, j \geq M_0$. Also, from (9.2), we get for all $\eta > 0$, there is a $M_1 \in \mathbb{N}$ so that

$$\rho\left(\varpi^{(i,j)}, \varpi\right) < \frac{\eta}{3}$$

for all $i, j \geq M_1$. In addition, since $\left(q_{rs}^{(i,j)}\right) \to \varpi^{(i,j)}$ for all $\eta > 0$, there is a $M_2 \in \mathbb{N}$ so that

$$\rho\left(q_{rs}^{(i,j)}, \varpi^{(i,j)}\right) < \frac{\eta}{3}$$

for all $i, j \geq M_2$. Take $M_3 = \max\{M_0, M_1, M_2\}$. For $\eta > 0$, we acquire

$$\rho(q_{rs}, \varpi) \to \rho\left(q_{rs}, q_{rs}^{(i,j)}\right) + \rho\left(q_{rs}^{(i,j)}, \varpi^{(i,j)}\right) + \rho\left(\varpi^{(i,j)}, \varpi\right) \leq \frac{\eta}{3} + \frac{\eta}{3} + \frac{\eta}{3} = \eta.$$

This demonstrates that (q_{rs}) is convergent to ϖ, namely, $(q_{rs}) \in c(S_2^n) \cap l_\infty^2(S_2^n)$. Therefore, we prove that $c(S_2^n) \cap l_\infty^2(S_2^n)$ is closed subset of the complete metric space $l_\infty^2(S_2^n)$. □

Theorem 9.9 *The space $c(S_2^n) \cap l_\infty^2(S_2^n)$ is not dense anywhere in the complete metric space $l_\infty^2(S_2^n)$.*

Proof. Since $c(S_2^n) \cap l_\infty^2(S_2^n)$ is a closed subset of $l_\infty^2(S_2^n)$ so $\overline{c(S_2^n) \cap l_\infty^2(S_2^n)} = c(S_2^n) \cap l_\infty^2(S_2^n)$. It is adequate to indicate that $\left(c(S_2^n) \cap l_\infty^2(S_2^n)\right)^o = \emptyset$. Contemplate an arbitrary point $(q_{rs}) \in c(S_2^n) \cap l_\infty^2(S_2^n)$. Then, for any $\kappa > 0$ there is a point (ϖ_{rs}) in the neighborhood $\mathcal{B}_{\rho_p}(q_{rs}, \kappa)$ so that $(\varpi_{rs}) \notin c(S^n)$ and $(\varpi_{rs}) \notin l_\infty^2(S_2^n)$. So $\mathcal{B}_{\rho_p}(q_{rs}, \kappa) \nsubseteq c(S_2^n) \cap l_\infty^2(S_2^n)$. As a result, $(q_{rs}) \notin \left(c(S_2^n) \cap l_\infty^2(S_2^n)\right)^\circ$. So, we acquire $\left(c(S_2^n) \cap l_\infty^2(S_2^n)\right)^\circ = \emptyset$. □

Now, we aim to put forward to the sequences spaces $c^{\mathcal{I}_2}(S_2^n)$, $c_0^{\mathcal{I}_2}(S_2^n)$, $l_\infty^{\mathcal{I}_2}(S_2^n)$ of FSSN in $\mathbb{R}^n$ w.r.t. L_p-metric. Take $\mathcal{I}_2$ as an admissible ideal in $\mathbb{N} \times \mathbb{N}$ and presume that $q = (q_{rs})$ be a sequence of FSSN in $\mathbb{R}^n$. We identify:

$$\begin{aligned}
&c^{\mathcal{I}_2}(S_2^n) = \{q = (q_{rs}) \in w^*(S_2^n) : \\
&\qquad \left\{(r,s) \in \mathbb{N} \times \mathbb{N} : \rho_p(q_{rs}, q_0) \geq \eta\right\} \in \mathcal{I}_2 \text{ for } \eta > 0 \text{ and some } q_0 \in S_2^n\};\\
&c_0^{\mathcal{I}_2}(S_2^n) = \{q = (q_{rs}) \in w^*(S_2^n) : \\
&\qquad \left\{(r,s) \in \mathbb{N} \times \mathbb{N} : \rho_p\left(q_{rs}, \overline{0}\right) \geq \eta\right\} \in \mathcal{I}_2 \text{ for } \eta > 0 \text{ and } \overline{0} \in S_2^n\};\\
&l_\infty^{\mathcal{I}_2}(S_2^n) = \left\{q = (q_{rs}) \in w^*(S_2^n) : \exists T > 0 \text{ so that } \left\{\rho_p\left(q_{rs}, \overline{0}\right) \geq T\right\} \in \mathcal{I}_2\right\};\\
&m^{\mathcal{I}_2}(S_2^n) = c^{\mathcal{I}_2}(S_2^n) \cap l_\infty^{\mathcal{I}_2}(S_2^n) \text{ and } m_0^{\mathcal{I}_2}(S^n) = c_0^{\mathcal{I}_2}(S_2^n) \cap l_\infty^{\mathcal{I}_2}(S_2^n).
\end{aligned}$$

Theorem 9.10 *The spaces $c^{\mathcal{I}_2}(S_2^n)$, $c_0^{\mathcal{I}_2}(S_2^n)$, $l_\infty^{\mathcal{I}_2}(S_2^n)$ are linear spaces.*

Proof. Assume that $q=(q_{rs})$ and $\varpi=(\varpi_{rs})$ be elements of $c^{\mathcal{I}_2}(S_2^n)$ that converge to q_0 and ϖ_0 respectively and $\phi\neq 0$, $\psi\neq 0$ be scalars. Then

$$\begin{aligned}\Upsilon(\eta)&=\left\{(r,s)\in\mathbb{N}\times\mathbb{N}:\rho_p(q_{rs},q_0)\geq\tfrac{\eta}{2}\right\}\in\mathcal{I}_2,\\ \Psi(\eta)&=\left\{(r,s)\in\mathbb{N}\times\mathbb{N}:\rho_p(\varpi_{rs},\varpi_0)\geq\tfrac{\eta}{2}\right\}\in\mathcal{I}_2.\end{aligned}$$

$$\begin{aligned}&\rho_p(\phi q+\psi\varpi,\phi q_0+\psi\varpi_0)\\ &=\left(\int_0^1\rho_H\left([\phi q_{rs}+\psi\varpi_{rs}]^\alpha,[\phi q_0+\psi\varpi_0]^\alpha\right)^p d\alpha\right)^{\frac{1}{p}}\\ &=\left(\int_0^1\rho_H\left(\phi[q_{rs}]^\alpha+\psi[\varpi_{rs}]^\alpha,\phi[q_0]^\alpha+\psi[\varpi_0]^\alpha\right)^p d\alpha\right)^{\frac{1}{p}}\\ &\leq\left(\int_0^1\rho_H\left([\phi q_{rs}]^\alpha+[\phi q_0]^\alpha\right)^p d\alpha\right)^{\frac{1}{p}}+\left(\int_0^1\rho_H\left([\psi\varpi_{rs}]^\alpha+[\psi\varpi_0]^\alpha\right)^p d\alpha\right)^{\frac{1}{p}}\\ &\leq|\phi|\left(\int_0^1\rho_H\left([q_{rs}]^\alpha+[q_0]^\alpha\right)^p d\alpha\right)^{\frac{1}{p}}+|\psi|\left(\int_0^1\rho_H\left([\varpi_{rs}]^\alpha+[\varpi_0]^\alpha\right)^p d\alpha\right)^{\frac{1}{p}}\\ &=|\phi|\rho_p(q,q_0)+|\psi|\rho_p(\varpi,\varpi_0).\end{aligned}$$

Now

$$\begin{aligned}\Pi(\eta)&=\left\{(r,s)\in\mathbb{N}\times\mathbb{N}:\rho_p(\phi q+\psi\varpi,\phi q_0+\psi\varpi_0)\geq\eta\right\}\\ &\subseteq\left\{(r,s)\in\mathbb{N}\times\mathbb{N}:|\phi|\rho_p(q,q_0)\geq\tfrac{\eta}{2}\right\}\cup\left\{(r,s)\in\mathbb{N}\times\mathbb{N}:|\psi|\rho_p(\varpi,\varpi_0)\geq\tfrac{\eta}{2}\right\}\\ &=\left\{(r,s)\in\mathbb{N}\times\mathbb{N}:\rho_p(q,q_0)\geq\tfrac{\eta}{2|\phi|}\right\}\cup\left\{(r,s)\in\mathbb{N}\times\mathbb{N}:\rho_p(\varpi,\varpi_0)\geq\tfrac{\eta}{2|\psi|}\right\}\\ &\subseteq\left\{\Upsilon\left(\tfrac{\eta}{2|\phi|}\right)\cup\Psi\left(\tfrac{\eta}{2|\psi|}\right)\right\}\in\mathcal{I}_2.\end{aligned}$$

This gives $(\phi q+\psi\varpi)\in c^{\mathcal{I}_2}(S_2^n)$. So, $c^{\mathcal{I}_2}(S_2^n)$ is linear space. □

Theorem 9.11 *The inclusions $c_0^{\mathcal{I}_2}(S_2^n)\subset c^{\mathcal{I}_2}(S_2^n)\subset l_\infty^{\mathcal{I}_2}(S_2^n)$ are strict.*

Proof. Obviously $c_0^{\mathcal{I}_2}(S_2^n)\subset c^{\mathcal{I}_2}(S_2^n)$. To demonstrate that $c^{\mathcal{I}_2}(S_2^n)\subset l_\infty^{\mathcal{I}_2}(S_2^n)$ contemplate the sequence $q=(q_{rs})\in w^*(S_2^n)$ so that

$$q_{rs}(m)=\begin{cases}m, & \text{if } 0\leq m<2,\\ 3-m, & \text{if } 2\leq m\leq 3,\\ 0, & \text{otherwise.}\end{cases}$$

Obviously, the sequence $(q_{rs})\in c^{\mathcal{I}_2}(S_2^n)$; however, $(q_{rs})\notin c_0^{\mathcal{I}_2}(S_2^n)$, namely $(q_{rs})\in c^{\mathcal{I}_2}(S_2^n)\diagdown c_0^{\mathcal{I}_2}(S_2^n)$. Now, consider a sequence $q=(q_{rs})\in c^{\mathcal{I}_2}(S_2^n)$. Then, there is a $q_0\in S_2^n$ such that $\mathcal{I}_2$-$\lim q_{rs}=q_0$. So, we get

$$\left\{(r,s)\in\mathbb{N}\times\mathbb{N}:\rho_p(q_{rs},q_0)\geq\eta\right\}\in\mathcal{I}_2.$$

We acquire

$$\rho_p\left(q_{rs},\overline{0}\right)\leq\rho_p(q_{rs},q_0)+\rho_p\left(q_0,\overline{0}\right).$$

This demonstrates that the sequence $q=(q_{rs})$ have to belongs to $l_\infty^{\mathcal{I}_2}(S_2^n)$. Subsequent example denotes the inclusion $c^{\mathcal{I}_2}(S_2^n)\subset l_\infty^{\mathcal{I}_2}(S_2^n)$. □

Example 9.2 *Contemplate a sequence of FSSN $q = (q_{rs})$, where*

$$q_{rs}(m) = \begin{cases} \frac{1+2m}{2}, & \text{if } \frac{-1}{2} \leq m < \frac{1}{2}, \\ 2(1-m), & \text{if } \frac{1}{2} \leq m \leq 1, \\ 0, & \text{otherwise.} \end{cases}$$

Take $\mathcal{I}_2$ as a non-maximal ideal. Determine a sequence $\varpi = (\varpi_{rs})$ by

$$\varpi_{rs} = \begin{cases} q_{rs}, & (r,s) \in K \\ 0, & \text{otherwise.} \end{cases}$$

Obviously $\varpi = (\varpi_{rs}) \in l_\infty^{\mathcal{I}_2}(S_2^n)$ however $(\varpi_{rs}) \notin c^{\mathcal{I}_2}(S_2^n)$.

Example 9.3 *Contemplate a sequence of FSSN $q = (q_{rs})$ as follows:*

$$q_{rs}(m) = \begin{cases} 1 - rsm, & \text{if } 0 \leq m < \frac{1}{rs}, \\ 1 + rsm, & \text{if } -\frac{1}{rs} \leq m \leq 0, \quad r = 2u,\ s = 2v \\ 0, & \text{otherwise.} \end{cases}$$

Otherwise,

$$q_{rs}(m) = \begin{cases} m+5, & \text{if } -5 \leq m \leq 0 \\ 1, & \text{if } 0 \leq m \leq 2 \\ -m+5, & \text{if } 2 \leq m \leq 5 \\ 0, & \text{otherwise.} \end{cases}$$

Hence, $(q_{rs}) \in l_\infty^{\mathcal{I}_2}(S_2^n)$ however $(\varpi_{rs}) \notin c^{\mathcal{I}_2}(S_2^n)$. So, the inclusions $c_0^{\mathcal{I}_2}(S_2^n) \subset c^{\mathcal{I}_2}(S_2^n) \subset l_\infty^{\mathcal{I}_2}(S_2^n)$ are strict.

Remark 9.1 *Identifying*

$$\tau = \left\{ T \subset c^{\mathcal{I}_2}(S_2^n) : \forall q \in T \text{ and } \eta > 0,\ \mathcal{B}_{\rho_p}(q,\eta) \subset T \right\},$$

τ is a topology on $c^{\mathcal{I}_2}(S_2^n)$ created by base B_{ρ_p}.

Theorem 9.12 *A sequence $q = (q_{rs}) \in w^*(S_2^n)$ is $\mathcal{I}_2$-convergent iff for each $\eta > 0$ there exist $M_\eta \in \mathbb{N}$, $N_\eta \in \mathbb{N}$ such that*

$$\{(r,s) \in \mathbb{N} \times \mathbb{N} : \rho_p(q_{rs}, q_{M_\eta N_\eta}) < \eta\} \in \mathcal{F}(\mathcal{I}_2).$$

Proof. Presume that $q = (q_{rs}) \in w^*(S_2^n)$. Take $\mathcal{I}_2$-$\lim q_{rs} = q_0$. Then, for each $\eta > 0$

$$W_\eta = \left\{ (r,s) \in \mathbb{N} \times \mathbb{N} : \rho_p(q_{rs}, q_0) < \frac{\eta}{2} \right\} \in \mathcal{F}(\mathcal{I}_2).$$

Fix $M_\eta, N_\eta \in W_\eta$. Then, the subsequent supplies for every $(r,s) \in W_\eta$;

$$\rho_p(q_{rs}, q_{M_\eta N_\eta}) \leq \rho_p(q_{rs}, q_0) + \rho_p(q_{M_\eta N_\eta}, q_0) < \frac{\eta}{2} + \frac{\eta}{2} = \eta.$$

Hence, we have

$$\{(r,s) \in \mathbb{N}\times\mathbb{N} : \rho_p\left(q_{rs}, q_{M_\eta N_\eta}\right) < \eta\} \in \mathcal{F}(\mathcal{I}_2).$$

Conversely, presume that

$$\Phi_\eta = \{(r,s) \in \mathbb{N}\times\mathbb{N} : \rho_p\left(q_{rs}, q_{M_\eta N_\eta}\right) < \eta\} \in \mathcal{F}(\mathcal{I}_2)$$

holds $\forall\eta > 0$. Then, we set

$$\Phi_\eta = \{(r,s) \in \mathbb{N}\times\mathbb{N} : (q_{rs}) \in \mathcal{B}_{\rho_p}\left(q_{M_\eta N_\eta}, \eta\right)\} \in \mathcal{F}(\mathcal{I}_2), \forall\eta > 0.$$

Let $\Omega_\eta = \mathcal{B}_{\rho_p}\left(q_{M_\eta N_\eta}, \eta\right)$. Fix an $\eta > 0$, then $\Phi_\eta \in \mathcal{F}(\mathcal{I}_2)$ and $\Phi_{\frac{\eta}{2}} \in \mathcal{F}(\mathcal{I}_2)$. So $\Phi_{\frac{\eta}{2}} \cap \Phi_\eta \in \mathcal{F}(\mathcal{I}_2)$. This causes that

$$\begin{aligned} &\Omega = \Omega_{\frac{\eta}{2}} \cap \Omega_\eta \neq \emptyset, \\ &\{(r,s) \in \mathbb{N}\times\mathbb{N} : (q_{rs}) \in \Omega\} \in \mathcal{F}(\mathcal{I}_2), \\ &\text{diam}\Omega \leq \text{diam}\Omega_\eta. \end{aligned}$$

Here, diamΩ indicates the diameter of the ball w.r.t. ρ_p metric. Continuing further by the aid of induction, we obtain the sequence of balls

$$\Omega_\eta = \mathcal{B}_{0,0} \supseteq \mathcal{B}_{1,1} \supseteq \ldots \supseteq \mathcal{B}_{r,s} \supseteq \ldots$$

that satisfy the subsequent feature

$$\text{diam}\mathcal{B}_{r,s} \leq \frac{1}{2}\text{diam}\mathcal{B}_{r-1,s-1}, \text{ for } (r,s) \in (\mathbb{N}\times\mathbb{N})\setminus\{1,1\}$$

and

$$\{(r,s) \in \mathbb{N}\times\mathbb{N} : (q_{rs}) \in \mathcal{B}_{r,s}\} \in \mathcal{F}(\mathcal{I}_2), \text{ for } (r,s) \in (\mathbb{N}\times\mathbb{N})\setminus\{1,1\}.$$

Afterward, there is a $\theta \in \cap_{(r,s)\in\mathbb{N}\times\mathbb{N}}\mathcal{B}_{r,s}$ so that $\theta = \mathcal{I}_2\text{-}\lim q_{rs}$. □

Theorem 9.13 *The spaces* $c_0^{\mathcal{I}_2}(S_2^n)$ *and* $c^{\mathcal{I}_2}(S_2^n)$ *are solid and monotone.*

Proof. Assume that $(q_{rs}) \in c_0^{\mathcal{I}_2}(S_2^n)$, for each $\eta > 0$. So, we have

$$\{(r,s) \in \mathbb{N}\times\mathbb{N} : \rho_p\left(q_{rs}, \overline{0}\right) \geq \eta\} \in \mathcal{I}_2.$$

Let (β_{rs}) be a sequence of $\mathbb{R}$ so as $|\beta_{rs}| \leq 1$ for $\forall r,s \in \mathbb{N}$. Then,

$$\rho_p\left(\beta_{rs}q_{rs}, \overline{0}\right) \leq |\beta_{rs}|\,\rho_p\left(q_{rs}, \overline{0}\right), \forall (r,s) \in \mathbb{N}\times\mathbb{N}$$

Therefore, for each $\eta > 0$, we have

$$\{(r,s) \in \mathbb{N}\times\mathbb{N} : \rho_p\left(\beta_{rs}q_{rs}, \overline{0}\right) \geq \eta\} \subseteq \{(r,s) \in \mathbb{N}\times\mathbb{N} : \rho_p\left(q_{rs}, \overline{0}\right) \geq \eta\} \in \mathcal{I}_2.$$

Hence, $(\beta_{rs}q_{rs}) \in c_0^{\mathcal{I}_2}(S_2^n)$. This means that $c_0^{\mathcal{I}_2}(S_2^n)$ is solid and so monotone. □

Theorem 9.14 *When $\mathcal{I}_2$ is not maximal, then $c^{\mathcal{I}_2}(S_2^n)$ is neither monotone nor normal.*

Proof. We put forward a counter-example in support of our statement. Contemplate a sequence $(q_{rs}) \in w^*(S_2^n)$

$$q_{rs}(m) = \begin{cases} 2m, & \text{if } 0 \le m \le \frac{1}{2}, \\ 1, & \text{if } \frac{1}{2} \le m \le \frac{3}{2}, \\ -2(m-2), & \text{if } \frac{3}{2} \le m \le 2, \\ 0, & \text{otherwise.} \end{cases}$$

Then, $(q_{rs}) \in c^{\mathcal{I}_2}(S^n)$. Since $\mathcal{I}_2$ is not maximal, as stated in Lemma 9.2, we determine a sequence $\varpi = (\varpi_{rs})$ as

$$\varpi_{rs} = \begin{cases} q_{rs}, & (r,s) \in K \subset \mathbb{N} \times \mathbb{N} \\ 0, & \text{otherwise,} \end{cases}$$

such that (ϖ_{rs}) lies in the canonical pre-image of (q_{rs}) of K-step spaces of $c^{\mathcal{I}_2}(S_2^n)$. However, $(\varpi_{rs}) \notin c^{\mathcal{I}_2}(S_2^n)$. So, $c^{\mathcal{I}_2}(S_2^n)$ is not monotone, hence $c^{\mathcal{I}_2}(S_2^n)$ is not normal. □

Theorem 9.15 *When $\mathcal{I}_2$ is neither maximal nor $\mathcal{I}_2 = \mathcal{I}_2^f$, then the spaces $c_0^{\mathcal{I}_2}(S_2^n)$ and $c^{\mathcal{I}_2}(S_2^n)$ aren't symmetric.*

Proof. Let $q = (q_{rs}) \in w^*(S_2^n)$, where

$$q_{rs}(m) = \begin{cases} 1 + \frac{m}{10}, & \text{if } -10 \le m < 0, \\ 1 - \frac{m}{10}, & \text{if } 0 \le m \le 10, \\ 0, & \text{otherwise.} \end{cases}$$

Then, for an infinite subset W including r, s included in $\mathcal{I}_2$, the sequence $(q_{rs}) \in c^{\mathcal{I}_2}(S_2^n)$. Utilizing Lemma 9.2, identify a sequence $\varpi = (\varpi_{rs})$ by rearranging the terms of (q_{rs}) by

$$\varpi_{rs} = \begin{cases} q_{rs}, & (r,s) \in K \\ 0, & \text{otherwise.} \end{cases}$$

Obviously, $(\varpi_{rs}) \notin c^{\mathcal{I}_2}(S_2^n)$. So $c^{\mathcal{I}_2}(S_2^n)$ isn't symmetric. In the same way, $c_0^{\mathcal{I}_2}(S_2^n)$ is not symmetric. □

Theorem 9.16 *The spaces $c^{\mathcal{I}_2}(S_2^n)$, $c_0^{\mathcal{I}_2}(S_2^n)$, $l_\infty^{\mathcal{I}_2}(S_2^n)$ are sequence algebra.*

Proof. When Υ and Ψ are FSSN, then product of Υ and Ψ is determined as $\tau_{\Upsilon.\Psi}(x) = \sup_{x=u.t}(\tau_\Upsilon(u), \tau_\Psi(t))$ for each $x \in \mathbb{R}$. Presume that $\mathcal{I}_2\text{-}\lim q_{rs} = q_0$ and $\mathcal{I}_2\text{-}\lim \varpi_{rs} = \varpi_0$. For $\alpha \in [0,1]$ and $\lambda, \kappa \ge 0$, we write

$$\rho_H\left([q_{rs}]^\alpha [\varpi_{rs}]^\alpha, [q_0]^\alpha [\varpi_0]^\alpha\right) \le \lambda \rho_H\left([q_{rs}]^\alpha, [q_0]^\alpha\right) + \kappa \rho_H\left([\varpi_{rs}]^\alpha, [\varpi_0]^\alpha\right).$$

So, we get

$$\rho_H(q_{rs}\varpi_{rs}, q_0\varpi_0) \leq \lambda\rho_H(q_{rs}, q_0) + \kappa\rho_H(\varpi_{rs}, \varpi_0).$$

Take $\eta > 0$. Then, we have

$$\begin{aligned} W\left(\tfrac{\eta}{2}\right) &= \left\{(r,s) \in \mathbb{N}\times\mathbb{N} : \rho_p(q_{rs}, q_0) \geq \tfrac{\eta}{2}\right\} \in \mathcal{I}_2, \\ \Psi\left(\tfrac{\eta}{2}\right) &= \left\{(r,s) \in \mathbb{N}\times\mathbb{N} : \rho_p(\varpi_{rs}, \varpi_0) \geq \tfrac{\eta}{2}\right\} \in \mathcal{I}_2. \end{aligned}$$

Contemplate the set

$$\Phi(\eta) = \left\{(r,s) \in \mathbb{N}\times\mathbb{N} : \rho_p(q_{rs}\varpi_{rs}, q_0\varpi_0) \geq \eta\right\}.$$

It is adequate to denote that $\Phi(\eta) \subseteq W(\eta_1) \cup \Psi(\eta_2)$. Now

$$\begin{aligned} \left\{(r,s) \in \mathbb{N}\times\mathbb{N} : \rho_p(q_{rs}\varpi_{rs}, q_0\varpi_0) \geq \eta\right\} &\subseteq \lambda\left\{(r,s) \in \mathbb{N}\times\mathbb{N} : \rho_p(q_{rs}, q_0) \geq \tfrac{\eta}{2}\right\} \\ &\cup \kappa\left\{(r,s) \in \mathbb{N}\times\mathbb{N} : \rho_p(\varpi_{rs}, \varpi_0) \geq \tfrac{\eta}{2}\right\}. \end{aligned}$$

Since

$$\Phi(\eta) \subseteq \left\{(r,s) \in \mathbb{N}\times\mathbb{N} : \rho_p(q_{rs}, q_0) \geq \frac{\eta}{2\lambda}\right\} \cup \left\{(r,s) \in \mathbb{N}\times\mathbb{N} : \rho_p(\varpi_{rs}, \varpi_0) \geq \frac{\eta}{2\kappa}\right\},$$

we acquire $\Phi(\eta) \subseteq W(\eta_1) \cup \Psi(\eta_2)$. □

Theorem 9.17 *The function $f : m^{\mathcal{I}_2}(S_2^n) \to \mathbb{R}$ defined by $f(q) = \mathcal{I}_2\text{-}\lim q$ is a Lipschitz function and so uniformly continuous.*

Proof. Let q, $\varpi \in m^{\mathcal{I}_2}(S_2^n)$ with $q \neq \varpi$ such that $\mathcal{I}_2\text{-}\lim q = f(q)$ and $\mathcal{I}_2\text{-}\lim \varpi = f(\varpi)$. Then, we get

$$\begin{aligned} R_q &= \left\{(r,s) \in \mathbb{N}\times\mathbb{N} : \rho_p(q, f(q)) \geq \|q - \varpi\|\right\} \in \mathcal{I}_2, \\ R_\varpi &= \left\{(r,s) \in \mathbb{N}\times\mathbb{N} : \rho_p(\varpi, f(\varpi)) \geq \|q - \varpi\|\right\} \in \mathcal{I}_2. \end{aligned}$$

So, we obtain

$$\begin{aligned} S_q &= \left\{(r,s) \in \mathbb{N}\times\mathbb{N} : \rho_p(q, f(q)) < \|q - \varpi\|\right\} \in \mathcal{F}(\mathcal{I}_2), \\ S_\varpi &= \left\{(r,s) \in \mathbb{N}\times\mathbb{N} : \rho_p(\varpi, f(\varpi)) < \|q - \varpi\|\right\} \in \mathcal{F}(\mathcal{I}_2). \end{aligned}$$

Then, we have $S = S_q \cap S_\varpi \in \mathcal{F}(\mathcal{I}_2)$ so $S \neq \emptyset$. Take $(r,s) \in S$ such that

$$\begin{aligned} \rho_p(f(q), f(\varpi)) &\leq \rho_p(f(q), q) + \rho_p(q, \varpi) \\ &+ \rho_p(\varpi, f(\varpi)) \leq 3\|q - \varpi\|. \end{aligned}$$

As a result, f is Lipschitz function. □

Theorem 9.18 *When q, $\varpi \in m^{\mathcal{I}_2}(S_2^n)$, then $(q.\varpi) \in m^{\mathcal{I}_2}(S_2^n)$ and $f(q.\varpi) = f(q)f(\varpi)$.*

Proof. Since q, $\varpi \in m^{\mathcal{I}_2}(S_2^n)$, for $\eta > 0$, the subsequent situation holds

$$W_q = \left\{(r,s) \in \mathbb{N}\times\mathbb{N} : \rho_p(q, f(q)) < \tfrac{\eta}{2\lambda}\right\} \in \mathcal{F}(\mathcal{I}_2),$$
$$W_\varpi = \left\{(r,s) \in \mathbb{N}\times\mathbb{N} : \rho_p(\varpi, f(\varpi)) < \tfrac{\eta}{2\kappa}\right\} \in \mathcal{F}(\mathcal{I}_2),$$

where $\lambda, \kappa > 0$ so that $\rho_p\left(q, \overline{0}\right) < \lambda$ and $\rho_p\left(\varpi, \overline{0}\right) < \kappa$. Consider the set

$$\mathcal{Y} = \left\{(r,s) \in \mathbb{N}\times\mathbb{N} : \rho_p(q\varpi, f(q)f(\varpi)) < \eta\right\}$$

and take $(r,s) \in W_q \cap W_\varpi$. Now, we use

$$\begin{aligned}
&\rho_p(q\varpi, f(q)f(\varpi)) \\
&\leq \rho_p(q\varpi, qf(\varpi)) + \rho_p(qf(\varpi), f(q)f(\varpi)) \\
&\leq \rho_p(q,0)\rho_p(\varpi, f(\varpi)) + \rho_p(f(\varpi),0)\rho_p(q, f(q)) \\
&< \tfrac{\eta}{2\lambda}\lambda + \tfrac{\eta}{2\kappa}\kappa = \eta.
\end{aligned}$$

Hence, $W_q \cap W_\varpi \in \mathcal{Y}$ such that $\mathcal{Y} \in \mathcal{F}(\mathcal{I}_2)$. As a result, $(q.\varpi) \in m^{\mathcal{I}_2}(S^n)$ and $f(q.\varpi) = f(q)f(\varpi)$. □

9.4 CONCLUSION

In this chapter, we examined the notions of convergent, Cauchy and bounded sequences for double sequences of FSSN in $\mathbb{R}^n$ w.r.t. L_p-metric. We prove that $l_\infty(S_2^n)$ with L_p-metric is complete. We investigated the ideal convergent sequence spaces $c^{\mathcal{I}_2}(S_2^n)$, $c_0^{\mathcal{I}_2}(S_2^n)$, $l_\infty^{\mathcal{I}_2}(S_2^n)$ of FSSN in $\mathbb{R}^n$ w.r.t. L_p-metric. Further, we obtained some algebraic and topological features of these spaces. These new results will further help the researchers to expand their work in the area of sequence spaces in view of fuzzy theory.

Bibliography

1. K. T. Atanassov. Intuitionistic fuzzy sets. *Fuzzy Sets Syst.*, 20(1):87–96, 1986.
2. S. Boyd and L. Vandenberghe. Convex optimization. *Cambridge University Press*, 2004.
3. P. Das, P. Kostyrko, W. Wilczyński, and P. Malik. $\mathcal{I}$ and $\mathcal{I}^*$-convergence of double sequences. *Math. Slovaca*, 58(5):605–620, 2008.
4. P. Debnath. Lacunary ideal convergence in intuitionistic fuzzy normed linear spaces. *Comput. Math. Appl.*, 63:708–715, 2012.
5. P. Debnath. Results on lacunary difference ideal convergence in intuitionistic fuzzy normed linear spaces. *J. Intell. Fuzzy Syst.*, 28(3):1299–1306, 2015.
6. P. Debnath. A generalised statistical convergence in intuitionistic fuzzy n-normed linear spaces. *Ann. Fuzzy Math. Inform.*, 12(4):559–572, 2016.
7. P. Debnath. A new type of convergence in intuitionistic fuzzy normed linear spaces. *J. New Theory*, 15:19–25, 2017.
8. P. Debnath. Some results on Cesàro summability in intuitionistic fuzzy n-normed linear spaces. *Sahand Commun. Math. Anal.*, 19(1):77–87, 2022.
9. P. Debnath and M. Sen. Some completeness results in terms of infinite series and quotient spaces in intuitionistic fuzzy n-normed linear spaces. *J. Intell. Fuzzy Syst.*, 26(6):975–982, 2014.

10. P. Debnath and M. Sen. Some results of calculus for functions having values in an intuitionistic fuzzy n-normed linear space. *J. Intell. Fuzzy Syst.*, 26(2):2983–2991, 2014.
11. P. Diamond. A note on fuzzy starshaped fuzzy sets. *Fuzzy Sets Syst.*, 37:193–199, 1990.
12. P. Diamond and P. E. Kloeden. Characterization of compact subsets of fuzzy sets. *Fuzzy Sets Syst.*, 29(3):341–348, 1989.
13. P. Diamond and P. E. Kloeden. Metric spaces of fuzzy sets. *Fuzzy Sets Syst.*, 35(2): 241–249, 1990.
14. P. Diamond and P. E. Kloeden. Metric spaces of fuzzy sets. *Corrigendum Fuzzy Sets Syst.*, 45:123,1992.
15. P. Diamond and P. E. Kloeden. *Metric Spaces of Fuzzy Sets: Theory and Applications*. World Scientific: Singapore, 1994.
16. C. Felbin. Finite dimensional fuzzy normed linear space. *Fuzzy Sets Syst.*, 48(2):239–248, 1992.
17. H. Huang and C. Wu. Characterizations of compact sets in fuzzy set spaces with l_p metric. *Fuzzy Sets Syst.*, 330:16–40, 2018.
18. A. K. Katsaras. Fuzzy topological vector spaces. *Fuzzy Sets Syst.*, 12:143–154, 1984.
19. V. A. Khan, E. E. Kara, U. Tuba, K. M. A. S. Alshlool, and A. Ahmad. Sequences of fuzzy star-shaped numbers. *J. Math. Comput. Sci.*, 23(4):321–327, 2021.
20. V. A. Khan, U. Tuba, SK. A. Rahamana, and A. Ahmad. Ideal convergent sequence spaces of fuzzy star-shaped numbers. *J. Intell. Fuzzy Syst.*, 40:11355–11362, 2021.
21. Y. K. Kim. Some notes on L_p-metric space of fuzzy sets. *Int. J. Fuzzy Log. Intell. Syst.*, 10(3):242–246, 2010.
22. N. Konwar and P. Debnath. $\mathcal{I}_\lambda$-convergence in intuitionistic fuzzy n-normed linear space. *Ann. Fuzzy Math. Inform.*, 13(1):91–107, 2017.
23. N. Konwar and P. Debnath. Continuity and Banach contraction principle in intuitionistic fuzzy n-normed linear spaces. *J. Intell. Fuzzy Syst.*, 33(4):2363–2373, 2017.
24. N. Konwar and P. Debnath. Some new contractive conditions and related fixed point theorems in intuitionistic fuzzy n-Banach spaces. *J. Intell. Fuzzy Syst.*, 34(1):361–372, 2018.
25. N. Konwar, B. Davvaz, and P. Debnath. Approximation of new bounded operators in intuitionistic fuzzy n-Banach spaces. *J. Intell. Fuzzy Syst.*, 35(6):6301–6312, 2018.
26. N. Konwar, B. Davvaz, and P. Debnath. Results on generalized intuitionistic fuzzy hypergroupoids. *J. Intell. Fuzzy Syst.*, 36(3):2571–2580, 2019.
27. P. Kostyrko, T. Šalát, and W. Wilczynski. $\mathcal{I}$-convergence. *Real Anal. Exch.*, 26(2):669–686, 2000.
28. K. Kumar and V. Kumar. On the $\mathcal{I}$ and $\mathcal{I}^*$-convergence of sequences in fuzzy normed spaces. *Adv. Fuzzy Syst.*, 3:341–365, 2008.
29. K. Kumar and V. Kumar. On the ideal convergence of sequences of fuzzy numbers. *Inf. Sci.*, 178:4670–4678, 2008.
30. M. Gürdal. On ideal convergent sequences in 2-normed spaces. *Thai. J. Math.*, 4(1):85–91, 2006.
31. K. Kumar and V. Kumar. On the ideal convergence of sequences in intuitionistic fuzzy normed spaces. *Selcuk J. Math.*, 10(2):27–41, 2009.
32. V. Kumar. On $\mathcal{I}$ and $\mathcal{I}^*$-convergence of double sequences. *Math. Commun.*, 12:171–181, 2007.
33. M. Mursaleen, S. A. Mohiuddine, and O. H.H. Edely. On the ideal convergence of double sequences in intuitionistic fuzzy normed spaces. *Comput. Math. Appl.*, 59:603–611, 2010.

34. M. Mursaleen and S. A. Mohiuddine. On ideal convergence of double sequences in probabilistic normed spaces. *Math. Rep.*, 12(62):359–371, 2010.
35. D. Qiu, L. hu, and Z. -W. Mo. On starshaped fuzzy sets. *Fuzzy Sets Syst.*, 160(11):1563–1577, 2009.
36. R. T. Rockafellar. *Convex Analysis*. Princeton University Press: London, 1971.
37. T. Šalát, B. C. Tripathy, and M. Ziman. On some properties of $\mathcal{I}$-convergence. *Tatra Mt. Math. Publ.*, 28(2):274–286, 2004.
38. E. Savas and M. Gürdal. Certain summability methods in intuitionistic fuzzy normed spaces. *J. Intell. Fuzzy Syst.*, 27(4):1621–1629, 2014.
39. E. Savas and M. Gürdal. Generalized statistically convergent sequences of functions in fuzzy 2-normed spaces. *J. Intell. Fuzzy Syst.*, 27(4):2067–2075, 2014.
40. E. Savas and M. Gürdal. A generalized statistical convergence in intuitionistic fuzzy normed spaces. *Sci. Asia*, 41:289–294, 2015.
41. A. Sahiner, M. Gürdal, and T. Yigit. Ideal convergence characterization of the completion of linear n-normed spaces. *Comput. Math. Appl.*, 61(3):683–689, 2011.
42. B. C. Tripathy and B. Sarma. On $\mathcal{I}$-convergent double sequences of fuzzy real numbers. *Kyungpook Math. J.*, 52(2):189–200, 2012.
43. C. Wu and Z. Zhao Some notes on the characterization of compact sets of fuzzy sets with l_p metric. *Fuzzy Sets Syst.*, 159(16):2104–2115, 2008.
44. H. Yang and Z. Daocheng. A special fuzzy star-shaped numbers space with endograph metric. *Fuzzy Sets Syst.*, 159(16):2104–2115, 2008.
45. L. A. Zadeh. Fuzzy sets. *Inform. Control*, 8:338–353, 1965.
46. Z. Zhao and C. Wu. A characterization for compact sets in the space of fuzzy star-shaped numbers with metric. *J. Intell. Fuzzy Syst.*, 38(2):1855–1864, 2020.
47. Z. Zhao and C. Wu. Some properties of space of fuzzy numbers with a kind of L_p-metric. *J. Nat. Sci. Heilongjiang Univ.*, 1:109–112, 2009.

10 Digitalization Investment Analysis in Maritime Industry with Interval–Valued Pythagorean Fuzzy Present Worth Analysis

Eda Boltürk
Istanbul Settlement and Custody Bank Inc.

CONTENTS

10.1 Introduction 141
10.2 Literature Review 142
10.3 Preliminaries: Interval-Valued Pythagorean Fuzzy Sets 144
10.4 Interval-Valued Pythagorean Fuzzy Present Worth Analysis 145
10.5 Application 145
10.6 Results and Discussion 146
10.7 Conclusion 148
Bibliography 148

10.1 INTRODUCTION

It can be said that digitalization studies and applications have become widespread after the COVID-19 Pandemic. Along with the digitalization process, companies that did not go through the digitalization processes had to keep up with these situations. The maritime sector is also affected after COVID-19 Pandemic, and the literature shows that some applications have been made.

In a changing world, companies need to plan their investments correctly in order to be more competitive in the market and to be as strong as before. Investment analysis is a very crucial subject for companies, especially in terms of benefits and cost. Many techniques are used in investment analysis, which is an important topic of the engineering economy. Some of them are: present worth analysis, future worth analysis, annual worth analysis, internal rate of return analysis, external rate of return

DOI: 10.1201/9781003312017-10

analysis, capital budget analysis, cost-benefit analysis, etc. These techniques offer investors the opportunity to evaluate alternatives from different perspectives. Investors who will be decision makers while making the evaluations can sometimes experience uncertainty, which may create some deviations in the evaluation of the investment. Fuzzy logic can be used to eliminate this problem.

Fuzzy sets theory was developed by Zadeh [1], and the extensions of these ordinary fuzzy sets have been developed by numerous fuzzy set researchers. These fuzzy set extensions have been used in estimating, decision-making, engineering economics, and controlling together with other intelligent systems. The extensions of ordinary fuzzy sets can be given as type-2 fuzzy sets [1], intuitionistic fuzzy sets in 1986 [2], fuzzy multisets [3], intuitionistic fuzzy sets of second type [4], neutrosophic sets [5], nonstationary fuzzy sets [6], hesitant fuzzy sets [7], Pythagorean fuzzy sets [8], picture fuzzy sets [9], q-rung orthopair fuzzy sets [3], fermatean fuzzy sets [10], spherical fuzzy sets [11], and circular intuitionistic fuzzy sets [12]. The present worth analysis method, which is one of the investment evaluation analyses, has been extended with fuzzy logic. In the literature, the present worth analysis is extended with fuzzy sets such as hesitant fuzzy present worth analysis [13], Pythagorean fuzzy present worth analysis [14], spherical fuzzy present worth analysis method [15], fermatean fuzzy present worth analysis [16], and picture fuzzy present worth analysis [17], interval-valued and circular intuitionistic fuzzy present worth analysis [18] in the literature.

Soft calculation techniques are used in many different fields, and there are similar studies in the literature [19]. To the best of our knowledge, there is no such study as interval-valued Pythagorean fuzzy present worth analysis. The aim of this chapter is to present interval-valued Pythagorean fuzzy present worth analysis and to demonstrate its applicability in maritime industry. Pythagorean fuzzy sets aid to eliminate the obtained uncertainty about the present worth analysis parameters. For this reason, new fuzzy extensions of the current value analysis including the uncertainty of membership functions have been developed.

This chapter is organized as follows: Literature review of maritime industry digitalization is given in Section 10.2. In Section 10.3, preliminary information about interval-valued Pythagorean fuzzy sets is given. In Section 10.4, the steps of the interval-valued Pythagorean fuzzy present worth analysis are shown. In Section 10.5, a numerical digitalization transformation project for a container ship company is analyzed in tables. In Section 10.6, results and discussion of application and proposed fuzzy extended present worth analysis are presented. In Section 10.7, the results and future suggestions are given.

10.2 LITERATURE REVIEW

Digitalization of maritime industry is discussed in the literature. Zhang and Tang [20] published the impact of digitalization on ship management. Giering and Dyck [21] gave insight into the current state of the maritime industry, and a "Maritime Digital Twin Architecture" is developed. Botnaryuk and Kalinina [22] analyzed the impact of the internet of things (IoT) and proposed collaboration between employers and educational institutions IoT in the maritime industry to optimize port terminal operations. Bartusevičienė and Valionienė [23] developed a case study approach to the digitalization challenges of future maritime professionals. Vanderheggen et al. [24] demonstrated and presented key aspects and components of digitalization process and experiences on merging information technology and operational technology environments in vessels with big data. Sandvik et al. [25] presented the digital servitization literature in the transitions to autonomous solutions. Tsiulin et al. [26] presented the case of document processing in maritime transport for document coordination between blockchain scenario and port community system in Denmark. Bartusevičienė and Valionienė [23] presented trends in digital shipping development along with logistics processes in the maritime industry. Räikkönen et al. [27] illustrated a model to evaluate the customer value of digital solutions in forest and maritime industry. Strandhagen et al. [28] identified challenges in shipbuilding supply chains and explored the impact of industry 4.0 technologies on shipbuilding sustainability. Danielsen [29] cited findings from an exploratory negotiation study targeting the skill sets needed for digital transformation launches and future engineer-to-order operations in maritime industry. Sullivan et al. [30] presented an approach to understand the advantages of Maritime 4.0 advantages in advanced manufacturing for vessel development and digitalization. Ellingsen and Aasland [31] demonstrated digitalizing the maritime industry through a technology acquisition study. Sanchez-Gonzalez et al. [32] presented the need for digitalization in the maritime transport industry with a state-of-the-art study. Westgarth and Rigby [33] presented the education and workforce of the future in the fourth maritime revolution. Gkerekos et al. [34] addressed digitalization in the UK maritime sector with a project aimed at adopting ease of adaptation and industry 4.0. Nasaruddin and Emad [35] analyzed the future roles of maritime professionals in digitalizing era with the effects of blockchain disruption. Akyuz et al. [36] showed the impact of machine learning impact studies on the future of maritime transport industry. Sencila and Alop [37] demonstrated an approach for autonomous shipping digitalization in maritime digitalization. Maydanova et al. [38] came to the fore in the blockchain technology application maritime industry. Sklyar et al. [39] studied the digitalization and digitalized states of a service ecosystem in maritime industry. Meskauskiene et al. [40] conducted a study as part of the waterway digitalization. Kitada et al. [41] presented the effects, results, and leadership of digitalization on ship management. Feibert et al. [42] demonstrated how an integrated perspective of business process management and digitization can improve supply chain performance for shipping companies. Heilig et al. [43] made an analysis of maritime ports with digital transformation and game framework. Calabria et al. [44] demonstrated digitalization of maritime traffic flow by comprising a project in sea traffic management. Meester the effects of digitalization in the maritime industry with big data analysis.

It can be easily seen from the literature that there are no study maritime digitalization studies with present worth analysis and interval-valued Pythagorean fuzzy sets in maritime digitalization. In addition, the literature shows that with the advancement of industry 4.0, digitalization in the maritime industry needs to be further investigated.

10.3 PRELIMINARIES: INTERVAL-VALUED PYTHAGOREAN FUZZY SETS

Preliminary information of interval-valued Pythagorean fuzzy sets is given in this section as follows:

Definition 10.1 *Given a finite universal set K, and interval-valued Pythagorean fuzzy sets $\tilde{P}$ on K is provided by [45], [46]:*

$$\tilde{A} = \{\langle a, \mu_{\tilde{a}}, v_{\tilde{x}}\rangle; a \in K\} \tag{10.1}$$

where $\mu_{\tilde{a}}(a) : K \to \varepsilon([0,1])$ and $\upsilon_{\tilde{a}}(a) : K \to \varepsilon([0,1])$ are the membership and non-membership functions, respectively. $\sup(\tilde{\mu}_{\tilde{a}}^2) + \sup(\tilde{v}_{\tilde{a}}^2)$ $\varepsilon([0,1])$*is the set of all closed intervals in $[0,1]$, and we call the two tuples $\tilde{\mu}_{\tilde{a}}(a), \tilde{v}_{\tilde{a}}(a)$ as interval-valued Pythagorean fuzzy number. If we let $\tilde{\mu}_{\tilde{a}}(a) = [a^-, a^+]$ and $\tilde{v}_{\tilde{a}}(a) = [a^-, a^+]$ then interval-valued Pythagorean fuzzy number can be defined as $\tilde{a} = ([p^-, p^+], [q^-, q^+]$, where $(p^+)^2 + (q^+)^2 \leq 1$.*

Definition 10.2 *Let $\tilde{A} = \langle [\mu_L^-, \mu_U^+], [v_L^-, v_U^+]\rangle$, be an interval-valued Pythagorean fuzzy number and $\tilde{A}_i$, $i = 1, 2, ..., k$ be a collection of interval-valued Pythagorean fuzzy numbers. Their aggregated value using interval-valued Pythagorean fuzzy weighted geometric (IVPFWG) operator is illustrated in Eq. (1.2) as an interval-valued Pythagorean fuzzy number [47].*

$$IVPFWG_\lambda(\tilde{A}_1, \tilde{A}_2, \tilde{A}_3, ..., \tilde{A}_k) = \left(\left[\prod_{i=1}^{k}(\mu_{A_i}^L)^{\lambda_i}, \prod_{i=1}^{k}(\mu_{A_i^U})^{\lambda_i}\right], \left[\sqrt{1 - \prod_{i=1}^{k}(1-(v_{A_i}^L)^2)^{\lambda_i}}, \sqrt{1 - \prod_{i=1}^{k}(1-(v_{A_i}^U)^2)^{\lambda_i}}\right]\right) \tag{10.2}$$

Definition 10.3 *Let $\tilde{A} = \langle [\mu_L^-, \mu_U^+], [v_L^-, v_U^+]\rangle$ be an interval-valued Pythagorean fuzzy number. π_L and π_U are the hesitancy degree of the lower and upper points of A, respectively calculated as in Eqs. (1.3) and (1.4) [48]:*

$$\pi_U^2 = 1 - (\mu_L^2 + v_L^2). \tag{10.3}$$

$$\pi_L^2 = 1 - (\mu_U^2 + v_U^2). \tag{10.4}$$

Definition 10.4 *Let $\tilde{A} = \langle [\mu_L^-, \mu_U^+], [v_L^-, v_U^+]\rangle$ be an interval-valued Pythagorean fuzzy number. The defuzzification of this number is calculated by Eq. (1.5) [48].*

$$IVPFN_D(\tilde{A}) = \frac{\mu_L^2 + \mu_U^2 + (1 - v_L^2 + \pi_U^2) + (1 - v_U^2 + \pi_L^2) + \mu_L \times \mu_U - \sqrt[4]{(1 - v_L^2 - \pi_U^2) \times (1 - v_u^2 - \pi_L^2)}}{6} \tag{10.5}$$

Definition 10.5 *Interval-valued Pythagorean fuzzy present worth analysis is obtained from interval-valued Pythagorean fuzzy numbers. Interval-valued Pythagorean fuzzy present worth formula is given as in Eq. (1.6).*

$$\begin{aligned}\widetilde{PW}_{IVPFN} =& \widetilde{FC}_{IVPFN} - \widetilde{AC}_{IVPFN}\left[\frac{(1+\tilde{i}_{IVPFN})^{\tilde{n}_{IVPFN}}-1}{\tilde{i}_{IVPFN}(1+\tilde{i}_{IVPFN})^{\tilde{n}_I VPFN}}\right]\\ &+\widetilde{AB}_{IVPFN}\left[\frac{(1+\tilde{i}_{IVPFN})^{\tilde{n}_{IVPFN}}-1}{\tilde{i}_{IVPFN}(1+\tilde{i}_{IVPFN})^{\tilde{n}_I VPFN}}\right]\\ &+\widetilde{SV}_{IVPFN}(1+\tilde{i}_{IVPFN})^{-\tilde{n}_{IVPFN}}\end{aligned} \tag{10.6}$$

10.4 INTERVAL-VALUED PYTHAGOREAN FUZZY PRESENT WORTH ANALYSIS

The steps of interval-valued Pythagorean fuzzy present worth analysis are given in Figure 10.1, respectively. First, the experts give their ideas with interval-valued Pythagorean fuzzy membership functions. Then each investment analysis parameter is aggregated with IVPFWG operator.The aggregated opinions are defuzzified with defuzzification formula. After that, defuzzified values are normalized and normalized possible values are obtained. Finally, the defuzzified values are used to compute final present worth of investment.

10.5 APPLICATION

A container ship company in the maritime industry decides to digitize its processes in order to be more competitive. This study is carried out by Expert A and Expert B, who carried out digitalization projects in the maritime industry. The weights of these experts are 0.6 and 0.4, respectively. They give opinions for each investment

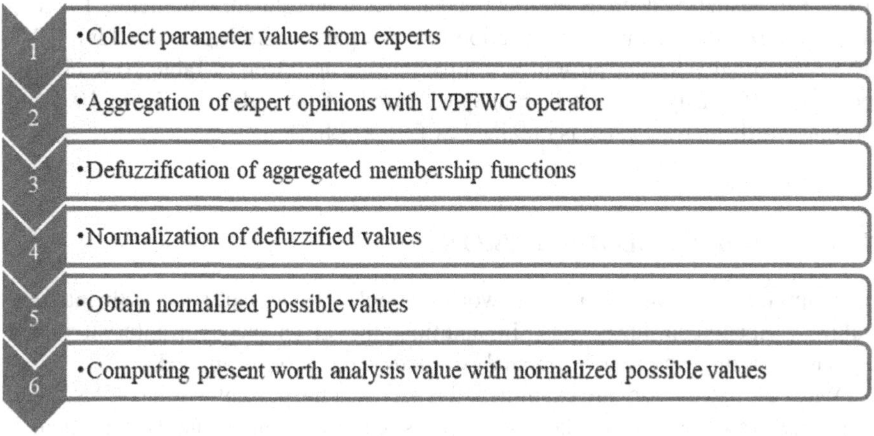
1
•Collect parameter values from experts
2
•Aggregation of expert opinions with IVPFWG operator
3
•Defuzzification of aggregated membership functions
4
•Normalization of defuzzified values
5
•Obtain normalized possible values
6
•Computing present worth analysis value with normalized possible values

Figure 10.4-1 The steps of interval-valued Pythagorean fuzzy present worth analysis.

Table 10.1
Investment Parameters of Expert A and B for Interval-Valued Pythagorean Fuzzy Sets

Parameters	Possible Value	Expert A	Expert B
First cost	€ 1,400	([0.10,0.30],[0.70,0.90])	([0.40,0.60],[0.40,0.60])
	€ 1,500	([0.50,0.70],[0.30,0.50])	([0.70,0.90],[0.10,0.30])
	€ 2,000	([0.60,0.80],[0.20,0.40])	([0.60,0.80],[0.20,0.40])
Annual benefit	€ 25,000	([0.50,0.70],[0.30,0.50])	([0.40,0.60],[0.40,0.60])
	€ 30,000	([0.40,0.60],[0.40,0.60])	([0.50,0.70],[0.30,0.50])
	€ 33,000	([0.20,0.40],[0.60,0.80])	([0.70,0.90],[0.10,0.30])
Annual cost	€ 500	([0.40,0.60],[0.40,0.60])	([0.20,0.40],[0.60,0.80])
	€ 600	([0.50,0.70],[0.30,0.50])	([0.70,0.90],[0.10,0.30])
	€ 550	([0.10,0.30],[0.70,0.90])	([0.40,0.60],[0.40,0.60])
Salvage value	€ 600	([0.50,0.70],[0.30,0.50])	([0.10,0.30],[0.70,0.90])
	€ 750	([0.20,0.40],[0.60,0.80])	([0.50,0.70],[0.30,0.50])
	€ 800	([0.40,0.60],[0.40,0.60])	([0.40,0.60],[0.40,0.60])
Interest rate	1.58	([0.20,0.40],[0.60,0.80])	([0.40,0.60],[0.40,0.60])
	1.54	([0.70,0.90],[0.10,0.30])	([0.50,0.70],[0.30,0.50])
	1.64	([0.40,0.60],[0.40,0.60])	([0.50,0.70],[0.30,0.50])
Life	3 year	([0.40,0.60],[0.40,0.60])	([0.70,0.90],[0.10,0.30])
	2 year	([0.50,0.70],[0.30,0.50])	([0.70,0.90],[0.10,0.30])
	4 year	([0.60,0.80],[0.20,0.40])	([0.40,0.60],[0.40,0.60])

problem as shown in Table 10.1. The numbers are taken from Haktanır and Kahraman's [48] interval-valued Pythagorean fuzzy correlation scale. These defined membership and non-membership degrees are given with interval-valued Pythagorean fuzzy sets. These values of Expert A and Expert B are aggregated as shown in Table 10.2. The hesitancy degrees are obtained for each investment parameter. The values of defuzzification and normalization for each parameters is given in Table 10.3. The defuzzified values of present worth parameters are given in Table 10.4. Finally, present worth analysis value is calculated based on the values in Table 10.4 and present worth analysis value is obtained as €15,273.8.

10.6 RESULTS AND DISCUSSION

This application shows us present worth formula can be extended with interval-valued Pythagorean fuzzy sets. In addition, the given steps of interval-valued Pythagorean fuzzy present worth analysis method can also be applied.

When the calculations are examined, it is seen that the present worth is €15,273.8. A positive value means that the investment is feasible. If this value were a negative value, we would conclude that this investment would not be possible. The weights of Expert A and Expert B are 0.6 and 0.4, respectively. In addition to the closeness

Table 10.2
Aggregated Memberships and Hesitancy Degrees for Investment Parameters

Parameters	Aggregated Memberships	Hesitancy Degree
First cost	([0.174,0.396],[0.614,0.831])	(0.390,0.770)
	([0.600,0.800],[0.200,0.400])	(0.447,0.775)
Annual benefit	([0.457,0.658],[0.344,0.544])	(0.520,0.820)
	([0.437,0.638],[0.364,0.564])	(0.524,0.822)
	([0.330,0.553],[0.488,0.692])	(0.464,0.808)
Annual cost	([0.303,0.510],[0.497,0.701])	(0.498,0.813)
	([0.572,0.774],[0.243,0.436])	(0.460,0.784)
	([0.174,0.396],[0.614,0.831])	(0.390,0.770)
Salvage value	([0.263,0.499],[0.527,0.753])	(0.429,0.808)
	([0.289,0.500],[0.513,0.719])	(0.482,0.808)
	([0.400,0.600],[0.400,0.600])	(0.529,0.825)
Interest rate	([0.264,0.470],[0.535,0.739])	(0.482,0.802)
	([0.612,0.814],[0.207,0.397])	(0.424,0.763)
	([0.437,0.638],[0.364,0.564])	(0.524,0.822)
Life	([0.500,0.706],[0.315,0.485])	(0.517,0.806)
	([0.572,0.774],[0.235,0.398])	(0.492,0.786)
	([0.510,0.713],[0.300,0.497])	(0.495,0.806)

Table 10.3
Defuzzification Values and Normalization Formulations for Investment Parameters

Parameters	Defuzzification Values	Normalization Values
First cost	0.366	0.190
	0.769	0.398
	0.795	0.412
Annual benefit	0.670	0.362
	0.651	0.352
	0.530	0.286
Annual cost	0.512	0.311
	0.769	0.467
	0.366	0.222
Salvage value	0.467	0.296
	0.494	0.313
	0.615	0.390
Interest rate	0.468	0.244
	0.800	0.417
	0.651	0.339
Life	0.713	0.323
	0.780	0.353
	0.716	0.324

Table 10.4
Defuzzified Values of Investment Parameter Interval-Valued Pythagorean Present Worth Analysis

Parameters	Values
First cost	€1,687.155
Annual benefit	€29,048.208
Annual cost	€557.794
Salvage value	€725.051
interest	1.584
Life	2.971 year

of these values, experts with very different experiences will be able to earn different points for the study and interpretation of the method.

This study was handled by two experts in digitalization application for maritime industry. More experts can be added for future studies. However, the proposed method can be used for other industries such as automotive, health, etc. In addition, the defuzzification process may be done in the last steps of application.

10.7 CONCLUSION

In this study, a new fuzzy engineering economics analysis called interval-valued Pythagorean fuzzy present value analysis is demonstrated. The interval-valued Pythagorean fuzzy present worth analysis extension is applied to a container ship company in digitalization in Industry 4.0. The application parameters are given in interval-valued Pythagorean fuzzy numbers and were determined by two experts specialized in both maritime industry and digitalization projects. The steps of the proposed model are given in Figure 10.1, and the interval-valued Pythagorean aggregation formula and defuzzification formula are used to obtain defuzzified and combined parameters. The defuzzified numbers are used to obtain the present worth value. In this study, an alternative was evaluated and the present worth was calculated as €15,273.8.

For future studies, interval-valued q-rung orthopair fuzzy and interval-valued Fermatean fuzzy present worth analysis can be used in the same application, and sensitivity analysis can be added.

Bibliography

1. L. A. Zadeh. Fuzzy sets. *Inf. Control*, 8 (3):338–353, 1965.
2. K. T. Atanassov. Intuitionistic fuzzy sets. *Fuzzy Sets Syst.*, 20(1):87–96, 1986.
3. R. R. Yager. On the theory of bags. *Int. J. Gen. Syst.*, 13(1):23–37, 1986.
4. K. T. Atanassov. More on intuitionistic fuzzy sets. *Fuzzy Sets Syst.*, 33(1):37–45, 1989.
5. F. Smarandache. *A Unifying Field in Logics. Neutrosophy: Neutrosophic Probability, Set and Logic*. American Research Press, Rehoboth, 1999.

6. J. M. Garibaldi and T. Ozen. Uncertain fuzzy reasoning: A case study in modelling expert decision making. *IEEE Trans. Fuzzy Syst.*, 15 (1):16–30, 2007.
7. V. Torra. Hesitant fuzzy sets. *Int. J. Intell. Syst.*, 25(6):529–539, 2010.
8. R. R. Yager. Pythagorean fuzzy subsets. *2013 Joint IFSA World Congress and NAFIPS Annual Meeting (IFSA/NAFIPS)*, Edmonton, Canada, pp. 57–61, 2013.
9. B. C. Cuong and V. Kreinovich. Picture fuzzy sets. *J. Comput. Sci. Technol.*, 30(4):409–420, 2014.
10. T. Senapati and R. R. Yager. Fermatean fuzzy sets. *J. Ambient Intell. Humaniz. Comput.*, 11(2):663–674, 2020.
11. F. Kutlu Gündoğdu and C. Kahraman. Spherical fuzzy sets and spherical fuzzy TOPSIS method. *J. Intell. Fuzzy Syst.*, 36 (1):337–352, 2019.
12. K. T. Atanassov. Circular intuitionistic fuzzy sets. *J. Intell. Fuzzy Syst.*, 39(5):5981–5986, 2020.
13. C. Kahraman, S. C. Onar, and B. Oztaysi. Present Worth Analysis Using Hesitant Fuzzy Sets. *Proceedings of the 9th Conference of the European Society for Fuzzy Logic and Technology (EUSFLAT 2015)*, Gijón, Spain. Atlantis Press, pp. 255–259, 2015.
14. C. Kahraman, S. C. Onar, and B. Oztaysi. Present worth analysis using pythagorean fuzzy set. In: Kacprzyk, J., Szmidt, E., Zadrożny, S., Atanassov, K., Krawczak, M. (eds), *Advances in Fuzzy Logic and Technology 2017. EUSFLAT IWIFSGN 2017. Advances in Intelligent Systems and Computing*, Warsaw, Poland, Springer, Cham, vol. 642, pp. 336–342, 2017.
15. E. Boltürk and S. Seker. Present worth analysis using spherical Fuzzy sets. In: Kahraman, C., Cebi, S., Cevik Onar, S., Oztaysi, B., Tolga, A.C., and Sari, I.U. (eds), *Intelligent and Fuzzy Techniques for Emerging Conditions and Digital Transformation. INFUS 2021. Lecture Notes in Networks and Systems*, Istanbul, Turkey. Springer, Cham, vol. 308, pp. 777–788, 2021.
16. D. Sergi and I. U. Sari. Fuzzy capital budgeting using fermatean fuzzy sets. *Proceedings of the INFUS 2020 Conference*, Istanbul, Turkey. Springer, pp. 448–456, 2020.
17. E. Boltürk. Container ship investment analysis using picture Fuzzy present worth analysis. *JEMS Maritime Sci.*, 9 (4):233–242, 2021.
18. E. Boltürk and C. Kahraman. Interval-valued and circular intuitionistic fuzzy present worth analyses. *Informatica*, 2022:1–19, 2022. doi: 10.15388/22-INFOR478
19. P. Debnath and S. A. Mohiuddine. *Soft Computing Techniques in Engineering, Health, Mathematical and Social Sciences*. CRC Press, Boca Raton, FL, 2021.
20. P. Zhang and L. Tang. *Ship Management: Theory and Practice*, Routledge, London, 2021.
21. J. E. Giering and A. Dyck. Maritime Digital Twin architecture. *Automatisierungstechnik*, 69 (12):1081–1095, 2021.
22. M. V. Botnaryuk, and S. A. Kalinina, . Impact of the Internet of Things on the formation of a model for optimizing port terminal operations. *Journal of Physics: Conference Series, International Conference on Actual Issues of Mechanical Engineering (AIME 2021)*, , Novorossiysk, Russia, vol. 2061(1), p. 012140, 2022.
23. I. Bartusevičienė, and E. Valionienė. An integrative approach for digitalization challenges of the future maritime specialists: A case study of the Lithuanian Maritime Academy. *TransNav*, 15 (2):349–355, 2021.
24. K. Vanderheggen, N. Meredith, J. Janssen, and A. Morandi. Bringing big data technology to wind turbine installation vessels. *SNAME Maritime Convention, Providence*, Rhode, Island, USA, 2021.

25. H. O. Sandvik, D. Sjödin, T. Brekke, and V. Parida. Inherent paradoxes in the shift to autonomous solutions provision: a multilevel investigation of the shipping industry. *Serv. Bus.*, 16(2):1–29, 2021.
26. S. Tsiulin, K. H. Reinau, and N. Goryaev. Conceptual comparison of port commmunity system and blockchain scenario for maritime document handling. *2020 Global Smart Industry Conference (GloSIC)*, Chelyabinsk, Russia, 66–71, 2020.
27. M. R äikkönen, J. Keski-Rahkonen, H. Kortelainen, M. Tikkanen, P. Valkokari, A. Vehanen, and S. Pirttikangas. Towards a framework for assessing the customer value of digital solutions. *30th European Safety and Reliability Conference, ESREL 2020 and 15th Probabilistic Safety Assessment and Management Conference, PSAM15 2020: Online*, Venice, Italy, pp. 2358–2365, 2020.
28. J. W. Strandhagen, S. V. Buer, M. Semini, E. Alfnes, and J. O. Strandhagen. Sustainability challenges and how Industry 4.0 technologies can address them: A case study of a shipbuilding supply chain. *Prod. Plan. Control*, 33(9-10):1–16, 2020.
29. A. V. Danielsen. Digital transformation and its potential effects on future management: Insights from an ETO context. *IFIP International Conference on Advances in Production Management Systems, Novi Sad, Serbia.* Springer International Publishing, pp. 146–153, 2020, Novi Sad, Serbia.
30. B. P. Sullivan, S. Desai, J. Sole, M. Rossi, L. Ramundo, and S. Terzi. Maritime 4.0–opportunities in digitalization and advanced manufacturing for vessel development. *Proc. Manuf.*, 42:246–253, 2020.
31. O. Ellingsen and K. E. Aasland. Digitalizing the maritime industry: A case study of technology acquisition and enabling advanced manufacturing technology. *J. Eng. Technol. Manag. - JET-M*, 54:12–27, 2019.
32. P.-L. Sanchez-Gonzalez, D. Díaz-Gutiérrez, T. J. Leo, and L. R. Núnez-Rivas. Toward digitalization of maritime transport? *Sensors*, 19(4):926, 2019.
33. R. Westgarth and J. Rigby. Future workforce and training in the fourth maritime revolution. *RINA, Royal Institution of Naval Architects - International Conference on Marine Industry 4.0, Papers*, Rotterdam, Netherlands, pp. 55-61, 2019.
34. C. Gkerekos, G. Theotokatos, L. Bujorianu, E. Boulougouris, D. Vassalos, B. Carballedo, S. McCluskey, T. Coats, and R. Sloan. Digitalisation in the uk maritime sector: A stakeholders' pulse check. *International Conference on Marine Industry 4.0*, Rotterdam, Netherlands, vol. 4, 2019.
35. M. M. Nasaruddin and G. R. Emad. Preparing maritime professionals for their future roles in a digitalized era: Bridging the blockchain skills gap in maritime education and training. *Proceedings of the International Association of Maritime Universities (IAMU) Conference*.Tokyo, Japan, pp. 87–97, 2019.
36. E. Akyuz, K. Cicek, and M. Celik. A Comparative research of machine learning impact to future of maritime transportation. *Proc. Comput. Sci.*, 158:275–280, 2019.
37. V. Sencila and A. Alop. Possibility to use gartner hype cycle approach for autonomous shipping. In: Ostasevicius, V. (Ed.), *Transport Means 2019: Proceedings of the 23rd International Scientific Conference.* Kaunas University of Technology Press, Kaunas, pp. 574–577, 2019.
38. S. Maydanova, I. Ilin, and A. Lepekhin. Capabilities evaluation in an enterprise architecture context for digital transformation of seaports network. *Proceedings of the 33rd International Business Information Management Association Conference, IBIMA 2019: Education Excellence and Innovation Management through Vision 2020*, Granada, Spain, pp. 5103–5111, 2019.

39. A. Sklyar, C. Kowalkowski, D. Sörhammar, and B. Tronvoll. Resource integration through digitalisation: A service ecosystem perspective. *J. Mark. Manag.*, 35 (11–12):974–991, 2019.
40. V. Meskauskiene, A. Öörni, and A. Sell. Transparency driven public sector innovation: Smart waterways and maritime traffic in Finland. *European, Mediterranean, and Middle Eastern Conference on Information Systems*, Limassol, Cyprus, 331–350, 2018.
41. M. Kitada, M. Baldauf, A. Mannov, P. A. Svendsen, R. Baumler, J.-U. Schröder-Hinrichs, D. Dalaklis, T. Fonseca, X. Shi, and K. Lagdami. Command of vessels in the era of digitalization. *Advances in Human Factors, Business Management and Society: Proceedings of the AHFE 2018 International Conference on Human Factors, Business Management and Society*, Orlando, FL. Springer, Cham, vol. 783, pp. 339–350, 2018.
42. D. C. Feibert, M. S. Hansen, and P. Jacobsen. An integrated process and digitalization perspective on the shipping supply chain—A literature review. *2017 IEEE International Conference on Industrial Engineering and Engineering Management (IEEM)*, Singapore, pp. 1352–1356, 2017.
43. L. Heilig, E. Lalla-Ruiz, and S. Vo. Digital transformation in maritime ports: Analysis and a game theoretic framework. *NETNOMICS: Econ. Res. Electron. Netw.*, 18(2):227–254, 2017.
44. L. Calabria. STM sea traffic management: Moving forward the digitalization of maritime traffic flow. *J. Marit. Res.*, 14(2):61–65, 2017.
45. X. Peng and Y. Yang. Fundamental properties of interval-valued Pythagorean fuzzy aggregation operators. *Int. J. Intell. Syst.*, 31(5):444–487, 2016.
46. X. Zhang. Multicriteria pythagorean fuzzy decision analysis: A hierarchical QUALIFLEX approach with the closeness index-based ranking methods. *Inf. Sci.*, 330:104–124, 2016.
47. K. Rahman, S. Abdullah, R. Ahmed, and M. Ullah. Pythagorean fuzzy Einstein weighted geometric aggregation operator and their application to multiple attribute group decision making. *J. Intell. Fuzzy Syst.*, 33(1):635–647, 2017.
48. E. Haktanır and C. Kahraman. A novel interval-valued Pythagorean fuzzy QFD method and its application to solar photovoltaic technology development. *Comput. Ind. Eng.*, 132:361–372, 2019.

11 Composite Mapping on Hesitant Fuzzy Soft Classes

Manash Jyoti Borah
Bahona College

Bipan Hazarika
Gauhati University

CONTENTS

11.1 Introduction 153
11.2 Background 154
11.3 Preliminary Results 155
11.4 Mapping on Hesitant Fuzzy Soft Classes 156
11.5 Conclusion 164
Bibliography 164

11.1 INTRODUCTION

Amidst many theories, the theory of probability, theory of fuzzy sets, theory of intuitionistic fuzzy sets, theory of rough sets, etc. are to be named a few. All these can be considered as essential mathematical tools for dealing with uncertain data, obtained in various fields of engineering, social science, physics, computer science, medical science, economics, multidisciplinary approach, and many other diverse fields. But all these theories in spite of having pros have their own shortcoming to overcome. The most apt theory for dealing with uncertainties is the theory of fuzzy sets. But, the same fine touch and extensions of the fuzzy sets need to be encountered in various practical applications and problems of real life. The concept of a hesitant fuzzy set is one of such extensions.

All the abovementioned theories are partly successful in dealing with different problems arising due to vagueness present in the real world. But there are also some aspects where these theories failed miserably to give satisfactory results possibly due to the inadequacy of the parameterization tool in them. Soft set theory, which is free from the difficulties of determining the membership function in fuzzy sets, plays an important role in dealing with uncertainty while modelling the problems in engineering, chemistry, physics, computer science, biology, economics, social sciences, and medical sciences.

DOI: 10.1201/9781003312017-11

11.2 BACKGROUND

The most appropriate theory for dealing with uncertainties is the theory of fuzzy set, which was introduced by L.A. Zadeh [39] in 1965. After that many researchers have studied the expansions of the fuzzy sets. Some of them are intuitionistic fuzzy sets [2], hesitant fuzzy sets [33–35,38], interval-valued intuitionistic hesitant fuzzy sets [9], type 2 hesitant fuzzy sets [31], intuitionistic fuzzy n-normed space [11,12] etc.

In 1999, Molodtsov [29] started the theory of soft sets as a new mathematical tool to deal with uncertainties while modelling the problems in different fields. In [30], Molodtsov et al. successfully applied soft sets in the applications such as game theory, operations research, probability, and theory of measurement. Maji et al. [26] came out with the first practical application of soft sets in decision-making problems. In 2003, Maji et al. [27] defined and introduced several fundamental perception of the soft set theory. Also Cagman et al. [10] established several fundamental perception of the soft set theory. In Refs. [20,21], Kharal and Ahmad studied the theory of a mapping on the classes of soft sets.

An extension of Zadeh [39]fuzzy set theory is the hesitant fuzzy set. These fuzzy sets allow the membership value that an element to a set presented by several possible values. In 2009, V. Torra [33,34] and Verma and Sharma [35] discussed the relationship between hesitant fuzzy set and showed that the envelope of hesitant fuzzy set is an intuitionistic fuzzy set. In 2011, Xu and Xia [38] defined the concept of hesitant fuzzy element, which can be considered as the primary unit of a hesitant fuzzy set, and is a simple yet effective tool used to express the decision maker's hesitant preferences in the computing of decision-making. So many researchers have done lots of research work on aggregation, distance, similarity and correlation measures, clustering analysis, and decision-making with hesitant fuzzy information. In 2013, Babitha and John [3] introduced another useful soft set hesitant fuzzy soft set. They introduced fundamental operations such as intersection, union, compliment and De Morgan's law was proved. In 2014, Wang et al. [36] applied hesitant fuzzy soft sets in multicriteria group decision-making problems.

In 2019, Li et al. [24] introduced the generalized hesitant fuzzy soft sets by integrating generalized fuzzy soft sets with hesitant fuzzy sets. Borah et al. [4,5] established some operations on hesitant fuzzy soft sets and interval-valued hesitant fuzzy soft sets. In 2019, Akram et al. [1] put forward the idea of hesitant fuzzy N-soft sets and established a decision-making process based on hesitant fuzzy N-soft sets and TOPSIS process. Ozlu and Karaaslan [31] studied the notion of type-2 hesitant fuzzy sets and introduced some distance measure methods between two type-2 hesitant fuzzy sets. They also introduced a decision-making process by integrating the proposed distance measures and TOPSIS method. Hao and Chiclana [18] studied new possibility distribution generation method with linguistic quantifier for hesitant fuzzy linguistic term set in 2020. For more relevant works, we refer to [6–8,13–17,19,22,23,25,32,37].

11.3 PRELIMINARY RESULTS

In this section, we recall some basic concepts and definitions regarding fuzzy soft sets, fuzzy soft image, fuzzy soft inverse image, hesitant fuzzy set, and hesitant fuzzy soft set.

Definition 11.1 *[28] Let $\mho$ be an initial universe and Γ be a set of parameters. Let $P(\mho)$ denote the power set of $\mho$ and A be a non-empty subset of Γ. Then Γ_A is called a fuzzy soft set over $\mho$ where $\Gamma : A \to P(\mho)$ is a mapping from A into $P(\mho)$.*

Definition 11.2 *[29] Γ_E is called a soft set over $\mho$ if and only if Γ is a mapping of E into the set of all subsets of the set $\mho$.*

In other words, the soft set is a parameterized family of subsets of the set $\mho$. Every set $\Gamma(\varepsilon)$, $\varepsilon \tilde{\in} E$, from this family may be considered as the set of ε-element of the soft set Γ_E or as the set of ε-approximate elements of the soft set.

Definition 11.3 *[20] Let $\mho$ be a universe and E a set of attributes. Then the collection of all fuzzy soft sets over $\mho$ with attributes from E is called a fuzzy soft class and is denoted by $\overbrace{(\mho, E)}$.*

Definition 11.4 *[20] Let $\overbrace{(P,E)}$and $\overbrace{(Q,E')}$ be classes of fuzzy soft sets over P and Q with attributes from E and E' respectively. Let $r : P \longrightarrow Q$ and $t : E \longrightarrow E'$ be mappings. Then a mappings $f = (r,t) : \overbrace{(P,E)} \longrightarrow \overbrace{(Q,E')}$ is defined as follows.*

For a fuzzy soft set D_A in $\overbrace{(P,E)}$, $f(D_A)$ is a fuzzy soft set in $\overbrace{(Q,E')}$ obtained as follows: for $\beta \tilde{\in} t(E) \tilde{\subseteq} E'$ and $y \tilde{\in} Q$,

$$f(D_A)(\beta)(y) = \begin{cases} \bigcup_{s \tilde{\in} r-1(y)} (\bigcup_{\alpha \tilde{\in} t^{-1}(\beta) \cap A} D_A(\alpha))(x) & \text{if } r^{-1}(y) \neq \phi, t^{-1}(\beta) \cap A \neq \phi \\ 0 & \text{otherwise} \end{cases}$$

$f(D_A)$ is called a fuzzy soft image of a fuzzy soft set D_A.

Definition 11.5 *[20]Let $r : P \longrightarrow Q$ and $t : E \longrightarrow E'$ be mappings. Let $f = (r,t) : \overbrace{(P,E)} \longrightarrow \overbrace{(Q,E')}$ be mappings and G_B, a fuzzy soft set in $\overbrace{(Q,E')}$, where $B \tilde{\subseteq} E'$. Then $f^{-1}(G_B)$, is a fuzzy soft set on $\overbrace{(P,E)}$, defined as follows. For $\alpha \tilde{\in} t^{-1}(B) \tilde{\subseteq} E$ and $x \tilde{\in} P$,*

$$f^{-1}(G_B)(\alpha)(x) = \begin{cases} G_B(t(\alpha))(r(x)), & \text{if } t(\alpha) \tilde{\in} B \\ 0 & \text{otherwise} \end{cases}$$

$f^{-1}(G_B)$ is called a fuzzy soft inverse image of G_B.

Definition 11.6 *[33] Given a fixed set Ω, then a hesitant fuzzy set (shortly HFS) in Ω is in terms of a function that when applied to Ω return a subset of $[0,1]$.*

We express the HFS by a mathematical symbol:
$K = \{< h, \omega_K(x) >: k \in \Omega\}$, *where* $\omega_K(x)$ *is a set of some values in [0,1], denoting the possible membership degrees of the element* $k \in \Omega$ *to the set* Ω. $\omega_K(x)$ *is called a hesitant fuzzy element (HFE) and K is the set of all HFEs.*

Definition 11.7 *[33] Let* $\omega_1, \omega_2 \in K$ *and three operations are defined as follows:*

(1) $\omega_1^C = \cup_{\gamma_1 \in \omega_1} \{1 - \gamma_1\}$;
(2) $\omega_1 \cup \omega_2 = \cup_{\gamma_1 \in \omega_1, \gamma_2 \in \omega_2} \max\{\gamma_1, \gamma_2\}$;
(3) $\omega_1 \cap \omega_2 = \cap_{\gamma_1 \in \omega_1, \gamma_2 \in \omega_2} \min\{\gamma_1, \gamma_2\}$.

Definition 11.8 *[36] Let* $\tilde{\mho}$ *be an initial universe and* $\tilde{E}$ *be a set of parameters. Let* $\tilde{F}(U)$ *be the set of all hesitant fuzzy subsets of* $\tilde{\mho}$. *Then* $F_{\tilde{E}}$ *is called a hesitant fuzzy soft set(HFSS) over* $\tilde{\mho}$, *where* $F : \tilde{E} \to F(\tilde{\mho})$.
A HFSS is a parameterized family of hesitant fuzzy subsets of $\tilde{\mho}$, *that is,* $F(\tilde{\mho})$. *For all* $\varepsilon \tilde{\in} \tilde{E}$, $F(\varepsilon)$ *is referred to as the set of* $\varepsilon-$ *approximate elements of the HFSS* $F_{\tilde{E}}$. *It can be written as* $F(\varepsilon) = \{< h, \mu_F(\varepsilon)(x) >: h \in \tilde{\mho}\}$.
Since HFE can represent the situation, in which different membership functions are considered possible (see [33]), $\mu_F(\varepsilon)(x)$ *is a set of several possible values, which is the hesitant fuzzy membership degree. In particular, if* $F(\varepsilon)$ *has only one element,* $F(\varepsilon)$ *can be called a hesitant fuzzy soft number. For convenience, a hesitant fuzzy soft number (HFSN) is denoted by* $\{< h, \mu_F(\varepsilon)(x) >\}$.

Example 11.1 *Suppose* $\tilde{\mho} = \{a_1, a_2\}$ *be an initial universe and* $\tilde{E} = \{e_1, e_2, e_3, e_4\}$ *be a set of parameters. Let* $\tilde{A} = \{e_1, e_2\}$. *Then the hesitant fuzzy soft set* $F_{\tilde{A}}$ *is given as* $F_{\tilde{A}} = \{F(e_1) = \{< a_1, \{0.6, 0.8\} >, < a_2, \{0.8, 0.4, 0.9\} >\}, F(e_2) = \{< a_1, \{0.9, 0.1, 0.5\} >, < a_2, \{0.2\} >\}\}$.

Definition 11.9 *[3] The union of two hesitant fuzzy soft sets* $U_{\tilde{A}}$ *and* $V_{\tilde{B}}$ *over* $(\tilde{\mho}, \tilde{E})$, *is the hesitant fuzzy soft set* $W_{\tilde{C}}$, *where* $\tilde{C} = \tilde{A} \cup \tilde{B}$ *and* $\forall e \tilde{\in} \tilde{C}$,

$$\mu_{W\tilde{(e)}} = \begin{cases} \mu_{U(e)}, & \text{if } e \tilde{\in} \tilde{A} - \tilde{B}; \\ \mu_{V(e)}, & \text{if } e \tilde{\in} \tilde{A} - \tilde{B}; \\ \mu_{U(e)} \cup \mu_{V(e)}, & \text{if } e \tilde{\in} \tilde{A} \cap \tilde{B}. \end{cases}$$

We write $U_{\tilde{A}} \tilde{\cup} V_{\tilde{B}} = W_{\tilde{C}}$.

11.4 MAPPING ON HESITANT FUZZY SOFT CLASSES

Definition 11.10 *Let* $\tilde{\mho}$ *be a hesitant fuzzy soft universe and* $\tilde{E}$ *a set of attributes. Then the collection of all hesitant fuzzy soft sets over* $\tilde{\mho}$ *with attributes from* $\tilde{E}$ *is called a hesitant fuzzy soft class and is denoted by* $\overline{(\tilde{\mho}, \tilde{E})}$.

Definition 11.11 *Let* $\overline{(\tilde{\mho}, \tilde{E})}$ *and* $\overline{(\tilde{\nabla}, \tilde{E}')}$ *be classes of hesitant fuzzy soft sets over* $\tilde{\mho}$ *and* $\tilde{\nabla}$ *with attributes from* $\tilde{E}$ *and* $\tilde{E}'$, *respectively. Let* $\rho : \tilde{\mho} \longrightarrow \tilde{\nabla}$ *and* $\varsigma : \tilde{E} \longrightarrow \tilde{E}'$ *be mappings. Then a hesitant fuzzy soft mapping* $f_{(\rho,\varsigma)} : \overline{(\tilde{\mho}, \tilde{E})} \longrightarrow \overline{(\tilde{\nabla}, \tilde{E}')}$ *is defined as follows. For a hesitant fuzzy soft set* $F_{\tilde{A}}$ *in* $\overline{(\tilde{\mho}, \tilde{E})}$, $f_{(\rho,\varsigma)}(F_{\tilde{A}})$ *is a hesitant fuzzy soft set in* $\overline{(\tilde{\nabla}, \tilde{E}')}$ *obtained as follows: for* $\eta \tilde{\in} \varsigma(\tilde{E}) \tilde{\subseteq} \tilde{E}'$ *and* $y \tilde{\in} \tilde{\nabla}$,

$f_{(\rho,\varsigma)}(F_{\tilde{A}})(\eta)(y) = \bigcup_{\alpha\tilde{\in}\varsigma^{-1}(\eta)\cap\tilde{A}, s\tilde{\in}\rho^{-1}(y)}(\alpha)\mu_s$; $f_{(\rho,\varsigma)}(F_{\tilde{A}})$ *is called a hesitant fuzzy soft image of a hesitant fuzzy soft set* $F_{\tilde{A}}$. *Hence* $(F_{\tilde{A}}, f_{(\rho,\varsigma)}(F_{\tilde{A}}))\tilde{\in}f_{(\rho,\varsigma)}$, *where* $F_{\tilde{A}}\tilde{\subseteq}\overline{(\tilde{\mho},\tilde{E})}, f_{(\rho,\varsigma)}(F_{\tilde{A}})\tilde{\subseteq}\overline{(\tilde{\nabla},\tilde{E}')}$.

Definition 11.12 *If* $f_{(\rho,\varsigma)} : \overline{(\tilde{\mho},\tilde{E})} \longrightarrow \overline{(\tilde{\nabla},\tilde{E}')}$ *is a hesitant fuzzy soft mapping, then hesitant fuzzy soft class* $\overline{(\tilde{\mho},\tilde{E})}$ *is called the domain of* $f_{(\rho,\varsigma)}$ *and the hesitant fuzzy soft class* $\{G_{\tilde{B}}\tilde{\in}\overline{(\tilde{\nabla},\tilde{E}')} : G_{\tilde{B}} = f_{(\rho,\varsigma)}(H_{\tilde{A}})$, *for some* $H_{\tilde{A}}\tilde{\in}\overline{(\tilde{\mho},\tilde{E})}\}$ *is called the range of* $f_{(\rho,\varsigma)}$. *The hesitant fuzzy soft class* $\overline{(\tilde{\nabla},\tilde{E}')}$ *is called co-domain of* $f_{(\rho,\varsigma)}$.

Definition 11.13 *Let* $f_{(\rho,\varsigma)} : \overline{(\tilde{\mho},\tilde{E})} \longrightarrow \overline{(\tilde{\nabla},\tilde{E}')}$ *be a hesitant fuzzy soft mapping and* $G_{\tilde{B}}$, *a hesitant fuzzy soft set in* $\overline{(\tilde{\nabla},\tilde{E}')}$, *where* $\rho : \tilde{\mho} \longrightarrow \tilde{\nabla}, \varsigma : \tilde{E} \longrightarrow \tilde{E}'$ *and* $\tilde{B}\tilde{\subseteq}\tilde{E}'$. *Then* $f^{-1}_{(\rho,\varsigma)}(G_{\tilde{B}})$ *is a hesitant fuzzy soft set in* $\overline{(\tilde{\mho},\tilde{E})}$ *defined as follows. For* $\alpha\tilde{\in}\varsigma^{-1}(\tilde{B})\tilde{\subseteq}\tilde{E}$ *and* $x\tilde{\in}\tilde{\mho}$, $f^{-1}_{(\rho,\varsigma)}(G_{\tilde{B}})(\alpha)(x) = (\varsigma(\alpha))\mu_{\rho(x)}$; $f^{-1}_{(\rho,\varsigma)}(G_{\tilde{B}})$ *is called a hesitant fuzzy soft inverse image of* $G_{\tilde{B}}$.

Example 11.2 *Let* $\tilde{\mho} = \{a_1,a_2,a_3\}$ *and* $\tilde{\nabla} = \{x,y,z\}, \tilde{E} = \{e_1,e_2,e_3,e_4\}, \tilde{E}' = \{e'_1,e'_2,e'_3\}$ *and* $\overline{(\tilde{\mho},\tilde{E})}, \overline{(\tilde{\nabla},\tilde{E}')}$ *classes of hesitant fuzzy soft sets. Let* $\rho(a_1) = y, \rho(a_2) = x, \rho(a_3) = y$ *and* $\varsigma(e_1) = e'_2, \varsigma(e_2) = e'_1, \varsigma(e_3) = e'_2, \varsigma(e_4) = e'_3$. *Let* $\tilde{A} = \{e_1,e_2,e_4\}$. *Let us consider a hesitant fuzzy soft set* $F_{\tilde{A}}$ *in* $\overline{(\tilde{\mho},\tilde{E})}$ *as*
$F_{\tilde{A}} = \{e_1 = \{< a_1,\{0.6,0.8\} >, < a_2,\{0.8,0.4,0.9\} >, < a_3,\{0.3\} >\}$
$e_2 = \{< a_1,\{0.9,0.1,0.2\} >, < a_2,\{0.5\} >, < a_3,\{0.2,0.4,0.6\} >\}$
$e_4 = \{< a_1,\{0.3\} >, < a_2,\{0.2,0.6\} >, < a_3,\{0.4,0.8\} >\}\}$.

Then the hesitant fuzzy soft image of $F_{\tilde{A}}$ *under* $f_{(\rho,\varsigma)} : \overline{(\tilde{\mho},\tilde{E})} \longrightarrow \overline{(\tilde{\nabla},\tilde{E}')}$ *is obtained as*
$f_{(\rho,\varsigma)}(F_{\tilde{A}})(e'_1)(x) = \bigcup_{\alpha\tilde{\in}\varsigma^{-1}(e'_1)\cap\tilde{A}, s\tilde{\in}\rho^{-1}(x)}(\alpha)\mu_s = \bigcup_{\alpha\tilde{\in}\{e_2\}, s\tilde{\in}\{a_2\}}(\alpha)\mu_s$
$= (e_2)\mu_{a_2} = \{0.5\}$
$f_{(\rho,\varsigma)}(F_{\tilde{A}})(e'_1)(y) = \bigcup_{\alpha\tilde{\in}\varsigma^{-1}(e'_1)\cap\tilde{A}, s\tilde{\in}\rho^{-1}(y)}(\alpha)\mu_s = \bigcup_{\alpha\tilde{\in}\{e_2\}, s\tilde{\in}\{a_1,a_3\}}(\alpha)\mu_s$
$= (e_2)(\mu_{a_1} \cup \mu_{a_3}) = \{0.2,0.4,0.9\}$
$f_{(\rho,\varsigma)}(F_{\tilde{A}})(e'_1)(z) = \bigcup_{\alpha\tilde{\in}\varsigma^{-1}(e'_1)\cap\tilde{A}, s\tilde{\in}\rho^{-1}(z)}(\alpha)\mu_s = \bigcup_{\alpha\tilde{\in}\{e_2\}, s\tilde{\in}\phi}(\alpha)\mu_s$
$= (e_2)\mu_\phi = \{0.0\}$
$f_{(\rho,\varsigma)}(F_{\tilde{A}})(e'_2)(x) = \bigcup_{\alpha\tilde{\in}\varsigma^{-1}(e'_2)\cap\tilde{A}, s\tilde{\in}\rho^{-1}(x)}(\alpha)\mu_s = \bigcup_{\alpha\tilde{\in}\{e_1,e_3\}\cap\{e_1,e_2,e_4\}, s\tilde{\in}\{a_2\}}(\alpha)\mu_s$
$= \bigcup_{\alpha\tilde{\in}\{e_1\}, s\tilde{\in}\{a_2\}}(\alpha)\mu_s = (e_1)\mu_{a_2} = \{0.8,0.4,0.9\}$.

By similar calculations we get

$f_{(\rho,\varsigma)}(F_{\tilde{A}}) = \{e'_1 = \{< x,\{0.5\} >, < y,\{0.2,0.4,0.9\} >, < z,\{0.0\} >\}$
$e'_2 = \{< x,\{0.8,0.4,0.9\} >, < y,\{0.6,0.8\} >, < z,\{0.0\} >\}$
$e'_3 = \{< x,\{0.2,0.6\} >, < y,\{0.4,0.8\} >, < z,\{0.0\} >\}\}$.

Again weconsider a hesitant fuzzy soft set $F_{\tilde{B}'}$ *in* $\overline{(\tilde{\nabla},\tilde{E}')}$ *as*
$F_{\tilde{B}'} = \{e'_1 = \{< x,\{0.2,0.4\} >, < y,\{0.3,0.1,0.8\} >, < z,\{0.4\} >\}$
$e'_2 = \{< x,\{0.5,0.3,0.7\} >, < y,\{0.7\} >, < z,\{0.7,0.8,0.2\} >\}$
$e'_3 = \{< x,\{0.9\} >, < y,\{0.6,0.8\} >, < z,\{0.8,0.3\} >\}\}$.

Therefore,

$f^{-1}_{(\rho,\varsigma)}(F_{\tilde{B}'})(e_1)(a_1) = (\varsigma(e_1))\mu_{\rho(a_1)} = (e'_2)\mu_y = \{0.7\}$
$f^{-1}_{(\rho,\varsigma)}(F_{\tilde{B}'})(e_1)(a_2) = (\varsigma(e_1))\mu_{\rho(a_2)} = (e'_2)\mu_x = \{0.5, 0.3, 0.7\}$
$f^{-1}_{(\rho,\varsigma)}(F_{\tilde{B}'})(e_1)(a_3) = (\varsigma(e_1))\mu_{\rho(a_3)} = (e'_2)\mu_y = \{0.7\}.$

By similar calculations, we get

$f^{-1}_{(\rho,\varsigma)}(F_{\tilde{B}'}) = \{e_1 = \{< a_1, \{0.7\} >, < a_2, \{0.5, 0.3, 0.7\} >, < a_3, \{0.7\} >\}$
$e_2 = \{< a_1, \{0.3, 0.1, 0.8\} >, < a_2, \{0.2, 0.4\} >, < a_3, \{0.3, 0.1, 0.8\} >\}$
$e_3 = \{< a_1, \{0.7\} >, < a_2, \{0.5, 0.3, 0.7\} >, < a_3, \{0.7\} >\}$
$e_4 = \{< a_1, \{0.6, 0.8\} >, < a_2, \{0.9\} >, < a_3, \{0.6, 0.8\} >\}\}.$

Definition 11.14 *Let $f_{(\rho,\varsigma)}$ be a hesitant fuzzy soft mapping of a hesitant fuzzy soft class $\overline{(\tilde{\mho}, \tilde{E})}$ into a hesitant fuzzy soft class $\overline{(\tilde{\nabla}, \tilde{E}')}$. Then*

(i) $f_{(\rho,\varsigma)}$ is said to be a one-one (or injection) hesitant fuzzy soft mapping if for both $\rho : \tilde{\mho} \longrightarrow \tilde{\nabla}$ and $\varsigma : \tilde{E} \longrightarrow \tilde{E}'$ are one-one.
(ii) $f_{(\rho,\varsigma)}$ is said to be a onto (or surjection) hesitant fuzzy soft mapping if for both $\rho : \tilde{\mho} \longrightarrow \tilde{\nabla}$ and $\varsigma : \tilde{E} \longrightarrow \tilde{E}'$ are onto.

If $f_{(\rho,\varsigma)}$ is both one-one and onto then $f_{(\rho,\varsigma)}$is called a hesitant one-one onto (or bijective) correspondence of hesitant fuzzy soft mapping.

Theorem 11.1 *Let $f_{(\rho,\varsigma)} : \overline{(\tilde{\mho}, \tilde{E})} \longrightarrow \overline{(\tilde{\nabla}, \tilde{E}')}$and $g_{(\xi,\psi)} : \overline{(\tilde{\mho}, \tilde{E})} \longrightarrow \overline{(\tilde{\nabla}, \tilde{E}')}$ are two hesitant fuzzy soft mappings. Then $f_{(\rho,\varsigma)}$ and $g_{(\xi,\psi)}$ are equal if and only if $\rho = \xi$ and $\varsigma = \psi$.*

Proof. Obvious.

Theorem 11.2 *Two hesitant fuzzy soft mappings $f_{(\rho,\varsigma)}$ and $g_{(\xi,\psi)}$ of a hesitant fuzzy soft class $\overline{(\tilde{\mho}, \tilde{E})}$ into a hesitant fuzzy soft class $\overline{(\tilde{\nabla}, \tilde{E}')}$ are equal if and only if $f_{(\rho,\varsigma)}(F_{\tilde{A}}) = g_{(\xi,\psi)}(F_{\tilde{A}})$ for all $(F_{\tilde{A}})\tilde{\in}\overline{(\tilde{\mho}, \tilde{E})}$.*

Proof. Let $f_{(\rho,\varsigma)} : \overline{(\tilde{\mho}, \tilde{E})} \longrightarrow \overline{(\tilde{\nabla}, \tilde{E}')}$and $g_{(\xi,\psi)} : \overline{(\tilde{\mho}, \tilde{E})} \longrightarrow \overline{(\tilde{\nabla}, \tilde{E}')}$ are two hesitant fuzzy soft mappings. Since $f_{(\rho,\varsigma)}$ and $g_{(\xi,\psi)}$ are equal, this implies $\rho = \xi$ and $\varsigma = \psi$.

Let $\eta\tilde{\in}\varsigma(\tilde{E})\tilde{\subseteq}\tilde{E}'$ and $y\tilde{\in}\tilde{\nabla}$,

$f_{(\rho,\varsigma)}(F_{\tilde{A}})(\eta)(y) = \bigcup_{\alpha\tilde{\in}\varsigma^{-1}(\eta)\cap\tilde{A}, s\tilde{\in}\rho^{-1}(y)}(\alpha)\mu_s = \bigcup_{\alpha\tilde{\in}\psi^{-1}(\eta)\cap\tilde{A}, s\tilde{\in}\xi^{-1}(y)}(\alpha)\mu_s$
$= g_{(\xi,\psi)}((F_{\tilde{A}}))(\eta)(y).$

Hence $f_{(\rho,\varsigma)}(F_{\tilde{A}}) = g_{(\xi,\psi)}(F_{\tilde{A}})$.

Conversely, Let $f_{(\rho,\varsigma)}(F_{\tilde{A}}) = g_{(\xi,\psi)}(F_{\tilde{A}})$, for all $F_{\tilde{A}}\tilde{\in}\overline{(\tilde{\mho}, \tilde{E})}$.

Let $(\tilde{R}, \tilde{T})\tilde{\in}f_{(\rho,\varsigma)}$, where $\tilde{R}\tilde{\subseteq}\overline{(\tilde{\mho}, \tilde{E})}$ and $\tilde{T}\tilde{\subseteq}\overline{(\tilde{\nabla}, \tilde{E}')}$.

Therefore $\tilde{T} = f_{(\rho,\varsigma)}(\tilde{R}) = g_{(\xi,\psi)}(\tilde{R})$, this gives $(\tilde{R},\tilde{T})\tilde{\in} g_{(\xi,\psi)}$.

Therefore $f_{(\rho,\varsigma)}\tilde{\subseteq} g_{(\xi,\psi)}$.

Similarly, it can be proved that $g_{(\xi,\psi)}\tilde{\subseteq} f_{(\rho,\varsigma)}$. Hence $f_{(\rho,\varsigma)} = g_{(\xi,\psi)}$.

Definition 11.15 *If* $f_{(\rho,\varsigma)} : \overline{(\tilde{\mho},\tilde{E})} \longrightarrow \overline{(\tilde{\nabla},\tilde{E}')}$ *and* $g_{(\xi,\psi)} : \overline{(\tilde{\nabla},\tilde{E}')} \longrightarrow \overline{(\tilde{\Theta},\tilde{E}'')}$ *are two hesitant fuzzy soft mappings, then their composite* $g_{(\xi,\psi)}\tilde{\circ} f_{(\rho,\varsigma)}$ *is a hesitant fuzzy soft mapping of* $\overline{(\tilde{\mho},\tilde{E})}$ *into* $\overline{(\tilde{\Theta},\tilde{E}'')}$ *such that for every* $F_{\tilde{A}}\tilde{\in}\overline{(\tilde{\mho},\tilde{E})}$, $(g_{(\xi,\psi)}\tilde{\circ} f_{(\rho,\varsigma)})(F_{\tilde{A}}) = g_{(\xi,\psi)}(f_{(\rho,\varsigma)}(F_{\tilde{A}}))$.*we defined as*

for $\eta\tilde{\in}\psi(\tilde{E}')\tilde{\subseteq}\tilde{E}''$ *and* $y\tilde{\in}\tilde{\Theta}$, $g_{(\xi,\psi)}(f_{(\rho,\varsigma)}(F_{\tilde{A}}))(\eta)(y)$
$= \bigcup_{\alpha\tilde{\in}\psi^{-1}(\eta)\cap f_{(\rho,\varsigma)}(\tilde{A}), s\tilde{\in}\xi-1(y)}(\alpha)\mu_s$.

Example 11.3 *From example 11.2 and considering hesitant fuzzy soft mapping* $g_{(\xi,\psi)} : \overline{(\tilde{\nabla},\tilde{E}')} \longrightarrow \overline{(\tilde{\Theta},\tilde{E}'')}$, *where* $\tilde{\Theta} = \{h_1,h_2,h_3\}, \tilde{E}'' = \{e_1'',e_3''\}$ *and* $\xi(x) = h_2, \xi(y) = h_3, \xi(z) = h_2 : \psi(e_1') = e_3'', \psi(e_2') = e_3'', \psi(e_3') = e_1''$.
Therefore
$g_{(\xi,\psi)}(f_{(\rho,\varsigma)}(F_{\tilde{A}}))(e_1'')(h_1) = \bigcup_{\alpha\tilde{\in}\psi^{-1}(e_1'')\cap f_{(\rho,\varsigma)}(\tilde{A}), s\tilde{\in}\xi^{-1}(h_1)}(\alpha)\mu_s$
$= \bigcup_{\alpha\tilde{\in}\{e_3'\}, s\tilde{\in}\phi}(\alpha)\mu_s = (e_3')\mu_\phi = \{0.0\}$
$g_{(\xi,\psi)}(f_{(\rho,\varsigma)}(F_{\tilde{A}}))(e_1'')(h_2) = \bigcup_{\alpha\tilde{\in}\psi^{-1}(e_1'')\cap f_{(\rho,\varsigma)}(\tilde{A}), s\tilde{\in}\xi^{-1}(h_2)}(\alpha)\mu_s$
$= \bigcup_{\alpha\tilde{\in}\{e_3'\}, s\tilde{\in}\{x,z\}}(\alpha)\mu_s = (e_3')(\mu_x\cup\mu_z) = \{0.2,0.6\}$
$g_{(\xi,\psi)}(f_{(\rho,\varsigma)}(F_{\tilde{A}}))(e_1'')(h_3) = \bigcup_{\alpha\tilde{\in}\psi^{-1}(e_1'')\cap f_{(\rho,\varsigma)}(\tilde{A}), s\tilde{\in}\xi^{-1}(h_3)}(\alpha)\mu_s$
$= \bigcup_{\alpha\tilde{\in}\{e_3'\}, s\tilde{\in}\{y\}}(\alpha)\mu_s = (e_3')\mu_y = \{0.4,0.8\}$.

By similar calculations we get

$(g_{(\xi,\psi)}\tilde{\circ} f_{(\rho,\varsigma)})(F_{\tilde{A}}) = g_{(\xi,\psi)}(f_{(\rho,\varsigma)}(F_{\tilde{A}})) = \{e_1'' = \{< h_1,\{0.0\}>, < h_2,\{0.2,0.6\}>,$
$< h_3,\{0.4,0.8\}>\}$
$e_2'' = \{< h_1,\{0.0\}>, < h_2,\{0.0\}>, < h_3,\{0.0\}>\}$
$e_3'' = \{< h_1,\{0.0\}>, < h_2,\{0.5,0.8,0.9\}>, < h_3,\{0.6,0.8,0.9\}>\}\}$.

Theorem 11.3 *Let* $f_{(\rho,\varsigma)} : \overline{(\tilde{\mho},\tilde{E})} \longrightarrow \overline{(\tilde{\nabla},\tilde{E}')}$ *and* $g_{(\xi,\psi)} : \overline{(\tilde{\nabla},\tilde{E}')} \longrightarrow \overline{(\tilde{\Theta},\tilde{E}'')}$ *are two hesitant fuzzy soft mappings. Then*

(i) if $f_{(\rho,\varsigma)}$ *and* $g_{(\xi,\psi)}$ *are one-one then so is* $g_{(\xi,\psi)}\tilde{\circ} f_{(\rho,\varsigma)}$.
(ii) if $f_{(\rho,\varsigma)}$ *and* $g_{(\xi,\psi)}$ *are onto then so is* $g_{(\xi,\psi)}\tilde{\circ} f_{(\rho,\varsigma)}$.
(iii) if $f_{(\rho,\varsigma)}$ *and* $g_{(\xi,\psi)}$ *are both bijections then so is* $g_{(\xi,\psi)}\tilde{\circ} f_{(\rho,\varsigma)}$.

Proof. Let us consider the hesitant fuzzy soft mappings $f_{(\rho,\varsigma)} : \overline{(\tilde{\mho},\tilde{E})} \longrightarrow \overline{(\tilde{\nabla},\tilde{E}')}$and $g_{(\xi,\psi)} : \overline{(\tilde{\nabla},\tilde{E}')} \longrightarrow \overline{(\tilde{\Theta},\tilde{E}'')}$. Let $\tilde{\mho} = \{a_1,a_2,a_3\}$ and $\tilde{\nabla} = \{x,y,z\}$, $\tilde{\Theta} = \{h_1,h_2,h_3\}, \tilde{E} = \{e_1,e_2,e_3\}, \tilde{E}' = \{e_1',e_2',e_3'\}, \tilde{E}'' = \{e_1'',e_2'',e_3''\}$ and $\overline{(\tilde{\mho},\tilde{E})}$, $\overline{(\tilde{\nabla},\tilde{E}')}, \overline{(\tilde{\Theta},\tilde{E}'')}$ classes of hesitant fuzzy soft sets. Let $\rho(a_1) = z, \rho(a_2) = x, \rho(a_3) = y$; $\varsigma(e_1) = e_2', \varsigma(e_2) = e_3', \varsigma(e_3) = e_1'$ and $\xi(x) = h_2, \xi(y) = h_3, \xi(z) = h_1 : \psi(e_1') = e_3'', \psi(e_2') = e_1'', \psi(e_3') = e_2''$. Also we consider a hesitant fuzzy soft set $L_{\tilde{A}}$ in $\overline{(\tilde{\mho},\tilde{E})}$

as

$L_{\tilde{A}} = \{e_1 = \{< a_1, \{0.6, 0.8\} >, < a_2, \{0.8, 0.4, 0.9\} >, < a_3, \{0.3\} >\}$
$e_2 = \{< a_1, \{0.0\} >, < a_2, \{0.0\} >, < a_3, \{0.0\} >$
$e_3 = \{< a_1, \{0.9, 0.1, 0.2\} >, < a_2, \{0.5\} >, < a_3, \{0.2, 0.4, 0.6\} >\}\}.$

Then the hesitant fuzzy soft image of $F_{\tilde{A}}$ under $f_{(\rho,\varsigma)} : \overline{(\tilde{\mho}, \tilde{E})} \longrightarrow \overline{(\tilde{\nabla}, \tilde{E}')}$is obtained as

$f_{(\rho,\varsigma)}(L_{\tilde{A}})(e_1')(x) = \bigcup_{\alpha \tilde{\in} \varsigma^{-1}(e_1') \cap \tilde{A}, s \tilde{\in} \rho^{-1}(x)} (\alpha)\mu_s$
$= \bigcup_{\alpha \tilde{\in} \{e_3\}, s \tilde{\in} \{a_2\}} (\alpha)\mu_s = (e_3)\mu_{a_2} = \{0.5\}$
$f_{(\rho,\varsigma)}(L_{\tilde{A}})(e_1')(y) = \bigcup_{\alpha \tilde{\in} \varsigma^{-1}(e_1') \cap \tilde{A}, s \tilde{\in} \rho^{-1}(y)} (\alpha)\mu_s$
$= \bigcup_{\alpha \tilde{\in} \{e_3\}, s \tilde{\in} \{a_3\}} (\alpha)\mu_s = (e_3)\mu_{a_3} = \{0.2, 0.4, 0.6\}$
$f_{(\rho,\varsigma)}(L_{\tilde{A}})(e_1')(z) = \bigcup_{\alpha \tilde{\in} \varsigma^{-1}(e_1') \cap \tilde{A}, s \tilde{\in} \rho^{-1}(z)} (\alpha)\mu_s$
$= \bigcup_{\alpha \tilde{\in} \{e_3\}, s \tilde{\in} \{a_1\}} (\alpha)\mu_s = (e_3)\mu_{a_1} = \{0.9, 0.1, 0.2\}.$

By similar calculations we get

$f_{(\rho,\varsigma)}(L_{\tilde{A}}) = \{e_1' = \{< x, \{0.5\} >, < y, \{0.2, 0.4, 0.6\} >, < z, \{0.9, 0.1, 0.2\} >\}$
$e_2' = \{< x, \{0.8, 0.4, 0.9\} >, < y, \{0.3\} >, < z, \{0.6, 0.8\} >\}$
$e_3' = \{< x, \{0.0\} >, < y, \{0.0\} >, < z, \{0.0\} >\}\}.$

Again,

$g_{(\xi,\psi)}(f_{(\rho,\varsigma)}(L_{\tilde{A}}))(e_1'')(h_1) = \bigcup_{\alpha \tilde{\in} \psi^{-1}(e_1'') \cap f_{(\rho,\varsigma)}(\tilde{A}), s \tilde{\in} \xi^{-1}(h_1)} (\alpha)\mu_s$
$= \bigcup_{\alpha \tilde{\in} \{e_2'\}, s \tilde{\in} \{z\}} (\alpha)\mu_s = (e_2')\mu_z = \{0.6, 0.8\}$
$g_{(\xi,\psi)}(f_{(\rho,\varsigma)}(L_{\tilde{A}}))(e_1'')(h_2) = \bigcup_{\alpha \tilde{\in} \psi^{-1}(e_1'') \cap f_{(\rho,\varsigma)}(\tilde{A}), s \tilde{\in} \xi^{-1}(h_2)} (\alpha)\mu_s$
$= \bigcup_{\alpha \tilde{\in} \{e_2'\}, s \tilde{\in} \{x\}} (\alpha)\mu_s = (e_2')\mu_x = \{0.8, 0.4, 0.9\}$
$g_{(\xi,\psi)}(f_{(\rho,\varsigma)}(L_{\tilde{A}}))(e_1'')(h_3) = \bigcup_{\alpha \tilde{\in} \psi^{-1}(e_1'') \cap f_{(\rho,\varsigma)}(\tilde{A}), s \tilde{\in} \xi^{-1}(h_3)} (\alpha)\mu_s$
$= \bigcup_{\alpha \tilde{\in} \{e_2'\}, s \tilde{\in} \{y\}} (\alpha)\mu_s = (e_2')\mu_y = \{0.3\}.$

By similar calculations we get

$(g_{(\xi,\psi)} \tilde{\circ} f_{(\rho,\varsigma)})(L_{\tilde{A}}) = g_{(\xi,\psi)}(f_{(\rho,\varsigma)}(L_{\tilde{A}})) = \{e_1'' = \{< h_1, \{0.6, 0.8\} >, < h_2, \{0.8, 0.4, 0.9\} >,$
$< h_3, \{0.3\} >\}$
$e_2'' = \{< h_1, \{0.0\} >, < h_2, \{0.0\} >, < h_3, \{0.0\} >\}$
$e_3'' = \{< h_1, \{0.9, 0.1, 0.2\} >, < h_2, \{0.5\} >, < h_3, \{0.2, 0.4, 0.6\} >\}\}.$

Therefore

(i) From the above example we see that, if $f_{(\rho,\varsigma)}$ and $g_{(\xi,\psi)}$ are one-one then so is $g_{(\xi,\psi)} \tilde{\circ} f_{(\rho,\varsigma)}$.
(ii) From the above example we see that,if $f_{(\rho,\varsigma)}$ and $g_{(\xi,\psi)}$ are onto then so is $g_{(\xi,\psi)} \tilde{\circ} f_{(\rho,\varsigma)}$.
(iii) From the above example we see that, if $f_{(\rho,\varsigma)}$ and $g_{(\xi,\psi)}$ are both bijections then so is $g_{(\xi,\psi)} \tilde{\circ} f_{(\rho,\varsigma)}$.

Theorem 11.4 *Let us consider three hesitant fuzzy soft mappings* $f_{(\rho,\varsigma)} : \overline{(\tilde{\mho},\tilde{E})} \longrightarrow \overline{(\tilde{\nabla},\tilde{E}')}$, $g_{(\xi,\psi)} : \overline{(\tilde{\nabla},\tilde{E}')} \longrightarrow \overline{(\tilde{\Theta},\tilde{E}'')}$. *and* $\sigma_{(\tau,\kappa)} : \overline{(\tilde{\Theta},\tilde{E}'')} \longrightarrow \overline{(\tilde{\Lambda},\tilde{E}''')}$. *Then* $\sigma_{(\tau,\kappa)}\tilde{\circ}(g_{(\xi,\psi)}\tilde{\circ}f_{(\rho,\varsigma)}) = (\sigma_{(\tau,\kappa)}\tilde{\circ}g_{(\xi,\psi)})\tilde{\circ}f_{(\rho,\varsigma)}$.

Proof. Let $F_{\tilde{A}}\tilde{\in}\overline{(\tilde{\mho},\tilde{E})}$. Now from definition we have
$[\sigma_{(\tau,\kappa)}\tilde{\circ}(g_{(\xi,\psi)}\tilde{\circ}f_{(\rho,\varsigma)})](F_{\tilde{A}}) = \sigma_{(\tau,\kappa)}[(g_{(\xi,\psi)}\tilde{\circ}f_{(\rho,\varsigma)})(F_{\tilde{A}})] = \sigma_{(\tau,\kappa)}[g_{(\xi,\psi)}(f_{(\rho,\varsigma)}(F_{\tilde{A}}))]$.

Also $[(\sigma_{(\tau,\kappa)}\tilde{\circ}g_{(\xi,\psi)})\tilde{\circ}f_{(\rho,\varsigma)}](F_{\tilde{A}}) = (\sigma_{(\tau,\kappa)}\tilde{\circ}g_{(\xi,\psi)})(f_{(\rho,\varsigma)}(F_{\tilde{A}})) = \sigma_{(\tau,\kappa)}[g_{(\xi,\psi)}(f_{(\rho,\varsigma)}(F_{\tilde{A}}))]$. Hence $\sigma_{(\tau,\kappa)}\tilde{\circ}(g_{(\xi,\psi)}\tilde{\circ}f_{(\rho,\varsigma)}) = (\sigma_{(\tau,\kappa)}\tilde{\circ}g_{(\xi,\psi)})\tilde{\circ}f_{(\rho,\varsigma)}$.

Definition 11.16 *A hesitant fuzzy soft mapping* $f_{(\rho,\varsigma)} : \overline{(\tilde{\mho},\tilde{E})} \longrightarrow \overline{(\tilde{\nabla},\tilde{E}')}$ *is said to be many one hesitant fuzzy soft mapping if two (or more than two) hesitant fuzzy soft sets in* $\overline{(\tilde{\mho},\tilde{E})}$ *have the same hesitant fuzzy soft image in* $\overline{(\tilde{\nabla},\tilde{E}')}$.

Example 11.4 *From example 11.2 and consider the hesitant fuzzy soft set* $M_{\tilde{A}}\tilde{\in}\overline{(\tilde{\mho},\tilde{E})}$,
$M_{\tilde{A}} = \{e_1 = \{< a_1, \{0.6, 0.5\} >, < a_2, \{0.8, 0.4, 0.9\} >, < a_3, \{0.6, 0.8\} >\}$
$e_2 = \{< a_1, \{0.3, 0.2, 0.7\} >, < a_2, \{0.5\} >, < a_3, \{0.4, 0.1, 0.9\} >\}$
$e_4 = \{< a_1, \{0.4\} >, < a_2, \{0.2, 0.6\} >, < a_3, \{0.3, 0.8\} >\}\}$.
Then the hesitant fuzzy soft image of $M_{\tilde{A}}$ *under* $f_{(\rho,\varsigma)} : \overline{(\tilde{\mho},\tilde{E})} \longrightarrow \overline{(\tilde{\nabla},\tilde{E}')}$ *is obtained as*
$f_{(\rho,\varsigma)}(M_{\tilde{A}})(e_1')(x) = \bigcup_{\alpha\tilde{\in}\varsigma^{-1}(e_1')\cap\tilde{A}, s\tilde{\in}\rho^{-1}(x)}(\alpha)\mu_s$
$= \bigcup_{\alpha\tilde{\in}\{e_2\}, s\tilde{\in}\{a_2\}}(\alpha)\mu_s = (e_2)\mu_{a_2} = \{0.5\}$
$f_{(\rho,\varsigma)}(M_{\tilde{A}})(e_1')(y) = \bigcup_{\alpha\tilde{\in}\varsigma^{-1}(e_1')\cap\tilde{A}, s\tilde{\in}\rho^{-1}(y)}(\alpha)\mu_s$
$= \bigcup_{\alpha\tilde{\in}\{e_2\}, s\tilde{\in}\{a_1,a_3\}}(\alpha)\mu_s = (e_2)(\mu_{a_1} \cup \mu_{a_3}) = \{0.2, 0.4, 0.9\}$
$f_{(\rho,\varsigma)}(M_{\tilde{A}})(e_1')(z) = \bigcup_{\alpha\tilde{\in}\varsigma^{-1}(e_1')\cap\tilde{A}, s\tilde{\in}\rho^{-1}(z)}(\alpha)\mu_s$
$= \bigcup_{\alpha\tilde{\in}\{e_2\}, s\tilde{\in}\phi}(\alpha)\mu_s = (e_2)\mu_\phi = \{0.0\}$
$f_{(\rho,\varsigma)}(M_{\tilde{A}})(e_2')(x) = \bigcup_{\alpha\tilde{\in}\varsigma^{-1}(e_2')\cap\tilde{A}, s\tilde{\in}\rho^{-1}(x)}(\alpha)\mu_s = \bigcup_{\alpha\tilde{\in}\{e_1,e_3\}\cap\{e_1,e_2,e_4\}, s\tilde{\in}\{a_2\}}(\alpha)\mu_s$
$= \bigcup_{\alpha\tilde{\in}\{e_1\}, s\tilde{\in}\{a_2\}}(\alpha)\mu_s = (e_1)\mu_{a_2} = \{0.8, 0.4, 0.9\}$.

By similar calculations we get

$f_{(\rho,\varsigma)}(M_{\tilde{A}}) = \{e_1' = \{< x, \{0.5\} >, < y, \{0.2, 0.4, 0.9\} >, < z, \{0.0\} >\}$
$e_2' = \{< x, \{0.8, 0.4, 0.9\} >, < y, \{0.6, 0.8\} >, < z, \{0.0\} >\}$
$e_3' = \{< x, \{0.2, 0.6\} >, < y, \{0.4, 0.8\} >, < z, \{0.0\} >\}\}$.

Therefore $f_{(\rho,\varsigma)}(M_{\tilde{A}}) = f_{(\rho,\varsigma)}(F_{\tilde{A}})$. *Hence* $f_{(\rho,\varsigma)}$ *is many one hesitant fuzzy soft mapping.*

Definition 11.17 *Let* $i_{(\rho,\varsigma)} : \overline{(\tilde{\mho},\tilde{E})} \longrightarrow \overline{(\tilde{\mho},\tilde{E})}$ *be a hesitant fuzzy soft mapping, where* $\rho : \tilde{\mho} \longrightarrow \tilde{\mho}$ *and* $\varsigma : \tilde{E} \longrightarrow \tilde{E}$. *Then* $i_{(\rho,\varsigma)}$ *is said to be a hesitant fuzzy soft identity mapping if both* ρ *and* ς *are identity mappings.*

Remark 11.1 $i_{(\rho,\varsigma)} : \overline{(\tilde{\mho},\tilde{E})} \longrightarrow \overline{(\tilde{\mho},\tilde{E})}$ *be a hesitant fuzzy soft identity mapping, then* $i_{(\rho,\varsigma)}(F_{\tilde{A}}) = F_{\tilde{A}}$, *where* $F_{\tilde{A}}\tilde{\in}\overline{(\tilde{\mho},\tilde{E})}$.

Theorem 11.5 *Let $f_{(\rho,\varsigma)} : \overline{(\tilde{\mho},\tilde{E})} \longrightarrow \overline{(\tilde{\nabla},\tilde{E}')}$ be a hesitant fuzzy soft mapping and let $i_{(l,m)} : \overline{(\tilde{\mho},\tilde{E})} \longrightarrow \overline{(\tilde{\mho},\tilde{E})}$ and $j_{(g,h)} : \overline{(\tilde{\nabla},\tilde{E}')} \longrightarrow \overline{(\tilde{\nabla},\tilde{E}')}$ are hesitant fuzzy soft identity mappings then $f_{(\rho,\varsigma)}\tilde{\circ}i_{(l,m)} = f_{(\rho,\varsigma)}$ and $j_{(g,h)}\tilde{\circ}f_{(\rho,\varsigma)} = f_{(\rho,\varsigma)}$.*

Proof. Consider the following example. We consider $F_{\tilde{A}}$ from example 11.2 and consider the hesitant fuzzy soft mappings $i_{(l,m)} : \overline{(\tilde{\mho},\tilde{E})} \longrightarrow \overline{(\tilde{\mho},\tilde{E})}$, where $l : \tilde{\mho} \longrightarrow \tilde{\mho}$ and $m : \tilde{E} \longrightarrow \tilde{E}$, such that $l(a_1) = a_1, l(a_2) = a_2, l(a_3) = a_3$; $m(e_1) = e_1, m(e_2) = e_2, m(e_3) = e_3, m(e_4) = e_4$. Therefore,

$$i_{(l,m)}(F_{\tilde{A}})(e_1)(a_1) = \bigcup_{\alpha\tilde{\in}m^{-1}(e_1)\cap\tilde{A},s\tilde{\in}l^{-1}(a_1)}(\alpha)\mu_s = \bigcup_{\alpha\tilde{\in}\{e_1\},s\tilde{\in}\{a_1\}}(\alpha)\mu_s$$
$$= (e_1)\mu_{a_1} = \{0.6, 0.8\}$$
$$i_{(l,m)}(F_{\tilde{A}})(e_1)(a_2) = \bigcup_{\alpha\tilde{\in}m^{-1}(e_1)\cap\tilde{A},s\tilde{\in}l^{-1}(a_2)}(\alpha)\mu_s = \bigcup_{\alpha\tilde{\in}\{e_1\},s\tilde{\in}\{a_2\}}(\alpha)\mu_s$$
$$= (e_1)(\mu_{a_2}) = \{0.8, 0.4, 0.9\}$$
$$i_{(l,m)}(F_{\tilde{A}})(e_1)(a_3) = \bigcup_{\alpha\tilde{\in}m^{-1}(e_1)\cap\tilde{A},s\tilde{\in}l-1(a_3)}(\alpha)\mu_s = \bigcup_{\alpha\tilde{\in}\{e_1\},s\tilde{\in}\{a_3\}}(\alpha)\mu_s$$
$$= (e_1)\mu_{a_3} = \{0.3\}.$$

By similar calculations we get

$$i_{(l,m)}(F_{\tilde{A}}) = \{e_1 = \{< a_1, \{0.6, 0.8\} >, < a_2, \{0.8, 0.4, 0.9\} >, < a_3, \{0.3\} >\}$$
$$e_2 = \{< a_1, \{0.9, 0.1, 0.2\} >, < a_2, \{0.5\} >, < a_3, \{0.2, 0.4, 0.6\} >\}$$
$$e_3 = \{< a_1, \{0.0\} >, < a_2, \{0.0\} >, < a_3, \{0.0\} >$$
$$e_4 = \{< a_1, \{0.3\} >, < a_2, \{0.2, 0.6\} >, < a_3, \{0.4, 0.8\} >\}\}.$$

Hence $i_{(l,m)}(F_{\tilde{A}}) = F_{\tilde{A}} \Rightarrow f_{(\rho,\varsigma)}(i_{(l,m)}(F_{\tilde{A}})) = f_{(\rho,\varsigma)}(F_{\tilde{A}}) \Rightarrow (f_{(\rho,\varsigma)}\tilde{\circ}i_{(l,m)})(F_{\tilde{A}}) = f_{(\rho,\varsigma)}(F_{\tilde{A}}) \Rightarrow f_{(\rho,\varsigma)}\tilde{\circ}i_{(l,m)} = f_{(\rho,\varsigma)}$.

Similarly we get $f_{(\rho,\varsigma)}(F_{\tilde{A}})\tilde{\in}\overline{(V,E')}$ and $j_{(g,h)}(f_{(\rho,\varsigma)}(F_{\tilde{A}})) = f_{(\rho,\varsigma)}(F_{\tilde{A}})$ $\Rightarrow (j_{(g,h)}\tilde{\circ}f_{(\rho,\varsigma)}(F_{\tilde{A}}) = f_{(\rho,\varsigma)}(F_{\tilde{A}})$.

Hence $j_{(g,h)}\tilde{\circ}f_{(\rho,\varsigma)} = f_{(\rho,\varsigma)}$.

Definition 11.18 *A one-one onto hesitant fuzzy soft mapping $f_{(\rho,\varsigma)} : \overline{(\tilde{\mho},\tilde{E})} \longrightarrow \overline{(\tilde{\nabla},\tilde{E}')}$ is called hesitant fuzzy soft invertible mapping. Its hesitant fuzzy soft inverse mapping is denoted by $f^{-1}_{(\rho^{-1},\varsigma^{-1})} : \overline{(\tilde{\nabla},\tilde{E}')} \longrightarrow \overline{(\tilde{\mho},\tilde{E})}$.*

Remark 11.2 *In a hesitant fuzzy soft invertible mapping $f_{(\rho,\varsigma)} : \overline{(\tilde{\mho},\tilde{E})} \longrightarrow \overline{(\tilde{\nabla},\tilde{E}')}$, for $F_{\tilde{A}}\tilde{\in}\overline{(\tilde{\mho},\tilde{E})}, G_{\tilde{B}}\tilde{\in}\overline{(\tilde{\nabla},\tilde{E}')}$, $f^{-1}_{(\rho^{-1},\varsigma^{-1})}(G_{\tilde{B}}) = F_{\tilde{A}}$, whenever $f_{(\rho,\varsigma)}(F_{\tilde{A}}) = G_{\tilde{B}}$.*

Example 11.5 *From proof of the Theorem 11.3. We consider $f_{(\rho,\varsigma)}(L_{\tilde{A}}) = G_{\tilde{B}}$. Therefore,*

$$f^{-1}_{(\rho^{-1},\varsigma^{-1})}(G_{\tilde{B}})(e_1)(a_1) = (\varsigma(e_1))\mu_{\rho(a_1)} = (e'_2)\mu_z = \{0.6, 0.8\}$$
$$f^{-1}_{(\rho^{-1},\varsigma^{-1})}(G_{\tilde{B}})(e_1)(a_2) = (\varsigma(e_1))\mu_{\rho(a_2)} = (e'_2)\mu_x = \{0.8, 0.4, 0.9\}$$
$$f^{-1}_{(\rho^{-1},\varsigma^{-1})}(G_{\tilde{B}})(e_1)(a_3) = (\varsigma(e_1))\mu_{\rho(a_3)} = (e'_2)\mu_y = \{0.3\}.$$

By similar calculations we get

$f^{-1}_{(\rho^{-1},\varsigma^{-1})}(G_{\tilde{B}}) = \{e_1 = \{< a_1, \{0.6, 0.8\} >, < a_2, \{0.8, 0.4, 0.9\} >, < a_3, \{0.3\} >\}$
$e_2 = \{< a_1, \{0.0\} >, < a_2, \{0.0\} >, < a_3, \{0.0\} >$
$e_3 = \{< a_1, \{0.9, 0.1, 0.2\} >, < a_2, \{0.5\} >, < a_3, \{0.2, 0.4, 0.6\} >\}\}.$
Hence $f^{-1}_{(\rho^{-1},\varsigma^{-1})}(G_{\tilde{B}}) = L_{\tilde{A}}$.

Theorem 11.6 *Let* $f_{(\rho,\varsigma)} : \overline{(\tilde{\mho}, \tilde{E})} \longrightarrow \overline{(\tilde{\nabla}, \tilde{E}')}$, *be a hesitant fuzzy soft invertible mapping. Therefore, its hesitant fuzzy soft inverse mapping is unique.*

Proof. Let $f^{-1}_{(\rho^{-1},\varsigma^{-1})}$ and $g^{-1}_{(\rho^{-1},\varsigma^{-1})}$ are two hesitant fuzzy soft inverse mappings of $f_{(\rho,\varsigma)}$. Therefore,
$f^{-1}_{(\rho^{-1},\varsigma^{-1})}(G_{\tilde{B}}) = F_{\tilde{A}}$, whenever $f_{(\rho,\varsigma)}(F_{\tilde{A}}) = G_{\tilde{B}}, F_{\tilde{A}} \tilde{\in} \overline{(\tilde{\mho}, \tilde{E})}, G_{\tilde{B}} \tilde{\in} \overline{(\tilde{\nabla}, \tilde{E}')}$, and $g^{-1}_{(\rho^{-1},\varsigma^{-1})}(G_{\tilde{B}}) = H_{\tilde{A}}$, whenever $g_{(\rho,\varsigma)}(H_{\tilde{A}}) = G_{\tilde{B}}, H_{\tilde{A}} \tilde{\in} \overline{(\tilde{\mho}, \tilde{E})}, G_{\tilde{B}} \tilde{\in} \overline{(\tilde{\nabla}, \tilde{E}')}$. Thus $f_{(\rho,\varsigma)}(F_{\tilde{A}}) = g_{(\rho,\varsigma)}(H_{\tilde{A}})$.
Since $f_{(\rho,\varsigma)}$ is one-one, therefore $F_{\tilde{A}} = H_{\tilde{A}}$. Hence $f^{-1}_{(\rho^{-1},\varsigma^{-1})}(G_{\tilde{B}}) = g^{-1}_{(\rho^{-1},\varsigma^{-1})}(G_{\tilde{B}})$ i.e $f^{-1}_{(\rho^{-1},\varsigma^{-1})} = g^{-1}_{(\rho^{-1},\varsigma^{-1})}$.

Theorem 11.7 *Let* $f_{(\rho,\varsigma)} : \overline{(\tilde{\mho}, \tilde{E})} \longrightarrow \overline{(\tilde{\nabla}, \tilde{E}')}$, $g_{(\xi,\psi)} : \overline{(\tilde{\nabla}, \tilde{E}')} \longrightarrow \overline{(\tilde{\Theta}, \tilde{E}'')}$, *are two one-one onto hesitant fuzzy soft mappings. If* $f^{-1}_{(\rho^{-1},\varsigma^{-1})} : \overline{(\tilde{\nabla}, \tilde{E}')} \longrightarrow \overline{(\tilde{\mho}, \tilde{E})}$, *and* $g^{-1}_{(\xi^{-1},\psi^{-1})} : \overline{(\tilde{\Theta}, \tilde{E}'')} \longrightarrow \overline{(\tilde{\nabla}, \tilde{E}')}$ *are hesitant fuzzy soft inverse mappings of* $f^{-1}_{(\rho^{-1},\varsigma^{-1})}$ *and* $g^{-1}_{(\xi^{-1},\psi^{-1})}$, *respectively, then the inverse of the mapping* $g^{-1}_{(\xi^{-1},\psi^{-1})} \tilde{\circ} f^{-1}_{(\rho^{-1},\varsigma^{-1})} : \overline{(\tilde{\mho}, \tilde{E})} \longrightarrow \overline{(\tilde{\Theta}, \tilde{E}'')}$ *is the hesitant fuzzy soft mapping* $f^{-1}_{(\rho^{-1},\varsigma^{-1})} \tilde{\circ} g^{-1}_{(\xi^{-1},\psi^{-1})} : \overline{(\tilde{\Theta}, \tilde{E}'')} \longrightarrow \overline{(\tilde{\mho}, \tilde{E})}$.

Proof. Obvious.

Theorem 11.8 *A hesitant fuzzy soft mapping* $f_{(\rho,\varsigma)} : \overline{(\tilde{\mho}, \tilde{E})} \longrightarrow \overline{(\tilde{\nabla}, \tilde{E}')}$, *is invertible if and only if there exists a hesitant fuzzy soft inverse mapping* $f^{-1}_{(\rho^{-1},\varsigma^{-1})} : \overline{(\tilde{\nabla}, \tilde{E}')} \longrightarrow \overline{(\tilde{\mho}, \tilde{E})}$, *such that* $f^{-1}_{(\rho^{-1},\varsigma^{-1})} \tilde{\circ} f_{(\rho,\varsigma)} = i_{(\rho,\varsigma)}$ *and* $f_{(\rho,\varsigma)} \tilde{\circ} f^{-1}_{(\rho^{-1},\varsigma^{-1})} = i'_{(\rho,\varsigma)}$, *where* $i_{(\rho,\varsigma)}$ *and* $i'_{(\rho,\varsigma)}$ *is hesitant fuzzy soft identity mapping on* $\overline{(\tilde{\mho}, \tilde{E})}$ *and* $\overline{(\tilde{\nabla}, \tilde{E}')}$, *respectively.*

Proof. Let $f_{(\rho,\varsigma)} : \overline{(\tilde{\mho}, \tilde{E})} \longrightarrow \overline{(\tilde{\nabla}, \tilde{E}')}$, be a hesitant fuzzy soft invertible mapping. Therefore by definition we have
$f^{-1}_{(\rho^{-1},\varsigma^{-1})}(G_{\tilde{B}}) = F_{\tilde{A}}$, whenever $f_{(\rho,\varsigma)}(F_{\tilde{A}}) = G_{\tilde{B}}, F_{\tilde{A}} \tilde{\in} \overline{(\tilde{\mho}, \tilde{E})}, G_{\tilde{B}} \tilde{\in} \overline{(\tilde{\nabla}, \tilde{E}')}$.
Since $(f^{-1}_{(\rho^{-1},\varsigma^{-1})} \tilde{\circ} f_{(\rho,\varsigma)})(F_{\tilde{A}}) = f^{-1}_{(\rho^{-1},\varsigma^{-1})}(f_{(\rho,\varsigma)}(F_{\tilde{A}})) = f^{-1}_{(\rho^{-1},\varsigma^{-1})}(G_{\tilde{B}}) = F_{\tilde{A}}$. Therefore $f^{-1}_{(\rho^{-1},\varsigma^{-1})} \tilde{\circ} f_{(\rho,\varsigma)} = i_{(\rho,\varsigma)}$.
Similarly, we prove that $f_{(\rho,\varsigma)} \tilde{\circ} f^{-1}_{(\rho^{-1},\varsigma^{-1})} = i'_{(\rho,\varsigma)}$.

Theorem 11.9 *If* $f_{(\rho,\varsigma)} : \overline{(\tilde{\mho},\tilde{E})} \longrightarrow \overline{(\tilde{\nabla},\tilde{E}')}$ *and* $g_{(\xi,\psi)} : \overline{(\tilde{\nabla},\tilde{E}')} \longrightarrow \overline{(\tilde{\Theta},\tilde{E}'')}$, *are two one-one onto hesitant fuzzy soft mapping then* $(g_{(\xi,\psi)}\tilde{\circ}f_{(\rho,\varsigma)})^{-1} = f^{-1}_{(\rho^{-1},\varsigma^{-1})}\tilde{\circ}g^{-1}_{(\xi^{-1},\psi^{-1})}$.

Proof. Since $f_{(\rho,\varsigma)}$ and $g_{(\xi,\psi)}$ are one-one onto hesitant fuzzy soft mapping, then there exists $f^{-1}_{(\rho^{-1},\varsigma^{-1})} : \overline{(\tilde{\nabla},\tilde{E}')} \longrightarrow \overline{(\tilde{\mho},\tilde{E})}$ and $g^{-1}_{(\xi^{-1},\psi^{-1})} : \overline{(\tilde{\Theta},\tilde{E}'')} \longrightarrow \overline{(\tilde{\nabla},\tilde{E}')}$ such that

$$f^{-1}_{(\rho^{-1},\varsigma^{-1})}(G_{\tilde{B}}) = F_{\tilde{A}}, \text{ whenever } f_{(\rho,\varsigma)}(F_{\tilde{A}}) = G_{\tilde{B}}, F_{\tilde{A}}\tilde{\in}\overline{(\tilde{\mho},\tilde{E})}, G_{\tilde{B}}\tilde{\in}\overline{(\tilde{\nabla},\tilde{E}')},$$

and

$$g^{-1}_{(\xi^{-1},\psi^{-1})}(H_{\tilde{C}}) = G_{\tilde{B}}, \text{ whenever } g_{(\xi,\psi)}(G_{\tilde{B}}) = H_{\tilde{C}}, H_{\tilde{C}}\tilde{\in}\overline{(\tilde{\Theta},\tilde{E}'')}, G_{\tilde{B}}\tilde{\in}\overline{(\tilde{\nabla},\tilde{E}')}.$$

Therefore, $(g_{(\xi,\psi)}\tilde{\circ}f_{(\rho,\varsigma)})(F_{\tilde{A}}) = g_{(\xi,\psi)}[f_{(\rho,\varsigma)}(F_{\tilde{A}})] = g_{(\xi,\psi)}(G_{\tilde{B}}) = H_{\tilde{C}}$.
As $g_{(\xi,\psi)}\tilde{\circ}f_{(\rho,\varsigma)}$ is one-one onto, therefore $(g_{(\xi,\psi)}\tilde{\circ}f_{(\rho,\varsigma)})^{-1}$ exists such that

$$(g_{(\xi,\psi)}\tilde{\circ}f_{(\rho,\varsigma)})(F_{\tilde{A}}) = H_{\tilde{C}} \Rightarrow (g_{(\xi,\psi)}\tilde{\circ}f_{(\rho,\varsigma)})^{-1}(H_{\tilde{C}}) = F_{\tilde{A}}.$$

Also $(f^{-1}_{(\rho^{-1},\varsigma^{-1})}\tilde{\circ}g^{-1}_{(\xi^{-1},\psi^{-1})})(H_{\tilde{C}}) = f^{-1}_{(\rho^{-1},\varsigma^{-1})}[g^{-1}_{(\xi^{-1},\psi^{-1})}(H_{\tilde{C}})] = f^{-1}_{(\rho^{-1},\varsigma^{-1})}(G_B) = F_{\tilde{A}}$.

Hence $(g_{(\xi,\psi)}\tilde{\circ}f_{(\rho,\varsigma)})^{-1}(H_{\tilde{C}}) = (f^{-1}_{(\rho^{-1},\varsigma^{-1})}\tilde{\circ}g^{-1}_{(\xi^{-1},\psi^{-1})})(H_{\tilde{C}}) \Rightarrow (g_{(\xi,\psi)}\tilde{\circ}f_{(\rho,\varsigma)})^{-1} = f^{-1}_{(\rho^{-1},\varsigma^{-1})}\tilde{\circ}g^{-1}_{(\xi^{-1},\psi^{-1})}$.

11.5 CONCLUSION

In this chapter, we have introduced and investigated the idea and theorems on hesitant fuzzy soft classes, hesitant fuzzy soft image, and hesitant fuzzy soft inverse image along with some examples. We hope these fundamental results will help the researchers to boost and foster the research on fuzzy soft set theory.

Bibliography

1. M. Akram, A. Adeel and J.C.R. Alcantud . Hesitant fuzzy N-soft sets: A new model with applications in decision-making. *J. Intell. Fuzzy Syst.*, 36(6):6113–6127, 2019.
2. K. Atanassov. Intuitionistic fuzzy sets. *Fuzzy Sets Syst.*, 20:87–96, 1986.
3. K.V. Babitha and S.J. Johan. Hesitant fuzzy soft sets. *J. New Results Sci.* 3:98–107, 2013.
4. M.J. Borah, B. Hazarika and X Zhang. Some aspects on hesitant fuzzy soft set. *Cogent. Math.*, 3(1):1–11, 2016.
5. M.J. Borah and B. Hazarika. Some operators on interval-valued hesitant fuzzy soft sets. Afrika Mat., 29(3):509–529, 2018.
6. M.J. Borah and B. Hazarika. Some applications of similarity of soft sets. *J. Intell. Fuzzy Syst.*, 33(6):3767–3777, 2017.
7. M.J. Borah, B. Hazarika, S.K. Panda and J.J. Nieto. Examining the correlation between the weather conditions and COVID-19 pandemic in India: A mathematical evidence. *Results Phys.*, 19:103587, 2020.

8. M.J. Borah, T.J. Neog and D.K. Sut. Relations on fuzzy soft sets. J. Math. Comput. Sci. 2(3):515–534, 2012.
9. S. Broumi and F. Smarandache. New operations over interval valued intuitionistic hesitant fuzzy set. *Math. Stat.*, 2(2):62–71, 2014.
10. N. Cağman and N. S. Enginoğlu. Soft set theory and uni-int decision making. *Euro. J. Opera. Res.*, 207:848–855, 2010.
11. P. Debnath. Some results on Cesaro summability in intuitionistic fuzzy n-normed linear spaces. *Sahand Commun. Math. Anal.*, 19(1):77–87, 2022.
12. P. Debnath. Results on lacunary difference ideal convergence in intuitionistic fuzzy normed linear spaces. *J. Intell. Fuzzy Syst.*, 28(3):1299–1306, 2015.
13. P. Debnath. Lacunary ideal convergence in intuitionistic fuzzy normed linear spaces. *Comput. Math. Appl.*, 63(3):708–715, 2012.
14. P. Debnath. Continuity and Banach contraction principle in intuitionistic fuzzy n-normed linear spaces. *J. Intell. Fuzzy Syst.*, 33(4):2363–2373, 2017.
15. P. Debnath. Approximation of new bounded operators in intuitionistic fuzzy n-Banach spaces. *J. Intell. Fuzzy Syst.*, 35(6):6301–6312, 2018.
16. P. Debnath. A generalized statistical convergence in intuitionistic fuzzy n-normed linear spaces. *Ann. Fuzzy Math. Inform.*, 12(4):559–572, 2016.
17. P. Debnath and S.A. Mohiuddine. *Soft Computing Techniques in Engineering, Health, Mathematical and Social Sciences.* CRC Press: Boca Raton, FL, 2021.
18. J. Hao and F. Chiclana. Attitude quantifier based possibility distribution generation method for hesitant fuzzy linguistic group decision making. *Inform. Sci.*, 518:341–360, 2020.
19. F. Karamaz and F. Karaaslan. Hesitant fuzzy parameterized soft sets and their applications in decision making. *J. Ambient Intell. Hum. Comput.*, 2020. doi: 10.1007/s12652-020-02258-7.
20. A. Kharal and B. Ahmad. Mapping on Fuzzy soft classes. *Adv. Fuzzy Syst.*, 2009. doi: 10.1155/2009/407890.
21. A. Kharal and B. Ahmad. Mapping on soft classes. *New Math. Nat. Comput.*, 7(3):471–481, 2011.
22. N. Konwar and P. Debnath. Intuitionistic fuzzy n-normed algebra and continuous product. *Proyecciones (Antofagasta)*, 37(1):68–83, 2018.
23. N. Konwar and P. Debnath. Some new contractive conditions and related fixed point theorems in intuitionistic fuzzy n-Banach spaces. *J. Intell. Fuzzy Syst.*, 35(6):6301–6312, 2018.
24. C. Li, D. Li and J. Jin. Generalized hesitant fuzzy soft sets and its application to decision making. *Int. J. Pattern Recogn.*, 33(12):1950019, 2019.
25. H.C. Liao and Z.S. Xu. Subtraction and divison operations over hesitant fuzzy sets. *J. Intell. Fuzzy Syst.*, 27(1):65–72, 2014.
26. P.K. Maji, R. Biswas and R. Roy. An application of soft sets in a decision making problem. *Comput. Math. Appl.*, 44:1077–1083, 2002.
27. P.K. Maji, R. Biswas, and R. Roy. Soft set theory. *Comput. Math. Appl.*, 45:555–562, 2003.
28. P.K. Maji, R. Biswas, and A.R. Roy. Fuzzy soft sets. *J. Fuzzy Math.*, 9(3):589–602, 2001.
29. D.A. Molodstov. Soft set theory-first result. *Comput. Math. Appl.*, 37:19–31, 1999.
30. D.A. Molodtsov, V.Y. Leonov and D.V. Kovkov. Soft sets technique and its application. *Nechetkie Sistemy i Myagkie Vychisleniya*, 1(1):8–39, 2006.

31. S. Ozlu and F. Karaaslan. Some distance measures for type 2 hesitant fuzzy sets and their applications to multi-criteria group decisionmaking problems. *Soft Comput.*, 2019. doi: 10.1007/s00500-019-04509–y.
32. S. Singh and Q. Zameeruddin, *Modern Algebra*. Vikas Publishing House Pvt Ltd: Delhi.
33. V. Torra. Hesitant fuzzy sets. *Inter. J. Intell. Syst.*, 25(6):529–539, 2010.
34. V. Torra and Y. Narukawa. On hesitant fuzzy sets and decision. *In Proceeding of the 18th IEEE Internatiuonal Conference on Fuzzy Systems*, Jeju Island, Republic of Korea, pp. 1378–1382, 2009.
35. R. Verma and B.D. Sharma. New operations over hesitant fuzzy sets. *Fuzzy Inform. Eng.*, 2:129–146, 2013.
36. J. Wang, X. Li and X. Chen. Hesitant fuzzy soft sets with application in multicrteria group decision making problems. *Sci. World J.*, 2015:1–14, 2015.
37. M. Xia and Z. Xu. Hesitant fuzzy information aggregation in decision making. *Inter. J. Appr. Reasoning*, 52:395–407, 2011.
38. Z. Xu and M. Xia. Distance and similrity measures for hesitant fuzzy sets. *Inform. Sci.*, 181:2128–2138, 2011.
39. L. A. Zadeh. Fuzzy sets. *Inform. Control.*, 8:338–353, 1965.

12 Ulam Stability of Mixed Type Functional Equation in Non-Archimedean IFN-Space

K. Tamilvanan
R.M.K. Engineering College

S. A. Mohiuddine
King Abdulaziz University

N. Revathi
Periyar University PG Extension Centre

CONTENTS

12.1 Introduction 167
12.2 Ulam Stability by Even Case: Direct Approach 169
12.3 Ulam Stability by Even Case: Fixed-Point Approach 171
12.4 Ulam Stability by Odd Case: Direct Approach 173
12.5 Ulam Stability by Odd Case: Fixed-Point Approach 175
Bibliography 177

12.1 INTRODUCTION

The stability of different functional equations in the setting of random normed spaces or fuzzy normed spaces has been investigated since the work [13] (for example, [12,14]. The work [15] shows that the Cauchy equation is stable in non-Archimedean fuzzy normed spaces when the t-norm T_M is used. The conclusions in Ref. [15] do not apply where the field of scalars is $\mathbb{R}$ or $\mathbb{C}$ since the vector space has just one element.

When is it necessary for a mapping that approximates the solution to a functional issue to be close to it? One of the most crucial aspects of functional equation stability research is the study of the stability of functional equations. A similar technique was described by Ulam [28] in 1940.

DOI: 10.1201/9781003312017-12

Hyers [16] studied virtually additive functions on Banach spaces which satisfy the Hyers stability, which is characterised by a non-negative constant, in 1941. In the instance of stability involving a sum of powers of norms, Aoki [1] generalised the classic Hyers stability discovery [16]. In 1978, Rassias [24] suggested a Hyers Theorem extension that allowed for an infinite Cauchy difference. Several authors have studied and generalised the stability problems of several functional equations in recent decades (see [10,11,16,18,19,20,27],[21,25,26]). For more relevant work, we refer to [3,4,7,8,9,17,22,23,29,31].

Here, we examine the Ulam stability of the mixed type additive-quadratic functional equation

$$\begin{aligned} \phi\left(\sum_{1\leq a\leq m} av_a\right) + \sum_{1\leq a\leq m} \phi\left(-av_a + \sum_{b=1;a\neq b}^{m} bv_b\right) &= (m-3)\sum_{1\leq a<b\leq m} \phi\left(av_a+bv_b\right) \\ &\quad - \left(m^2-5m+2\right)\sum_{1\leq a\leq m} a^2\left[\frac{\phi(v_a)+\phi(-v_a)}{2}\right] \\ &\quad - \left(m^2-5m+4\right)\sum_{1\leq a\leq m} a\left[\frac{\phi(v_a)-\phi(-v_a)}{2}\right] \end{aligned} \tag{12.1}$$

where $\phi(0)=0$, and m is a non-negative integer with $m>4$ in non-Archimedean IFN spaces over a field by using direct and fixed-point techniques.

We may use the alternative fixed point theorem to get several significant conclusions in fixed point theory, and we can refer to certain essential preliminaries in [2,6,18],[30].

The subsequent Diaz and Margolis [5] results are noted for future use.

Theorem 12.1 *Let (P,d) be a generalised complete metric space and let $M: P \to P$ be a strictly contractive function with $L<1$. Then, for every $v_1 \in P$, either*

$$d\left(M^n v_1, M^{n+1} v_1\right) = \infty, \quad n \geq n_0;$$

or there is a positive integer n_0 satisfies

(i) $d\left(P^n v_1, P^{n+1} v_1\right) < \infty, \quad n \geq n_0;$
(ii) the sequence $\{P^n v_1\}_{n\in\mathbb{N}}$ converges to a fixed point v_1^* of P;
(iii) v_1^* is the only one fixed point of P in $S^* = \{v_2 \in P | d(S^{n_0} v_1, v_2) < \infty\}$;
(iv) $d(v_2, v_2^*) \leq \frac{1}{1-L} d(Sv_2, v_2)$, for every $v_2 \in P^*$.

Throughout all the sections, we assume that $\mathbb{K}$ as a valued field, two vector spaces are W and F over a field $\mathbb{K}$ and complete non-Archimedean IFN space $(F, N_{\mu,\nu}, T)$

over a field $\mathbb{K}$. We can define the mapping $\phi : W \to F$ by

$$\begin{aligned} D\phi(v_1,v_2,\cdots,v_m) &= \phi\left(\sum_{1\le a\le m} av_a\right) + \sum_{1\le a\le m}\phi\left(-av_a + \sum_{b=1;a\neq b}^{m} bv_b\right) \\ &\quad -(m-3)\sum_{1\le a<b\le m}\phi\left(av_a+bv_b\right) \\ &\quad +\left(m^2-5m+2\right)\sum_{1\le a\le m} a^2\left[\frac{\phi(v_a)+\phi(-v_a)}{2}\right] \\ &\quad +\left(m^2-5m+4\right)\sum_{1\le a\le m} a\left[\frac{\phi(v_a)-\phi(-v_a)}{2}\right] \end{aligned} \tag{12.2}$$

12.2 ULAM STABILITY BY EVEN CASE: DIRECT APPROACH

Theorem 12.2 *Suppose that a function* $\Phi_{\mu,\nu} : W^m \times [0,\infty) \to [0,1]$ *satisfies*

$$\lim_{i\to\infty}\Phi_{\mu,\nu}(2^iv_1,2^iv_2,\cdots,2^iv_m,|2|^{2i}t) = 1 \tag{12.3}$$

and

$$\begin{aligned} \lim_{l\to\infty} T_{i=l}^{\infty} \quad & T \quad (\Phi_{\mu,\nu}(0,2^iv,0,\cdots,0,|2|^{2i+1}t)) \\ &= \lim_{l\to\infty} T_{i=1}^{\infty}T(\Phi_{\mu,\nu}(0,2^{l+i-1}v,0,\cdots,0,|2|^{2i+2l-1}t)) \\ &= 1 \end{aligned} \tag{12.4}$$

for every $v_1,v_2,\cdots,v_m \in W$ *and every* $t>0$. *If a function* $\phi : W \to F$ *fulfills Eq. (12.2) and*

$$\phi(0)=0 \tag{12.5}$$

and

$$N_{\mu,\nu}\left(D\phi(v_1,v_2,\cdots,v_m),t\right) \ge \Phi_{\mu,\nu}(v_1,v_2,\cdots,v_m,t) \tag{12.6}$$

for every $v_1,v_2,\cdots,v_m \in W$ *and every* $t \in [0,\infty)$, *then there exists only one quadratic function* $Q_2 : E \to F$ *fulfilling*

$$N_{\mu,\nu}\left(\phi(v)-Q_2(v),t\right) \ge T_{i=1}^{\infty}T\left(\Phi_{\mu,\nu}(0,2^{i-1}v,0,\cdots,0,|2|^{2i-1}dt)\right) \tag{12.7}$$

where $d=(m^2-5m+2)$, *for every* $v\in W$ *and every* $t>0$.

Proof. Fix for every v in W and every $t>0$. Switching $(v_1,v_2,\cdots,v_m)$ by $(0,v,0,\cdots,0)$ in Eq. (12.6), we obtain

$$N_{\mu,\nu}\left(d\phi(2v)-2^2d\phi(v),t\right) \ge \Phi_{\mu,\nu}(0,v,0,\cdots,0,t). \tag{12.8}$$

From inequality Eq. (12.8), we get

$$N_{\mu,\nu}\left(\frac{1}{2^2}\phi(2v)-\phi(v),t\right) \ge T\left(\Phi_{\mu,\nu}(0,v,0,\cdots,0,|2|^2dt)\right). \tag{12.9}$$

Therefore, one can get

$$N_{\mu,\nu}\left(\frac{1}{2^{2(l+m)}}\phi(2^{l+m}v)-\frac{1}{2^{2l}}\phi(2^{l}v),t\right)$$
$$\geq T_{i=l}^{l+m-1}T\left(\Phi_{\mu,\nu}(0,2^{i}v,0,\cdots,0,|2|^{2i+1}dt)\right).$$

From Eq. (12.4), the sequence $\left\{\frac{\phi(2^{i}v)}{2^{2i}}\right\}_{i\in\mathbb{N}}$ is Cauchy in a complete non-Archimedean intuitionistic fuzzy normed space.

Thus, we may define a function $Q_2 : W \to F$ by

$$\lim_{i\to\infty} N_{\mu,\nu}\left(\frac{1}{2^{2i}}\phi(2^{i}v)-Q_2(v),t\right)=1.$$

For every l in $\mathbb{N}$ and $l \geq 1$, we obtain

$$\begin{aligned}N_{\mu,\nu}\left(\phi(v)-\frac{1}{2^{2l}}\phi(2^{l}v),t\right) &\geq T_{i=1}^{l}N_{\mu,\nu}\left(\frac{1}{2^{2(i-1)}}\phi(2^{i-1}v)-\frac{1}{2^{2i}}\phi(2^{i}v),t\right)\\ &\geq T_{i=1}^{l}T\left(\Phi_{\mu,\nu}(0,2^{i-1}v,0,\cdots,0,|2|^{2(i-1)}dt)\right).\end{aligned}$$

Therefore,

$$\begin{aligned}N_{\mu,\nu}\left(\phi(v)-Q_2(v),t\right) &\geq T\left(N_{\mu,\nu}\left(\phi(v)-\frac{1}{2^{2l}}\phi(2^{l}v),t\right),\right.\\ &\quad\left.N_{\mu,\nu}\left(\frac{1}{2^{2l}}\phi(2^{l}v)-Q_2(v),t\right)\right)\\ &\geq T\left(T_{i=1}^{l}T\left(\Phi_{\mu,\nu}\left(0,2^{i-1}v,0,\cdots,0,|2|^{2i-1}dt\right)\right)\right),\\ &\quad N_{\mu,\nu}\left(2^{-2l}\phi\left(2^{l}v\right)-Q_2\left(v\right),t\right)\Big).\end{aligned}$$

Taking the limit $l \to \infty$ in the above inequality, we arrive Eq. (12.7). Hence, the mapping Q_2 is quadratic. Assume that an one more quadratic function $Q_2' : W \to F$ fulfilling Eq. (12.7). Hence, by $\phi(2v) = 2^2\phi(v)$ and Eqs. (12.4), (12.7), it follows that

$$\begin{aligned}N_{\mu,\nu}\left(Q_2'(v)-Q_2(v),t\right) &= N_{\mu,\nu}\left(Q_2\left(2^{l}v\right)-Q_2'\left(2^{l}v\right),|2|^{2i+2l-1}t\right)\\ &\geq T\left(T_{i=1}^{\infty}T\left(\Phi_{\mu,\nu}\left(0,2^{l+i-1}v,0,\cdots,0,|2|^{2l+2i-1}dt\right),\right.\right.\\ &\quad T_{i=1}^{\infty}T\left(\Phi_{\mu,\nu}\left(0,2^{l+i-1}v,0,\cdots,0,|2|^{2l+2i-1}dt\right),\right.\\ &\quad\left.\left.\Phi_{\mu,\nu}\left(0,2^{l+i-1}v,0,\cdots,0,|2|^{2l+2i}dt\right)\right)\right)\\ &\to 1 \ (\text{as } l\to\infty),\end{aligned}$$

and thus, $Q_2 = Q_2'$. Hence, the proof is completed. □

Theorem 12.3 *Suppose that a function $\Phi_{\mu,v} : W^m \times [0,\infty) \to [0,1]$ satisfies*

$$\lim_{i\to\infty} \Phi_{\mu,v}(2^{-i}v_1, 2^{-i}v_2, \cdots, 2^{-i}v_m, |2|^{-2i}t) = 1 \tag{12.10}$$

and

$$\begin{aligned} \lim_{l\to\infty} T_{i=l}^{\infty} \quad T \quad & (\Phi_{\mu,v}(0, 2^{-i-1}v, 0, \cdots, 0, |2|^{-2i-1}t) & (12.11)\\ = \quad & \lim_{l\to\infty} T_{i=1}^{\infty} T(\Phi_{\mu,v}(0, 2^{-l-i-1}v, 0, \cdots, 0, |2|^{-2i-2l-1}t)) \\ = \quad & 1 & (12.12) \end{aligned}$$

for every $v_1, v_2, \cdots, v_m \in W$ and all $t > 0$. If an even function $\phi : W \to F$ fulfilling Eqs. (12.5) *and* (12.6)*, then there exists only one quadratic function $Q_2 : W \to F$ fulfilling*

$$N_{\mu,v}(\phi(v) - Q_2(v), t) \geq T_{i=1}^{\infty} T\left(\Phi_{\mu,v}(0, 2^{-i-1}v, 0, \cdots, 0), |2|^{-2i-1}dt)\right)$$

where $d = m^2 - 5m + 2$, for every $v \in W$ and every $t > 0$.

12.3 ULAM STABILITY BY EVEN CASE: FIXED-POINT APPROACH

Theorem 12.4 *Suppose that a function $\Phi_{\mu,v} : W^m \times [0,\infty) \to [0,1]$ such that Eq.* (12.3) *satisfies and*

$$\Phi_{\mu,v}\left(2v_1, 2v_2, \cdots, 2v_m, |2|^2 Lt\right) \geq \Phi_{\mu,v}(v_1, v_2, \cdots, v_m, t), \quad v_1, v_2, \cdots, v_m \in W \tag{12.13}$$

where $L \in (0,1)$. If an even mapping $\phi : W \to F$ fulfilling Eqs. (12.5) *and* (12.6)*, then there exist only one quadratic function $Q_2 : W \to F$ fulfilling*

$$N_{\mu,v}(\phi(v) - Q_2(v), t) \geq T\left(\Phi_{\mu,v}\left(0, v, 0, \cdots, 0, |2|^2(1-L)dt\right)\right) \tag{12.14}$$

where $d = (m^2 - 5m + 2)$, for every $v \in W$ and every $t > 0$.

Proof. We consider a set

$$P := \{n : W \to F\}$$

and introduce the generalised metric m on P:

$$\begin{aligned} m(n,r) \quad = \quad & \inf\{c \in [0,\infty) : N_{\mu,v}(n(v) - r(v), dt) \\ \geq \quad & T\left(\Phi_{\mu,v}\left(0, v, 0, \cdots, 0, |2|^2 dt\right)\right), \quad v \in W\} \end{aligned}$$

for every $n, r \in P$. A standard verification (see for instance [8]) shows that (P,m) is a complete generalised metric space.

We may define a mapping $M : P \to P$ by

$$Mn(v) = \frac{1}{2^2} n(2v)$$

for every $n \in P$ and every $v \in W$.

For evry $n,r \in P$ and $c_{n,r} \in [0,\infty)$ with $m(n,r) \leq c_{n,r}$. Then,

$$N_{\mu,v}(n(v) - r(v), c_{n,r}t) \geq T\left(\Phi_{\mu,v}(0,v,0,\cdots,0,|2|^2 dt)\right),$$

which together with Eq. (12.13) gives

$$N_{\mu,v}(Mn(v) - Mr(v), t) \geq T\left(\Phi_{\mu,v}\left(0,v,0,\cdots,0,\frac{|2|^2 dt}{Lc_{n,r}}\right)\right)$$

and subsequently, $m(Mn, Mr) \leq Lc_{n,r}$, as a result, M is strictly contractive. Furthermore, from Eq. (12.9) that

$$N_{\mu,v}(M\phi(v) - \phi(v), t) \geq T\left(\Phi_{\mu,v}(0,v,0,\cdots,0,|2|^2 dt)\right)$$

and thus, $m(M\phi,\phi) \leq 1 < \infty$. Thus, by Theorem 12.1, M has a only one fixed point $Q_2 : W \to F$ in $P^* = \{n \in P : m(\phi,n) < \infty\}$ satisfies

$$\frac{1}{2^2} Q_2(2v) = Q_2(v) \tag{12.15}$$

and

$$Q_2(v) = \lim_{l\to\infty} 2^{-2l}\phi\left(2^l v\right)$$

for every $v \in W$. Furthermore, as $\phi \in P^*$, Theorem 12.1, and $m(M\phi,\phi) \leq 1$, we have

$$m(\phi, Q_2) \leq \frac{1}{1-L} m(M\phi,\phi) \leq \frac{1}{1-L} \tag{12.16}$$

and Eq. (12.14) follows. The Theorem 12.2 can be utilised to prove that Q_2 is a quadratic function.

Finally, consider this $Q_2' : W \to F$ is one more quadratic mapping which fulfilling Eq. (12.14). Then, Q_2' fulfills Eq. (12.15). As a result, it is a M fixed point.

Thus, by Eq. (12.14), we have

$$m\left(Q_2', \phi\right) < \infty,$$

and thus $Q_2' \in P^*$. Theorem 12.1 shows that $Q_2 = Q_2'$, i.e., the Q_2 is unique. □

Theorem 12.5 *Suppose that a function* $\Phi_{\mu,v} : W^m \times [0,\infty) \to [0,1]$ *satisfies Eq.* (12.10) *holds and*

$$\Phi_{\mu,v}\left(0,2^{-1}v,0,\cdots,0,|2|^{-2}Lt\right) \geq \Phi_{\mu,v}(0,v,0,\cdots,0,t), \quad v \in W$$

for $L \in (0,1)$. *If an even mapping* $\phi : W \to F$ *fulfilling Eqs.* (12.5) *and* (12.6), *then there exists only one quadratic mapping* $Q_2 : W \to F$ *fulfilling*

$$N_{\mu,v}(\phi(v) - Q_2(v), t) \geq T\left(\Phi_{\mu,v}\left(0,v,0,\cdots,0,|2|^2\left(\frac{1}{L}-1\right)dt\right)\right)$$

for every $v \in W$ *and every* $t > 0$.

12.4 ULAM STABILITY BY ODD CASE: DIRECT APPROACH

Theorem 12.6 *Suppose that a function $\Phi_{\mu,\nu} : W^m \times [0,\infty) \to [0,1]$ satisfies*

$$\lim_{i\to\infty} \Phi_{\mu,\nu}(2^i v_1, 2^i v_2, \cdots, 2^i v_m, |2|^i t) = 1 \tag{12.17}$$

and

$$\begin{aligned}\lim_{l\to\infty} T_{i=l}^{\infty} \quad T \quad & (\Phi_{\mu,\nu}(0,2^i v,0,\cdots,0,|2|^{i+1}t)) \\ &= \lim_{l\to\infty} T_{i=1}^{\infty} T(\Phi_{\mu,\nu}(0,2^{l+i-1}v,0,\cdots,0,|2|^{i+l-1}t)) \\ &= 1 \end{aligned}\tag{12.18}$$

for every $v_1, v_2, \cdots, v_m \in W$ and every $t > 0$. If an odd function $\phi : W \to F$ is satisfying Eq. (12.2) and fulfilling

$$\phi(0) = 0, \tag{12.19}$$

and

$$N_{\mu,\nu}(D\phi(v_1,v_2,\cdots,v_m),t) \geq \Phi_{\mu,\nu}(v_1,v_2,\cdots,v_m,t) \tag{12.20}$$

for every $v_1, v_2, \cdots, v_m \in W$ and every $t \in [0,\infty)$, then there is only one additive function $A_1 : W \to F$ such that

$$N_{\mu,\nu}(\phi(v) - A_1(v),t) \geq T_{i=1}^{\infty} T\left(\Phi_{\mu,\nu}(0,2^{i-1}v,0,\cdots,0,|2|^{i-1}ct)\right) \tag{12.21}$$

where $c = (m^2 - 5m + 4)$, for every $v \in W$ and every $t > 0$.

Proof. Fix for every v in W and every $t > 0$. Switching $(v_1, v_2, \cdots, v_m)$ by $(0, v, 0, \cdots, 0)$ in Eq. (12.20), we have

$$N_{\mu,\nu}(c\phi(2v) - 2c\phi(v),t) \geq \Phi_{\mu,\nu}(0,v,0,\cdots,0,t). \tag{12.22}$$

From inequality Eq. (12.22), we get

$$N_{\mu,\nu}\left(\frac{1}{2}\phi(2v) - \phi(v),t\right) \geq T\left(\Phi_{\mu,\nu}(0,v,0,\cdots,0,|2|ct)\right). \tag{12.23}$$

Therefore, one can get

$$N_{\mu,\nu}\left(\frac{1}{2^{(l+m)}}\phi(2^{l+m}v) - \frac{1}{2^l}\phi(2^l v),t\right) \geq T_{i=l}^{l+m-1} T\left(\Phi_{\mu,\nu}(0,2^i v,0,\cdots,0,|2|^{i+1}ct)\right).$$

From Eq. (12.18), the sequence $\left\{\frac{\phi(2^i v)}{2^{2i}}\right\}_{i\in\mathbb{N}}$ is Cauchy in a complete non-Archimedean intuitionistic fuzzy normed space.

Thus, we may define a function $A_1 : W \to F$ by

$$\lim_{i\to\infty} N_{\mu,\nu}\left(\frac{1}{2^i}\phi(2^i v) - A_1(v),t\right) = 1.$$

For every l in $\mathbb{N}$ and $l \geq 1$, we obtain

$$\begin{aligned} N_{\mu,v}\left(\phi(v)-\frac{1}{2^l}\phi(2^l v),t\right) &\geq T_{i=1}^{l} N_{\mu,v}\left(\frac{1}{2^{(i-1)}}\phi(2^{i-1}v)-\frac{1}{2^i}\phi(2^i v),t\right) \\ &\geq T_{i=1}^{l} T\left(\Phi_{\mu,v}(0,2^{i-1}v,0,\cdots,0,|2|^{(i-1)}ct)\right). \end{aligned}$$

Therefore,

$$\begin{aligned} N_{\mu,v}(\phi(v)-A_1(v),t) &\geq T\left(N_{\mu,v}\left(\phi(v)-\frac{1}{2^l}\phi(2^l v),t\right),\right. \\ &\quad \left. N_{\mu,v}\left(\frac{1}{2^l}\phi(2^l v)-A_1(v),t\right)\right) \\ &\geq T\left(T_{i=1}^{l} T\left(\Phi_{\mu,v}\left(0,2^{i-1}v,0,\cdots,0,|2|^{i-1}ct\right)\right)\right), \\ &\quad N_{\mu,v}\left(2^{-l}\phi\left(2^l v\right)-A_1(v),t\right)\right). \end{aligned}$$

Taking the limit $l \to \infty$ in the above inequality, we arrive Eq. (12.21). Hence, the mapping A_1 is additive. Assume that $A_1^{'} : W \to F$ is one more additive function which fulfilling Eq. (12.21). Hence, by $\phi(2v) = 2\phi(v)$ and Eqs. (12.18), (12.21), it follows that

$$\begin{aligned} N_{\mu,v}\left(A_1(v)-A_1^{'}(v),t\right) &= N_{\mu,v}\left(A_1\left(2^l v\right)-A_1^{'}\left(2^l v\right),|2|^{l+i-1}t\right) \\ &\geq T\left(T_{i=1}^{\infty} T\left(\Phi_{\mu,v}\left(0,2^{l+i-1}v,0,\cdots,0,|2|^{l+i-1}ct\right),\right.\right. \\ &\quad T_{i=1}^{\infty} T\left(\Phi_{\mu,v}\left(0,2^{l+i-1}v,0,\cdots,0,|2|^{l+i-1}ct\right),\right. \\ &\quad \left.\left.\left.\Phi_{\mu,v}\left(0,2^{l+i-1}v,0,\cdots,0,|2|^{l+i}ct\right)\right)\right)\right) \\ &\to 1 \ (\text{as } l \to \infty), \end{aligned}$$

and therefore, $A_1 = A_1^{'}$. □

Theorem 12.7 *Suppose that a mapping $\Phi_{\mu,v} : W^m \times [0,\infty) \to [0,1]$ such that*

$$\lim_{i\to\infty} \Phi_{\mu,v}(2^{-i}v_1, 2^{-i}v_2, \cdots, 2^{-i}v_m, |2|^{-i}t) = 1 \tag{12.24}$$

and

$$\lim_{l\to\infty} T_{i=l}^{\infty} \quad T \quad (\Phi_{\mu,v}(0,2^{-i-1}v,0,\cdots,0,|2|^{-i-1}t) \tag{12.25}$$

$$= \lim_{l\to\infty} T_{i=1}^{\infty} T(\Phi_{\mu,v}(0,2^{-l-i-1}v,0,\cdots,0,|2|^{-i-l-1}t))$$

$$= 1 \tag{12.26}$$

for every $v_1, v_2, \cdots, v_m \in W$ and every $t > 0$. If an odd function $\phi : W \to F$ fulfilling Eqs. (12.19) *and* (12.20)*, then there is only one additive mapping $A_1 : W \to F$ fulfils*

$$N_{\mu,v}(\phi(v)-A_1(v),t) \geq T_{i=1}^{\infty} T\left(\Phi_{\mu,v}(0,2^{-i-1}v,0,\cdots,0),|2|^{-i-1}ct\right)\right)$$

where $c = m^2 - 5m + 4$, for every $v \in W$ and every $t > 0$.

12.5 ULAM STABILITY BY ODD CASE: FIXED-POINT APPROACH

Theorem 12.8 *Suppose that a function* $\Phi_{\mu,\nu} : W^m \times [0,\infty) \to [0,1]$ *satisfies* (12.17) *satisfies and*

$$\Phi_{\mu,\nu}(2v_1, 2v_2, \cdots, 2v_m, |2|Lt) \geq \Phi_{\mu,\nu}(v_1, v_2, \cdots, v_m, t), \quad v_1, v_2, \cdots, v_m \in W \tag{12.27}$$

where $L \in (0,1)$. *If an odd mapping* $\phi : W \to F$ *fulfilling Eqs.* (12.19) *and* (12.20), *then there is only one additive mapping* $A_1 : W \to F$ *fulfils*

$$N_{\mu,\nu}(\phi(v) - A_1(v), t) \geq T(\Phi_{\mu,\nu}(0, v, 0, \cdots, 0, |2|(1-L)ct)) \tag{12.28}$$

where $c = m^2 - 5m + 4$, *for every* $v \in W$ *and every* $t > 0$.

Proof. Consider a set

$$P := \{n : W \to F\}$$

and introduce a generalised metric m on P:

$$\begin{aligned} m(n,r) &= \inf\{c \in [0,\infty) : N_{\mu,\nu}(n(v) - r(v), ct) \\ &\geq T(\Phi_{\mu,\nu}(0, v, 0, \cdots, 0, |2|ct)), \ v \in W\} \end{aligned}$$

for every $n, r \in P$. A typical verification (for example [8]) establishes that (P, m) is a complete generalised metric space. Next, we may define a mapping $M : P \to P$ by

$$Mn(v) = \frac{1}{2} n(2v)$$

for every $n \in P$ and every $v \in W$.

Let $n, r \in P$ and $c_{n,r} \in [0,\infty)$ with $m(n,r) \leq c_{n,r}$. Then,

$$N_{\mu,\nu}(n(v) - r(v), c_{n,r}t) \geq T\Big(\Phi_{\mu,\nu}(0, v, 0, \cdots, 0, |2|ct)\Big),$$

which together with Eq. (12.27) gives

$$N_{\mu,\nu}(Mn(v) - Mr(v), t) \geq T\left(\Phi_{\mu,\nu}\left(0, v, 0, \cdots, 0, \frac{|2|ct}{Lc_{n,r}}\right)\right).$$

Subsequently, $m(Mn, Mr) \leq Lc_{n,r}$, as a result, M is strictly contractive. Furthermore, it follows from Eq. (12.23) that

$$N_{\mu,\nu}(M\phi(v) - \phi(v), t) \geq T\Big(\Phi_{\mu,\nu}(0, v, 0, \cdots, 0, |2|ct)\Big).$$

Thus, $m(M\phi, \phi) \leq 1 < \infty$. By Theorem 12.1, M has only one fixed point $A_1 : W \to F$ in the set $P^* = \{n \in P : m(\phi, n) < \infty\}$ satisfies

$$\frac{1}{2} A_1(2v) = A_1(v) \tag{12.29}$$

and

$$A_1(v) = \lim_{l \to \infty} 2^{-l} \phi\left(2^l v\right)$$

for every $v \in W$. Furthermore, as $\phi \in P^*$, Theorem 12.1, and $m(M\phi, \phi) \leq 1$, we have

$$m(\phi, A_1) \leq \frac{1}{1-L} m(M\phi, \phi) \leq \frac{1}{1-L} \tag{12.30}$$

and Eq. (12.28) follows. The Theorem 12.2 can be utilised to prove that the function A_1 is additive.

Finally, consider that $A_1^{'} : W \to F$ is an another additive function which satisfying Eq. (12.28). Then, $A_1^{'}$ fulfills Eq. (12.29). Thus, it is a fixed point of M.

Thus, by Eq. (12.28), we obtain

$$m\left(\phi, A_1^{'}\right) \leq \frac{1}{1-L} < \infty,$$

and hence $A_1^{'} \in P^*$. Theorem 12.1 proves that $A_1^{'} = A_1$, i.e., A_1 is the unique function. Hence this completes the proof of the Theorem. □

Theorem 12.9 *Suppose that a function* $\Phi_{\mu,\nu} : W^m \times [0, \infty) \to [0, 1]$ *such that Eq.* (12.24) *holds and*

$$\Phi_{\mu,\nu}\left(0, 2^{-1}v, 0, \cdots, 0, |2|^{-1}Lt\right) \geq \Phi_{\mu,\nu}\left(0, v, 0, \cdots, 0, t\right), \quad v \in W$$

where $L \in (0, 1)$. *If an odd mapping* $\phi : W \to F$ *fulfilling Eqs.* (12.19) *and* (12.20), *then there is only one additive mapping* $A_1 : W \to F$ *fulfils*

$$N_{\mu,\nu}\left(\phi(v) - A_1(v), t\right) \geq T\left(\Phi_{\mu,\nu}\left(0, v, 0, \cdots, 0, |2|ct(L^{-1} - 1)\right)\right)$$

for every $v \in W$ *and every* $t > 0$.

Corollary 12 *Let* $\varepsilon, \lambda > 0$ *be two real constants and* $s \in (0, 1) \cup (1, \infty)$. *If an odd mapping* $\phi : W \to F$ *fulfilling Eq.* (12.19) *and*

$$\|D\phi(v_1, v_2, \cdots, v_m\| \leq \lambda\left[\|v_1\|^s + \|v_2\|^s + \cdots + \|v_m\|^s\right].$$

Then, there exists only one additive function $A_1 : W \to F$ *fulfilling*

$$\|\phi(v) - A_1(v)\| \leq \frac{\lambda\left(\|v\|^s\right)|2|}{\||2|^s - |2|\|}$$

for all $v_1 \in W$.

Bibliography

1. T. Aoki. On the stability of the linear transformation in Banach spaces. *J. Math. Soc. Japan*, 2:64–66, 1950.
2. P. Debnath. Results on lacunary difference ideal convergence in intuitionistic fuzzy normed linear spaces. *J. Intell. Fuzzy Syst.*, 28:1299–1306, 2015.
3. P. Debnath. A generalized statistical convergence in intuitionistic fuzzy n-normed linear spaces. *Ann. Fuzzy Math. Inform.*, 12:559–572, 2016.
4. P. Debnath. Some results on cesáro summability in intuitionistic fuzzy n-normed linear Spaces. *Sahand Commun. Math. Anal.*, 19:7—87, 2022.
5. J. B. Diaz and B. Margolis. A fixed point theorem of the alternative, for contractions on a generalized complete metric space. *Bull. Am. Math. Soc.*, 74:305–309, 1968.
6. D. H. Hyers. On the stability of the linear functional equation. *Proc. Nat. Acad. Sci. U. S. A.*, 27:222–224, 1941.
7. K.-W. Jun and H.-M. Kim. On the stability of Euler-Lagrange type cubic mappings in quasi-Banach spaces. *J. Math. Anal. Appl.*, 332:1335–1350, 2007.
8. S. O. Kim and K. Tamilvanan. Fuzzy stability results of generalized quartic functional equations. *Mathematics*, 9:120, 2021.
9. H. Koh and D. Kang. Solution and stability of Euler-Lagrange-Rassias quartic functional equations in various quasinormed spaces. *Abstr. Appl. Anal.*, 2013:8 pp., 2013
10. N. Konwar and P. Debnath. Some new contractive conditions and related fixed point theorems in intuitionistic fuzzy n-Banach spaces. *J. Intell. Fuzzy Syst.*, 35:6301–6312, 2018.
11. N. Konwar and P. Debnath. Intuitionistic fuzzy n-normed algebra and continuous product. *Proyecciones (Antofagasta)*, 37:68-83, 2018.
12. D. Mihet. The fixed point method for fuzzy stability of the Jensen functional equation. *Fuzzy Sets Syst.*, 160:1663–1667, 2009.
13. A. K. Mirmostafaee, M. Mirzavaziri and M. S. Moslehian. Fuzzy stability of the Jensen functional equation. *Fuzzy Sets Syst.*, 159:730–738, 2008.
14. A. K. Mirmostafaee and M. S. Moslehian. Fuzzy versions of Hyers-Ulam-Rassias theorem. *Fuzzy Sets Syst.*, 159:720–729, 2008.
15. A. K. Mirmostafaee and M. S. Moslehian. Stability of additive mappings in non-Archimedean fuzzy normed spaces. *Fuzzy Sets Syst.*, 160:1643–1652, 2009.
16. S. A. Mohiuddine. Stability of Jensen functional equation in intuitionistic fuzzy normed space. *Chaos Solitons Fractals* 42:2989–2996, 2009.
17. S. A. Mohiuddine, A. Alotaibi and M. Obaid. Stability of various functional equations in non-Archimedean intuitionistic fuzzy normed spaces. *Discrete Dyn. Nat. Soc.*, 2012:16 p., 2012.
18. S. A. Mohiuddine and H. Sevli. Stability of pexiderized quadratic functional equation in intuitionistic fuzzy normed space. *J. Comput. Appl. Math.*, 235:2137–2146, 2011.
19. S. A. Mohiuddine, J. M. Rassias and A. Alotaibi. Solution of the Ulam stability problem for Euler-Lagrange-Jensen k-cubic mappings. *Filomat*, 30(2):305–312, 2016.
20. S. A. Mohiuddine, J. M. Rassias and A. Alotaibi. Solution of the Ulam stability problem for Euler-Lagrange-Jensen k-quintic mappings. *Math. Meth. Appl. Sci.*, 40:3017–3025, 2017.
21. C. Park, K. Tamilvanan, Batool Noori, M. B. Moghimi and Abbas Najati. Fuzzy normed spaces and stability of a generalized quadratic functional equation. *AIMS Math.*, 5:7161–7174, 2020.

22. J. M. Rassias. On the stability of the Euler-Lagrange functional equation. *Chin. J. Math.*, 20:185–190, 1992.
23. J. M. Rassias. Solution of the Ulam stability problem for quartic mappings. *Glas. Mat. Ser. III*, 34:243–252, 1999.
24. T. M. Rassias. On the stability of the linear mapping in Banach spaces. *Proc. Am. Math. Soc.*, 72:297–300, 1978.
25. T. M. Rassias and K. Shibata. Variational problem of some quadratic functionals in complex analysis. *J. Math. Anal. Appl.*, 228:234–253, 1998.
26. K. Tamilvanan, J. R. Lee and C. Park. Ulam stability of a functional equation deriving from quadratic and additive mappings in random normed spaces. *AIMS Math.*, 6:908–924, 2021.
27. K. Tamilvanan, R. T. Alqahtani and S. A. Mohiuddine. Stability results of mixed type quadratic-additive functional equation in β-Banach modules by using fixed-point technique. *Mathematics*, 10:493, 2022.
28. S. M. Ulam. *A Collection of Mathematical Problems*, Interscience Tracts in Pure and Applied Mathematics, no. 8. Interscience Publishers, New York, 1960.
29. T. Z. Xu, J. M. Rassias and W. X. Xu. Stability of a general mixed additive-cubic functional equation in non-Archimedean fuzzy normed spaces. *J. Math. Phys.*, 51:093508, 2010.
30. T. Z. Xu and J. M. Rassias. Stability of general multi-Euler-Lagrange quadratic functional equations in non-Archimedean fuzzy normed spaces. *Adv. Differ. Equ.*, 2012:19 pp., 2012.
31. A. Zivari-Kazempour and M. E. Gordji. Generalized Hyers-Ulam stabilities of an Euler-Lagrange-Rassias quadratic functional equation. *Asian-Eur. J. Math.*, 5:1250014, 2012.

13 Optimum Design of 3D Steel Frames with Composite Slabs Using Adaptive Harmony Search Method

Mehmet Polat Saka
Middle East Technical University

Ibrahim Aydogdu
Akdeniz University

Refik Burak Taymus
Yuzuncu yil University

Zong Woo Geem
Gachon University

CONTENTS

13.1 Introduction ... 180
13.2 Discrete Optimum Design of Space Steel Frames with Composite Slabs to LRFD-AISC ... 181
13.2.1 The Objective Function ... 182
13.2.2 Strength Constraints ... 182
13.2.3 Displacement Constraints ... 183
13.2.3.1 Deflection Constraints ... 183
13.2.3.2 Drift Constraints ... 184
13.2.4 Geometric Constraints ... 184
13.2.4.1 Column-to-Column Geometric Constraints ... 185
13.2.4.2 Beam-to-Column Geometric Constraints ... 185
13.2.5 Design Constraints for Composite Slab ... 185
13.2.5.1 Shear Yield Check ... 187
13.2.5.2 Bending Check ... 187

DOI: 10.1201/9781003312017-13

13.3 Soft Computing Techniques 188
13.3.1 Adaptive Harmony Search Method 189
13.3.1.1 Initialization of a Parameter Set 189
13.3.1.2 Initialization of Harmony Memory Matrix 189
13.3.1.3 Evaluation of Harmony Memory Matrix 190
13.3.1.4 Generating a New Harmony Vector 190
13.3.1.5 Update of Harmony Memory and Adaptivity 191
13.3.1.6 Termination 191
13.3.2 Biogeography Based Optimization Algorithm with Levy Flight 192
13.3.2.1 Levy Flight Strategy 193
13.3.3 Whale Optimization Algorithm 194
13.3.3.1 Encircling Prey 194
13.3.3.2 Bubble-Net Attack 195
13.3.3.3 Search for Prey 195
13.3.3.4 Steps of Whale Optimization Algorithm 196
13.4 Design Examples 196
13.4.1 Steel Building with Irregular Plan and without composite Slabs (IFWOS) 198
13.4.2 Steel Building with Regular Plan and without Composite Slab (RFWOS) 200
13.4.3 Steel Building with Irregular Plan and Composite Slabs (IFWS) 201
13.4.4 Steel Building with Regular Plan and Composite Slabs (RFWS) 203
13.5 Discussion 205
13.6 Conclusions 207
Bibliography 208

13.1 INTRODUCTION

Structural optimization is well established today and a large number of optimum design algorithms for steel and reinforced concrete structures are available in the literature [17]– [19]. These algorithms make it possible to design structures in such a way that they need the least amount of material to be built while their response under the external loads is within the provisions of design codes. The use of the least amount of material is important because buildings and construction industry accounts for 38% of carbon dioxide emission [25]. Therefore, it is of prime importance from the sustainability point of view that structures are required to be designed and built using sufficient amount of material but not more. Structural optimization algorithms strive to achieve this goal.

The design process of steel structures can be automated by using optimum design algorithms. This automation provides the appropriate steel profiles from the available catalog for the members of steel frame in such a way that the cost or the weight of steel frame is the minimum and design code provisions are satisfied. The mathematical formulation of this design problem as an optimization problem yields discrete nonlinear programming problem [17]– [19]. Soft computing techniques are shown to be effective in obtaining the solution of such combinatorial problems. There are a large number of optimum design algorithms for steel structures in the literature that are based on several different metaheuristic algorithms [14,15,21], [26]– [27]. In these research works, most of the optimum design algorithms developed consider two- or three-dimensional steel frames under various loading conditions. The literature survey carried out indicates that only two publications are available that consider the composite slabs in the design of three-dimensional steel frames [4,7]. In Ref. [4], genetic algorithm-based minimum weight approach is presented for two-dimensional steel frames where the frame beams are considered as composite beams. Beam-column connections are taken as semi-rigid connections. The optimum design algorithm selects appropriate W-section from the catalog and the design satisfies AISC-ASD [2] specifications. The study has not taken into account the effect of composite slab in the response of the three-dimensional structure. In Ref. [7], a parametric study dealing with typical office buildings braced horizontally and with regularly spaced columns is presented. In the first step, two common structural arrangements for the girders are compared for material economy. In the second step, and for the most convenient girder arrangement, the type of column layout, the spans and the structural steel grade are varied. The study does not use any of the mathematical optimization techniques.

In this chapter, the optimum design problem of complete three-dimensional steel frame with its composite slabs is formulated according to LRFD-AISC [3] provisions. The weight of steel building is taken as objective function to be minimized. Design variables are selected as designation of W-sections to be assigned to frame member groups, slab thickness, stud diameter, stud height, deck type, and designations of W-sections for intermediate steel beams in composite slabs. The solution of the optimum design problem is obtained by making use of Adaptive Harmony Search (AHS) algorithm, Biogeography optimization with levy Flight (LFBBO) and Whale Optimization (WO) algorithm. Two three-dimensional six-story steel frames with composite slabs are considered as design examples to evaluate the performance of metaheuristic algorithms selected in obtaining the optimum solution of the design problem.

13.2 DISCRETE OPTIMUM DESIGN OF SPACE STEEL FRAMES WITH COMPOSITE SLABS TO LRFD-AISC

The design of space steel frames with composite slabs necessitates the selection of steel sections for the columns and beams of the steel frame from a W-section tables as well as the thickness of concrete slab, the diameter and height of studs and W-sections for the intermediate steel beams present in the composite slab. This selection should be carried out such that the steel frame and the composite slab satisfy the serviceability and strength requirements specified by the code of practice while the economy is observed in the overall or material cost of the frame. When the design constraints are implemented from LRFD-AISC, the following discrete programming problem is obtained.

13.2.1 THE OBJECTIVE FUNCTION

The objective function is taken as the minimum weight of the structure, which is expressed as in the following.

$$\text{Minimize } W = W_{\text{frame}} + W_{\text{slab,steel}} = \left(\sum_{r=1}^{ngf} m_r \sum_{s=1}^{t_r} \ell_s\right) + \sum_{r=1}^{ngs} m_r \sum_{sc=1}^{t_{rs}} \ell_{sc} \quad (13.1)$$

where W defines the weight of the structure. W_{frame} is the weight of steel frame and $W_{\text{slab,steel}}$ is the weight of the steel parts of the slab. m_r is the unit weight of the steel section selected from the standard steel sections table adopted for group r. t_r is the total number of members in group r, ngf is the total number of frame member groups, ngs is the total number of slab groups. l_s is the length of steel members belongs to group r. l_{sc} is the length of steel beams in composite slab belongs to rs. t_{rs} is the total number of steel members in group rs.

Initially, the concrete slab thickness is taken as design variable in the optimum design problem. However, it is noticed that in the optimum designs the thickness of concrete slab was the smallest value in the design pool in both examples. This makes the weight of concrete slab constant during the design process. Therefore, it is found appropriate to exclude the weight of the concrete slab from the objective function.

13.2.2 STRENGTH CONSTRAINTS

The strength capacity of W-sections that are selected for beam-column members of the three-dimensional frame should satisfy the following inequalities given in Chapter H of LRFD-AISC [3].

$$g_1(x) = \left(\frac{P_u}{\emptyset_c P_n} + \frac{8}{9}\left(\frac{M_{ux}}{\emptyset_b M_{nx}} + \frac{M_{uy}}{\emptyset_b M_{ny}}\right)\right)_{i,j} - 1.0 \leq 0 \quad \text{for} \left(\frac{P_u}{\emptyset_c P_n}\right)_{i,j} \geq 0.2 \quad (13.2)$$

$$g_1(x) = \left(\frac{P_u}{2\emptyset_c P_n} + \left(\frac{M_{ux}}{\emptyset_b M_{nx}} + \frac{M_{uy}}{\emptyset_b M_{ny}}\right)\right)_{i,j} - 1.0 \leq 0 \quad \text{for} \left(\frac{P_u}{\emptyset_c P_n}\right)_{i,j} < 0.2 \quad (13.3)$$

$$i = 1, 2, \ldots NM; \; j = 1, 2, \ldots N_{lc}$$

where M_{nx} is the nominal flexural strength at strong axis (x-axis). M_{ny} is the nominal flexural strength at weak axis (y-axis). M_{ux} is the required flexural strength at strong axis (x-axis), M_{uy} is the required flexural strength at weak axis (y-axis), P_n is the nominal axial strength (Tension or compression), and P_u is the required axial strength (tension or compression) for member i. The values of M_{ux} and M_{uy} are to be obtained by carrying out $P-\Delta$ analysis of the steel frame. In Chapter C of LRFD-AISC, an alternative way is suggested for the computations of M_{ux} and M_{uy} values. This method requires two first-order elastic analyses of the frame. In the first, the frame is analyzed under the gravity loads only where the sway of the frame is prevented to obtain M_{nt} values. In the second, the frame is analyzed only under the lateral loads to find M_{lt} values. These moment values are combined as given in the following.

$$M_u = B_1 M_{nt} + B_2 M_{lt} \tag{13.4}$$

where B_1 is the moment magnifier coefficient and B_2 is the sway moment magnifier coefficient. The details of how these coefficients are calculated are given in Chapter C of LRFD-AISC [3].

For composite beams, the strength constraints are computed as described in Section 13.2.5 of the chapter.

13.2.3 DISPLACEMENT CONSTRAINTS

The steel design codes restrict the lateral displacements of steel frames and deflection of its beams due to serviceability requirements. According to the ASCE Ad Hoc Committee report [9], the accepted range of drift limits by first-order analysis is 1/750 to 1/250 times the building height H with a recommended value of $H/400$.The typical limits on the inter-story drift are 1/500 to 1/200 times the story height. Based on this report, the deflection limits recommended are proposed in Ref. [8,9] for general use, which is repeated in Table 13.1.

13.2.3.1 Deflection Constraints

The mid-span deflections of beams in a steel space frame are required to be limited not to cause cracks in brittle finishes that they may support due to excessive displacements. Deflection constraints are expressed by the following inequality.

$$g_{dj} = \frac{\delta_{jl}}{\delta_j^u} - 1 \le 0 \; j = 1,\ldots,n_{sm}; l = 1,\ldots,n_{lc} \tag{13.5}$$

where δ_{jl} is the maximum deflection of jth member under the lth load case, δ_j^u is

Table 13.1
Displacement Limitations for Steel Frames

	Item	Deflection Limit
1	Floor girder deflection for service live load	L/360
2	Roof girder deflection	L/240
3	Lateral drift for service wind load	H/400
4	Inter-story drift for service wind load	H/300

the upper bound on this deflection which is defined in the code as *span*/360 for beams carrying brittle finishers, n_{sm} is the total number of members where deflections limitations are to be imposed and n_{lc} is the number of load cases.

13.2.3.2 Drift Constraints

These constraints are of two types. One is the restriction applied to the top-story sway and the other is the limitation applied on the inter-story drift.

- **13.2.3.2.1 Top-Story Drift**
  Top-story drift limitation is expressed as in the following equation.

$$g_{td\,j} = \frac{(\Delta_{\text{top}})_{jl}}{H/\text{Ratio}} - 1 \leq 0; j = 1,\ldots,n_{jtop}; l = 1,\ldots,n_k \tag{13.6}$$

  where H is the height of the frame, n_{jtop} is the number of joints on the top story, n_{lc} is the number of load cases, $(\Delta_{\text{top}})_{jl}$ is the top-story drift of the jth joint under l^{th} load case and ratio is the drift ratio given the ASCE Ad Hoc Committee report [26].
- **13.2.3.2.2 Inter-Story Drift**
  In multi-story steel frames, the relative lateral displacements of each floor is required to be limited. This limit is defined as the maximum inter-story drift which is specified as h_{sx}/Ratio where h_{sx} is the story height and ratio is a constant value given in ASCE Ad Hoc Committee report [26].

$$g_{id\,j} = \frac{(\Delta_{oh})_{jl}}{h_{sx}/Ratio} - 1 \leq 0; j = 1,\ldots,n_{st}; l = 1,\ldots,n_{lc} \tag{13.7}$$

  where n_{st} is the number of story, n_{lc} is the number of load cases and $(\Delta_{oh})_{jl}$ is the story drift of the jth story under l^{th} load case.

13.2.4 GEOMETRIC CONSTRAINTS

In practice, it is preferred to have smaller W-section for the upper floor columns compared to the lower floor columns in steel frames due to ease of constructibility reasons. In the case where upper column W-section is larger than the lower floor W-section, it becomes necessary to carry out special joint arrangement which is not economical. The same applies to the beam-to-column connections. The W-section selected for any beam should have a flange width smaller than or equal to the flange width of the W-section selected for the column to which the beam is to be connected. These are shown in Figure 13.1 and named as geometric constraints. These limitations are included in the design optimization model to satisfy practical requirements. Two types of geometric constraints are considered in the mathematical model. These are column-to-column geometric constraints and beam-to-column geometric limitations.

13.2.4.1 Column-to-Column Geometric Constraints

The depth and the unit weight of W-sections selected for the columns of two consecutive stores should be either equal to each other or the one in the upper story should be smaller than the one in the lower story. These limitations are included in the design problem as in the following.

$$g_{cdi} = \frac{D^a{}_i}{D^b{}_i} - 1 \leq 0;\ i = 1, \ldots, n_{ccj} \tag{13.8}$$

$$g_{cmi} = \frac{m^a{}_i}{m^b{}_i} - 1 \leq 0\ i = 1, \ldots, n_{ccj} \tag{13.9}$$

where n_{ccj} is the number of column-to-column geometric constraints defined in the problem , m_i^a is the unit weight of W-section selected for above story, m_i^b is the unit weight of W-section selected for below story, D_i^a is the depth of W-section selected for above story, and D_i^b is the depth of W-section selected for below story.

13.2.4.2 Beam-to-Column Geometric Constraints

When a beam is connected to a flange of a column, the flange width of the beam should be less than or equal to the flange width of the column so that the connection can be made without difficulty. In order to achieve this, the flange width of the beam should be less than or equal to $(D - 2t_b)$ of the column web dimensions in the connection where D and t_b are the depth and the flange thickness of W-section respectively as shown in Figure 13.1.

$$g_{bci} = \frac{(B_f)_{bi}}{D_{ci} - 2(t_{bc})_i} - 1 \leq 0; i = 1, \ldots, n_{j1} \tag{13.10}$$

or

$$g_{bbi} = \frac{(B_f)_{bi}}{(B_f)_{ci}} - 1 \leq 0;\ i = 1, \ldots, n_{j2} \tag{13.11}$$

where n_{j1} is the number of joints where beams are connected to the web of a column. n_{j2} is the number of joints where beams are connected to the flange of a column. D_{ci} is the depth of W-section selected for the column at joint i, $(t_b)_{cj}$ is the flange thickness of W-section selected for the column at joint i. $(B_f)_{ci}$ is the flange width of W-section selected for the column at joint i and is the $(B_f)_{bi}$ flange width of W-section selected for the beam at joint i.

13.2.5 DESIGN CONSTRAINTS FOR COMPOSITE SLAB

The details of composite slab are shown in Figure 13.2. The design checks for composite beams are carried out as per the provisions of ANSI/AISC [1]. There are two main checks specified in the design code. These are shear yield check and construction bending check, which are repeated below.

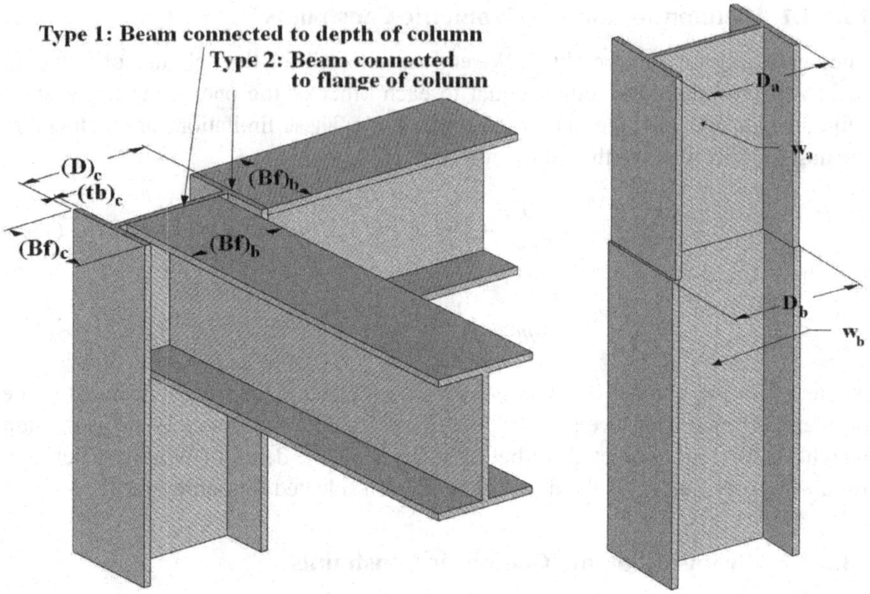

Figure 13.2-1 Geometric constraints.

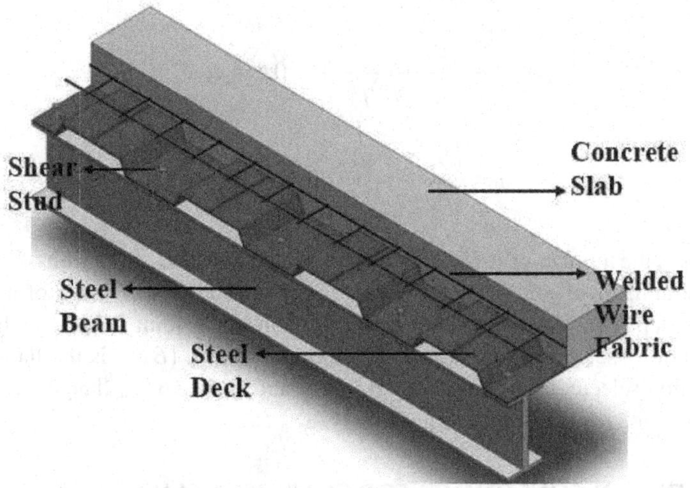

Figure 13.2-2 Typical composite slab.

13.2.5.1 Shear Yield Check

The composite beam subjected to shear forces should have sufficient strength to withstand this force. This is assured with the following constraint.

$$\frac{V_u}{\phi_v V_n} \leq 1.0 \tag{13.12}$$

where

$$\phi_v = \begin{cases} 1 & \text{if} \frac{h}{t_w} \leq 2.24\sqrt{\frac{E}{F_y}} \\ 0.9 & \text{otherwise} \end{cases} \tag{13.13}$$

$$V_n = 0.6F_yA_wC_v \tag{13.14}$$

In the above expressions, V_u is the ultimate shear force, h is height of the composite beam, t_w is web thickness of the composite beam, E is young modulus of the composite steel beam section, F_y is yield strength of the composite steel beam section, A_w is web area of the composite beam, and C_v is the web shear coefficient. A_w can be calculated from Eq. (13.15).

$$A_w = \begin{cases} d\backslash \cdot t_w \\ (d - C_{top} - C_{bottom}) \cdot t_w \end{cases} \tag{13.15}$$

where d is depth of a structural steel section from the outside face of the top flange to the outside face of the bottom flange, C_{top} is cope depth at top of beam, and C_{bottom} is cope depth at bottom of beam.

13.2.5.2 Bending Check

The composite section subjected to flexural moment should have sufficient strength to withstand to this bending moment. This is provided with the following constraint.

$$\frac{|M_u|}{\phi M_n} \leq 1.0 \tag{13.16}$$

where M_u is the ultimate flexural bending moment, ϕ is equal to 0.9, and M_n is the nominal flexural bending moment as a function of C_b and L_b which are defined in LRFD.

Optimum solution of the above-described programming problem requires the selection of the appropriate W-sections to the beams and column groups of the steel frame and intermediate beams of composite slab from the W-section catalog as well as appropriate slab thickness, deck type, stud diameter, and height for the composite slab. The design pool adopted for composite slab design variables is given in Table 13.2. This selection has to be made in such a way that Eq. (13.1) is to be minimized while the design constraints given from Eqs. (13.2) to (13.16) are satisfied.

Table 13.2
Design Pool for Composite Slabs

Design variables for composite slab	
Concrete Slab thickness (mm)	70,80,90,100,110,120,130,140,150
Stud diameters (mm)	13,16,19,22,25
Stud heights (mm)	50–200, 50–450
Steel Deck Type (four different types)	B Formlock, W2 Formlock, W3 Formlock, N Formlock
Steel profile	W-sections table (273 W-sections)

This programming problem is discrete nonlinear programming problem. It is shown in the literature that soft computing techniques (metaheuristics) are quite efficient to determine its optimum solution [14,15], [17]– [19], [21], [26]– [28]. There are several soft computing techniques available in the literature that are used in finding the solution of such design optimization problems. In this chapter, three of them are employed due to their successful applications in structural optimization problems. These are Adaptive Harmony Search (AHS) algorithm, Biogeography optimization with Levy Flight (LFBBO) and Whale Optimization (WO) algorithm. The working steps of these algorithms are given in the next section.

13.3 SOFT COMPUTING TECHNIQUES

In the application of the all-soft computing techniques before initiating the design process, a set of steel sections selected from an available profile list are collected in a design pool. Each steel section is assigned a sequence number that varies between 1 and total number of sections (N_{sec}) in the list. It is important to note that during the optimization process, the selection of sections for design variables is carried out using these numbers.

Soft computing techniques in general solves unconstrained optimization problems. For the constrained optimization problems, it becomes necessary to transform the constrained problem into unconstrained problem. This is achieved by making use of penalty function methods. There are several penalty function methods in the literature. Here, static penalty function method is used due to its previous successful applications [6].

$$V = \sum_{i=1}^{nc} C_i;\ C_i = \left\{ \begin{matrix} 0 \text{ for } g_i(x) \leq 0 \\ g_i(x) \text{ for } g_i(x) > 0 \end{matrix} \right\} \tag{13.17}$$

In Eq. (13.17), C_i is the violation of the ith problem constraint: $g_i(x)$ and nc represents the total number of constraints.

If the total violation, (V) is greater than zero, and structure weight is penalized using penalty function described in Eq. (13.18).

$$\Phi = W \cdot (1+V)^2 \tag{13.18}$$

where Φ is penalized weight of the structure. If V is calculated as zero, then the solution satisfies all the design constraints, and penalized weight of the structure directly equals to its unpenalized (real) weight.

13.3.1 ADAPTIVE HARMONY SEARCH METHOD

Adaptive harmony search algorithm is an enhanced version of the standard harmony search method [12]. The standard harmony search method considers two parameters in conceiving the new solution. These are harmony memory considering rate and pitch adjusting rate. In the implementation of the technique, appropriate constant values are assigned to these parameters following a sensitivity analysis for each problem considered. The success of the optimization process is directly related on a chosen parameter value set. The adaptive harmony search algorithm incorporates a new approach for adjusting these parameters automatically during the search for the most efficient optimization process [16]. The basic steps of the adaptive harmony search algorithm are outlined in the following.

13.3.1.1 Initialization of a Parameter Set

First, a harmony search-related optimization parameter set is specified. As described later in the section, this parameter set consists of four entities known as a harmony memory size (μ), a harmony memory considering rate (η), a pitch adjusting rate (ρ), and a maximum search number (N_s). Out of these four parameters, η and ρ are dynamic parameters that vary from one solution vector to another and are set to initial values of $\eta^{(0)}$ and $\rho^{(0)}$ for all the solution vectors in the initial harmony memory matrix. It is worthwhile to mention that in the standard harmony search algorithm, these parameters are treated as static quantities, and hence they are assigned to suitable values chosen within their recommended ranges of $\eta\ \varepsilon\ [0.70, 0.95]$ and $\rho\ \varepsilon\ [0.20, 0.50]$ [10,11,13].

13.3.1.2 Initialization of Harmony Memory Matrix

A harmony memory matrix **H** is generated and randomly initialized next. The harmony memory matrix simply represents a design population for the solution of a problem under consideration and incorporates a predefined number of solution vectors referred to as harmony memory size (μ). Each solution vector (harmony vector,$\mathbf{I}^i$ where **I** represents sequence number of W-sections in the catalog) consists of N_d design variables, and is represented in a separate row of the matrix; consequently, the size of **H** is $\mu X N_d$.

$$H = \begin{bmatrix} I_1^1 & I_2^1 & \dots & I_{N_d}^1 \\ I_1^2 & I_2^2 & \dots & I_{N_d}^2 \\ \dots & \dots & \dots & \dots \\ I_1^\mu & I_2^\mu & \dots & I_{N_d}^\mu \end{bmatrix} \begin{matrix} \varphi(I^1) \\ \varphi(I^2) \\ \dots \\ \varphi(I^\mu) \end{matrix} \tag{13.19}$$

13.3.1.3 Evaluation of Harmony Memory Matrix

The structural analysis of each solution is then performed with the set of steel sections selected for design variables, and force and deformation responses are obtained under the applied loads. The objective function values of each candidate solution are calculated according to Eq. (13.18). The solutions evaluated are sorted in the matrix in the descending order of objective function values, that is, $\Phi(I^1) \leq \Phi(I^2) \leq ,\cdots,\Phi(I^\mu)$.

13.3.1.4 Generating a New Harmony Vector

In harmony search algorithm, the generation of a new solution (harmony) vector is controlled by two parameters (η and ρ) of the technique. The harmony memory considering rate (η) refers to a probability value that biases the algorithm to select a value for a design variable either from harmony memory or from the entire set of discrete values used for the variable. The goal is to encourage a more explorative search by allowing transitions to designs in the vicinity of the current solutions. This phenomenon is known as pitch adjustment in HS, and is controlled by pitch adjusting rate parameter (ρ). In the adaptive harmony search algorithm a new set of values is sampled for η and ρ parameters each time prior to generation of a new harmony vector. To generate a new harmony vector, two-step procedure is followed consisting of (i) sampling of control parameters and (ii) improvisation of the design vector.

13.3.1.4.1 Sampling of Control Parameters

For each harmony vector to be generated during the search process, first a new set of values are sampled for η and ρ control parameters by applying a logistic normal distribution-based variation to the average values of these parameters within the harmony memory matrix, as formulated in Eqs. (13.20) and (13.21).

$$\eta^k = (1 + \frac{1-\bar{\eta}}{\bar{\eta}} \cdot e^{-\gamma \cdot N(0,1)}) \tag{13.20}$$

$$\rho^k = (1 + \frac{1-\bar{\rho}}{\bar{\rho}} \cdot e^{-\gamma \cdot N(0,1)}) \tag{13.21}$$

In Eqs. (13.20) and (13.21), η^k and ρ^k represent the sampled values of the control parameters for a new harmony vector. The notation N(0,1) designates a normally distributed random number having expectation 0 and standard deviation 1. The symbols $\overline{\eta}$ and $\overline{\rho}$ denote the average values of control parameters within the harmony memory matrix, obtained by averaging the corresponding values of all the solution vectors within the **H** matrix, that is,

$$\bar{\eta} = \frac{\sum_{i=1}^{\mu} \eta^i}{\mu}, \bar{\rho} = \frac{\sum_{i=1}^{\mu} \rho^i}{\mu} \tag{13.22}$$

Finally, the factor γ in Eqs. (13.20) and (13.21) refers to the learning rate of control parameters, which is recommended to be selected within a range of $[0.25, 0.50]$. In the numerical examples, this parameter is set to 0.35.

13.3.1.4.2 Improvisation of the Design Vector

Upon sampling of a new set of values for control parameters, the new harmony vector $I^k = \left[I_1^k, I_2^k, \ldots, I(N_d)^k\right]^T$ is improvised in such a way that each design variable is selected at random from either harmony memory matrix or the entire discrete set. Which one of these two sets is used for a variable is determined probabilistically in conjunction with harmony memory considering rate (η^k) parameter of the solution. To implement the process a uniform random number r_i is generated between 0 and 1 for each variable I_i^k. If r_i is smaller than or equal to η^k, the variable is chosen from harmony memory in which case it is assigned any value from the ith column of the **H** matrix. Otherwise (if $r_i > \eta^k$), an arbitrary value is assigned to the variable from the entire design set.

$$I_i^k = \begin{Bmatrix} I_i^k \in \{I_i^1, I_i^2, \ldots, I_i^\mu\} & \text{if } r_i \leq \eta^k \\ I_i^k \in \{1, \ldots, N_{\text{sec}}\} & \text{if } r_i > \eta^k \end{Bmatrix} \tag{13.23}$$

If a design variable attains its value from harmony memory, it is checked whether this value should be pitch-adjusted or not. In pitch adjustment, the value of a design variable ($I_i^{k'}$) is altered to its very upper or lower neighboring value obtained by adding ± 1 to its current value. This process is also operated probabilistically in conjunction with pitch adjusting rate (ρ^k) parameter of the solution, Eq. (13.24).

$$I_i^{k'} = \begin{cases} I_i^k \pm 1 \; if \; r_i \leq \rho^k \\ I_i^k \quad if \; r_i > \rho^k \end{cases} \tag{13.24}$$

13.3.1.5 Update of Harmony Memory and Adaptivity

After generating the new harmony vector, its objective function value is calculated as per Eq. (13.18). If this value is better (lower) than that of the worst solution in the harmony memory matrix, it is included in the matrix while the worst one is discarded out of the matrix. It follows that the solutions in the harmony memory matrix represent the best μ design points located thus far during the search. The harmony memory matrix is then sorted in ascending order of objective function value. Whenever a new solution is added to the harmony memory matrix, the $\overline{\eta}$ and $\overline{\rho}$ parameters are recalculated using Eq. (13.22).

13.3.1.6 Termination

The steps 13.3.1.4 and 13.3.1.5 are iterated in the same manner for each solution sampled in the process, and the algorithm terminates when a predefined number of solutions (N_s) is sampled.

13.3.2 BIOGEOGRAPHY BASED OPTIMIZATION ALGORITHM WITH LEVY FLIGHT

The BBO algorithm was initially developed by Simon [29] and is based on the geographical behavior of individuals in the habitat such as migration, existence, and extinctions. In the algorithm, two main parameters, HSI (high suitability index) and SIV (suitability index variable), control these behaviors. HSI is related to the life conditions of the islands which can be modeled as fitness value of the solution vector. SIV describes habitability of individuals in the islands, which is independent design variable of the solution vector.

The mathematical modeling of the algorithm consists of two main phases: migration and mutation. In the migration phase, individuals move from one habitat to another, which requires generation of new solution vectors by modifying former solutions. The movements are performed by using the roulette wheel selection method. The movement probabilities of individuals are determined using their immigration and emigration rates which are related to the fitness values of the solution vectors. In mutation phase, the mutation probabilities of all the individuals are determined first. If the mutation takes place, any design variable of the individual is randomly changed.

For structural optimization, each habitat represents structural design and the individuals in the habitat represent design groups (variables) of the structure. The BBO algorithm is described in detail as follows:

- **Step 1**
  Initial habitats (structural designs) are generated randomly. The number of initial designs is equal to the number of habitats (NH). Then, some procedures are applied in the same way described in step 1 of the ABC algorithm.
- **Step 2**
  The migration phase is performed in this step. First, structural designs are sorted in ascending order; emigration (μ) and immigration (Λ) rates of the designs are calculated as follows:

$$\mu_i = \frac{NH+1-i}{NH+1};\ \lambda_i = 1-\mu_i;\ i = 1,2,\ldots,NH \tag{13.25}$$

Then, the new design is generated by changing the former designs according to μ and Λ. The generation process can be described in simple pseudocode as follows:

$$If\ (rnd < \lambda_k)\ Then$$
$$Do\ j = 1, NG$$
$$RandN = rnd * \sum_{i=1}^{NH} \mu_i \tag{13.26}$$
$$Select = \mu_1$$
$$SelectIndex = 1$$

$$DoWhile(RandN > Select.and.SelectIndex < NH)$$
$$SelectIndex = SelectIndex + 1$$
$$Select = Select + \mu_S electIndex$$
$$EndDo \qquad (13.27)$$
$$xCand_j = X_S electIndex, j$$
$$EndDo$$
$$Endif$$

- **Step 3**
  Selected designs are mutated in this phase. Selection criteria of the designs are dependent on their mutation rates. Mutation rates and selection criteria of the designs are calculated as follows:

$$m_i = m_{max}\left(\frac{1-P_i}{P_{\max}}\right);\ i = 1,2,\ldots,NH \qquad (13.28)$$

$$\text{If rnd} < \text{mi, mutation is performed} \qquad (13.29)$$

  where P_i is a selection probability of the ith habitat (design) by Simon [29]. In the mutation process, randomly determined group of the structural design is modified randomly.
  At the end of step 3, elite designs having best solutions are stored for the next generations. Steps 2 to 3 are repeated until a pre-assigned maximum number of iterations are completed.

13.3.2.1 Levy Flight Strategy

LF, also called Levy motion, demonstrated a type of non-Gaussian stochastic process whose step size is distributed based on a Levy stable distribution [22]. When generating new solution x^{t+1} for solution i, a LF is performed

$$x^{t+1} = x^t + \alpha \oplus Levy(\beta) \qquad (13.30)$$

where $\alpha \geq 0$ is the step size which is relevant to the scales of the problem and β is stability (Levy) index. In most conditions, we let $\alpha = 1$. The product $\oplus$ means entry-wise multiplications. LF essentially provides a random walk while its random step is drawn from a Levy distribution for large steps as depicted in the following.

$$\alpha \oplus levy(\beta)\ 0.01\frac{u}{v^{\frac{1}{\beta}}}(x_j - x_j^{best}) \qquad (13.31)$$

where u and v values are obtained from normal distributions;

$$u\,N\left(0,\ \sigma_u^2\right),\ \ v\,N(0,\ \sigma_v^2) \qquad (13.32)$$

with

$$\sigma_u = \left[\frac{\Gamma(1+\beta) sin\left(\frac{\pi\beta}{2}\right)}{\Gamma\left(\frac{1+\beta}{2}\right) \beta \, 2^{\frac{\beta-1}{2}}} \right]^{1/\beta} \qquad \sigma_V = 1 \tag{13.33}$$

where Γ is the gamma function $\Gamma(z) = \int_0^\infty t^{z-1} \cdot e^{-z} dt$ that is the extension of the factorial function with its argument shifted down by 1 to real and complex numbers. That is, if k is a positive integer $\Gamma(k) = (k-1)!$

There are a few ways to implement LFs; the method chosen in this chapter is one of the most efficient and simple ways based on the Mantegna algorithm; all the equations are detailed in Refs. [5,23].

13.3.3 WHALE OPTIMIZATION ALGORITHM

The whale optimization algorithm mimics the hunting behavior of humpback whales [24]. Humpback whales hunts school of krill or small fishes close to surface. They dive down into the sea and then start creating bubbles in a spiral form around the prey and swim up to surface. The later maneuver includes three different stages: coral loop, lob tail, and capture loop. In whale optimization algorithm the spiral bubble-net feeding maneuver is mathematically modeled in order to perform optimization. The algorithm consists of three stages: encircling prey, bubble-net attack and search for prey [24,30].

13.3.3.1 Encircling Prey

The humpback whales encircle the prey, when they identify its location. They consider the current best candidate solution is the best obtained so far. After assigning the best candidate solution, the other agents try to update their positions toward the best search agents according to Eqs. (13.33) and (13.34).

$$D = |C \otimes X_b^k - X^k| \tag{13.34}$$

$$X^{k+1} = X_b^k - A \otimes D \tag{13.35}$$

where k is the current iteration, A and C are coefficient vectors, X_b^k is the position of vector of the best solution and X^k is the position vector of a solution in iteration k. $\oplus$ is an element-by-element multiplication. X_b^k needs to be updated in each iteration if there is a better solution. The vectors A and D are calculated as follows:

$$A = 2a \otimes r - a \tag{13.36}$$

$$C = 2 \otimes r \tag{13.37}$$

where α is linearly decreased from 2 to 0 over the course of iterations and $\mathbf{r}$ is a random vector in [0,1]. The change of α can be as follows.

$$a = 2 - 2\frac{k}{k_{\max}} \tag{13.38}$$

where $k_{\max}$ is the maximum number of iterations.

13.3.3.2 Bubble-Net Attack

The bubble-net attack behavior of humpback whales consists of two mechanisms.

- **Shrinking encircling mechanism**
  In this mechanism, the value of **A** is a random value in interval $[-a, a]$ and the value of a is decreased from 2 to 0 over the course of iterations by using Eq. (13.35). When the range of the random variable A is set at [-1,1], the new position of the whale individual can be defined anywhere between the original position and the current best position by using Eqs. (13.33) and (13.34).
- **Spiral updating position mechanism**
  In this mechanism, the distance between the whale location and the prey (current best solution) location is first calculated, and then a logarithmic spiral equation is established between the positions of the whales and the prey (current optimal solution) to simulate the spiral movement of humpback whales. This is achieved using Eq. (13.38).

$$X^{k+1} = D' \otimes e^{bl} \otimes cos(2\pi l) + X_b^k \tag{13.39}$$

where $D' = |X_b^k - X^k|$ is the distance between the prey (best solution) and the ith whale, b is a constant parameter that controls the shape of the logarithmic spiral, l is a random number ranged -1 to 1.
It should be remembered that as the humpback whales attack their prey, they move along a spiral path while they are encircling. To simulate this behavior, it is assumed that the shrinking encircling mechanism and the spiral updating position mechanism have the same probability of 0.5. Equation (13.39) is used to choose between these two mechanisms to update the position of whales.

$$X^{k+1} = \begin{Bmatrix} X_b^k - A \otimes D & \text{if} \quad p < 0.5 \\ D' \otimes e^{bl} \otimes cos(2\pi l) + X_b^k & \text{if} \quad p > 0.5 \end{Bmatrix} \tag{13.40}$$

where p is a random probability from 0 to 1.

13.3.3.3 Search for Prey

In the exploration phase, the humpback whales search for prey (best solution) randomly and change their position according to the position of other whales. In order to force the search agent to move away from reference whale, **A** is used with values greater than 1 or less than 1. The algorithm search the domain by making use of Eqs. (13.40) and (13.41).

$$D = |C \otimes X_{\text{rand}} - X| \tag{13.41}$$

$$X^{k+1} = X_{\text{rand}} - A \otimes D \tag{13.42}$$

where X_{rand} is a random position vector chosen from the current population.

13.3.3.4 Steps of Whale Optimization Algorithm

The steps of the whale optimization algorithm is as follows [29,30]:

Step 1: Select the initial values for parameter a, coefficient A and C and the maximum number of iterations, kmax.

Step 2: Initialize the iteration counter $k = 1$. Generate the initial population of size n randomly.

Step 3: Calculate the fitness function of each agent in the population. Determine the whale with the best fitness function value and save it.

Step 4: When $p < 0.5$ and $A < 1$, the position of the current whale individual is updated by Eqs. (13.33) and (13.34); when $A \geq 1$, individuals of random whales are selected and the current position of the individual whales is updated by Eqs. (13.40) and (13.41).

Step 5: When $p \geq 0.5$, the position of the current whale individual is updated by Eq. (13.38).

Step 6: Check if any whale individual's updated position exceeds the search space and amend the whale's position beyond the search space.

Step 7: Repeat steps 3–7 until the maximum number of iterations is reached.

13.4 DESIGN EXAMPLES

The optimum design algorithm developed is used in the design of two steel six-story building examples, one with a regular and the other with an irregular floor plan, respectively. Both buildings are modeled with composite slabs and without composite slabs. The geometry and dimensions of both steel building are given in Figures 13.3 and 13.4. In the model without composite slabs, rigid diaphragms are applied to each floor in order to be able to take care of earthquake loads. This is due to the fact that space frame systems without slabs horizontal seismic loads are applied at the center of mass and distributed to the entire frame system by means of rigid diaphragms. The design example with regular plan and composite slab has 775 joints, 390 beam-column members, and 96 composite slabs each of which has 5 composite beams. In the design example with regular plan without composite slabs there are 175 joints, 390 beam-column members. In the irregular model with composite slabs, there are 627 joints, 318 beam-column members, and 72 composite slabs each of which has 5 composite beams. The design example with irregular plan without composite slabs has 147 joints, 318 beam-column members. It should be noticed that in the

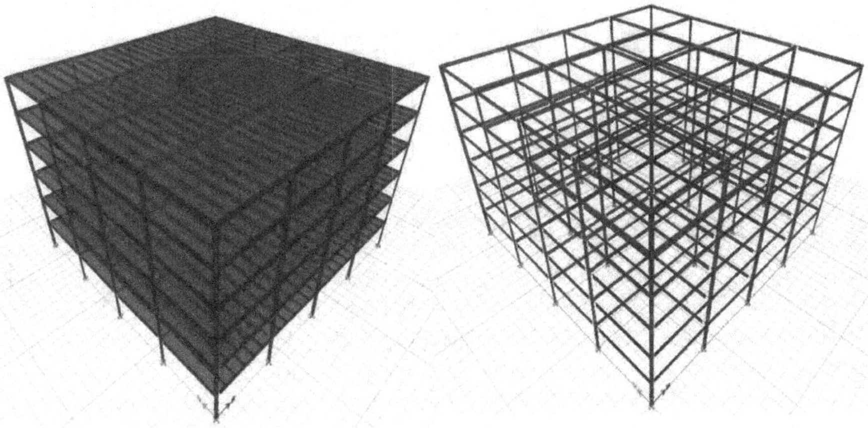

Figure 13.4-3 3-D views of six-story steel building with regular plan.

design examples without composite slabs rigid diaphragm is introduced for handling the earthquake loads. The design pool for the beams and columns of both buildings is established by selecting W-section from LRFD-AISC catalog from 100×19.3 to $1,100 \times 499$; total of 273 sections. The design pool for the design variables of composite slabs is given in Table 13.2. The intermediate steel beams of composite slab are spaced at 1.2 m. Table 13.3 shows element grouping adopted in the design examples. The default values given in SAP2000 are used for the elasticity modulus and Poisson ratios. The following loading values are considered.

- Steel building with composite slabs:
  Dead Load (D) (Beam + Column + Composite Slabs),
  Live Load (L): 2.39 kN/m^2
  Snow Load (S): 0.755 kN/m^2
- Steel building without composite slabs:
  Dead Load (Beam + Column + 2.88 kN/m^2)
  Live Load: 2.39 kN/m^2
  Snow load: 0.755 kN/m^2
- (iii) The lateral loading is the earthquake load applied in both X and Y directions by mode superposition method in both examples. The design load combinations used are: Load case 1: 1.4D, 1.2D + 1.6L + 0.5S
  Load case 2: 1.2D + 1.6S + 0.5L
  Load case 3: 1.2D +0.2L + 0.5S + 1Ex
  Load case 4: 1.2D +0.2L + 0.5S + 1Ey

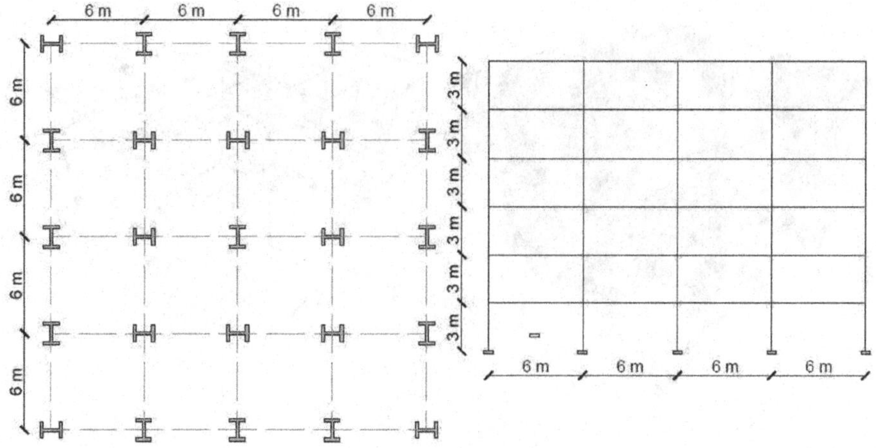

Figure 13.4-4 Side and plan views of six-story steel building with irregular plan.

Table 13.3
Element Grouping in the Design Examples

Group ID	Group Name	Design Example without Composite Slab Group Elements	Design Example with Composite Slabs Group Elements
Group 1	Corner Columns-1	Corner Columns for Floors 1-2-3	Corner Columns for Floors 1-2-3
Group 2	Edge Beams-1	Edge Beams for Floors 1-2-3	Edge Beams for Floors 1-2-3
Group 3	Edge Columns-1	Edge Columns for Floors 1-2-3	Edge Columns for Floors 1-2-3
Group 4	Inner Columns-1	Inner Columns for Floors 1-2-3	Inner Columns for Floors 1-2-3
Group 5	Inner Beams-1	Inner Beams for Floors 1-2-3	Inner Beams for Floors 1-2-3
Group 6	Corner Columns-2	Corner Columns for Floors 4-5-6	Corner Columns for Floors 4-5-6
Group 7	Edge Beams-2	Edge Beams for Floors 4-5-6	Edge Beams for Floors 4-5-6
Group 8	Edge Columns-2	Edge Columns for Floors 4-5-6	Edge Columns for Floors 4-5-6
Group 9	Inner Columns-2	Inner Columns for Floors 4-5-6	Inner Columns for Floors 4-5-6
Group 10	Inner Beams-2	Inner Beams for Floors 4-5-6	Inner Beams for Floors 4-5-6
Group 11	Composite Beams-1	-	Composite Beams for Floors 1-2-3
Group 12	Composite Beams-2	-	Composite Beams for Floors 4-5-6
Group 13	Decks	-	All the Slabs

13.4.1 STEEL BUILDING WITH IRREGULAR PLAN AND WITHOUT COMPOSITE SLABS (IFWOS)

The steel building with regular plan and without composite slab is first designed by the optimum design algorithm presented. The optimum W-sections attained for the frame members by the three soft computing techniques selected are listed in Table 13.4.

Table 13.4 reveals the fact that in this particular example LFBBO has found the lightest design. The optimum weights of AHS and WO algorithms are 8.4% and 9% heavier than LFBBO's result respectively.

Table 13.5 gives the maximum constraint values of the optimum designs for the IFWOS model. It can be noticed from these constraint values that column-to-column geometric constraint and inter-story drift constraints are dominant in the design problem. All inter-story limit constraints are very close to their upper bound values. It can also be noticed that all strength constraints and top-story drift constraints are more than 50% of their upper limit values in all the final designs.

Design histories of each soft computing technique are illustrated in Figure 13.5. It can be observed from the figure that LFBBO converged faster than AHS and WO algorithms. The difference between the best result of LFBBO found before reaching 1/3 of the optimization iterations and the best result found at the final iteration is only 3%. AHS and WO lagged behind LFBBO since they could not improve their solutions in the initial stage of the optimization process.

Table 13.4
The Optimum Designs Obtained for IFWOS Model

Group ID	LFBBO	AHS	WO
Group 1	W1000X249	W1000X272	W530X182
Group 2	W410X38.8	W410X38.8	W250X25.3
Group 3	W1000X249	W1000X296	W1000X222
Group 4	W920X201	W840X210	W1000X350
Group 5	W460X60	W410X38.8	W530X66
Group 6	W690X125	W920X238	W530X150
Group 7	W410X38.8	W410X46.1	W250X28.4
Group 8	W760X161	W760X134	W760X134
Group 9	W690X125	W530X182	W690X323
Group 10	W410X38.8	W410X46.1	W530X66
Global Best Weight (kN)	1202.569	1303.046	1311.082

Table 13.5
Critical Constraint Values in the Optimum Designs of IFWOS Model

	LFBBO	AHS	WO
Maximum strength ratio	0.712	0.699	0.953
Maximum inter-story drift (limit: 10 mm)	9.87	9.96	9.78
Maximum top-story drift (limit : 60 mm)	47.64	47.42	46.65
Maximum beam to colum geometric constraint ratios	0.55	0.467	0.625
Maximum column-to-column geometric constraint ratios	1	1	1

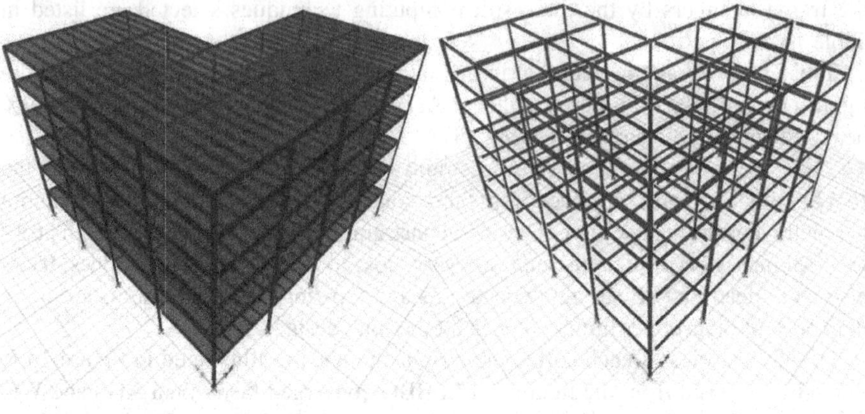

Figure 13.4-5 Design histories of the optimization algorithms for the IFWOS.

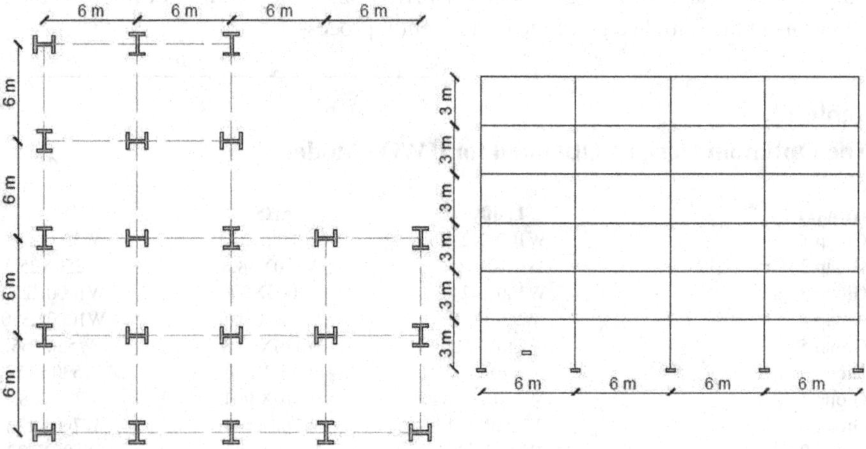

Figure 13.4-6 Design histories of the optimization algorithms for the RFWOS.

13.4.2 STEEL BUILDING WITH REGULAR PLAN AND WITHOUT COMPOSITE SLAB (RFWOS)

The steel building with regular plan and without composite slab is the next example designed by the optimum design algorithm presented. The optimum W-sections attained for the frame members by the three soft computing techniques selected are listed in Table 13.6.

Table 13.6 shows that AHS algorithm has reached the lightest optimum design. The minimum weight determined by AHS is 1591.65 kN. The other optimum designs obtained by AHS and WO are 1.4% and 2.48% heavier than the one attained by AHS.

Table 13.7 gives critical constraint values in the optimum designs for the RFWOS model. Once again, inter-story drift and column-to-column geometric constraints are

Table 13.6
The Optimum Designs Obtained for RFWOS Model

Group ID	LFBBO	AHS	WO
Group 1	W530X82	W530X109	W840X176
Group 2	W360X44	W410X38.8	W360X39
Group 3	W920X271	W840X251	W760X173
Group 4	W840X299	W530X182	W760X220
Group 5	W410X46.1	W530X82	W610X92
Group 6	W250X22.3	W250X38.5	W360X101
Group 7	W310X28.3	W360X32.9	W200X31.3
Group 8	W760X134	W690X140	W460X144
Group 9	W690X289	W530X182	W360X179
Group 10	W530X66	W410X67	W530X74
Global Best Weight (kN)	1613.94	1591.65	1654.09

Table 13.7
Critical Constraint Values in the Optimum Designs of RFWOS Model

	LFBBO	AHS	WO
Maximum strength ratio	0.889	0.535	0.436
Maximum inter-story drift (limit: 10 mm)	10	9.746	9.86
Maximum top-story drift (limit : 60 mm)	47.03	47.36	47.65
Maximum beam-to-column geometric constraint ratios	1	0.863	0.67
Maximum column-to-column geometric constraint ratios	1	1	1

dominant constraints in the design problem in all the metaheuristic algorithms. In addition to this fact, in the optimum design of the LFBBO algorithm beam-to-column geometric constraint also reached its limit value.

Design histories of three metaheuristic algorithms are shown in Figure 13.4. It is apparent from the figure that LFBBO and AHS have similar convergence behavior up to the first 2500th iteration. However, in the last 500 iterations, AHS has improved the optimum solution and found the best result among three optimization algorithms used. WO has lower convergence rate than LFBBO and AHS and was only able to make significant progress only in the last 700 iterations.

13.4.3 STEEL BUILDING WITH IRREGULAR PLAN AND COMPOSITE SLABS (IFWS)

The optimum W-sections attained for the frame members of the steel building with irregular plan and composite slabs by three optimum design algorithms are listed in Table 13.8. It is seen from the table that the lightest optimum design is obtained by LFBBO as 1426.91 kN. The optimum design determined by AHS method is 1.8% and the one obtained by WO is 11.2% heavier than the one attained by LFBBO.

Table 13.8
The Optimum Designs Obtained for IFWS Model

Group ID	LFBBO	AHS	WO
Group 1	W760X220	W690X217	W840X251
Group 2	W460X52	W460X60	W410X38.8
Group 3	W690X125	W840X176	W920X238
Group 4	W920X238	W460X193	W840X193
Group 5	W310X38.7	W410X38.8	W360X32.9
Group 6	W760X173	W690X140	W460X193
Group 7	W360X32.9	W250X25.3	W250X32.7
Group 8	W460X89	W530X123	W610X217
Group 9	W840X193	W460X177	W310X179
Group 10	W410X38.8	W460X60	W310X44.5
Group 11	W250X17.9	W200X15	W200X19.3
Group 12	W250X17.9	W200X15	W200X15
Global Best Weight (kN)	1426.91	1453.8	1587.38

Table 13.9
Critical Constraint Values

	LFBBO	AHS	WO
Maximum strength ratio	0.891	0.994	0.986
Maximum inter-story drift (limit: 10 mm)	9.98	9.45	9.86
Maximum top-story drift (limit: 60 mm)	47.91	45.82	46.54
Maximum beam-to-column geometric constraint ratios	0.661	0.721	0.6
Maximum column-to-column geometric constraint ratios	1	1	1

The critical constraint values in the optimum designs presented in Table 13.8 are given in Table 13.9. The inter-story drift and column-to-column geometric constraints are dominant in the design problem in all the optimum design algorithms. It is interesting to notice that strength constraints also close to 1 which implies that they are the next dominant constraints.

The optimum values of composite slab design variables are listed in Table 13.10. All the design algorithms selected B formlock for steel deck, 50 mm concrete slab thickness and 50 mm shear stud height. While the shear stud diameter is selected 13 mm by LFBBO and WO, 16 mm is adopted by AHS.

The design histories of the LFBBO, AHS, and WO algorithms for the IFWS model are given in Figure 13.7. It is apparent in the figure that LFBBO has the best convergence rate and reaches the best result at the 1500th iterations. AHS and WO convergence rates are slower than LFBBO and they attained their optimum solutions in the last 500 iterations. It is noticed that the optimum design obtained by AHS is quite close to the one attained LFBBO.

Table 13.10
Optimum Values of Composite Slab Design Variables for the IFWS Model

	LFBBO	AHS	WO
Decks	B Formlok	B Formlok	B Formlok
Slab depth (mm)	50	50	50
Shear stud diameter (mm)	13	16	13
Shear stud height (mm)	50	50	50

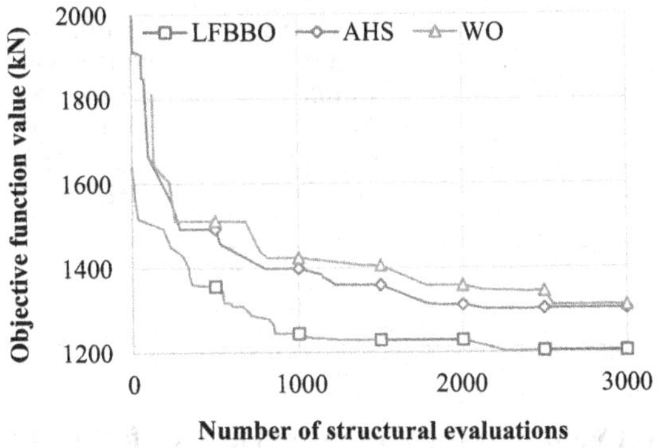

Figure 13.4-7 Design histories of the optimization algorithms for the IFWS.

13.4.4 STEEL BUILDING WITH REGULAR PLAN AND COMPOSITE SLABS (RFWS)

The optimum W-sections attained for the frame members of the steel building with regular plan and composite slabs by three optimum design algorithms are listed in Table 13.11. The lightest optimum design is obtained by LFBBO as 1573.60 kN. The other optimum designs attained by AHS and WO are 6.4% and 10.8% heavier than the one obtained by LFBBO, respectively.

The critical constraint values in the optimum designs presented in Table 13.11 are given in Table 13.12. The inter-story drift and column-to-column geometric constraints are again dominant in the design problem in all the optimum design algorithms. It is interesting to notice that strength constraints are also close to 1 which implies that they are the next dominant constraints.

In Table 13.13, the optimum values of design variables for composite slab are listed. It is noticed that all the metaheuristic algorithms have ended up with the same values except AHS which selected 100 mm shear stud height.

Figure 13.8 shows the design histories of the optimization algorithms presented for the RFWS model. LFBBO and AHS showed a similar convergence behavior. The WO algorithm showed a weak improvement until the 2000th iteration and reached its optimum design at the 2100th iteration.

Table 13.11
The Optimum Designs Obtained for the RFWS Model

Regular Plan with Composite Slab	LFBBO	AHS	WO
Group 1	W360X91	W760X161	W310X158
Group 2	W250X17.9	W310X28.3	W310X21
Group 3	W610X82	W690X192	W920X271
Group 4	W530X196	W610X155	W1000X249
Group 5	W530X74	W460X52	W410X38.8
Group 6	W200X46.1	W460X144	W250X101
Group 7	W250X28.4	W250X17.9	W310X28.3
Group 8	W530X82	W610X113	W610X92
Group 9	W530X150	W610X155	W1000X249
Group 10	W410X38.8	W410X38.8	W410X38.8
Group 11	W200X15	W200X19.3	W200X15
Group 12	W250X17.9	W200X15	W200X15
Global Best Weight (kN)	1573.609	1680.515	1764.2

Table 13.12
Critical Constraint Values in the Optimum Designs for the RFWS Model

	LFBBO	AHS	WO
Maximum strength ratio	0.986	0.956	0.986
Maximum inter-story drift (limit: 10 mm)	9.51	9.95	9.71
Maximum top-story drift (limit: 60 mm)	49.2	49.12	48.03
Maximum beam-to-column geometric constraint ratios	0.932	0.614	0.782
Maximum column-to-column geometric constraint ratios	1	1	1

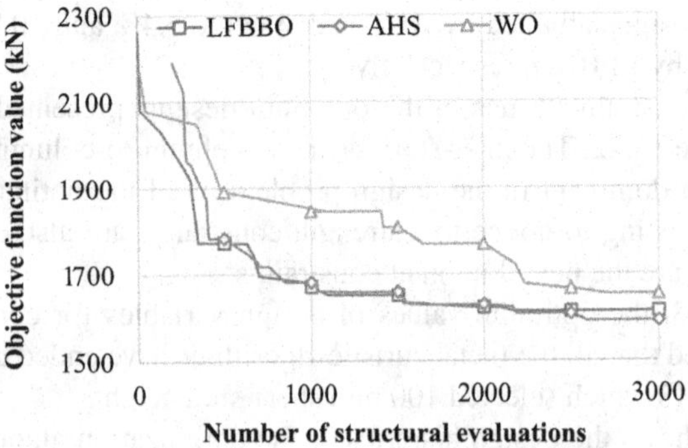

Figure 13.4-8 Design histories of the optimization algorithms for the RFWS.

Table 13.13
Optimum Values of the Composite Slab Design Variables for the RFWS Model

Decks	LFBBO BFormlok	AHS BFormlok	WO BFormlok
Slab depth (mm)	50	50	50
Shear stud diameter (mm)	13	13	13
Shear stud height (mm)	50	100	50

13.5 DISCUSSION

In this chapter, four steel buildings with regular and irregular plans and with and without composite slabs are designed using the optimum design algorithm presented. The minimum weights of the buildings obtained are summarized in Table 13.14.

It is apparent from the table that out of four design cases, LFBBO has reached the lightest optimum designs in three cases and AHS has found the lightest optimum design in one case only. However, in all other cases, the final result obtained by AHS are close to the one found by LFBBO. In all cases, WO has provided the heaviest designs. One reason for this is that while the standard version of WO is used in the design algorithms, the enhanced versions of BBO and HS algorithms are employed in the other optimum algorithms. The parameter a given in Eq. (13.37) needs to be adjusted. Because this equation is intended to control the diversification of the method. However, it becomes dominant in the initial stages of the iterations which causes serious problems in the development of the best solution. Later toward the final stages of optimization process, it gets smaller. When this happens, the convergence rate of the algorithm improves as can be observed in Figures 13.5 to 13.8.

The critical values of design constraints indicate that column-to-column geometric constraints and inter-story drift constraints are dominant in the design problems. The dominance of inter-story drift is understandable because of earthquake loads

Table 13.14
The Comparison of Optimum Weights of Steel Buildings

	Soft Computing Algorithms		
Model	LFBBO	AHS	WO
Irregular plan without composite slabs	1202.57	1303.05	1311.08
Irregular plan with composite slabs	1426.91	1453.8	1587.38
Regular plan without composite slabs	1613.94	1591.65	1654.09
Regular plan with composite slabs	1573.61	1680.52	1764.2

Table 13.15
Optimum Weights of Beams and Columns in the Optimum Designs

Model	Optimization Method	LFBBO	AHS	WO
IFWOS	The weight of beam and columns	1202.57	1303.05	1311.08
IFWS	The weight of beam and columns	1047.85	1136.24	1222.44
	The weight of composite beams	379.06	317.559	364.944
RFWOS	The weight of beam and columns	1613.94	1591.65	1654.09
RFWS	The weight of beam and columns	1573.61	1193.92	1340.79
	The weight of composite beams	461.845	486.592	423.412

considered among the load cases. The satisfaction of column-to-column geometric constraints is always important due to practical considerations. Having a larger W-section for the upper columns requires expensive column-to-column connections which is undesirable in practice. Therefore, it is of prime importance that w-sections for the upper columns should be smaller sections than the upper ones, if not possible, at least the same as the lower columns. Because of these, the dominance of these two constraints, strength and tops story drift constraints were not at their limits (Figures 13.9 and 13.10).

The optimum values of the design variables for composite slabs remained at their lower values in the design pool because they are not properly included in the objective function. It would be appropriate to express the objective function as cost of the building and include the cost of the concrete slabs, steel deck, and shear studs in the objective function. In this case, more realistic optimum results may be obtained for these design variables. Furthermore, considering the spacing of intermediate steel beams as design variables will make the formulation of the design optimization problem more general.

In Table 13.15, a comparison is carried out at the level of the optimum weights of beams and columns in both steel buildings with and without composite slabs. It

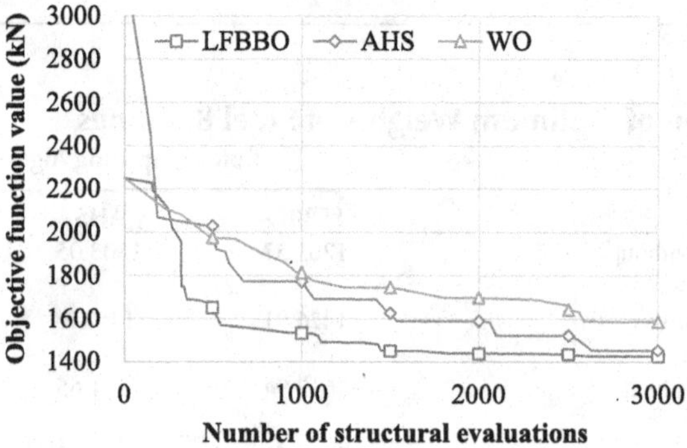

Figure 13.5-9 Design histories of the optimization algorithms for the IFWS.

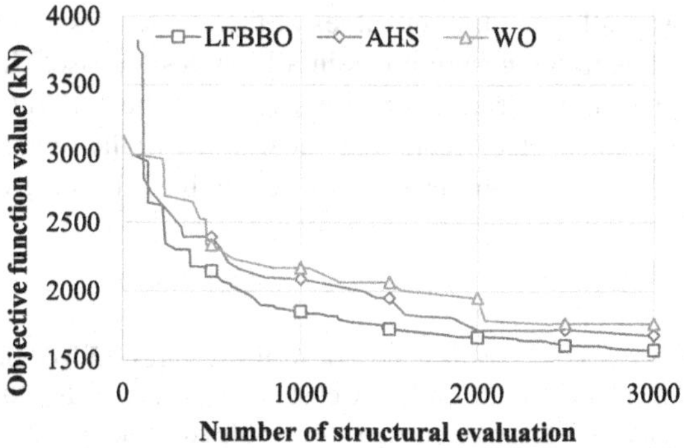

Figure 13.5-10 Design histories of the optimization algorithms for the RFWS.

is clear from the table that consideration of the composite slabs in the optimum design of space steel frames yields economy in the steel material required in beam and column members of the frames. The weight difference between with and without composite slabs is 14.7% in LFBBO and AHS and 7.2% in WO in steel building with irregular plan, and 2.5% in LFBBO, 33.3% in AHS and 23.3% in WO in steel building with regular plan. Naturally, the savings is more in steel building with regular plans. It is apparent that in the optimum design of steel buildings slabs should be taken into account in the formulation of the design optimization problem.

13.6 CONCLUSIONS

It is shown in this chapter that design of complete steel buildings, space steel frames, and composite slabs can be formulated as a design optimization problem where the design constraints are implemented from LRFD-AISC. The steel building is subjected to combined loading conditions which include dead, live, snow, and earthquake loads. The effect of considering the composite slabs in the optimum design of space steel buildings with regular and irregular plans is studied. It is shown that consideration of composite slabs in the design process provides economy in the required material for beams and columns of space steel frames. It is found that saving may reach around 33% in steel buildings with regular plans and 14.7% in steel buildings with irregular plans.

Among the soft computing techniques considered in this study, LFBBO and AHS performed better than WO. However, it should be noticed that while the standard versions of WO are used in developing the optimum design algorithms, in case of BBO and HS their enhanced versions are employed. The performance of WO algorithm has shown that it needs improvements to increase its convergence rate. This improvement could be inclusion of levy flight and/or chaos theories.

It is found that minimum weight design is not very appropriate as an objective function in the consideration of composite slabs, because such formulation does not allow to include the design variables for the composite slab in the objective function properly. This is why all the optimum values of these variables are determined to be their minimum values in the design pools in all the design cases. It would be more appropriate to express the objective function as cost of the building and include the cost of the concrete slabs, steel deck, and shear studs in the objective function. In this case, more realistic optimum results may be obtained for these design variables.

Bibliography

1. ANSI/AISC 360-16. AISC specifications for steel structures, 15th edition, steel construction manual. American Institute of Steel Construction, Chicago, IL, 2016.
2. AISC-ASD. Manual of steel construction: Allowable stress design. American Institute of Steel Construction, Chicago, IL, 1989.
3. AISC-LRFD. Load and resistance factor design, volume 1, structural members specifications codes, third edition. American Institute of Steel Construction, Chicago, IL, 2001.
4. M. Artar and A. T. Daloglu. Optimum design of composite steel frames with semi-rigid connections and column bases via genetic algorithm. *Steel Compos. Struct.*, 19(4):1035–1053, 2015.
5. I. Aydogdu, A. Akin, and M. P. Saka. Design optimization of real world steel space frames using artificial bee colony algorithm with levy flight distribution. *Adv. Eng. Software*, 92:1–14, 2016.
6. I. Aydogdu, S. Carbas, and A. Akin. Effect of levy flight on the discrete optimum design of steel skeletal structures using metaheuristics. *Steel Compos. Struct.*, 24(1):93–112, 2017.
7. L. F. Costa-Neves, C. S. S. R. Costa, L. R. O. Lima, and S. Jordao. Optimum design of steel and concrete composite building structures. *Proc. Inst. Civ. Eng. Struct. Build.*, 167(11):678–690, 2014.
8. B. Ellingwood. Serviceability guidelines for steel structures. *Eng. J. Am. Inst. Steel Constr.*, 26(1st quarter):1–8, 1989.
9. B. Ellingwood, D. E. Allen, M. Elnimeiri, T. V. Galambos, H. Iyengar, L. E. Robertson, J. Stockbridge, and C. J. Turkstra. Structural serviceability: A critical appraisal and research needs. *J. Struct. Eng.*, 112(12):2646–2664, 1986.
10. Z. W. Geem. Improved harmony search from ensemble of music players. In: *Lecture Notes in Artificial Intelligence*, volume 4251, pp. 86–93. Berlin, Germany: Springer, 2006.
11. Z. W. Geem. Optimal cost design of water distribution networks using harmony search. *Eng. Optim.*, 38(03):259–277, 2006.
12. Z. W. Geem, J. H. Kim, and G. V. Loganathan. A new heuristic optimization algorithm: harmony search. *Simulation*, 76(2):60–68, 2001.
13. Z. W. Geem, J. H. Kim, and G. V. Loganathan. Harmony search optimization: Application to pipe network design. *Int. J. Model. Simul.*, 22(2):125–133, 2002.
14. O. Hasancebi, S. Carbas, E. Dogan, F. Erdal, and M. P. Saka. Comparison of non-deterministic search techniques in the optimum design of real size steel frames. *Comput. Struct.*, 88(17–18):1033–1048, 2010.
15. O. Hasancebi, S. Carbas, E. Dogan, F. Erdal, and M. P. Saka. Performance evaluation of metaheuristic search techniques in the optimum design of real size pin jointed structures. *Comput. Struct.*, 87(5–6):284–302, 2009.
16. O. Hasancebi, F. Erdal, and M. P. Saka. Adaptive Harmony Search Method for Structural Optimization. *J. Struct. Eng.*, 136(4):419–431, 2010.

17. A. Kaveh. *Advances in Metaheuristic Algorithms for Optimal Design of Structures*. Cham: Springer, 2014.
18. A. Kaveh. *Applications of Metaheuristic Optimization Algorithms in Civil Engineering*. Cham: Springer, 2017.
19. A. Kaveh and A. D. Eslamlou. *Metaheuristic Optimization Algorithms in Civil Engineering: New Applications*. Cham: Springer, 2020.
20. A. Kaveh and M. I. Ghazaan. *Meta-Heuristic Algorithms for Optimal Design of Real-Size Structures*. Berlin: Springer, 2018.
21. N. D. Lagaros. A general purpose real-world structural design optimization computing platform. *Struct. Multidiscip. Optim.*, 49(6):1047–1066, 2014.
22. P. Lévy. L'addition des variables aléatoires définies sur une circonférence. *Bulletin de la S. M. F*, 67:1–41, 1939.
23. R. N. Mantegna. Fast, accurate algorithm for numerical simulation of levy stable stochastic processes. *Phys. Rev. E*, 49(5):4677–4683, 1994.
24. S. Mirjalili and A. Lewis. The whale optimization algorithm. *Adv. Eng. Software*, 95:51–67, 2016.
25. P. Neill. Features, net-zero, news. *Environ. J*, 2020.
26. M. P. Saka, I. Aydogdu, O. Hasancebi, and Z. W. Geem. Harmony search algorithms in structural engineering. In: X.-S. Yang and S. Koziel (eds), *Computational Optimization and Applications in Engineering and Industry*, pp. 145–182. Berlin, Germany: Springer, 2011.
27. M. P. Saka, E. Dogan, and I. Aydogdu. Review and analysis of swarm-intelligence based algorithms. In: X.S. Yang, Z. Cui, R. Xiao, A.H. Gandomi, and M. Karamanoglu (eds.), *Swarm Intelligence and Bio-Inspired Computation,* , pp. 25–47. Amsterdam, Netherlands: Elsevier, 2013.
28. M. P. Saka and Z. W. Geem. Mathematical and metaheuristic applications in design optimization of steel frame structures: An extensive review. *Math. Probl. Eng.*, 2013:1–33, 2013.
29. D. Simon. Biogeography-based optimization. *IEEE Trans. Evol. Comput.*, 12(6):702–713, 2008.
30. Z. Yan, S. Wang, B. Liu, and X. Li. Application of whale optimization algorithm in optimal allocation of water resources. In *E3S Web Conference*, vol. 53, 04019, 2018, Handan, China.

14 Fostering Sustainability in Open Innovation, to Select the Right Partner on Green Product Development

Ricardo Santos
University of Aveiro

Polinho Katina
University of South Carolina Upstate

José Soares
University of Lisbon

Anouar Hallioui
Sidi Mohamed Ben Abdellah University

Joao Matias
University of Aveiro

Fernanda Mendes
ESAI

CONTENTS

14.1 Introduction 212
14.2 Literature Review 213
14.3 Research Method 215
14.4 Variables Definition 220
14.5 System Development 222
14.6 Case Study 222
14.7 Final Conclusions 229
Bibliography 230

DOI: 10.1201/9781003312017-14

14.1 INTRODUCTION

Finding appropriate Open Innovation (OI)'s partners in a variety of areas of knowledge is critical to achieving success when innovating in a collaborative environment [1]. In recent years, scholars have mostly directed their research on the effects of the social environment on behalf of the innovation levels [2,3]. Some studies even highlighted the needs of granting SMEs employees some autonomy when establishing a workgroup from persons with various competencies in order to produce positive work environments and high levels of innovation from such collaborators (e.g. [4]).

In addition, the growth of social networks (SN), on behalf of SMEs context, has allowed their members to share information with other SMEs in order to acquire certain competencies, including some experience-related [5,6].

Furthermore, according to several studies in the literature (e.g.,[7]), Open Innovation Networks (OINs) can lead to efficient asset allocation while also boosting an organization's performance.

Several studies have been conducted, through the development of approaches, regarding partner's selection in the context of OIN, to support OI's managers on its performance, with the majority of them, analyzing OINs by using various perceptions like knowledge's importance (e.g. [8]), key-positions of OIN (e.g. [9]), the availability of external resources to use in OIN environment (e.g. [10].]), cooperation through the production of new knowledge or skills to face eventual contingencies (e.g.[11]) regarding new product development in OIN's context.

Some works (e.g. [4]), uses SN to identify external assets for Small Medium Enterprises (SMEs), with others (e.g. [3,10]) using SN to contact specialists.

Such studies highlight the need of selecting OI's partners in order to assist managers in coordinating their OIN in order to improve their innovative performance.

The most recent innovations in information systems have resulted in a plethora of professional apps, most of which have been used by human resources (HR) experts to find decent OI's partners to suit team-building activities [8].

However, there are a few limited approaches to support managers on OI's partner's assessment-based criteria, on behalf of the three dimensions of sustainability (economic, social, and ecologic), due to the increasing requests within SMEs on behalf of sustainable development, such as social and environmental responsibilities, on behalf of the three dimensions of sustainability (α - Economic, β - Social and γ - Ecologic/Environmental), there is an absence of techniques to assist the board of management in OI's partner's assessment and selection [12].

Furthermore, the existence of some subjectivity within managers' perceptions of other OI's partners' assessments, is another issue to be considered since the subjectivity increases with the managers on OIN conducting the same review. The use of approaches based on fuzzy logic theory, can bring some improvements in order to solve this problem.

As a result, we hope to fill a gap in the literature by presenting a model that integrates all of these issues into a single approach to promote sustainable choices.

The suggested model's resilience will be tested in a project built in the OIN environment to provide "green" energy regarding an industrial facility. It will be shown some of the advantages of this strategy as well as some limitations, which will be considered to provide some future research directions.

As a result, this chapter is organized as follows: The literature review is described in Section 14.2, the research method is described in Section 14.3, variables definition, described in Section 14.4, while system deployment is described in Section 14.5 with the validation of the model, being done by using a case study, with the results provided and discussed in Section 14.6. In the end, Section 14.7 makes the final conclusions, including some recommendations for future work.

14.2 LITERATURE REVIEW

Given the initial needs, selecting the "suitable OI's partner" has become a difficult process for OIN's managers due to the increasing complexity of each project (e.g., growth in the number of OI's partners participating) [13].

Some researchers have primarily focused on selecting an appropriate provider for the OIN (e.g. [14–17]). Typically, these studies follow several processes, the first of which begins with the problem characterization, followed by the identification of potential OI's candidates for a new OI's product/component, and their selection based on a set of previously stated criteria [13].

The best OI's candidate is then chosen to utilize analytical techniques based on multicriteria decision making (MCDM) approaches to select and assess a pool of potential candidates, which are then ranked according to the decision maker's (DM) preferences.

The use of MCDM methods allows for the resolution of complex and highly uncertain situations involving various and competing interests and purposes [18–22]. Several papers on MCDM approaches have been presented and contested in recent years. The applicability of such approaches was then demonstrated by picking and weighting the most appropriate alternatives based on the DM's needs [23], demonstrating therefore their great effectiveness and efficiency in decision-making.

MCDM, on the other hand, typically demands that the DMs examine and explain their judgments (based on their perceptions) in order to evaluate the alternatives against a set of criteria [24].

As a result, if we regard OI's partner selection as an MCDM problem, such a process, while often unpredictable due to the DM's subjectivity, is strategic, implying some risks and ambiguous parameters. When we consider that such judgments must be made in groups, as in the case of OI's partner selection for Open Innovation (OI) projects, the situation might become much more complicated.

Nonetheless, several scientists (e.g., [25,26]) have emphasized the importance of creating MCDM methods to address the challenges associated with Decision Making in Group (DMG) on OI's partner selection. DMG is typically used in this situation to bring together a group of experts whose interaction allows them to obtain a consensus [27,28].

Because there is a shared purpose in obtaining some consensus on picking the best OI's partner for the OIN [29], as there is for the OI, a process that allows for consensus on selecting the best OI's partner for the OIN is necessary.

As previously stated, various studies examined the effective deployment of OI's techniques, with many of them obtaining alternative titles such as "management in open innovation" (e.g. [30–32]) or even " open innovation in practice " (e.g. [33]).

In terms of OI's partner search and selection, as well as project planning, several studies, on the other hand, may be deemed fairly extensive.

Many of them provide an overview or even different frameworks to frame OI as a concept (e.g. [34–38]), or even analyzing the effects of OI on organizations on a macro perspective level (considering the OIN as a whole) or even at a micro perspective level (considering each OI's partner involved), which includes general lessons concerning when and what to do, but does not account for how to search as well as select the "suitable" partner for an OI [31]. As an example, [38] highlights the need of discovering suitable OIN's partners and provides broad guidelines on how to locate them.

Other research, for example, in-depth case studies on a specific type of OI and OIN partner, such as crowdsourcing (e.g. [39,40]), or even those related to cross-industry innovation [41], have integrated additional information to address some of these constraints. Some studies have even looked at the relationship between the number of OIN partners and the overall performance of the OIN as a result of the innovation [42,43].

This is in line with previous research, which has found that having too much breadth has a poor influence on the OIN's innovation performance, whether in terms of novelty or efficiency archived [44,45].

While this stresses the necessity of a well-intentioned OIN partner, the literature also mentions bias in local search, as companies prefer to commit to well-established companies [42].

The research from [41] offers some suggestions for OIN partner selection in the context of managing OINs on SMEs, including variables for "hard skills" and capabilities, such as resources, competencies, and risk appetite, as well as partners' shared ambitions and personal relationships.

The work of [43] gives some help by offering a sort of "checklist" of socio-technical selection factors.

Despite the wide diversity of OIN strategies recorded in the literature, most of them focus on a single OI type and do not include OIN partners in a holistic approach based on sustainable development principles. Additionally, Fuzzy Logic-based approaches have been employed to express linguistic terms in DM processes concerning other studies involved [29].

Other research considers combining other approaches with fuzzy to increase the final approach's versatility. According to the literature evaluation undertaken in this study, the most widely used techniques that combine fuzzy logic to handle MCDM issues are those that use AHP (Analytical Hierarchical Process) and TOPSIS processes.

The AHP approach was first devised by Saaty [24], and it is a well-known decision-making procedure that is frequently utilized in operations and management science research.

This approach allows for the prioritization of Multicriteria Decision-Making (MCDM) exercises/problems by reducing complicated structures to a simpler structure in order to pick from a variety of different and feasible solutions/alternatives [38].

Some ways have created MCDM procedures that integrate AHP (Analytical Hierarchical Process) with Fuzzy Logic (e.g. [34]), as well as other methods such as TOPSIS (e.g. [34]). The flexibility to incorporate a wide variety of criteria and associated aspects, the ability to account for trade-offs among the detected traits [28], and the ability to swiftly determine the optimal scenario/alternative [24] are all advantages of employing the AHP technique.

However, despite its popularity, TOPSIS has significant drawbacks when compared to AHP, particularly when dealing with human perception and establishing relative priority around each criterion, because AHP, rather than TOPSIS, can better convey the DM's demands through the associated weights.

The integrated TOPSIS approach proposed by [29,30], which was used to evaluate different renewable energy production technologies in Turkey, as well as the approach from Ref. [32], which was used to rank the scenarios/alternatives in MCDM problems, are examples of applications of some of the MCDM approaches mentioned previously.

We located a few limited studies including industrial applications, particularly when applied to real-world scenarios, in the fields of Open Innovation (OI) and Open Innovation Networks (OIN), where sustainable development is a prior issue to account for, based on works published in the literature.

Furthermore, few research on OI partner selection use both human perception and OI criteria in order to find eligible organizations for an OIN.

The bulk of the few current applications (e.g. [27,35]) are largely focused on supplier selection, and it appears that there is a gap in the employment of an integrated approach that combines AHP and Fuzzy Logic in the selection of the best OI's partner.

In this regard, the purpose of this study is to advance the state-of-the-art by providing a real-world application/case study that illustrates how companies may make decisions in the face of ambiguity when choosing the correct OI's partner for an OIN.

14.3 RESEARCH METHOD

The majority of the few existing applications are primarily concerned with supplier selection (e.g. [28,34,41]), which suggests the existence of a gap in the use of a full integrated strategy that relates AHP with Fuzzy Logic to select the best OI's partners on performing sustainable decisions. In this regard, the goal of this research is to add to the literature by offering an industrial world application that demonstrates how businesses may make judgments in the face of uncertainty when selecting the right OI's partner for an open innovation network (OIN).

According to some studies, sustainable measures can be split into three dimensions of sustainability; α - Economic, β - Social, and γ - Environment.

Thus, and by considering the criteria generally used on OI's partner selection for OIN, we've identified through the literature, a collection of criteria, which we have classified, based on the three aspects stated before, namely;

Economic: Includes some issues primarily regarding the organization's economic well-being [5,6], like the facility location, supply chain channels (distribution points, transportation modes, etc.), availability of operation's scale, operation costs involved, financial situation and credibility, facility capacity, and feedstock supply reliability, between other criteria to be accounted.

Social: Include any elements that may have an influence on the OIN's social viability, like social responsibility acts (e.g., workers', health insurance, local population, family members, etc.), work conditions, reputation, knowledge and information access, knowledge relevance and the number of employees.

Environmental/Ecologic: This category encompasses all criteria that may have an impact on the OIN's environmental viability, including issues primarily related to the organization's environmental compliance [2,5], like greenhouse gas emissions (GHG), water quality, measures related to the circular economy, among other criteria used here.

A technique was devised based on those qualities to assess each OI's partner's possibility as a candidate for inclusion in an OIN. Table 14.1 depicts a proposed framework based on a set of criteria categorized according to the previously described sustainability factors.

Thus, based on the criterion shown in Table 14.1, an attribute x may be defined as an alternative (partner's candidate) i and is associated to a criterion j, related to a dimension g, which gives $\left(x_{ij}^{D_j}\right)$. For each criterion j , there is a sustainable dimension, correlates to a series of sub-criteria, which are then used to evaluate each candidate's potential using Multi Attribute Value Theory (MAVT). As a result, there is a dimension/criteria D, which may be expressed as Economic (α), Social (β), and Ecological/Environmental (γ), in relation to a specific sub-criterion j, which is employed here (D_j). Each characteristic $x_{ij}^{D_j}$ can be specified in general, i.e.:

$$x_i = \{x_{i1}, x_{i2}, x_{i3}, .., x_{in_D}\} \wedge n_D = \{n_\alpha, n_\beta, n_\gamma\} \wedge n_\alpha, n_\beta, n_\gamma, i, j \in \mathrm{N} \tag{14.1}$$

$$D_j \in \left\{\{\alpha_1, \alpha_2, .., \alpha_{n_\alpha}\} \cup \left\{\beta_1, \beta_2, .., \beta_{n_\beta}\right\} \cup \{\gamma_1, \gamma_2, .., \gamma_{n_\gamma}\}\right\} \tag{14.2}$$

As a result, each characteristic $\left(x_{ij}^{D_j}\right)$ may be joined in just 1 evaluation table (Table 14.2a). Because each alternative $\left(x_{ij}^{D_j}\right)$ has different a scale and unit involved, the related alternative values were converted to their related value $\left(v_{ij}^{D_j}\left(x_{ij}^{D_j}\right)\right)$ by using MVAT.

As a result, each characteristic/attribute $\left(x_{ij}^{D_j}\right)$ may be combined an evaluation table such as Table 14.2a). For each alternative $\left(x_{ij}^{D_j}\right)$, it was obtained the correspondent value $\left(v_{ij}^{D_j}\left(x_{ij}^{D_j}\right)\right)$, and by recurring to the "favorable" and "unfavorable"

Table 14.1
Adopted Criteria, Considered for the Model's Definition

		Attributes\Accomplishment level	0% Weak accomplishment	25% Low accomplishment	50% Reasonable accomplishment	75% Strong accomplishment	100% High accomplishment
Criterion	a. Economics	Finance credibility (and situation) situation on market					
		Asset's availability					
		Facility's location					
		Production's scale availability					
		Available supply chain's channels					
		Total (score)	0 5 10	15 20 25 30 35	40 45 50 55 60	65 70 75 80 85	90 95 100
	b. Social	Social reputation (company's "transparency")					
		Knowledge relevance					
		Work conditions					
		External resources (social network)					
		Knowledge relevance					
		Total (score)	0 5 10	15 20 25 30 35	40 45 50 55 60	65 70 75 80 85	90 95 100
	c. Environment	Production's carbon footprint					
		Circular economy policies					
		Compliance with environmental standards					
		Production's water footprint					
		Total (score)	0 5 10	15 20 25 30 35	40 45 50 55 60	65 70 75 80 85	90 95 100
Total Score			0 5 10	15 20 25 30 35	40 45 50 55 60	65 70 75 80 85	90 95 100

values of $x_{ij}^{D_j}$, i.e.:

$$x_{ij}^{(D_j)} \longrightarrow \left(\frac{\left| x_{ij}^{(D_j)} - x_{ij(\text{unfavorable})}^{(D_j)} \right|}{\left| x_{ij(\text{favorable})}^{(D_j)} - x_{ij(\text{unfavorable})}^{(D_j)} \right|} \right) \longrightarrow v_{ij}^{(D_j)}(x_{ij}^{(D_j)}) \tag{14.3}$$

The new values, referred to each $v_{ij}^{(D_j)}\left(x_{ij}^{(D_j)}\right)$, have created a new pay-off table as a consequence of converting Table 14.2a to 14.2b with the help of (14.3)

Table 14.2
Model's Formulation (Pay-Off Table): (a) $x_{ij}^{(D_j)}$; (b) $v_{ij}\left(x_{ij}^{(D_j)}\right)$.

x_{ij}^{Dj}	$\alpha 1$	$\alpha 2$	...	αn_α	$\beta 1$	$\beta 2$	...	βn_β	$\gamma 1$	$\gamma 2$	...	γn_γ
X_1	$x_{11}^{\alpha 1}$	$x_{12}^{\alpha 2}$	...	$x_{1\gamma}^{\alpha n_\alpha}$	$x_{11}^{\beta 1}$	$x_{12}^{\beta 2}$	...	$x_{1}^{\beta n_\beta}$	$x_{11}^{\gamma 1}$	$x_{12}^{\gamma 2}$	...	$x_{1n_\gamma}^{\gamma n_\gamma}$
X_2	$x_{21}^{\alpha 1}$	$x_{22}^{\alpha 2}$	...	$x_{2n_\alpha}^{\alpha n_\alpha}$	$x_{21}^{\beta 1}$	$x_{22}^{\beta 2}$	...	$x_{2n_\beta}^{\beta n_\beta}$	$x_{21}^{\gamma 1}$	$x_{22}^{\gamma 2}$	...	$x_{2n_\gamma}^{\gamma n_\gamma}$
...	...	...	$\ddots$	...	...	...	...	...	...	...	...	...
X_n	$x_{n1}^{\alpha 1}$	$x_{n2}^{\alpha 2}$	...	$x_{nn_\alpha}^{\alpha n_\alpha}$	$x_{n1}^{\beta 1}$	$x_{n2}^{\beta 2}$	...	$x_{nn_\beta}^{\beta n_\beta}$	$x_{n1}^{\gamma 1}$	$x_{n2}^{\gamma 2}$	...	$x_{nn_\gamma}^{\gamma n_\gamma}$

a)

$v_{ij}^{Dj}(x_{ij}^{Dj})$	$\alpha 1$	$\alpha 2$	...	αn_α	$\beta 1$	$\beta 2$	...	βn	$\gamma 1$	$\gamma 2$	...	γn
x_1	$v_{11}^{\alpha 1}(x_{11}^{\alpha 1})$	$v_{12}^{\alpha 2}(x_{12}^{\alpha 2})$	...	$v_{1n_\alpha}^{\alpha n_\alpha}(x_{1n_\alpha}^{\alpha n_\alpha})$	$v_{11}^{\beta 1}(x_{11}^{\beta 1})$	$v_{12}^{\beta 2}(x_{12}^{\beta 2})$	...	$v_{1n_\beta}^{\beta n_\beta}(x_{1n_\beta}^{\beta n_\beta})$	$v_{11}^{\gamma 1}(x_{11}^{\gamma 1})$	$v_{12}^{\gamma 2}(x_{12}^{\gamma 2})$	...	$v_{1n_\gamma}^{\gamma n_\gamma}(x_{1n_\gamma}^{\gamma n_\gamma})$
x_2	$v_{21}^{\alpha 1}(x_{21}^{\alpha 1})$	$v_{22}^{\alpha 2}(x_{22}^{\alpha 2})$	...	$v_{2n_\alpha}^{\alpha n_\alpha}(x_{2n_\alpha}^{\alpha n_\alpha})$	$v_{21}^{\beta 1}(x_{21}^{\beta 1})$	$v_{22}^{\beta 2}(x_{22}^{\beta 2})$	...	$v_{2n_\beta}^{\beta n_\beta}(x_{2n_\beta}^{\beta n_\beta}$	$v_{21}^{\gamma 1}(x_{21}^{\gamma 1})$	$v_{22}^{\gamma 2}(x_{22}^{\gamma 2})$	...	$v_{2n_\gamma}^{\gamma n_\gamma}(x_{2n_\gamma}^{\gamma n_v}$
...	...	...	$\ddots$	...	...	...	...	...	...	...	...	...
x_n	$v_{n1}^{\alpha 1}(x_{n1}^{\alpha 1})$	$v_{n2}^{\alpha 2}(x_{n2}^{\alpha 2})$	...	$v_{nn_\alpha}^{\alpha n_\alpha}(x_{nn_\alpha}^{\alpha n_\alpha})$	$v_{n1}^{\beta 1}(x_{n1}^{\beta 1})$	$v_{n2}^{\beta 2}(x_{n2}^{\beta 2})$	...	$v_{nn_\beta}^{\beta n_\beta}(x_{nn_\beta}^{\beta n_\beta})$	$v_{n1}^{\gamma 1}(x_{n1}^{\gamma 1})$	$v_{n2}^{\gamma 2}(x_{n2}^{\gamma 2})$	...	$v_{nn_\gamma}^{\gamma n_\gamma}(x_{nn_\gamma}^{\gamma n_\gamma})$

b)

It was accomplished utilizing the previously mentioned qualities and fuzzy logic approaches, the correspondent value functions, $V_i^\alpha(x_i^\alpha)$, $V_i^\beta\left(x_i^\beta\right)$ and $V_i^\gamma(x_i^\gamma)$, for each sustainability dimension, were created utilizing the previously stated characteristics and fuzzy logic approaches. Then, by using a MAVT additive model, we've obtained a unique expression that allows to combine all the aspects that were generated, allowing each alternative/potential mate to be assessed. Parts of this expression (regarding each dimension j) are then multiplied by a factor ω_D, which expresses the proportional priority assigned to each sustainability dimension, yielding the following expression, i.e.:

$$\begin{aligned} V_i(X_i) &= V_i\left(V_i^\alpha(x_i^\alpha), V_i^\beta\left(x_i^\beta\right), V_i^\gamma(x_i^\gamma)\right) \\ &= \omega_\alpha . V_i^\alpha(x_i^\alpha) + \omega_\beta . V_i^\beta\left(x_i^\beta\right) + \omega_\gamma . V_i^\gamma(x_i^\gamma) \end{aligned} \tag{14.4}$$

Where $\omega_\alpha, \omega_\beta$ and ω_γ are obtained through AHP approach.

The proposed architecture tries to address all of the issues stated before with fuzzy inference systems in order to aid managers in developing an OIN product (Figure 14.1). Furthermore, the purpose of integrating Fuzzy Systems is to combine the ambiguity and subjectivity connected with human perception on examining each probable mate according to a set of previously specified criteria.

Each OIN's partner candidate I as shown in Figure 14.1, has a set of individual scores, each of which corresponds to a given criteria/dimension D, and is related to each sub-criterion *j*, and is then used as an input for each correspondent fuzzy system (each of which is related to a specific dimension/criteria). The aggregate score of

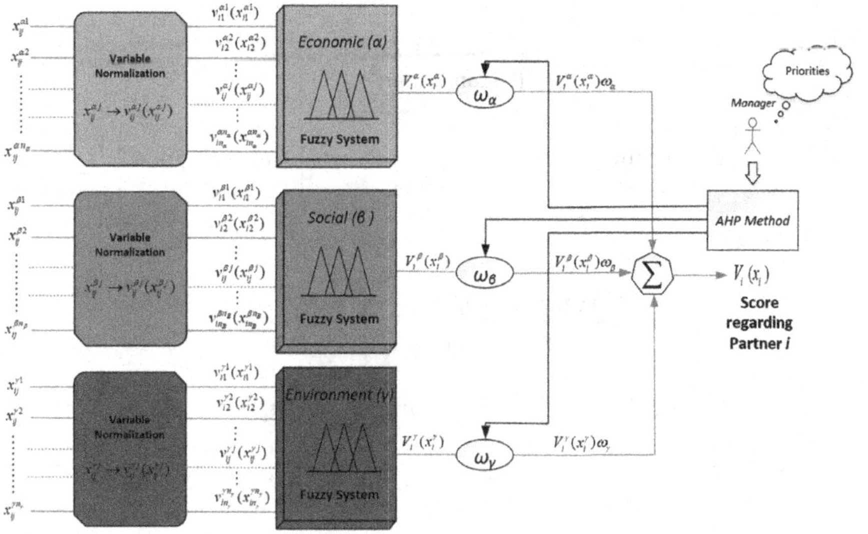

Figure 14.3-1 Model developed.

each criterion for each alternative/potential mate $V_i^D\left(x_i^D\right)$ is determined using a fuzzy inference mechanism and a set of inference rules in response to a statement of the kind "If...And...Then". By offering a formal approach for encoding, manipulating, and applying human heuristic knowledge on how to aid the decision agent when it is requested to make sensible judgments, a fuzzy-logic-based system may be utilized to handle decision-making difficulties (e.g., [9]). Figure 14.2 depicts a block diagram that may be used to describe each of the fuzzy system in Figure 14.1.

The antecedents, which are related to the rule type utilized in this technique, correlate to each of the sub-criteria stated in Table 14.3.

As a result, each $V_i^D\left(x_i^D\right)$ of the dimensions considered here (α,β, and γ) is then achieved by using $V_{ij}^{Dj}\left(x_{ij}^{Dj}\right)$ inputs, namely:

$$V_i^D\left(x_i^D\right) = v_{i1}^{D1}(x_{i1}^{D1}) \cap v_{i2}^{\alpha 2}(x_{i2}^{\alpha 2}) \cap \ldots. \cap v_{ij}^{Dj}(x_{ij}^{Dj}) \cap \ldots. \cap v_{in_D}^{Dn_D}(x_{in_D}^{Dn_D}) \tag{14.5}$$

As a result, and through, $V_j^\alpha\left(x_i^\alpha\right)$, $V_j^\beta\left(x_i^\beta\right)$ and $V_j^\gamma\left(x_i^\gamma\right)$, an expression to evaluate each partner's candidate i i.e.:

$$\begin{aligned} V_i(x_i) &= V_i\left(V_i^\alpha\left(x_i^\alpha\right), V_i^\beta\left(x_i^\beta\right), V_i^\gamma\left(x_i^\gamma\right)\right) \\ &= \omega_\alpha . V_i^\alpha\left(x_i^\alpha\right) + \omega_\beta . V_i^\beta\left(x_i^\beta\right) + \omega_\gamma . V_i^\gamma\left(x_i^\gamma\right) \end{aligned} \tag{14.6}$$

Where ω_α, ω_β and ω_γ are obtained from AHP method, to perform the following constraint:

$$\omega_\alpha + \omega_\beta + \omega_\gamma = 1 \tag{14.7}$$

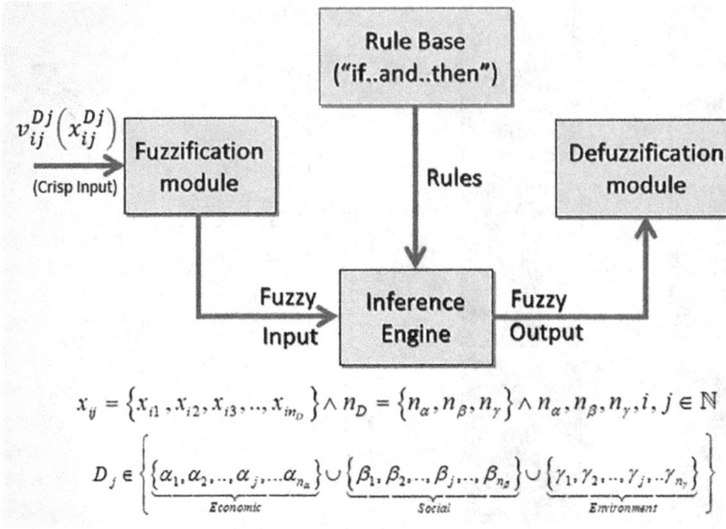

Figure 14.3-2 Fuzzy system block diagram.

Table 14.3
Fuzzy Linguistic Levels, Concerning $V_{ij}^{Dj}\left(x_{ij}^{Dj}\right)$ Values

Linguistic level	Membership Function	Parameters [φ, χ, ψ]
Weak accomplishment	There is a week accomplishment level, considering this criterion	(0, 0, 0.25)
Low accomplishment	There is some accomplishment level, considering this criterion	(0, 0.25, 0.50)
Reasonable accomplishment	There is a reasonable accomplishment level, considering this criterion	(0.25, 0.50, 0.75)
Strong Accomplishment	There is a strong accomplishment level, considering this criterion	(0.5, 0.75, 1.0)
High accomplishment	There is a high accomplishment level, considering this criterion	(0.75, 1, 1)

14.4 VARIABLES DEFINITION

In terms of linguistic variables, the number of linguistic levels should not exceed nine, due to the risk of surpassing the decision-perception agent's boundaries while discerning such values [13,15].

As a result and based on the Fuzzy Systems shown in Figures 14.1 and 14.2, a set of linguistic terms, as well as their related pertinence expressions, were defined in terms of $V_{ij}^{Dj}\left(x_{ij}^{Dj}\right)$ and $V_{ij}^{Dj}\left(x_i^{Dj}\right)$ values (Tables 14.1 and 14.2). Every pertinence function employs a triangular type whose parameters, γ,β and α are respectively presented on both tables.

Table 14.4
Fuzzy Linguistic Levels, Concerning $V_{ij}^{Dj}\left(x_i^{Dj}\right)$ Values Regarding Dimension D

Linguistic level	Membership Function	Parameters [φ, χ, ψ]
Weak Preference	There is a weak preference, considering this dimension	(0, 0, 0.25)
Low Preference	There is some preference, considering this dimension	(0, 0.25, 0.50)
Reasonable Preference	There is a reasonable preference, considering this dimension	(0.25, 0.50, 0.75)
Strong Preference	There is a strong preference, considering this dimension	(0.5, 0.75, 1.0)
High Preference	There is a high preference, considering this dimension	(0.75, 1, 1)

Every pertinence function employs a triangular type, whose parameters, γ, β and α are respectively presented on both tables. The same functions are graphically presented below on Figure 14.3, respectively regarded to model's inputs $\left(v_{ij}^{Dj}\left(x_{ij}^{Dj}\right)\right)$ and model's outputs $\left(V_i^D\left(x_i^D\right)\right)$.

We used a collection of intervals to turn the numerical outputs into "linguistic" ones, where each one is associated with a specific color, in order to provide a graphical result to the board of managers, regarding the score of each OIN's partner's candidate, and regarding each criterion j considered, given the inference mechanism

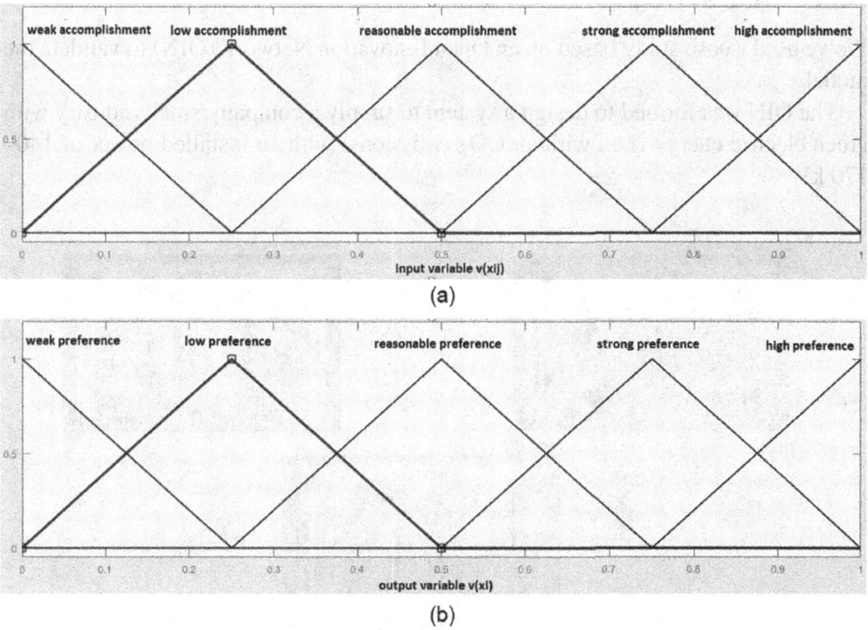

Figure 14.4-3 Pertinence expressions, regarding: (a) model's inputs $\left(v_{ij}^{Dj}\left(x_{ij}^{Dj}\right)\right)$ (b) model's outputs $\left(V_i^D\left(x_i^D\right)\right)$.

used in this work and based on the generated crisp values achieved from each fuzzy system considered here.

In order to provide the board of managers with a graphical result connected to the overall preference degree level (overall score regarding OI's partner I linked to each applicant), a similar technique was used.

Thus, by constructing a sequence of intervals and then aggregating them using expressions, the linguistic values were changed into a quantitative form by employing the parameters in Tables 14.3 and 14.4. (8).

14.5 SYSTEM DEVELOPMENT

Each fuzzy system has been developed using Matlab® software (version R2019a), which incorporates the previously stated membership functions and inference rules, as shown in Figure 14.3 (Table 14.1).

As previously indicated, triangle functions were employed for each of the Fuzzy Systems developed here, with the relevant parameters obtained from Table 14.1. The inference rules were implemented using Mamdani's inference mechanism due to its intuitive manner, which is well-suited to human inputs and general acceptance in the literature [15]. (Figure 14.4).

For the defuzzification related to each one FS considered, it was used the centroid method, owing to its widespread adoption in other research in the literature [15].

14.6 CASE STUDY

We've used a case study based on an Open Innovation Network (OIN) to validate the model.

The OIN was formed to design a system to supply a company/small industry with green electric energy (i.e., without CO_2 emissions) with an installed power of 140–170 kW.

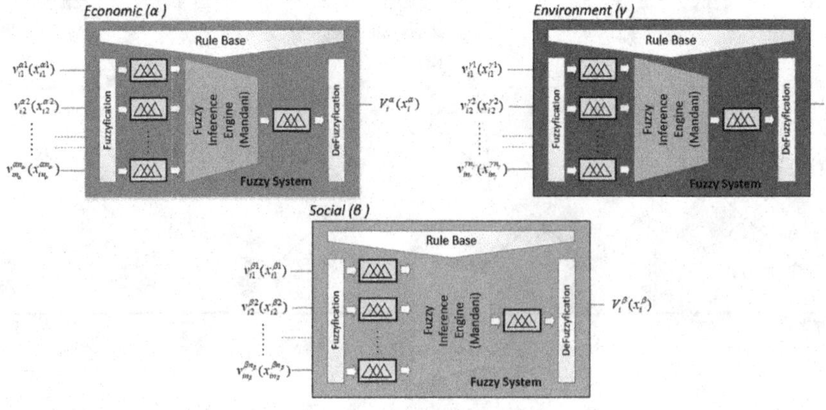

Figure 14.4-4 Model's dimensions by using fuzzy approach.

The system combines photovoltaic and hydrogen systems, to ensure that the industry produces its own energy, even during the night periods.

This approach was first tested in a prototype to supply a small company with 145 kW, and it's made up of several components (e.g., PV panels, DC-DC converters, Fuel Cell, H_2 tanks, O_2 tanks, Electrolyzer), as well as other parts regarding data acquisition, system supervision, and control (Figure 14.5).

Each OI's partner (or a group of them) designs each part/component to be integrated with the system. There are public and private entities involved here, and its nature can be varied (e.g. Company, Faculty, R&D, etc.).

The share of resources and skills, involved in the OIN, allows the system's development, among 19 partners, originated from different countries.

The OIN was mapped using the methodology presented in Ref. [13], and the transfer of different resources and competences involved here (Figure 14.6).

For this case study, we have considered some of the processes involved here (Table 14.5), to provide some assistance to the OIN's board of management, through the selection of two OI's partners that needed to be integrated on different parts of the OIN developed here.

As a consequence, in Table 14.5, it's presented the processes used here, together with the OI's partners involved. As it can be seen through the same table, the OIN's manager needs to select two OI's partners, respectively regarded for the activities K02Pr11 and K04Pr16.

Through the Table 14.5, it was achieved the OI's partners needed to fulfill the OIN's needs. Figure 14.7 describes this situation more clearly, by showing in more detail the required OI's partners to be integrated in the OIN.

In this situation, the OIN requires two additional OI's partners, with one (P15) required for the communications regarding the SCADA system (K02Pr11 activity),

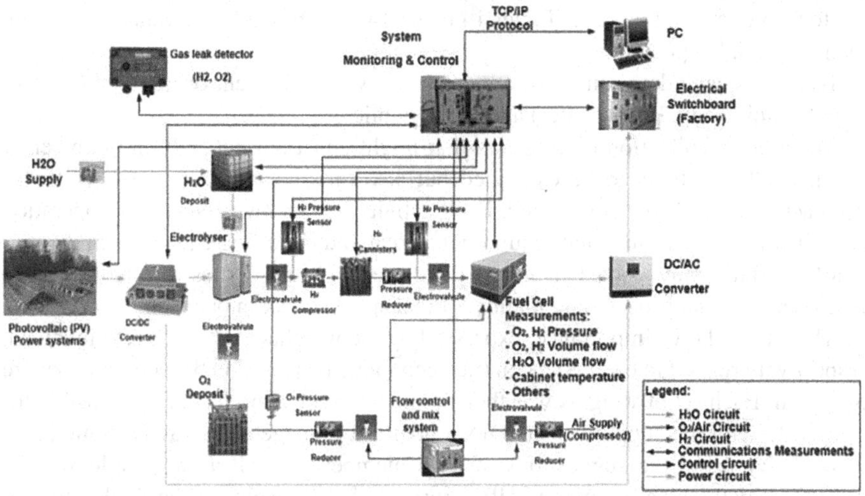

Figure 14.6-5 OIN regarding the developed system.

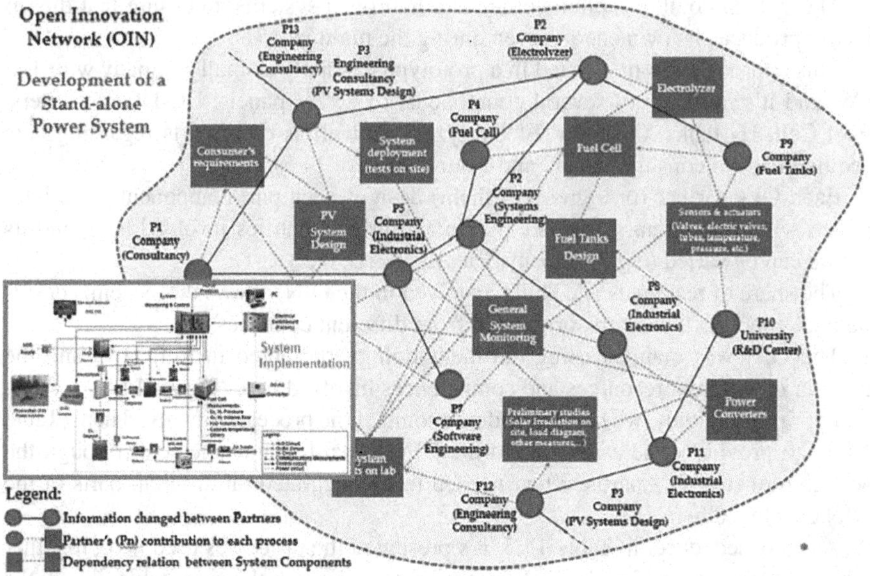

Figure 14.6-6 Competencies changed in the OIN regarding the development system.

and another one (P16), required for the Interface with the Electrolyzer (K04Pr16 activity).

A team leader was responsible for each selection process on behalf of the OIN's created.

Each team leader has formed a group of candidates (possible OI's partners) in order to further create two lists (Tables 14.6 and 14.7) of possible candidates regarding the two available positions.

Each OI's candidate can be an organization, with a different origin/type (e.g. enterprise, university, R&D center) and being public or private.

There are a collection of concerns that might constrain not only the number of possible OI's partners to be examined but also the assessment process itself, for each activity/task to be considered. Each activity has its own issues (e.g. operation costs involved, environmental requirements to attend regarding each system component/material, competencies involved), therefore the discrepancies within the relative importance of that process and mainly, of that specific task in particular.

Thus, the relative importance, expressed by the weights ($\omega\alpha$, $\omega\beta$, $\omega\gamma$) involved, respectively related to each criterion (i.e., economic (α), social (β), ecologic (γ)) are not equal. Each set of weights was then defined by each team leader, responsible for each task, with the support of the OIN's board of management, having 5 members in total. By using the suggestions of each member, as well as by employing the analytical hierarchical process (AHP) approach, it was achieved the final values of these weights, represented in Figure 14.8.

Table 14.5
Some of the Activities Involved in the OIN (Based on Ref. [39])

Process	Activity	Ref.	Partners Involved
...	...	...	...
Marketing (Pr5)	Marketing Plan	K04Pr5	P5, P6
	Consumer's needs	K05Pr5	P7, P9
	....	...	...
	Publicity (e.g. commercials)	K4Pr5	P3
...	...	...	...
PV Panels (Pr8)	System's deployment	K02Pr8	P6, P7
	Preliminary tests	K03Pr8	P4, P9
System's assembly (Pr9)	General operations	K01Pr9	P2,P5, P7
Tanks (Pr10)	System's deployment	K07Pr10	P14
	Modelling	K08Pr10	P5
	Preliminary tests	K09Pr10	P12
SCADA system (Pr11)	Software development	K10Pr11	P2, P8
	Communications	K02Pr11	P11, P12, [P15?]
	Preliminary tests	K03Pr11	P10
...	...	...	...
Fuel Cell (Pr16)	System's deployment	K01Pr16	P9
	Fuel Cell's modelling	K02Pr16	P11, P12
	Interface with SCADA	K03Pr16	P13, P11
	Interface with Electrolyzer	K04Pr16	P6, P10, P11, [P16?]
	Preliminary tests	K05Pr16	P11
...	...	...	...
Power converters (Pr20)	System development	K01Pr20	P2, P10
	System's tests	K02Pr20	P10
...	...	...	...
Valvules & actuators (Pr25)	System development	K01Pr25	P8, P11
	System's tests	K02Pr25	P10

Further, the definition of the correspondent weights, the correspondent crisp values x_{ij}^{Dj}, regarding each attribute, are then normalized by using MAVT approach $v_{ij}^{Dj}\left(x_{ij}^{Dj}\right)$, and then inserted into a fuzzy system, associated each one to a sustainability dimension (Figure 14.4).

Table 14.8 provides the input and output values for the K02Pr11 and K04Pr16 activities, respectively, where each color, is regarding to a linguistic level, concerning each model's attribute $\left(x_{ij}^{Dj}\right)$. Thus, by using a set of intervals and correlated them with the crisp values $\left(v_{ij}^{Dj}\left(x_{ij}^{Dj}\right)\right)$ at the model's entrance, and by using inference

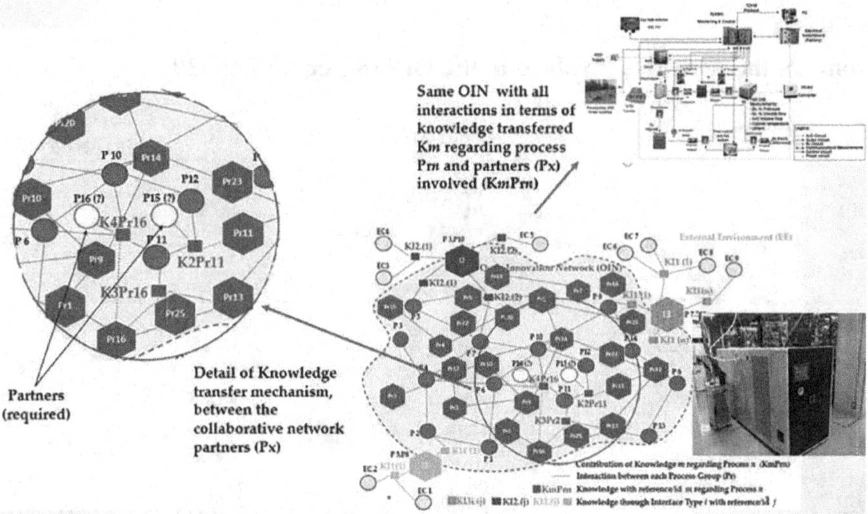

Figure 14.6-7 Knowledge transferred mechanism (detailed view) between the OI's partners.

Table 14.6
Candidates' List Regarding the P15's, Concerning Task K02Pr11

Task/activity	Required	Candidates	
		Name	Organization
K02Pr11	P15	P15.1	University
		P15.2	Company
		P15.3	University
		P15.4	Company
		P15.5	R&D Center
		P15.6	University
		P15.7	Company
		P15.8	R&D Center
		P15.9	University

rules shown before in Tables 14.3 and 14.4, it was achieved three different outputs $\left(V_i^D\right)$, each one regarding to a sustainable dimension D (Table 14.8).

Based on these results, and by using the FS outputs $(V_i^{\alpha}(x_i^{\alpha}), V_i^{\beta}\left(x_i^{\beta}\right), V_i^{\gamma}(x_i^{\gamma}))$, we have obtained the overall ones, presented in Tables 14.9 and 14.10 related to all candidates considered on both activities. Both tables include the weights ω_{α}, ω_{β}, and ω_{γ}, where it was previously accomplished with the use of AHP approach

Table 14.7
Candidates' List Regarding the P15's, Concerning Task K04Pr16

Task/activity	Required	Candidates: Name	Candidates: Organization
K04Pr16	P16	P16.1	University
		P16.2	Company
		P16.3	Company
		P16.4	R&D Center
		P16.5	R&D Center
		P16.6	University
		P16.7	R&D Center
		P16.8	Company

Table 14.8
Inputs/Outputs Regarding the Activity/Tasks K02Pr11 and K04Pr16

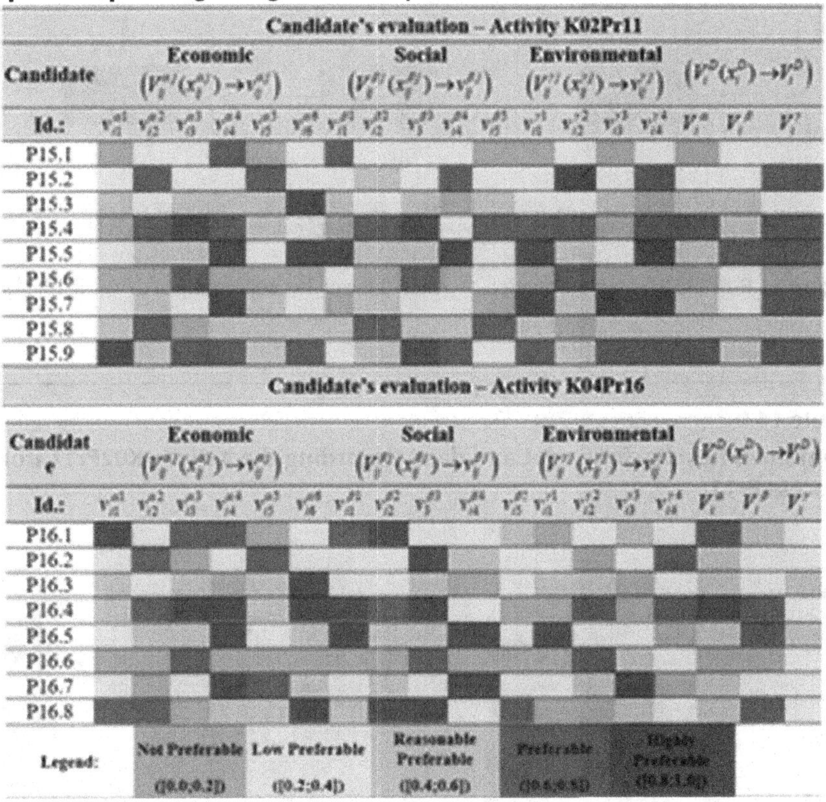

For the establishment of the manager's order of preference, the candidates were re-ordered, according to their score on both tables (Tables 14.9 and 14.10).

Thus, in terms of K02Pr11's activity (Table 14.9), P15.4 has the greatest fitness to occupy the P15's position (company). The total score, regarding the 2nd well-placed (P15.9), on the other hand, is quite close to P15.4, and it has a higher score in the environmental dimension when compared to P15.4. Given the available information in Table 14.9, as well as OIN's environmental concerns and its priorities, this situation can be reassessed by the managers, which can opt for P15.9 instead of P15.4.

In any case, these findings suggest that the board of management (decision-makers) can test various scenarios based on the relative importance previously assigned by the OIN to each of the sustainable dimensions considered here, and thus see the marginal benefit of emphasizing one dimension over another when comparing candidates' scores.

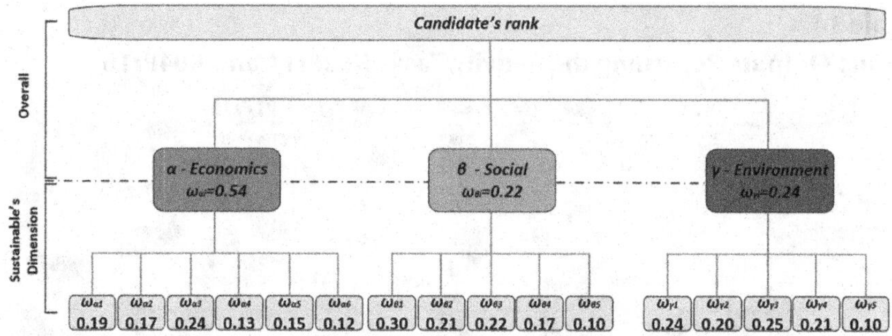

Figure 14.6-8 AHP's implementation to obtain the weights concerning activity K02Pr11.

Table 14.9
Combined Results, for each Candidate, Regarding the Activity K02Pr11 from Process Pr11.

overall rank									ordered rank		
Id.:	Organization	$V_i^{\alpha}(x_i^{\alpha})$	$V_i^{\beta}(x_i^{\beta})$	$V_i^{\gamma}(x_i^{\gamma})$	ω_α	ω_β	ω_γ	$V_i(x_i)$	Id.:	Organization	$V_i(x_i)$
P15.1	University	0.14	0.23	0.22	0.54	0.22	0.24	0.18	P15.4	Company	0.65
P15.2	Company	0.37	0.21	0.66	0.54	0.22	0.24	0.40	P15.9	University	0.64
P15.3	University	0.56	0.53	0.21	0.54	0.22	0.24	0.47	P15.5	University	0.57
P15.4	Company	0.71	0.47	0.66	0.54	0.22	0.24	0.65	P15.7	R&D Center	0.50
P15.5	University	0.47	0.64	0.74	0.54	0.22	0.24	0.57	P15.3	University	0.47
P15.6	University	0.11	0.35	0.16	0.54	0.22	0.24	0.15	P15.8	University	0.46
P15.7	R&D Center	0.56	0.22	0.61	0.54	0.22	0.24	0.50	P15.2	Company	0.40
P15.8	University	0.41	0.48	0.56	0.54	0.22	0.24	0.46	P15.1	University	0.18
P15.9	University	0.67	0.52	0.68	0.54	0.22	0.24	0.64	P15.6	University	0.15
							Order of preference:	1st	2nd	3rd 4th	5th

Table 14.10
Combined Results, for each Candidate, Regarding the Activity K04Pr16 from Process Pr16

		overall rank								ordered rank	
Id.:	Organization	$V_i^{e}(x_i^{e})$	$V_i^{s}(x_i^{s})$	$V_i^{v}(x_i^{v})$	ω_{e}	ω_{s}	ω_{v}	$V_i(x_i)$	Id.:	Organization	$V_i(x_i)$
P16.1	University	0.73	0.41	0.22	0.55	0.24	0.21	0.55	P16.4	R&D Center	0.74
P16.2	Company	0.54	0.24	0.35	0.55	0.24	0.21	0.43	P16.5	R&D Center	0.58
P16.3	Company	0.54	0.33	0.51	0.55	0.24	0.21	0.48	P16.1	University	0.55
P16.4	R&D Center	0.95	0.71	0.32	0.55	0.24	0.21	0.74	P16.3	Company	0.48
P16.5	R&D Center	0.56	0.61	0.59	0.55	0.24	0.21	0.58	P16.8	Company	0.47
P16.6	University	0.16	0.17	0.37	0.55	0.24	0.21	0.21	P16.2	Company	0.43
P16.7	R&D Center	0.51	0.28	0.23	0.55	0.24	0.21	0.40	P16.7	R&D Center	0.40
P16.8	Company	0.53	0.48	0.37	0.55	0.24	0.21	0.47	P16.6	University	0.21
						Order of preference:		1st	2nd	3rd	4th 5th

In terms of K04Pr16's activity (Table 14.10), and to occupy the OI's partner's position P16, the candidate P16.4 (university) has the greatest fitness for Pr16's aims. In this situation, the first candidate has a high level of advantage over the second one (P16.5) in all aspects of sustainability, except in the environment's dimension, where the candidate P16.5, is more suitable.

An alternative for this decision should be the management board choosing OI's partner P16.1 in order to face contingencies with the unavailability of candidate P16.4 (best positioned to the place), if the dimension with high priority is the economic one. However, in terms of overall score, the candidate with the second highest position should be the candidate P16.5, with the second-best score regarding social dimension.

In the case of both candidates with the same overall score, it is also possible to decide based on their individual scores, regarding each dimension, which one is more suitable for the position, given the OIN's priorities.

It is also possible to choose two candidates from the same list if the goal is to select two OI's partners.

As previously stated, it may also be possible to consider the second-best positioned candidate to solve a contingency problem (e.g., candidate P16.4 resigned after further negotiations), allowing the second-best positioned candidate to fill the position, which in this case (K04Pr16) would be the R&D Center (candidate P16.5).

14.7 FINAL CONCLUSIONS

In this effort, a strategy was devised to assist OIN's management in selecting partners for the creation of new goods, based on the three identified sustainable aspects (Economic, Social, and Ecologic).

The approach may be used to evaluate a group of potential OI partners and prioritize them based on their overall score as well as their individual ratings for each sustainability factor.

Based on the OIN's priorities, this last issue allows to determine each candidate's suitability in terms of sustainability.

Furthermore, the method also provides alternatives by selecting other candidates with highest scores, to deal with potential contingencies, associated with the unavailability of the initially selected OI's partner (e.g., resignation, disagreement with the proposed conditions during the final negotiations).

By using fuzzy logic, it can even be possible to deal with the subjectivity degree around each manager's perception, when it is preformed the OI's partner's assessment, by considering the same criterion previously defined.
However, there are some limitations present that allows to define some future work and make some improvements. One recommendation is to incorporate neural networks to forecast OIN's management priorities in case of unavailability of the management board to define new priorities for selecting new OI's partners in the future and given the changes in the market.

Bibliography

1. N. Mansor, S.N. Yahaya, K. Okazaki, Risk factors affecting new product development (NPD), *Int. J. Recent Res. Appl. Stud.*, 27(1):18–25, 2016.
2. T. Obradović, B. Vlačić, M. Dabić. Open innovation in the manufacturing industry: A review and research agenda, *Technovation*, 102, 2021.
3. L. Wang, X. Wang, N.J. Philipsen. Network structure of scientific collaborations between China and the EU member states, *Scientometrics* 113(2):765–781, 2017.
4. W.U. Hameed, Q.A. Nisar, H. Wu, Relationships between external knowledge, internal innovation, firms' open innovation performance, service innovation and business performance in the Pakistani hotel industry, *Int. J. Hospitality Manage.*, 92, 2021.
5. C.K. Prahalad , G. Hamel , The core competence of the corporation, *Harvard Bus. Rev.* 68(3):275–292, 2010.
6. M.L. Weitzman , Recombinant growth, *Q. J. Econ.*, 113(2):331–360, 1998.
7. L. Santamaría, M.J. Nieto, A. Rodríguez, Failed and successful innovations: The role of geographic proximity and international diversity of partners in technological collaboration, *Technol. Forecasting Social Change*, 166, 2021.
8. M. Coscia , G. Rossetti , D. Pennacchioli , F.Giannotti , You Know Because I Know: A multidimensional network approach to human resources problem, In *ACM Int. Conf. Adv. Social Networks Anal. Mining*, 4(3):434–441, 2013
9. F. Wei, N. Feng, S. Yang, Q. Zhao, A conceptual framework of two-stage partner selection in platform-based innovation ecosystems for sterilization, *J. Cleaner Prod.*, 262(3):221–245, 2020.
10. M.L.A. Hsu , F.H. Chen , The cross-level mediating effect of psychological capital on the organizational innovation climate–employee innovative behavior relationship, *J. Creat. Behav.* 51(2):128–139, 2017.
11. J.E. Perrysmith, Social yet creative: The role of social relationships in facilitating individual creativity, *Acad. Manag. J.* 49(1):85–101, 2006.
12. T.M. Amabile, Social psychology of creativity: A consensual assessment technique, *J. Pers. Soc. Psychol.* 43(5):997–1013, 1982.
13. T.M. Amabile , R. Conti , H. Coon , J. Lazenby , M. Herron , Assessing the work environment for creativity, *Acad. Manag. J.* 39(5):1154–1184, 1996.
14. C.N. Gonzalez-Brambila , F.M. Veloso , D. Krackhardt , The impact of network embeddedness on research output, *Res. Policy*, 42(9):1555–1567, 2013.

15. K.V. Andersen, The problem of embeddedness revisited: Collaboration and market types, *Res. Policy* 42(1):139–148, 2013.
16. T. Zhou , L.Lü, Y.C. Zhang , Predicting missing links via local information, *Eur. Phys. J. B* 71(4):623–630, 2009.
17. C.H. Liao , How to improve research quality? Examining the impacts of collaboration intensity and member diversity in collaboration networks, *Sci. Tometrics* 86(3):747–761, 2011.
18. E.Y. Li , C.H. Liao , H.R. Yen , Co-authorship networks and research impact: A social capital perspective, *Res. Policy* 42(9):1515–1530, 2020.
19. H. Wi , S. Oh , J. Mun , M. Jung , A team formation model based on knowledge and collaboration, *Exp. Syst. Appl.* 36(5):9121–9134, 2009.
20. R. Santos, A. Abreu, J. Soares, F. Mendes, J.M.F. Calado, A soft computing framework to support consumers in obtaining sustainable appliances from the market. *Appl. Sci.* 10:3206, 2020.
21. A. Abreu, J. Martins, J. M. F. Calado, Fuzzy Logic model to support risk assessment in innovation ecosystems, *In 13th CONTROLO*, Ponta Delgada, pp. 104–109, 2018.
22. A. Bozzon , M. Brambilla , S. Ceri , M. Silvestri , G. Vesci , Choosing the right crowd: Expert finding in social networks, *In ACM International Conference on Extending Database Technology*, pp. 637–648, 2013, Genoa, Italy.
23. P. Ávila, A. Mota, A. Piresa, J. Bastos, Putnik, G., J. Teixeira, Supplier's selection model based on an empirical study, *Proc. Technol.* 5:625–634, 2012.
24. Z. Emden, R. J. Calantone, C. Droge, Collaborating for new product development: Selecting the partner with maximum potential to create value. *J. Prod. Innovation Manage.* 23(4):330–341, 2006.
25. M. Zolghadri, C. Eckert, S. Zouggar, P. Girard, Power-based supplier selection in product development projects. *Comput. Ind.*, 62:487–500, 2011.
26. K.H. Tsai, Collaborative networks and product innovation performance: Toward a contingency perspective. *Res. Policy* 38(5):765–778, 2009.
27. R. Rajesh, V. Ravi, Supplier selection in resilient supply chains: A grey relational analysis approach, *J. Cleaner Prod.* 86:343–359, 2015.
28. P. Kraljic, Purchasing must become supply management, *Harvard Bus. Rev.*, 61(5):109–117, 1983.
29. T. Kaya, C. Kahraman, Multicriteria decision making in energy planning using a modified fuzzy TOPSIS methodology. *Expert Syst. Appl.* 38:6577–6585, 2011.
30. L. Abdullah, L. Najib, Sustainable energy planning decision using the intuitionistic fuzzy analytic hierarchy process: Choosing energy technology in Malaysia, *Int. J. Sustainable Energy*, 37(5):362–377, 2014.
31. F.R.L. Junior, L. Osiro, L.C.R. Carpinetti, A comparison between fuzzy AHP and Fuzzy TOPSIS methods to supplier selection, Appl. Soft Comput., 21:194–209, 2014.
32. G. Büyüközkan, G. Cifci, S. Güleryüz, Strategic analysis of healthcare service quality using fuzzy AHP methodology, *Expert Syst. Appl.*, 38:9407–9424, 2011.
33. D. Kannan, R. Khodaverdi, L. Olfat, A. Jafarian, A. Diabat, Integrated fuzzy multi criteria decision making method and multiobjective programming approach for supplier selection and order allocation in a green supply chain, *J. Cleaner Prod.* 47:355–367, 2013.
34. Z. Yue. TOPSIS-based group decision-making methodology in intuitionistic fuzzy setting, *Inform. Sci.* 37(1):141–153, 2014.
35. Z. Xu, H. Liao. Intuitionistic fuzzy analytic hierarchy process, *IEEE Trans. Fuzzy Logic* 22(4), 2014.

36. F.E. Boran, K. Boran, T. Menlik. The evaluation of renewable energy technologies for electricity generation in Turkey using intuitionistic fuzzy TOPSIS. *Energy Sources Part B* 7:81–90, 2012.
37. D. Joshi, S. Kumar. Intuitionistic fuzzy entropy and distance measure based TOPSIS method for multi-criteria decision making, *Egypt. Inf. J.* 15(2):97–104, 2014.
38. L. Lin, X.H. Yuan, Z.Q. Xia. Multicriteria fuzzy decision-making methods based on intuitionistic fuzzy sets, *J. Comput. Syst. Sci.* 73(1):84–88, 2007.
39. A.S.M.E. Dias, A. Abreu, H.V.G. Navas, R. Santos. Proposal of a holistic framework to support sustainability of new product innovation processes, *Sustainability* 12:3450, 2020.
40. M.R. Guertler, N. Sick. Exploring the enabling effects of project management for SMEs in adopting open innovation: A framework for partner search and selection in open innovation projects, *Int. J. Project Manage.* 39(2):102–114, 2021.
41. V. Uren, T. Miller, R. Da Campo, A. Dadzie, A model for partner selection criteria in energy from waste projects, *J. Cleaner Prod.* 279, 2021.
42. R. Santos, A. Abreu, A. Dias, J.M.F. Calado, V. Anes, J. Soares. A framework for risk assessment in collaborative networks to promote sustainable systems in innovation ecosystems, *Sustainability* 12:6218, 2020
43. E.Y. Li , C.H. Liao , H.R. Yen. Co-authorship networks and research impact: A social capital perspective, *Res. Policy* 42(9):1515–1530, 2013.
44. R. Santos, A. Abreu, V. Anes. Developing a green product-based in an open innovation environment, case study: Electrical vehicle. In: *Collaborative Networks and Digital Transformation*, Camarinha-Matos, L., Afsarmanesh, H., Antonelli, D., (Eds). IFIP Advances in Information and Communication Technology, Springer: Cham, Switzerland, 568, 2019.
45. A. Abreu, R. Santos, J.M.F. Calado, J. Requeijo. A Fuzzy Logic model to enhance quality management on R&D units, *KnE Eng.* 5(6):285–298, 2020.

Index

F-contraction, 47
α-admissible mapping, 47
χ-admisible self-mapping, 50
χ-admissible mapping, 50
ω-Cauchy sequence, 57
b metric space, 30

adaptive harmony search algorithm, 190
additive function, 173, 176
Analytical Hierarchical Process, 215
approximate fixed point property, 8

Banach space, 125, 168
Banach's fixed point theorem, 46
Biogeography optimization, 181, 188

Cauchy sequence, 18, 20–22, 24, 109, 110
Cauchy-Schwarz inequality, 73, 77
composite beam, 187
composite slab, 185
cone, 109
cone metric space, 108
conjugate gradient method, 68, 70
contraction mapping, 32
convex analysis, 125
COVID-19 Pandemic, 141
cubic inverse soft set, 87, 90, 94

defuzzification, 144, 146, 148, 222
digitalization, 141, 143
double controlled metric space, 46

Electrolyzer, 224
extended b-metric space, 46
extended fuzzy b-metric space, 23
extended parametric b-metric, 16

fixed point, 3, 6, 17, 19, 20, 22, 29, 30, 33, 35, 58, 168, 172, 175, 176
fixed point property, 1
Fredholm integral equation, 62
functional equation, 167
fuzzy b-metric space, 23
fuzzy functional analysis, 122
fuzzy logic, 214
fuzzy metric space, 30, 31, 59
fuzzy normed linear space, 122
fuzzy normed space, 108
fuzzy number, 108, 125
fuzzy present worth analysis, 148
fuzzy set, 30, 31, 88, 142, 154
fuzzy sets, 153
fuzzy soft image, 155
fuzzy soft inverse image, 155
fuzzy soft set, 88
fuzzy-contractive, 32

G-Cauchy, 32
generalized triple-controlled fuzzy metric space, 45
generalized triple-controlled modular metric space, 45

harmony memory matrix, 189
Hausdorff metric, 127
hesitant fuzzy element, 156
hesitant fuzzy set, 153, 154
hesitant fuzzy soft class, 156, 158
hesitant fuzzy soft identity mapping, 161
hesitant fuzzy soft image, 157
hesitant fuzzy soft inverse mapping, 163
hesitant fuzzy soft invertible mapping, 162
hesitant fuzzy soft mapping, 156, 157, 159
hesitant fuzzy soft number, 156
hesitant fuzzy soft set, 156
Hyers stability, 168

ideal convergence, 126
interval-valued fuzzy set, 88

interval-valued Pythagorean fuzzy number, 144
interval-valued Pythagorean fuzzy set, 144, 146
intuitionistic n-fuzzy approximate fixed point, 3, 9
intuitionistic n-fuzzy asymptotic regular, 4
intuitionistic n-fuzzy continuous, 10, 11
intuitionistic n-fuzzy contraction, 5
intuitionistic n-fuzzy nonexpansive mapping, 8, 9, 11
intuitionistic n-fuzzy weak contraction operator, 7
intuitionistic fuzzy n-norm, 8
intuitionistic fuzzy n-normed linear space, 1
intuitionistic fuzzy n-normed space, 154
intuitionistic fuzzy norm, 5
intuitionistic fuzzy normed space, 1, 108, 126
intuitionistic fuzzy set, 142, 153
inverse interval-valued soft set, 87
inverse soft set, 88

Jacobian matrix, 68

lacunary ideal convergence, 108
lacunary invariant convergent, 111
lacunary invariant statistical convergent, 112
lacunary statistical convergence, 108
Levy motion, 193
linguistic variable, 220

Mamdani's inference mechanism, 222
Mantegna algorithm, 194
Max-Min decision matrix, 104
metaheuristic algorithm, 181, 201, 203
metric space, 29, 30, 108
mixed type additive-quadratic functional equation, 168
modular b-metric space, 47
modular metric space, 47
multi-criteria decision, 101
multicriteria decision making, 213

nominal flexural bending moment, 187
non-Archimedean fuzzy normed space, 167
non-Archimedean intuitionistic fuzzy normed space, 170, 173
non-Gaussian stochastic process, 193
nonexpansive mappings, 5

Open Innovation Network, 212
Open Innovation Networks, 215
optimization algorithm, 194
optimum design algorithm, 200

parametric b-metric space, 18
parametric metric space, 16
partial ordering, 109
photovoltaic, 223

rational-type fuzzy contraction, 30, 32, 33, 40, 42
relative lateral displacement, 184

sequential extended parametric b-metric space, 15
Small Medium Enterprise, 212
soft approximation, 98
soft definable, 98
soft set, 87, 98
soft-rough, 98
spectral gradient method, 69, 70
statistical convergence, 108
sustainability, 212, 229
sustainability dimension, 218
sustainable development, 214, 215
sustainable dimension, 226

TOPSIS, 214

Ulam stability, 168

W-section, 184, 201
weak-Wardowski contraction, 46, 56
weak-Wardowski fuzzy contraction, 62
weakly compatible map, 30